ALSO BY TONY HISS

H2O—*Highlands to Ocean: A First Close Look at the Outstanding Landscapes and Waterscapes of the New York/New Jersey Metropolitan Region*
(with Christopher Meier)

Building Images: Seventy Years of Photography at Hedrich Blessing

The View from Alger's Window

Disarming the Prairie
(with Terry Evans)

Prairie Passage: The Illinois and Michigan Canal Corridor
(with Edward Ranney)

All Aboard with E. M. Frimbo
(with Rogers E. M. Whitaker)

A Region at Risk: The Third Regional Plan for the New York— New Jersey—Connecticut Metropolitan Area
(with Robert D. Yaro)

The Experience of Place

Laughing Last

Know-How: A Fix-It Book for the Clumsy but Pure of Heart
(with Guy Alland and Marion Waskiw)

The Giant Panda Book

ILLUSTRATOR

The Bird Who Steals Everything Shining

EDITOR

Henry Chung's Hunan Style Chinese Cookbook

IN MOTION

IN MOTION

The Experience of Travel

TONY HISS

Alfred A. *Knopf* NEW YORK 2010

Grateful acknowledgment is made to the following for permission to reprint previously published material:

Alfred A. Knopf: Excerpts from The Magic Mountain by Thomas Mann, translated by John E. Woods, translation copyright © 1995 by Alfred A. Knopf, a division of Random House, Inc. Reprinted by permission of Alfred A. Knopf, a division of Random House, Inc., Alfred Publishing Co. Inc.: Excerpt from "Let Down" by Thomas Edward Yorke, Jonathan Richard Guy Greenwood, Philip James Selway, Colin Charles Greenwood, and Edward John O'Brien, copyright © 1997, by Warner/Chappell Music Ltd. (PRS). All rights reserved. Reprinted by permission of Alfred Publishing Co. Inc., Doubleday: Excerpts from The Dance of Life by Edward T. Hall, copyright © 1983 by Edward T. Hall. Reprinted by permission of Doubleday, a division of Random House, Inc. Dutton and Octagon Press Ltd.: Excerpt from "Where it Went" by Hasan of Basra, excerpt from "Profiting by Experience" and "Two Reeds" by Jalaludin Rumi, and excerpt from "Safety and Riches" by Saadi of Shiraz from The Way of the Sufi by Idries Shah, copyright © 1968 by Idries Shah. Reprinted by permission of Dutton, a division of Penguin Group (USA) Inc. and Octagon Press Ltd. Octagon Press Ltd.: Excerpts from Adventures in Afghanistan by Louis Palmer (London: Octagon Press, 1990). Reprinted by permission of Octagon Press Ltd. Random House, Inc. and Random House Canada: Excerpts from The Head Trip: Adventures on the Wheel of Consciousness by Jeff Warren, copyright © 2007 by Jeff Warren. Reprinted by permission of Random House, Inc. and Random House Canada. Richard Curtis Associates Inc.: Excerpts from China to Me by Emily Hahn (New York: Doubleday, 1944). Reprinted by permission of Richard Curtis Associates Inc. David Wagoner and the University of Illinois Press: Excerpts from "Speeding" from The House of Song: Poems by David Wagoner, copyright © 2002 by David Wagoner. Reprinted by permission of David Wagoner and the University of Illinois Press.

Library of Congress Cataloging-in-Publication Data
Hiss, Tony.
In motion : the experience of travel / by Tony Hiss.
p. cm.
ISBN 978-0-679-41597-8
1. Travel—Psychological aspects.   I. Title.
G151.H57 2010
910.01—dc22   2010004143

Manufactured in the United States of America

FIRST EDITION

TO LOIS AND JACOB

CONTENTS

Two reeds drink from one stream. One is hollow, the other is sugar-cane.

—JALALUDIN RUMI (1207–1273)

Deep in the sea are riches beyond compare.
But if you seek safety, it is on the shore.

—SAADI OF SHIRAZ (1184–1291)

IN MOTION

DEEP TRAVEL

Although I was only leaving the house for a few minutes and only to run a few errands (mail a couple of bills; pick up an iced coffee at the local bagel shop), and although it was a perfectly ordinary day, like hundreds of others that unfold in any year, year after year, something was no longer the same. Before the door had even closed behind me, the familiar world outside immediately seemed— unexplored. That comes closest to describing the unexpected sensation that had arrived. "Fresh" and "new" were part of it, but only a part, even though there were undoubtedly now some things present that hadn't ever previously appeared on my block, such as the particular play of light on the buildings across the street, and the array of zigzaggy clouds in the sky overhead, and the patterns formed by the various groups of people walking by.

But it was the familiar objects, the ones that were still what they had always been, that seemed the most transformed. It wasn't as if they had changed shape or color, but they now seemed charged with purpose, beckoning, calling out, and almost glowing or shimmering, with each detail etched in the sharpest kind of focus. Each thing I looked at seemed now to have a story curled inside it, and to represent something that many people from many places and times had thought about over long periods with great care and deliberation and a kind of intelligence that takes generations to accumulate and then get sifted through and refined and pared down. The corner mailbox, for instance. I live in Greenwich Village, in New York City—have done so for most of my life—and the corner mailbox has been there for as long as I can remember.

Battered, blue, durable, unprepossessing—already obsolete some might say. Square on the bottom with a rounded top and a squeaky, pull-down handle that needs a certain decisiveness to open and close, it was something I've often used but had never at any time given the kind of close examination that it in fact—what? needed; deserved; wanted? *Wanted*—that seemed as close to it as anything. I was at the moment wide-awake in a way that reached out in all directions. Awareness and attention had been intensified, reorganized, redeployed, and I was abruptly eager to know more.

That was one thing. Yet, inanimate as it remained, it seemed in this same moment almost as if the mailbox, too, were reaching out in my direction, that it was broadcasting on a wavelength I wasn't normally tuned to, and that when I listened as well as looked, if that was the right way of putting it, let me understand that it was as eager as I was, and pleased to have its role and purpose and its previously overlooked impressiveness better known and securely remembered. But there was more than one role or function involved, as I could already make out. On the one hand, it was just a few cubic feet of public space set aside and protected—from the elements; from any marauders—so that outgoing mail could accumulate for several hours. On the other hand, it was the near end of a global force, an energy stream in constant motion and powered by millions of workers in all countries that can redistribute envelopes and packages to any spot in the world. Then, too, it was also a place of irrevocability, because once it had received something for transmittal, there was no getting that thing back.

Nor was the mailbox alone in the revelations that were being made available. Everywhere I looked were objects that, as I could start to see, played a part in sustaining or enriching the life of the area—the bright green awning over the bagel shop, for instance. When had it first occurred to people that they could move shadows around without the use of clouds or hills or trees, and could extend shade beyond the edge of a building and out over part of a street? The small, red, two-headed "siamese standpipe" next to the tall building on the nearby corner, and the round wooden bin up on that building's roof with a conical hat—in a modern city like New York, no building could stand more than six stories high without these odd devices. The standpipes keep the buildings safe from fires; they're linked to a network of other pipes in a building and when they're connected to hydrants by a Fire Department pumper, it's then possible to bring a high-pressure stream of water to any floor. The rooftop water tanks, by contrast, make tall buildings habitable by furnishing them with running water. Fresh water that reaches New York by running through aqueducts that stretch toward the city from the Catskill Mountains will rise to about the sixth floor without any assistance, but that water has to be pumped to tanks on top of all taller buildings to provide sufficient pressure for water to flow to their upper floors.

I could go on; there were so many things to notice, so many explorations and side trips that could now be undertaken. Because of my fascination, a ten-minute trip to the bagel shop seemed, once I got home with the iced coffee I'd gone out for, to have lasted far longer, and I felt as though I had come home enriched and refreshed and in some small way slightly better equipped for my next trip outside. I had also arrived with food for thought that, as it turned out, I was still digesting days later.

But the most extraordinary part of this little trip, as I can now see, was that nothing extraordinary had happened. Nothing beyond our reach, at least, and nothing at all magical, if "magical" means either something that's just imaginary or something that at bottom is no more than a trick or a deception. Having since that day examined many such "changeover" trips, my own and those of both renowned and of anonymous travelers, taking a look at big trips and little ones, at journeys to nearby places and to faraway, exotic destinations, I've come to understand that the only difference between such greatly rewarding trips and the more conventional ones that get you there and bring you back and nothing much more is that, during the memorable trips, people somewhere along the way enter a different part of their own minds, and begin to make use of an awareness that has its own range of interests and concerns and methods. And when the mind is in motion in this way, the experience of travel changes.

The switchover often enough happens automatically or inadvertently or seemingly by accident, and frequently without anyone quite noticing that anything in particular has happened inside, except that outside things seem somehow different, or that the day itself seems more alive and full of possibility. But the very same kind of awareness change can also be deliberately evoked in several ways. By the successive moments and stages of a trip, for one thing, if the people who construct roads and paths and train lines and every conceivable kind of vehicle and right-of-way know what they are doing. In addition, and much more immediately, this is something that people can choose to do all by themselves and for themselves and at almost any moment, as soon as someone finds out how to get in touch with—actually, it's easier than it sounds, since it's more like resuming contact with— what is a built-in, active, oddly ignored, complex, discriminating, many-dimensioned, and remarkably ancient capacity. We grow up fully equipped for such adventuring.

This book, among other things, is about that innate capacity: how it's often naturally activated by being in motion and by traveling; what its uses are; how it can play a larger role in everyday life; why we're lucky enough to have it; and where it long ago may have come from in the first place.

Sometimes I look ahead to what still seems like an impossibly ambi-tious destination for all the traveling billions of people undertake, day by day, year after year, locally, globally, and, increasingly, beyond the earth. At that point—when will it arrive? in whose lifetime?—the sim-ple act and fact of moving around will be enjoyed, savored, treasured, as one of the most satisfying parts of being alive. People will know and expect travel to be fundamentally rewarding and nourishing, not just every now and then but almost invariably, the way eating, sleeping, and friendships are.

Because ordinary moving around will be familiar as a springboard for fully engaging the mind and the senses, people will turn to it for delight, variety, and renewal; for unexpected ideas and completed thoughts. The transportation systems of the time—presumably a still somewhat familiar mixture of roads and cars, planes and trains, along with other vehicles not yet invented—will be people's partners in this process, seeing it as a core part of their business. After all, they, too, will share the same common understanding that our minds are in motion whenever our bodies are. The one is evoked by the other.

As travel comes to be seen as a "whole-person event," so to speak, a continuum of actions and experiences with "interior travel" and "exte-rior travel" as its inseparable parts, we will see a similar reshaping of the now rather fuzzy concept of sustainability. It is already more than clear to many people, for instance, that today's transportation systems waste energy, cost too much, disrupt communities, add poisons to the planet and greenhouse gases to the air. Many people would also agree that today's ways of moving around force them to waste time—and that is the point where confusion cuts in. The widely shared if unvoiced assumption is that the time we spend moving around, except during vacations and getaways, is a burden, a necessary evil, a delayed goal, something we have to put up with.

There: it's insidious, deep-seated, and almost inescapable to say "the time we spend moving around," rather than "the time we give to moving around." The message being delivered is that this is time subtracted from our finite daily allotment, a begrudged and regretted expenditure, endured rather than loved, something of an insult, a sour period that leaves behind the sense of an unrecoverable absence. This sets travel apart as a "disbenefit" or a "disutility" (two words economists use) or at best a "derived demand" (another one of their phrases), meaning an intermediate step, something with no intrinsic value, a postponed pleasure, an imposed surcharge on existence, part of paying our dues, part of the price we pay for civilization—something that feels like the tucked-away "preride" holding pens at Disney World, which you can't see from a distance but where you will be asked to stand in a snaking line between stanchions, standing and shuffling forward for an hour before getting to an exhilarating ten minutes on a roller coaster.

The many miseries, frustrations, and disappointments of present-day travel are a consequence of this distorted way of thinking, not the evidence that proves its truth. At its worst, this is a "parcel theory," making little distinction between moving people and shipping packages, making accommodations for bodies but not for bodies with heads and hearts. It sometimes feels as if we must hate ourselves—on a New York subway platform at rush hour in a heat wave—to treat ourselves so. Even at its humane best, when it pampers, soothes, comforts, and distracts travelers, this inadequate, foreshortened, and still grimly frozen model of how people respond to motion treats the human mind as no more than a flightless bird, unable to be sent soaring by travel.

When this grotesque old misconception melts away, fixing travel's problems will take on new clarity and an even larger purpose. Addressing travel in whole-person terms will mean thinking about what transportation systems can do to sustain both our brains and our health, while also considering how they can use far less energy and add far less pollution to the air and land and water around us. The mechanical parts of transportation as they change and change again will always respect and support the "bionical parts," so to speak, meaning the living, leaping minds within us, as distinct from automatic, predetermined, involuntary, clockwork responses. Such comprehensive thinking, a new practical discipline shared as a common concern by engineers, scientists, designers, planners, and the rest of us, will prove even more useful in the near future, since it looks as though we will want to keep our minds in play whenever possible, with all of our wits about us, to make it through the twenty-first century unscathed.

Many writers about travel have noticed that the word itself, in its original Old French form, *travaillier,* had only harsh meanings, such as "toil," "trouble," and "torment," and seems to trace back to an even older Latin word, *tripalium,* the name of a three-staked Roman instrument of torture. Modern travel, the movements of hundreds of millions of people day by day, also includes the extraordinary, often torturous circumstances of millions of migrants and refugees, many of whom are in motion only involuntarily, fearing for their lives. Ordinary twenty-first-century travel itself has been accompanied by an undercurrent of fear since its first year, when 9/11 forced us to realize that any vehicle at all, even a passenger plane, can be used as a bomb. Sometimes the feeling of vulnerability fades, but its vibration is never quite stilled, and there are times when, even without a headline, we can feel it stealing back over us like some thickening of the air, a small, dark cloud or a patch of fog or mist, shifting, changeable, and capable, even when not directly overhead, of shadowing landscape and landmarks, draining off light and color, blurring clarity.

These ugly realities add to the difficulty of the turnaround ahead, and to the urgency of getting it right. Travel already confers so many blessings—moving goods and foods around and spreading ideas and innovations, lightening our load, extending humanity's reach, bringing together people who might never otherwise meet, challenging stay-at-home thinking. As we set our sights even higher, and restore its extra, innermost dimension, we will welcome it, seek it out, rely on it at any moment of any day, confidently, routinely, implicitly, as an ever-present opportunity, a built-in launchpad and catapult for lifting the wings of the human spirit.

The larger understanding about people in motion is approaching, though it could take a generation or more to arrive, and will need leadership from citizens' movements yet to arise. Meanwhile, we live in "the meantime," as all people have in all ages. What can be done within this meantime to bring present and future closer together? In the Jeffersonian language Americans grow up with, the pursuit of happiness, one of our inalienable rights, seems to divide future and present into realms almost without a common border—with its emphasis on working for something that doesn't yet exist.

At times, though, the present is more porous than it may appear, and there are outposts of the future in our midst, and passageways that lead back and forth. One of these corridors, paradoxically, is also a legacy from the past, a form of fulfillment that does not need to be pursued, because it is part of our endowment. It was formerly, perhaps, better known than it is now. It opens in a moment, standing ready to be reclaimed and put into regular use. Fortunately, among its other uses, it serves as the travelers' elixir. At the moment and just for now, as we work our way through this particular meantime, it mostly comes in individual portions.

There is one quite specific thing anyone can already do—easily, immediately, personally, and on any day of any week—that can transform the nature of the time spent in motion. It happens whenever we increase the portion of a trip of any length during which we are making use of an ancient, innate, ground-shifting variant of ordinary waking consciousness that, for this book, we can call Deep Travel—since, though not limited to aiding travelers, one of the occasions on which it seems to announce its availability or spring to the ready, even without being summoned or chosen, is while we are moving around.

It has its own distinctive taste. People who like it tend to look for ways of getting more of it. It often surprises us, stealing over us unawares. But it can be sought out, chosen, practiced, remembered, returned to.

What can be gained from greater familiarity with this different way of being awake? Well, no one can tell you even the half of it, but in my own traveling through Deep Travel I have found that it can, among many effects, give me the sense that even a long-familiar route, like a walk through nearby streets, exists within such a fullness of brand-new or at least new-to-me information and questions that I wonder how I ever had the capacity to exclude them from consideration.

One spring morning, for instance, with nothing on my mind and walking home on East Sixteenth Street, a quiet residential block near Union Square Park in Manhattan, after dropping my son off at school, I saw three people staring wide-eyed at an apartment building fire escape overhead. Blue and white feathers drifted slowly toward the sidewalk. A peregrine falcon—the cliff-dwelling hawk known to birders as the "embodiment of freedom"—was plucking and eating a pigeon. Peregrines, with fierce black eyes, blue-gray backs, and striped bellies, can fly two hundred miles an hour when swooping to kill. They are crow-sized; this one looked enormous.

Above the fire escape I could see puffy white clouds and a pale blue sky, as I had a minute before. When I looked down again, however, the concrete sidewalk and the asphalt street seemed suddenly insubstantial, no more than a paper-thin, makeshift, temporary cover—like a throw rug, almost, or a picnic blanket—hiding the island's original underpinnings, dirt and boulders that have been a continuing presence at least since the last glaciers retreated. I seemed connected to a different "now," a longer time frame, peregrine time, so to speak, an uninterrupted, postglacial present moment more than ten thousand years old. It made me want to learn more, so much so that I then took three years to write a book about it, *H2O: Highlands to Ocean,* which was able to show the ongoing strength of the founding assets of the whole New York metropolitan area, its waterscapes and water-sculpted landscapes.

Since these natural areas, which stretch from the highlands of the Appalachian Mountains to the Atlantic Ocean, across parts of three states, remain unnamed, they got a name, the "H2O Area." These areas are still so plentiful and so bountiful, even if often hidden by four hundred years of growth, that everyone within the region actually has two addresses, a street address and an H2O address. DDT spraying after World War II almost eliminated the peregrines from the area, but captive-breeding programs have restored them. With Manhattan's endless supply of pigeons, these falcons now accept Manhattan skyscrapers as cliffs they will nest in. The bird I saw probably lived near the top of the seven-hundred-foot tall MetLife Tower on Twenty-third Street; the pigeon it ate probably came from Union Square.

If Deep Travel is sometimes a cure for boredom, at other times it is a life-changing experience.

Segueing or slipping into Deep Travel can initially seem disconcerting to some people because, although it is a kind of simple internal lane changing or focus readjustment, like shifting your gaze from your laptop to the view out the window, it has an all-at-once impact more like that of an abrupt border crossing—something with the suddenness of the transition line that extends across the center of Korea, where only a razor-wire-topped fence separates urban sprawl and rapid industrialization from deeply forested wilderness with mountains where Amur leopards, Asiatic black bears, and probably tigers, as well, prowl beneath spreading Mongolian oaks. The Korean Demilitarized Zone, a long, narrow belt of no-man's-land that has divided North from South ever since war ended in 1953, has become an improbable wildlife refuge that is now the winter home for a tenth of the world's cranes. Should the two countries ever reunite, the DMZ could become a "Peace Park," a Central Park for the entire Korean Peninsula that would also be both a kind of 155-mile-long "megazoo" and a seed bank, the principal local source for rare plants that have already disappeared from other parts of eastern Asia.

There is one thing more, and although it explains why the changeover can be instantaneous, it can in itself take some getting used to. The most striking difference between gliding into Deep Travel and crossing into the DMZ—if you were ever allowed to do so; it's the world's most heavily armed border—is that once you enter Deep Travel nothing "out there" that you can respond to has changed by even a molecule. You have not moved away from sprawl and into an oak forest, from factories to a tiger's lair, from the ordinary to the extraordinary. If a moment before you were moving through suburban sprawl, the same sprawl still surrounds you. The change here is all within, but one of its effects, until you examine it more closely, is to make you think that the world beyond you has just rearranged itself. You yourself have taken a nearly imperceptible action, and yet it can feel like something vast has happened to you—and even for your benefit. It is indeed for you, but it is a gift you have given yourself. There is no need for the world to raise shutters or open doors or throw back curtains that were never there to begin with; instead, for the time being, you have put to one side a mental filter that normally limits, dampens, flattens, or discounts what the senses can say and search for.

With all that, there is also a sense that, dramatic and abrupt as the change is, it has not led you into anything foreign or strange but, on the contrary, has brought you back in touch with exactly what was always there but had been just out of reach, or perhaps not quite remembered. It is a resumption, a rejoining. You are back in touch with, have taken up the thread of something that, once it has reappeared, is altogether familiar, even after a long absence.

Analogies can go only so far. Deep Travel has some of the qualities of sunlight after rain—details stand out—but in other ways it more resembles moonlight, because it changes your sense of what has become possible and of what might happen next. The unexpected, the seldom considered are at your fingertips. This gives it some similarity to lucid dreaming, the one dreaming state in which people know they are dreaming. Stephen LaBerge, a Stanford-trained psychophysiologist who for more than thirty years has carefully studied and induced or evoked this highly prized, elusive, but (with practice) available aspect of sleep, suggests that one function of dreams is to present us with exaggerated visions of the assumptions we make about the world and how it operates and what it means. In an ordinary dream we forget that we are in the presence of assumptions and behave as though our safety is in question and the laws of physics still apply. In a lucid dream, we suddenly and without threat or danger have a chance to challenge these assumptions—having remembered that they are only constructed, not real, we can override them in any way we choose to: by flying, by asking strangers we meet to give us a gift. The realization, the revelation, is that what we had thought of as the familiar, sensations based on events happening outside, is in fact the unfamiliar—mental images generated entirely from memories stored within. It is an exhilarating, energizing discovery. In a lucid dream we feel that we have woken up while still asleep and dreaming.

Deep Travel, on the other hand, has the feeling of waking up further while already fully awake. Again, the familiar becomes unfamiliar, but this time not because it has become unreal. Quite the contrary, it seems in some sense to have taken on new substance and content, to have so much more to say that is worth hearing—almost the way falling in love gives another person a glow that had been invisible before. So rather than your doubting what you see, it has taken on so many more qualities and possibilities than seemed to be present that it can no longer simply be taken for granted. All around you, the known, usually a set of already-told tales, has been eclipsed by the only just met up with, the yet-to-be discovered. Doubts about the strength of our ordinary assumptions in this case arise in retrospect and by contrast. Previous impressions, normally so unchallengeably solid and reliable, seem oddly inadequate in the presence of what Deep Travel brings forth— and seem static, brittle, thin, crudely formed, more like discardable placeholders than true perceptions.

As a subject, Deep Travel remains underinvestigated, perhaps at least a generation away from the attentive scrutiny lucid dreaming has now been given—although, because it is something almost everyone does on a regular basis, even if only fleetingly (unlike lucid dreaming, which must be patiently sought and cannot be summoned at will), maybe our knowledge and familiarity will be assembled far more quickly. The potential exists for millions of reports from travelers and trained investigators and transportation experts alike, and to make the beginnings of an organized and informal effort I invite you to post your own personal findings and experiences on the Web site I have set up to accompany this book, www.howwetravel.org, as a place where people can compare notes. This book itself relies heavily and gratefully on what others have noticed as they move around. Fortunately, the traces of Deep Travel can be found in many places, including the writings and conversations of people from many generations who could not put that particular name to what they understood.

Assessing or "ground truthing" what someone says about Deep Travel is a relatively simple matter. It does not require a "replicable experiment," since it just happens to people by chance and by choice here and there and in uncontrolled settings. Nor does it need a "confirmed sighting," complete with photographs and tape recordings, like the ongoing search for possible surviving ivory-billed woodpeckers in the forested bottomland swamps of the southeastern United States. The "Lord God bird"—the nickname comes from what so many people said when they first saw how big the bird was and caught sight of its vivid red, white, and black plumage—has been presumed extinct by many ornithologists since shortly after the end of World War II. This position is still reluctantly adhered to by a majority despite repeated and tantalizing twenty-first-century glimpses across three states. Any Deep Travel report you run across can be checked against what you remember from your own experiences and sense of this capacity's operations to see if they have a similar taste, or "emit the same light," so to speak.

Even at this early point, in addition to being able to set down one quick first rule of action—No Self-Propelled Flying in Deep Travel!— we would probably among us already know enough to agree on some of the interconnected reasons why Deep Travel, when it arises, makes such a powerful impact. It arrives in the mind as a complete package, but it has a number of aspects. Psychologists and cognitive scientists, for example, often estimate that human senses, with all their refinement and sensitivity, are able to respond to and conjure up mental images for us of only about one-trillionth of the energy that envelops us. No one has tried to calculate how much of that available energy we are responding to when we refocus our minds to take advantage of Deep Travel. It probably does not and could not jump to two-trillionths—but we definitely sense something like a doubling or tripling of the information potentially being provided to us. Presumably this happens because we have internally multiplied and reinforced the intensity of the awareness we are training on the world around us.

This puts us in the position, as we have seen, of expecting to find out still more about the things and people around us, and maybe even of gaining a different understanding of them. This openness is quite evenly distributed and omnidirectional. It extends both to objects and subjects we ordinarily find fascinating and to those previously thought dull or trivial. Without exactly seeking such a thing, we have adopted a different mental posture, one with fewer streaks of certainty running through it. The willingness to have been mistaken, the wish to absorb further, the sense that there is something still to be learned steals over us only when we consider what is in front of us valuable and worthy of our respect. Inwardly, this attitude has another name: humbleness, a willingness to think that what we know about the people and things and places and all the aspects of creation we encounter during the course of a day can still be added to and has not yet been perfected.

This book is an introduction, a foreword to the rebalanced awareness, the "tripled world" of Deep Travel, a preliminary travelers' guide for exploring this different pathway through exploring. It does not come with ownership papers or a lifetime guarantee, since those are reassurances and ratifications that people can confer on themselves. It does reassert a modern claim to this ancient and original human talent, neglected but still intact. If it sounds confusing or paradoxical to think about being introduced to something that is already and has always been ours, then these pages can perhaps serve as a reminder, some hints and prompts, or notes to self, or refrigerator magnets. If journeys of a thousand miles must begin with a single step, a sojourn in Deep Travel starts off more modestly than that, with nothing anyone else can even see—a mental sidestep.

As a first and incomplete survey of what happens to minds in motion, this book exists to make future discussions more complete, by pointing to the ingredient still missing from current conversations. How will Deep Travel fit in and find its place among more established interests? The old story of the teacher and the seventeen camels suggests one possibility. The teacher on his deathbed left the camels to his three students with instructions they found incomprehensible: the oldest was to receive half, the middle one a third, and the youngest one a ninth. Their problem remained unsolved until a traveler arrived with a single camel, which he offered to add to the total. Now the oldest student could get nine camels (half of eighteen), the next six (a third), and the youngest two (one-ninth)—leaving the traveler's camel left over to be returned to him. We can share the word with others and still make use of it in our own lives.

One of the problems of the moment is that many people actually already know a good deal about Deep Travel but have it filed away in a different part of their minds, as something that just happens to them every now and again—accidentally, or so unpredictably and even randomly that it almost feels like *it* is looking for *them,* rather than the other way around. A curiosity, the product of chance, not choice. A by-product, not subject to direct control. Unreliable, fleeting, and therefore in the end maybe—disappointing. Alternatively, some people who know it think of it, even after they have become return visitors, as a bonus that might be awarded under special circumstances that need preplanning and careful arrangement—such as emerging from a fog-bank swirling around the lower tracks of the old cog railway that climbs Mount Washington, in New Hampshire, and into gusty winds nearer the summit; or waking up before dawn at a lodge in Machu Picchu, the mountaintop Inca citadel in Peru that the Spanish were never able to find and plunder.

People have an easier time, I have been finding, recognizing their long familiarity with Deep Travel, and reconnecting to Deep Travel memories that have stayed with them after the details of a trip have been forgotten, if the subject is brought up more broadly as one of the unexpected discoveries or unearned rewards travelers can sometimes find along the way. Introduced this way, Deep Travel becomes common currency, since it is probably not an exaggeration to think that we have all had such encounters, casually and occasionally, moments that take us out of ourselves rather than just away from the place we were leaving. Moments when something has shifted. So that while still on the way to our original destination, we seem at the same time to have headed off in a less familiar direction as well, and find we have been led or pushed or pulled toward, into, straight through to, beyond, and then, while still in motion, have emerged onto . . . well, there is no accepted vocabulary for it, which has been another good reason for not talking about it. So it's like . . . emerging onto a platform that was not there a moment before. Yet once reached, it can seem as simple and sturdy as that.

A moving platform—that will do, since "magic carpet," another phrase that might fit, sounds too much like something one might hope to find but even while wishing for it knows it can never be real. Once out on that platform, we are aware that we have somehow been jarred loose from pieces of our ordinary thinking; we are not quite sure what might happen next, for better or worse. A threshold has somehow been crossed; a horizon has receded. Comparing notes with people who have been taken unawares by Deep Travel, I've found that there is no particular point during a trip when this inner lightning is most likely to strike. Many hours after leaving home, one man told me, and glancing out the window of a delayed, cramped, and crowded jet as it began its descent, he caught sight of something almost straight down that seemed to pull the whole flight together in a different way and change the focus of his day. He had noticed the plane's own shadow, a black speck skimming and scudding across the ground below, like a porpoise following the wake of a boat.

Some more experienced Accidental Deep Travelers have come to associate certain routes or ways of getting around with a greater likelihood of being overtaken at some point by a different frame of mind. Sometimes they share this knowledge; sometimes they keep it to themselves, like a fly fisherman who has discovered a deep pool that trout keep returning to. I myself, for instance, grew up loving train rides, because so many of them, even very ordinary ones, seemed to be twofers that lifted me out of myself while also taking me to the destination printed on my ticket. You probably have your own list of favorite entry points.

Before finding out how readily accessible and plentiful Deep Travel can be, back in my hunter-gatherer days—that is to say, when I assumed, like many people, that it was a scarce commodity that perhaps came in finite amounts—I used to rely on a bumpy Amtrak branch line north of Albany, New York, as a promising source of supply. Since the track was so deteriorated—this being America—that trains were held to an average speed of 24 miles an hour on one stretch between two stations, this was clearly a travel option most people would avoid, and on some days could almost outrun. But there was always the chance of that extra dessert, as I thought of it. I remember climbing on board in Rutland, Vermont, early one winter morning not that long ago for a return trip to New York City after a meeting in Vermont the day before. The coach/café car I was in was at least twenty-five years old, a silvery cylinder with small, slitty windows. The design of this and other "Amfleet" cars, frequently derided by passengers as "cigar tubes" or "Amcans," dates back to abject and despondent days in the 1960s when railroaders in this country thought the only way of getting Americans back onto a train was to fool them into thinking they had boarded a wingless airplane. That morning the old Amcan was fiercely overheated and mostly empty, but it was clean, and the reading-light switches overhead and the seat-back adjusters all worked. The snack bar was fully stocked, coffee was brewing, and the two conductors seemed relaxed and friendly—so that as I looked around and ticked off in my head an itemized checklist of grim possibilities, something all longtime Amtrak riders instinctively do immediately after boarding, the positives far outweighed the negatives.

Outside it was bitingly cold, with a bright blue sky and sun glinting off snowbanks. My state of mind was every bit as ordinary as the train itself, at one moment closely focused on possible Amflaws, and at the next daydreamy and abstracted. I had some work with me, but I didn't take it out. The doors closed, and the train glided forward, at first almost imperceptibly; the conductor punched my ticket and, as an afterthought, propped open the door to the vestibule, which began to draw off some of the heat. Snow-covered backyards at the back end of Rutland gave way a few minutes later to patchy woods, which flowed past at an almost stately pace, since the train was swaying gently through one of several speed-restricted areas. Two centuries after the early industrial revolution implanted the idea of speed as a measure of progress, a 30-mile-an-hour ride is a poky dawdle, tame and lame, but it is in fact exactly the same pace that terrified and exhilarated early railway passengers in the 1830s, when trains became the high-tech, high-speed replacement for stagecoaches. There are several sliding scales at work within us. Once unleashed from the speeds imposed on us by human and horses' legs, we have over and over again recalibrated our expectations of how fast we think we "ought" to be able to go. Yet at the same time we have kept in close check our sense of how fast we "ought to feel" we are moving, by swaddling ourselves deep within bulky vehicles, muffling and walling ourselves off most of the time— except on roller coasters—from the speeds we actually generate.

There were no conversations in the café car to overhear or ignore. It could have been an almost ideal moment for a short nap. Instead, all at once and quite out of the blue, I felt a surge of buoyancy, as if my whole body were popping up through murky water into sunshine. My thoughts, previously drifting by in ones and twos, were multitudinous and seemed airborne, sometimes racing ahead of the still-lumbering train, sometimes darting off and slicing behind a line of snow-clad hills that had just appeared off to my right as the train crossed a broad, shallow valley. Before even thinking about it, I had pulled a notebook out of my briefcase and was jotting down some notes about . . . the speed of trains and the speed of thought. I was certainly far more awake than I had been a few minutes before, and was surprised to realize that one of the things I had become aware of, now that I had moved over from one travel world into another, was a strong rise in a sense of uncertainty, a condition, like speed, that we generally manage to ignore.

It was not unpleasant, and I could see what was happening. My attention had certainly been brought to a higher level of alertness. Looking around more carefully, I noticed that the small "here" within easy reach, the "here" inside the café car, was of course entirely unchanged—the heat and stuffiness continued. So did the smell of fresh coffee and the fact that the foam-rubber padding in the seat back was somehow molded to hit the shoulders just about an inch and a half below where it would have felt most comfortable. As on all trips, this limited "here" had become unmoored as soon as we set out and no longer had an easily defined location at any given instant. Which meant that like all travelers, I no longer knew, and hadn't known for some minutes, exactly where I was.

The difference was that now I was thinking about it. And, along with this, I understood—couldn't avoid understanding at that point— that I didn't know precisely and couldn't say for certain what might happen in the next instant. Or the one after that. Now, this not being able to know for sure is a constant part of everyone's situation, awake and asleep, in motion and at rest, as long as life continues. It's far easier not to think about it, and also far easier to think of it as something that doesn't need to be thought about, especially when we're not moving around, when the wider "here," the one beyond the window, generally seems as unmoving or immutable or at least as slow to change as the "here" within arm's length. But once we're in Deep Travel, this aspect of reality, this acknowledgment of how much is temporary, including ourselves, cannot be discarded or deflected and returns to the fore-front of the mind.

At the same time, another kind of travelers' awareness also arises. On a train, for instance, or any kind of organized transportation, even an elderly Amtrak local making a slow, post-9/11 run across southern Vermont, you also gain a counterbalancing sense of steadiness, of the likelihood of arrival, of a slowly accumulated and carefully tended trail of forethought. You don't have to know the railroad's history to know you're not by yourself or to realize that even the leaders of your small caravan, the engineer and conductor, the train crew, are themselves never acting alone, and are constantly being helped along, guided, and have been thought about by a long chain of current and former col-leagues that stretches back, in this case, to the original nineteenth-century way finders, grade levelers, and track layers, who laid out the route unfolding before you, a path that has a definite terminus and a published time of arrival. In these circumstances, remembering that you don't know where you are or what will happen next brings with it the reassurance that for the time being you don't have do anything about this situation. The railroad's intention is not to move your mind forward, but it is in the process of moving your body forward safely and in relative comfort. It's no more than a "half a loaf" setting, but it's one that the mind can nibble on. Energized, untethered, unhurried, and protected, your mind can be free to explore any subject at all, because all possibilities lie open.

To someone looking at me, as the conductor did on a swing through the car to check temperature, nothing detectable had happened—I was still sitting quietly in the same chair. As were the few other passengers near me. I have no way of knowing how many of them had also changed places within themselves during the first ten minutes since the train had pulled out of the Rutland depot. It's perhaps worth noting that it hadn't happened to me earlier in the morning when I checked out of my hotel, or during the half hour right after that when I was focused on not missing my train, which turned out to be more complicated than expected because it involved arranging a lift down to the station in the hotel van.

I have found out that for some people, at least, this changing-over process is quite commonplace. When I happened to mention my Rutland ride, for instance, to Hillary Brown, a New York City green architect I know—she designs buildings that don't pollute and are healthy to work in—she said she would send me a note about her own travel experiences. A few days later she e-mailed me this:

Think time.

Curiously, some of my most mentally productive hours have been spent in long-distance transit—trains or buses. I enjoy a good interval of speeding scenery. It induces a spatial detachment and the time suspension necessary for bold thoughts to race ahead. It's much like being carried by music, which buoys you along at its own speed, jostling your emotions. Sensations of speed encourage the mind to dart, and the eyes to fasten momentarily on speeding objects and crystalize new understandings around them. Feeling gently cradled, hustled by occasional weightlessness, the mind is freed and the eyes can skim the moving horizon for insight, thinking ever more audacious thoughts. Body and mind together tunnel into new terrain.

The histories of several modern scientific breakthroughs also support the importance of "think time"—although that is not the focus of these accounts. It was a 1972 bus ride, for instance, that disproved the then still prevalent notion that there were deep genetic differences between human beings with different skin color. Richard Lewontin, a noted evolutionary biologist then teaching at the University of Chicago, was on deadline with a scholarly article on the subject. "I had to take a very long bus trip to Bloomington, Indiana," he later told a student, "and I had long had the habit, when going on trains and buses, of writing papers. I needed to write this paper." So he packed a standard textbook on human blood groups and a math table used to calculate genetic diversity, and began his analysis. His results, since confirmed many times over, conclusively showed that the idea of "races" within human-ity has no biological standing or value, since there is over ten times more genetic variety *among* people who share the same skin color than there is *between* people from far-distant areas, such as Africa and Europe, or North America and China.

Probably the most famous episode of scientific "think time" travel took place in a Honda Civic on a two-lane highway, as Kary B. Mullis, a biochemist, drove north through redwood country about a hundred miles north of San Francisco on a Friday night in the spring of 1983. During the drive Mullis invented the polymerase chain reaction, or PCR, a technique that, by making it possible to copy billions of pieces of DNA in a few hours, has led to DNA testing in criminal cases, and to DNA sampling of fossilized bones to pin down hereditary links between, say, mammoths and elephants, among dozens of other appli-cations. It also brought Mullis a Nobel Prize in chemistry. In his 1993 Nobel lecture in Stockholm before the king of Sweden and assembled guests, Mullis, who openly tells interviewers, "I do my best thinking while driving," recounted the setting, still vividly remembered, of his PCR-discovery drive ten years before: "As I drove through the moun-tains that night, the stalks of the California buckeyes heavily in blos-som leaned over into the road. The air was moist and cool and filled with their heady aroma." Ideas tumbled out, he said, producing three "Eureka" moments. Once he stopped the car to make a few calcula-tions, and toward the end of his trip, he recalled, "I stopped the car again. 'Dear Thor!' I exclaimed. I had solved the most annoying prob-lems in DNA chemistry in a single lightning bolt."

M ost statistics about regular weekday transportation patterns don't yet attempt to come to grips with the preciousness and spaciousness that travel time can bring forward in people's minds, but it's possible to make a few rough, back-of-an-envelope calculations that can give us a better idea of what's potentially at stake here on a daily basis. A starting point might be the central finding of a "A Look Under the Hood of a Nation on Wheels," a 2005 poll about U.S. traffic jointly commissioned by ABC News, *Time* magazine, and the *Washington Post,* which reported that 220 million American adults find themselves driving around in their cars for an average of about a hour and a half of each day. (This figure may in the future need some adjusting to fit the travel habits of a country where gas may routinely cost four dollars a gallon or more, but at present it seems to capture what's still happening day after day.)

Just over half of this hour and a half in cars—almost forty-nine minutes—is needed for getting to work and back, while errand running and other chores and quick trips fill up the rest of the time. People who have children at home drive even longer and need almost an extra quarter of an hour on the road for drop-offs and pickups. The U.S. Census Bureau, looking at this same daily commuting data in its annual American Community Survey, has found one way of making it stand out in people's minds: by presenting it as a slice of a year. They add up a year's worth of driving to and from work, and then have a figure they can compare to another known annual quantity: vacation time. It stacks up as a 2:5 ratio, since most Americans get two weeks' paid vacation a year and put in the equivalent of five workweeks reaching and heading home from the jobs that offer them a two-week vacation.

There's another way of weighing and taking the measure of this hour and a half (or hour and three-quarters) a day on the road. Let's say, arbitrarily enough, that the same 220 million people who do this amount of driving also average eight hours of sleep at night. Now we can give travel time a different focus and think about it as one of the substantial dimensions of our waking lives. The drivers in the poll, for instance, who are said to represent 90 percent of Americans, are committing approximately a tenth of their waking lives to travel time (more precisely between 9.4 to 10.8 percent, depending on circumstances).

Let's set aside for a moment one enormous problem, the question of how and why Americans got into this situation—of how, that is, we reached a point where jobs and homes and schools and stores are half an hour away from each other, and why driving is so often the only way of getting from one to the next. Some people think of the still-increasing distances between where people spend the different parts of their day as "the elephant in the transportation center," if you will, an overarching threat to prosperity and community that Americans, despite repeated warnings, have avoided coming to terms with throughout six decades of growth since the end of World War II. Standing next to it all this time, however, has been a second elephant, maybe even a mammoth, with its own impact on well-being and also undealt with but until now practically invisible: the almost constant opportunities that travel offers us to put our minds in motion, or keep them there, or even accelerate their activeness.

According to the ABC/*Time*/*Post* poll, American drivers have very mixed responses during their time on the road. Almost three-quarters say it often makes them feel "independent," and almost two-thirds say they sometimes feel "frustrated." Although 48 percent frequently feel "relaxed," 43 percent occasionally feel "angry." A 2001 survey that took a close look at the "travel behavior" of people who live in the San Francisco Bay Area turned up an equally wide range of feelings (including, it would seem, considerable numbness). Although more than two-thirds of a large group of Californians who filled out a detailed questionnaire—drivers and nondrivers alike—reject the idea that "The Only Good Thing about Traveling Is Arriving at Your Destination," less than a third actually like their daily trips, and a majority find that their time in motion adds up to only a "neutral" experience. Almost half believe that "Getting There Is Half the Fun"; on the other hand, more than half either agree or can't say they disagree (another "neutral" vote) when presented with the bleakest summary statement on this multiple-choice survey form about the value of moving around: "Travel Time Is Generally Wasted Time."

Wasted time feels like time unlived, time marred or defaced or denied, time that has been stolen or was never properly delivered or somehow escaped, time that has been subtracted from the ledger of a lifetime. With that in mind, here's the figure I keep drawing from the most reliable aggregate travel data: If the great majority of Americans are devoting an hour and a half or more a day to travel, and if this represents 10 percent of their time awake, and if we arrive at a point where Travel Time Is Never Wasted Time, so that this portion of a day becomes at least as valuable to us as what happens before and after, then by rescuing, recapturing, restoring, and resecuring this period of the day, we will have rearranged our waking lives in effect so they will last longer. Less time will be siphoned off or rushed through or blotted out as a way of getting travel over with. And, no matter what calendar age we reach, we will have amplified something the calendar cannot measure, our "available lifespan," so to speak. By about 10 percent, it would seem, if current travel times hold.

Modern Europeans and Americans can expect to live more than twice as long as the people who were born on these continents in the 1750s, at the beginning of the industrial revolution. And it has recently been suggested by an English epidemiologist, David Barker, that this, along with the fact that most of today's Westerners are half again as tall as their forebears, traces back in large part to the fact that our mothers eat better, giving us a "nutritional boost" even before birth, allowing us to grow stronger and more durable hearts. "The embryo," Barker says, "is very sensitive to the nutrients it's bathed in." Longer lives are a legacy of our arrival in the world. An "attentional boost," on the other hand, a gift we can give ourselves, can nourish our journey through the world.

Knowing about this different form of life extension can help us start riding both of the elephants in the transportation center, yoking them together and then steering them side by side toward a destination now just over the horizon. Many would-be elephant riders, people interested in shrinking the daily distances between homes, jobs, schools, and shops, have as their primary focus a process of parallel reductions, lopping travel time to make profound cuts in the gas burned, the pollution emitted, the amount of concrete paving poured—and perhaps at the same time to reassemble people, to cut down on some of the sense of being cut off and cast adrift that can intensify as the locations at either end of travel time become more remote from one another.

Meanwhile other people, once they have come to connect motion and minds in motion and to see opportunities for Deep Travel within even the most familiar of daily rounds, sense a similarly urgent need to protect human possibilities by guarding and adding further dimension to the travel time we have, whatever its total amount—although the percentage of the day given over to it may have an irreducible component. According to one way of looking at things, all these looming necessities—lessening the weight of the human footprint on the planet (as economists now describe the cumulative impacts of our actions on land, air, and water); strengthening communities that have been flung outward; and celebrating and exploring the imprint travel has on the human mind—already have a point of overlap.

The idea of the "travel-time budget," or TTB, an intriguing and controversial discovery by a 1970s World Bank mobility researcher, Vacov Zahavi, arose from observations that in all societies, as two pioneering Australian transportation writers, Peter Newman and Jeff Kenworthy, later summarized the finding, "a portion of each person's daily time, around one hour is 'budgeted' to necessary travel needs. The concept of the travel-time budget appears to hold true in all cities, whether bicycle modes dominate, such as in the Netherlands, whether public transport dominates, such as in Singapore, or whether the private motorized modes dominate, such as in the U.S. and Australian cities." As a result, as they put it, "the city will always be 'one hour wide.'"

Other researchers, looking backward across the centuries, have found the same time correspondences, with only occasional variation: Werner Bróg, a German investigator of mobility patterns around the world, reports that "in a historical context, the average travel time for work trips has been stable for the past 600 years." The Domesday Book, the first great census of England, compiled in 1086 at the order of William the Conqueror, reported, according to the distinguished American geographer William L. Garrison, that those who worked away from home needed "about 20 minutes" to reach their fields or pastures. And Cesare Marchetti, an Italian physicist, who considers travel time a modern global invariant—"from Australia to Zambia," as he says—has also, glancing deeper into the past, noted that, "interestingly, the travel-time budget was also about one hour 5,000 years ago."

This data, if it holds up—and there are those who think that the TTB is no more than a mismeasurement—could give us a whole new perspective on travel time. We might, for instance, have to think of it as an enduring phenomenon of sedentism, if you will. "Sedentism" is a word anthropologists use to describe settling down, staying in one place—or at least returning to the same place at the end of the day. It was once thought that learning how to grow crops 10,000 to 11,000 years ago was what first made staying put both possible and necessary, but excavations in Israel and Syria in the 1950s and 1960s brought the

Natufians to contemporary attention. These hunter-gatherers of the wooded eastern Mediterranean hills, and similar groups north and east of there in the grasslands near the Euphrates, between 13,500 and 14,500 years ago took advantage of conditions that sprang up in the first millennia that followed the Last Glacial Maximum 20,000 years ago, and stopped in their tracks.

They ceased their wanderings and built villages, and continued to hunt and gather. The woods provided acorns and pistachios and almonds, gazelles to hunt, and "wild gardens" of naturally growing cereals and peas and lentils they could harvest with stone sickles. They even domesticated dogs, the first companion animal and helper. Steven Mithen, an English archaeologist, has described the transformation in a poetic book about the long period between the melting of the glaciers and the rise of cities, *After the Ice: A Global Human History, 20,000—5,000 BC*: here were hunter-gatherers who "enjoyed the most attractive environmental conditions that had existed for many thousands of years, since long before the LGM. At no other times had animals and plants been so abundant, so diverse, and so predictable in their availability. . . . This provided them with the opportunity to give up the mobile lifestyle that had served human society since its first appearance 3.5 million years ago on the African savannah."

Mithen is not sure why they would have wanted to: "Why create the social tensions that inevitably arise when one has permanent next-door neighbors within a village? Why expose oneself to human waste and garbage and the health risks that accompany a more sedentary lifestyle? Why risk the depletion of the animals and plants near one's own village?" There are no signs of any of the external pressures that might have halted the Natufians in one spot—overpopulation, ill health, low-grade wars with neighboring groups. Following the lead of François Valla, the French archaeologist who excavated one Natufian village, Mithen thinks the pressures were more likely to have been internal. Settlement may have been the result of a dream, an urge, an effort, and even a makeshift strategy to increase the vividness with which life could be lived, something that "simply emerged" from the seasonal gatherings of presedentist groups. Valla said his guess about this was based on forceful writings by a famous French sociologist, Marcel Mauss, who lived with more recent Arctic hunter-gatherers a hundred years ago and found their periodic get-togethers "characterized by intense communal life, by feasts and religious ceremonies, by intellectual discussion, and by lots of sex. In comparison, the rest of the year, when people lived in small, far-flung groups, was rather dull."

So at bottom, perhaps, what was being brought to a standstill by withdrawing from constant movement across the face of the earth was a calendar, a cycle of encounters hitherto only infrequent that had now been arrested and then held steady during its peak days. The abundance around them was a stepping stone toward greater abundance within.

The Natufian villages didn't last. They were abandoned during a sudden return of more glacial conditions, called the Younger Dryas, which took 1,500 years to retreat. The Eden-like plentifulness that had allowed or tempted the Natufians to linger disappeared, and in the hardships imposed by colder times, the intensified life of the villages melted away. People in the eastern Mediterranean hills resumed their wanderings. The warmer world that we know, the world whose seasons and features we recognize, appeared about 11,000 years ago— geologists call it the "Holocene epoch," meaning "entirely recent"; one anthropologist calls it the "long summer." The steady-state nature of this more recent period has helped erase memories of both the warm and bountiful spring and then the sharp return of winter that preceded it. Regrouped villages reappeared with the Holocene, but under the new and still prevailing circumstances of more restricted abundance and part-time plentifulness, they were the villages of farmers. Farmers who worked hard, coaxing a living from the landscape. Farmers who walked to their fields and back, budgeted their time, and were subject to an inexorable annual calendar of planting and harvesting.

With this background in mind, the purpose and function of having a continuing daily travel-time budget can perhaps be explained in several different ways. There is what we might call the "victor's viewpoint," an after-the-fact, somewhat complacent, and still prevalent account put together by generations of sedentists to help them understand and appreciate their new situation. Endless travel, in this formulation, is something humans and their predecessors had to endure ever since various prehuman ancestors stood upright millions of years ago; when permanent settlements came, this burden could finally be set down—although people are still willing to tolerate a fraction, a remnant of their previous travel, even as much as an hour's worth each day, to keep settled life stable and prevent the resumption of wandering.

On the other hand, travel behavior studies, like the Bay Area survey mentioned earlier, have turned up evidence that, despite thousands of years at anchor at fixed abodes, with street addresses to return to each night, people seem to have retained an unquenched thirst for daily doses of travel—or what the survey report calls an "unobserved desired level of mobility." They insist on reporting positives, in other words. Among the hundreds of Bay Area residents questioned, for example, "the average reported ideal one-way commuting time was just over 16 minutes." Meaning that on a round-trip basis these people would, by and large, like to retain at least half of a one-hour travel-time budget. (A few—3 percent—would prefer "a zero to two-minute commute" one way; almost half wanted round-trips that would last at least forty minutes.) If François Valla is correct, and nonstop travel was abandoned to increase the pace and intensity of human mental life by containing it within an unmoving spot, how would we then explain the persistence of the travel urge over the past 11,000 years, a force that remains vigorous even after being pruned and circumscribed or shunted aside? Perhaps it's simply because travel, even when no longer a constant state, continues to serve as a unique stimulus with its own unsurpassed and still much-prized ability to lead our minds in new directions.

Patricia L. Mokhtarian, the co-compiler of the Bay Area travel survey, is a transportation engineering pioneer. A professor and researcher at the University of California at Davis's Institute of Transportation Studies, she has spent more than thirty years studying travel behavior, devoting much of her research time to combating the notion that travel is nothing more than a "disutility," or a "bad," as she calls it, an activity people undertake only when required to, a behavior we have, in effect, outgrown—or moved beyond—but have learned to devote to a higher purpose.

It's been a continuing struggle, she has written in various papers. "Since the origin of transportation as a field of scientific inquiry," one of her scholarly articles begins, "the tenet that 'travel is a derived demand' has been accepted with little question." A second paper expands on the pervasiveness of this viewpoint and its consequences:

"The truism that travel is a 'derived demand'—meaning that travel is not pursued for its own sake but only as a means of accessing desired activities in other locations—appears in virtually every textbook on transportation planning, engineering, or economics, and has dominated our professional approach to transportation planning and policymaking for decades."

With travel so widely, and seemingly so scientifically, assumed to be a "bad" to be endured, a cost to be grudgingly paid, "improving" travel then becomes a matter of minimizing it, making trips shorter so that less travel needs to happen. When planning a new highway, for instance, as Mokhtarian notes, "the assumed monetary value of travel time savings typically constitutes the largest share of the quantified benefits of a proposed improvement." Which means that, as they proudly design and build a new road, most transportation engineers, in some odd corner of their minds, also think of themselves as being in the business of making travel go away.

From the survey data she's been gathering about "attitudes toward mobility"—with positives about travel that repeatedly turn up and are never extinguished, even when negatives soar—Mokhtarian thinks it's self-evident that people arrive in the world with "an intrinsic desire for travel." Which establishes that travel—to give this finding a simultaneous translation into language her colleagues can recognize—"has an intrinsic positive utility." Whatever the circumstances, she has found instances where people have chosen moving around solely "for its own sake." Sometimes this takes the form of what she calls "excess travel," meaning trips that deliberately last longer than they need to, whether for looking at scenery, or exploring, or relaxing, or "just for the fun of it," or suddenly taking "a new route to a familiar destination," or going out of your way on purpose, even to a farther-away destination, "to experience more of your surroundings."

Mokhtarian measures what people do, the "activities that generate the travel," as she says, rather than trying to record the less quantifiable change of focus that may precede them—the shift in attention that adds color and depth back to scenery or makes a familiar place one to explore by pointing out how much of it has gone unnoticed; so she doesn't directly focus on the invisible, interior personal activities that can regenerate interest in the observable personal activities that then generate the travel. But without discussing it by name, she has come up with an excellent informal litmus test for determining whether Deep Travel has put in an appearance—something she calls the "Teleportation Test," based on the old *Star Trek* quick-exit plea, "Beam me up, Scotty." As Mokhtarian puts it, "The question is, 'if you could snap your fingers or blink your eyes and instantly teleport yourself to the desired destination, would you do so?' "

A meticulous observer, Mokhtarian sees the need for a Teleportation Test because of the differentiations she finds even among trips that people self-report as enjoyable. Some of the pleasures people find while traveling have their own distinctive flavors that have been stirred in from other sources rather than being directly offered by travel begun "for its own sake." For instance, "when a respondent reports that she 'loves' vacation travel, it is unlikely that she is referring to the fifteen hours in one or more crowded and noisy airplanes, the six hours waiting in uncomfortable airports eating overpriced and unpalatable food, and the three hours of ground-access travel in peak-period urban traffic. It is more likely that a halo effect is at work, so that she is confounding the positive appeal of the destination with the travel required to reach it."

Similarly, "in reporting an affinity for traveling, individuals may in part be considering the utility of activities they can conduct while traveling. In some cases, it is in fact the 'anti-activity,' " Mokhtarian thinks, that becomes most important—such as talking or texting on a cell phone, reading, listening to a talk show on the radio, music on an iPod, or a book on tape, or watching TV or videos. She notes, "The phenomenon of 'carcooning' is one manifestation of this aspect, in which the personal vehicle is customized for the traveler's comfort, almost as a sanctuary-escape from the world."

These are very helpful distinctions. The first situation is an example of what we might call "*already-there* travel," in which people, inside their minds, have already set their clocks forward into a future time zone, and more strongly feel the lure of what will or could or might happen at some point later on than they do the pull of what is already disclosing itself around them or the possibilities of what could or might happen at any moment along the way. *I Know Where I'm Going!* a magical English fairy tale of a movie from 1945, is entirely based on the great good fortune that can await someone, in this case a headstrong twenty-five-year-old English girl, who gets deflected from a seemingly implacable course of "already-there travel."

Harlan Ellison, the science-fiction writer, has often said that there are only two plots in literature: a person goes on a journey; a stranger comes to town. *I Know Where I'm Going!* uses both plots to tell a travel story that is about fighting off falling in love. Joan Webster, the heroine, is on her way from Manchester to Kiloran, a small island in the Scottish Hebrides, fiercely determined to marry a rich older man she has never cared for. A three-day gale strands her on the larger Isle of Mull, half an hour from her destination, and "by the time the storm dies down," as one of the film's writers, Emeric Pressburger, later explained, "her life has changed, and she no longer wants to go to the island." Her typed itinerary scheduling her every moment is blown into the ocean, and things she has had no time for, like the details of life on Mull, famous for its sands and the gray seals along its shores, for its moors and the sheep that graze them, for the 250 species of birds flying overhead, begin to catch at her. She hears the gray seals singing, she joins the islanders at a joyous ceilidh dance, she meets a young man who adores her. Marooned on Mull, thwarted and cut off from her goals, with all her assumptions tattered and then blown away, four days later she finds that her life has been rescued by this misfortune, not ruined, as she had thought, and that she has been saved from herself in the nick of time. Using the Mokhtarian Teleportation Scale, this is a trip that would have been avoided, if possible. At great cost.

"Carcooning," on the other hand, identified by Mokhtarian as a different kind of pleasurable travel where travel is not what provides the pleasure, is more a matter of a postponed departure than of a premature arrival. It represents what we could call "*never-left-at-all* travel," or "*still-back-here* travel." As Mokhtarian suggests, this is partly a matter of continuing to do exactly the same things we were doing while stationary, almost without interruption, and partly a question of just how "transparent" and "breathable" the vehicles that enclose us are or are capable of being. Meaning, to what extent do they pass along or intensify or filter or suppress the view unfolding in front of us? A generation ago, the profoundly curious American anthropologist Edward T. Hall found himself transfixed by the serene detachment from the passing scene promised in an American magazine ad "showing a car full of happy people *floating on a cloud above the road!*" Modern American cars impose "real sensory deprivation" on their users, Hall wrote in *The Hidden Dimension,* a 1960s book about how people use space that still seems daring in its insights, since "soft springs, soft cushions, soft tires, power steering, and monotonously smooth pavements create an unreal experience of the earth."

In general, Mokhtarian suspects that among the larger category of people who say they enjoy traveling, those whose focus stays behind them, meaning "still-back-here travelers," most of whose attention is still caught up in the kind of things they were doing before leaving or can do when not traveling—phoning, listening to iPods, and so on—might opt for teleportation if it became available. "Already-there travelers," people whose focus is anticipatory and has leapt so far ahead of them that they are already tasting the future, she thinks would almost always prefer to be beamed to their destination. There will also, of course, be people who move back and forth from one of these travel states to another, or from either or both of them into Deep Travel. There is little doubt that Deep Travelers, whether they started off with a plan of traveling for its own sake or at some point along the way found themselves responding directly to a trip, reveling in it, undistracted by what they have left behind or have not yet reached, will be people who would prefer to continue on with their journey, who wouldn't miss it for the world, so to speak, even if there were a fast-forward button within easy reach.

This brings up a further layer of travel distractability, here in the unteleported world, that Mokhtarian hasn't yet examined: the extent to which roads and streets and trails, the guided paths, the support systems for our current vehicles that stretch in intersecting and ever-lengthening and widening strips and stripes across the landscape (forming the most frequently encountered part of what engineers call the "infrastructure," or physical underpinnings, of a country) in and of themselves dilute or mute or otherwise reshape the sights, sounds, and sensations of travel—and even the underlying "awayness" and "otherness" that travel brings with it. Architects often talk about buildings as our "third skin"—with clothes being our "second skin." A few of the words we use for clothing or for things around the house, such as "muffler," for example, or "comforter," suggest the dual body and mind functions of these extra skins, which by their very presence can change both what reaches us from outside and what we make of it. If a car often acts as a kind of third-skin extender, so to speak, a room linker, a detachable, rolling pod that, as it shuttles us between interiors, can set up and sustain in our minds a practically unbroken semblance of indoorsiness en route, the corridors that enfold these vehicles have likewise often taken on the role of a "fourth skin." They've become something else that, as it makes travel easier, can tug on our minds—perhaps shielding us from a distraction, perhaps more thoughtlessly restricting our awareness and shrinking the world in ways we can't even quite notice.

You can, for instance, drive along Main Street in the stately old college town of Middlebury, Vermont, on the downtown block that leads off the village green—it takes no more than a minute or two, even when there's traffic—and sense only a slight gap in the nineteenth-century brick storefronts and offices lining the street. In fact, you have just crossed over the top of the reason why Middlebury sprang into existence more than two hundred years ago: a dramatically noisy, eighteen-foot-tall waterfall on Otter Creek, Vermont's longest waterway, that tumbles down into a sudden gorge and churning eddy just behind Main Street. Early in the industrial revolution, Middlebury Falls was the power source for the country's second woolen mill and for dozens of sawmills and gristmills and cotton mills and nail factories, and other shops, all silent now, including a blacksmith's forge where in the 1820s John Deere, who later moved to Illinois and invented the "plow that broke the plains"—made of polished steel that could cut through the thick clay soils of the prairies—served his apprenticeship.

Like many towns, Middlebury never completely forgot its origins or the central position of its most commanding and once-inescapable physical feature, but over a hundred years ago, at a moment of high Victorian prosperity, it reached a point where it no longer put them on display. An older, open-sided, wooden Main Street bridge only twelve feet above the falls burned, and a local benefactor decided to replace it in stone with a copy of a bridge built across the Tiber River almost eighteen hundred years earlier that let Romans reach the tomb of the emperor Hadrian. The new Middlebury bridge was ten feet higher than the old one, so the entire block of Main Street had to be raised by ten feet. The gorge, called Frog Hollow, is not off-limits, if you know how to find it. A small street winds down into it, and one of the old mills has reopened as a state Craft Center. From the Craft Center windows you can look up at the surging waterfall and, just behind it, at the sturdy stone arches of the mock-Roman bridge—which, you realize down below, are from Main Street, when you're crossing them, as invisible as the falls they hide. Up on Main Street the sounds of traffic are interrupted every fifteen minutes by chimes from the five-tiered spire of the Congregational Church on the village green, but I get a sense that the rhythm of the day is incomplete. The roar of the falls, a pulse that never ceases, remains undetectable.

A much-admired and far more spectacular bridge, the recently opened Millau Bridge, or Millau Viaduct, in the south of France, whose four-lane roadway stretches evenly and horizontally across the sky, looking from a distance almost like a thin, graceful gray crayon line drawn by a remarkably steady hand, brings with it a similar and quite fixable "fourth skin" problem, an unnoticed mental tourniquet that needs careful loosening. The Millau Viaduct is the tallest bridge in the world, and it crosses the steep-sided, eight-hundred-foot deep Tarn River Valley, an expanse of sloping forests, sheep pastures, ancient villages, and the town of Millau itself that's more than a mile and a half wide, without even dipping toward it, staying instead up at the height of the two plateaus that flank the valley. As the last link in a superhighway, the A75, from Paris to Barcelona, the new bridge is part of an ongoing project to eliminate traffic jams between Paris and the beaches of the Riviera and, more ambitiously, to stitch Europe more tightly together with new roads and high-speed trains, the twenty-first-century equivalent of the old Roman aqueducts. Only now it is people, rather than water, who find themselves mingled and poured through the countryside in long geometric lines that can ignore geography to stay level.

The viaduct's lines are so open and clean that it could easily be considered a Roman aqueduct turned inside out, with air substituting for stone. In a Roman aqueduct, the strength of the ground rises upward, stone by stone, until its final rock has been piled high enough to support the water pipe on top. The Millau Viaduct seems suspended from the sky. Seven slender pillars rise from the valley floor, pierce the center of the roadway, and then soar above it as masts that radiate parallel lines of "stay cables" that reach down to hold the roadway in place. The design is the work of the London "starchitect" Norman Foster and his office, and like many great buildings it seems from afar to change its shape and take on new meanings with shifts in the light or the weather. Half a million people came to look at the bridge while it was still under construction. "Looking up from the valley floor," wrote one of these admiring visitors, Frank Renout, a reporter for the *Christian Science Monitor,* "you might struggle to see the bridge's underside: often, only the pillars are visible, as fog tends to engulf the roadway that spans the empyrean. Standing on one of the surrounding mountains the picture is reversed: a futuristic expressway floating on top of the clouds."

With so many superlatives incorporated into its design, you might think that driving over the Millau Bridge would be as memorable as its setting or its construction—and Norman Foster has told reporters that this was always his aim, to provide something soaring and cloud piercing as the crowning achievement of all his firm's ingenuity: "You do fly across the bridge, literally above the clouds." Yet, curiously, the travel experience currently being offered, although unusual, is tantalizingly abstract and reserved, more earthbound than airborne. Part of this probably comes from the fact that the mission of the bridge, as a link in an expressway, is to hurry you without pause across the Tarn River Valley, toward the Mediterranean beaches fifty miles to the south—which probably also means that many of the people using the bridge are "already-there travelers," for whom reaching the bridge may primarily register as a sort of homing signal that broadcasts a message of "less than an hour left to go."

There is no lingering on the Millau Viaduct. It is not open to pedestrians. The bridge carries a high-speed, white-striped, blacktop roadway that looks identical to the highway segments beyond the bridge on either side, with two vehicle lanes and a service lane in either direction, separated by a median strip. There is a speed limit of 110 kilometers an hour (over 68 miles an hour); this is something of a compromise: the original speed limit was 130 kilometers (over 80), but bridge officials noticed that cars were slowing down as they got close to the bridge so that people could take pictures of it out their windows. What changes most dramatically once you're out on the bridge is the median strip, which is entirely taken up by the bridge's seven masts, each almost three hundred feet high, and the eleven stay cables that branch triangularly from either side of each mast. All are painted a cool, metallic gray-white, and their rigid and alternating vertical and diagonal lines flicker past gauntly, rhythmically, and almost hypnotically on the left during the minute and twenty seconds or so that it takes to cross the valley below. It's like speeding past the world's longest sculpture garden, an allée of gigantic, minimalist, leafless trees.

The other distinctive feature of the bridge's roadway are the fences that line its outer edges from one end to the other—and it is these sleek fences, elegant in themselves, that give the Millau Viaduct such an oddly rough fourth skin. They dazzle the eye but fail to unlock the mind's eye.

The fences are altogether necessary and even as currently designed they are—almost right. There are actually two of them on either side of the bridge: a simple, open, low, metal inner fence that separates the roadway from a narrow pathway used by bridge maintenance workers, and a higher and more elaborate outer fence, taller than a person, that curves protectively inward, cradling the roadway. Considering that one of the seven pylons holding up the roadway is almost as tall as the Eiffel Tower, and that cars and trucks on the bridge are moving by at almost 70 miles an hour, these fences must, and of course do, have the kind of third-skin strength that can withstand and contain a serious accident. The outer fences are more innovative, metal-and-glass adaptations of old-time, wooden farm-field post-and-rail fences, a design made up of horizontal slats—kept far enough apart so you can see through the gaps—that get nailed to vertical posts. On the Millau Bridge the posts are metal, narrow, and gray-white like the masts and cables, and the slats are rounded, striped semicylinders of reinforced glass. The use of glass suggests that Foster and his associates were aware of and wanted to do right by the bridge's fourth-skin obligations.

The outer fences have a practical purpose—they are windscreens that can cut strong, midair wind gusts in half, gentling them to the kind of flows we expect to encounter at ground level. Since the architects could have deflected the winds with solid steel panels, perhaps their thought was that by using glass they could offer a somewhat muted celebration of the bridge's "midairness," providing glimpses of what's out there while still shielding drivers from the vertigo of the situation by keeping them semi-enclosed. A mother might loosely hold a couple of fingers in front of a small child's eyes, concealing while revealing, to make the view from the top of a high hill seem safer. But what's been built doesn't quite do this. Applying a fourth-skin or Deep Travel test beforehand would have shown . . . but of course we don't have fourth-skin or Deep Travel tests yet.

Such tests— they are coming, and will become part of routine design procedures, like safety tests—would have shown that the glass half tubes chosen have a couple of flaws. In the meantime, we have

YouTube, which has put these defects on display. As a series of YouTube videos shot independently by people crossing the Millau Viaduct makes plain, the bridge's glass railings, when looked at straight on, as only a passenger in a car or truck can do, turning right to look out the side window, are at best only semi-transparent, changing as the light hits them, and the curves in them bend and change the shape of what you're seeing. Strangely, the landscape down below, seen through alternating horizontal stripes of glass railings and the open gaps between them, takes on an indistinct and wavering and murky look, like something being peered at underwater.

For drivers, on the other hand, there's a totally different effect. Looking up ahead, they see the fence stretching out in front as completely opaque, a curving, gray-white, enveloping solid. If passengers intermittently feel underwater, drivers seem to be moving along something more like a sunken country road, with high embankments on either side and the sky above.

So it's an uneasy mixture, for the moment. Expressway, abstract sculpture park, submarine views, sunken road. And the sky. The Millau Viaduct brilliantly displays the sky. The bridge isn't going anywhere— it was built to last at least a century—so there's plenty of time for thinking about a fourth-skin retrofit here, and for getting it right, which would be a matter of making sure that views *from* the bridge become as captivating and sought after as views *of* the bridge have been ever since its pylons began to rise from the Tarn Valley floor. The sky is already an immediate and compelling presence, so that needs no further work. The masts and the cables are a given. But then the possibilities begin. Is speed as essential to the bridge's success as has been assumed? Could the speed limit, already reduced, decrease by 10 kilometers at every pylon until you reach the center pylon? That way you'd be going less than 45 miles an hour out on the middle of the bridge. This idea was part of a fourth-skin solution arrived at in the White Mountains of New Hampshire: speeds on Interstate Highway 93 drop from 65 miles per hour to 45 for an eight-mile stretch as the road passes through Franconia Notch, a spectacular mountain pass.

Is there room for people to walk or ride bikes on the Millau Bridge? Does the roadway itself have to be black? I doubt it. I'm not suggesting making it see-through, like the glass-bottomed walkway the Hualapai Indians extended seventy feet out from the rim of the Grand Canyon in 2007; some visitors to the Hualapai Skywalk can't bring themselves to trust the strength of the reinforced glass under their feet or the horseshoe-shaped steel girders that support it, and freeze in their tracks or shuffle forward without looking down at all. Painting the road surface a dark blue or some slowly changing palette of colors—with perhaps a different color at each mast—might suggest entering a new realm without distracting drivers. Or maybe a dark green when passing over the valley's forested slopes, a lighter green when drivers are over the fields and pastures along the flatter lands near the bottom, and a stripe of blue when crossing the Tarn River itself. Finding different glass for the fences that are now half porthole and half wall seems like the easiest place to start—in order to create barriers that hold winds and cars back but let minds through.

BEYOND THE TURNSTILE

In some ways, Deep Travel, when it puts in a sudden appearance, is like having jumped into a different "first skin"—it feels as if at any moment we can molt the outside edge we were born with or let it melt away, leaving something more transparent and flexible and responsive, less armored against or oblivious to the world we no longer seem so shut off from. It's a great discovery, finding that we've been gifted with senses that are already capable—without any retrofitting—of acting either as a wall or an open door. Even more remarkably, we don't actually have to do anything cumbersome or effortful, like shedding a skin or a shell, to effect this changeover. Sometimes Deep Travel seems to reach out for us—the way Joan Webster, the heroine of *I Know Where I'm Going!* couldn't avoid seeing a rainbow on Mull or hearing the seals singing. At other moments it simply arrives for no obvious reason. But when this happens, what is it that we do, or that is done to us? Where and what within us is the mechanism, the trigger, the shift key, the entry point?

When I first began to try to think this through, I assumed, never having seen these questions in print, that there wasn't much information on the subject. I realized with a start one day that some classic travel books I'd already looked though and been disappointed in—were they ignoring the matter or avoiding it?—needed to be read again, with attention this time on a different and more indirect language. Careful observations of minute changes of mood or awareness were being presented in images that were also metaphors and symbols that could be registered and decoded or deciphered if you retraced the sequence of feelings and sensations that the words conjured up. In this way, outside events—real ones, I didn't doubt—could offer some clues to the course taken by inside events. Perhaps this is one reason why certain travel scenes are so gripping to read: they seem to be clear-eyed descriptions of two overlapping journeys. Have you ever been swimming sidestroke and looked out at the world so that one eye sees through air and the other through water?

There is a wonderful passage, for instance, in *My Khyber Marriage,* a Scotswoman's best-selling book about Afghanistan published more than ninety years ago (and still in print), that now seems to me a detailed account of her dramatic arrival in a new land that also has something unusual to say about reaching and passing through a Deep Travel entry point.

Morag Murray Abdullah, a sort of real-life Joan Webster in reverse, had met her true love, the son of an Afghan tribal chieftain, in Edinburgh and was traveling with him to his parents' home in a kind of no-man's-land just beyond the Khyber Pass in the Hindu Kush—despite terrifying warnings from friends at home that leaving what was then British India behind meant that she was about to be poisoned or sold into slavery:

> After two days' rest we left Peshawar by road through the Khyber Pass. The great rocks, towering boulder upon boulder to heights ranging from 600 to 1000 feet, strike a peculiar terror in the traveler. In some places the pass is so narrow that four camels cannot walk abreast. At the actual frontier there is a "turnstile" through which one passes into "No Man's Land." That turnstile looks unimportant. It should be massive and stand for what it is, the gate leading to what is one of the least known and most remarkable countries in the world—a strip of land neither Indian nor Afghan, inhabited by clans who owe allegiance to none but their own chiefs, and live in loopholed towers, always armed and sleeping with their rifles at their sides.
>
> Into this land of mystery I passed through the insignificant turnstile. Certainly I must confess I felt a little the truth of what I had been told in far-away Edinburgh. I stood for a few seconds in wonderment at it all. Was it a dream? Would I awake to find myself in Edinburgh again? I looked back at the last outpost of my own people and knew there would be no possibility of my return if the odds went against me. It is a

moment I do not wish anyone to experience, unless they are certain of their ability to face confidently what lies over those hills.

My husband I think sensed my feelings. "Welcome," he said, "to the land of my fathers."

An insignificant turnstile, not something massive, leads into the land of mystery. Don't look for something elaborate or exciting. Stay simple.

Then I began to find similar hints in a number of travel books. It wasn't fair to think of it as information, because the authors themselves may not have been aware of addressing the "second traveler" within us, the Deep Traveler. Nevertheless, there they were—descriptions that seemed to resonate on several levels. I found I was paying particular attention to side trips, to stories about how making a detour or taking a shortcut, turning aside unexpectedly from the main road or veering off at an odd angle from the stated purpose of a trip, or sometimes about being guided down a path that seemed not to beckon or to have no destination led instead to extraordinary discoveries. These last accounts— about being directed into an improbable course—seemed to add another element, the suggestion that our "second traveler" is active even before we find ourselves moving into Deep Travel. Maybe the "second vehicle" available to us is always warmed up and ready to go, and this is why we can hop into it almost without pause. And maybe there are always at least two paths leading off from practically every resting place and each front door.

Louis Palmer, a traveler who visited Afghanistan several generations after Morag Murray Abdullah, seems from his writings to have been frequently escorted by companions he met along the road to almost wildly improbable and quite unguessable locations. His *Adventures in Afghanistan* is about joining a group sent to resupply Afghan resistance fighters in the early 1990s, shortly after Soviet troops had withdrawn but before the fall of the local Communist regime. On one occasion Palmer gets taken to a hidden castle in an area of northeastern Afghanistan deserted since a Mongol massacre centuries before. The approach is twisting and takes some time, pulling him along unfamiliar paths: first he is driven through "what looked like a mine-shaft, at a fairly precipitate angle, down into the earth." After a right turn, this track becomes "a gully or very narrow, shallow valley, roofed over with what looked like matting, with light streaming down in a checker pattern as we drove slowly along. It was like being under the sea."

After three miles of this, he writes, "we emerged into a large flat expanse" and "before us stood a turreted, apparently deserted wall, with a crowd of very nondescript-looking hillmen in padded jackets and high red boots and shaggy fur caps, standing at the crumbling entrance to . . . what?"

Passing through an inner courtyard, he recalls, there is another right turn, and "there, immediately in front of me, I saw standing open a huge door of oiled olive-wood, with great iron decorations on it and tiling beyond." He has to take off his boots because "the tiling of the walkway was the bed of a stream or, at any rate, the bottom of a channel of running water. As I stepped onto it, in my turn, I saw that the tiles were patterned to resemble fish and flowers. We were in a passage then, this time perfumed with the odor of sandalwood." From there he finally emerges into "one beautiful room after another, something reminiscent of the architecture of the Taj Mahal, and up a flight of marble steps into a lofty, airy hall, surrounded by marble columns and with excellent carpets on the floor."

In a second adventure, Palmer is invited to meet with an Arab group descended from fighters who had invaded the country in the seventh century and who now live in a miniature, secluded valley guarding a healing spring. This time, "bowling along the excellent highway" north of Kabul, he is met by an escort and, leaving the highway, finds himself "moving along a dried-up river bed, one of those which flood with seasonal rains, and heading for a thick clump of trees a mile or so away. As we approached, I saw that a cavern or tunnel opened just before the trees." He continues:

I switched on the headlamps, and saw that we were going downhill, through a passageway some fifteen feet wide, with boulders on either side, where guards were dimly to be seen from time to time, each armed with a rifle.

It all looked, and felt, distinctly sinister, like the way into a robbers' den such as might have been described, or imagined, in some tale of ancient times.

Then, suddenly, around a curve, we were in daylight, in a valley full of poplar trees, with a small stream on one side, and high cliffs all around, dotted with stone-built square edifices.

It really was an astonishing sight: a secret place if ever there was one. People were walking about; men, women and children, looking at products on sale at a number of stalls, while goats and sheep, chickens and donkeys, wandered here and there, as if they had no owners.

Suddenly I started to feel afraid, probably as a result of the contrast between the darkness and the light, the uncertainty and now the total ordinariness of the scene in front of me.

When Palmer's fear subsides he finds himself made welcome in this miniature valley. He stays for three days, drinks from the mineral spring on two of the days—the water, he reports, "tasted very fresh, though slightly mineral"—and finds before he leaves that rheumatic pains he's had for the past five years have faded away.

Sometimes an entire trip can seem in retrospect like a metaphor for the transition at the entry point into Deep Travel. Martin Hanlon, a Queens College sociologist who studies the impact that interstate highways have had on American cities, has been carrying in his mind for decades the imprint that one train ride in 1970 left on him. When he mentioned it to me one day, I asked him to write it down:

Many years ago my wife and I were working in Nairobi, Kenya, where we were often house parents to fellow volunteers who got more exciting assignments out in the bush. For our first vacation, we decided to travel to Mombasa—Kenya's historic port city on the Indian Ocean, about 300 miles away. Renting a car was financially out of the question; bus service was unreliable; most people took "Matatus"—grossly overloaded Peugeot station wagons driven by insanely fast drivers. We chose instead the Nairobi-to-Mombasa train.

The train pulled out of Nairobi's central station just before dusk. Nairobi is just south of the equator, so evening always comes about seven, year-round. We settled into our mahogany-and-brass second-class compartment, a comfortable, shabby, colonial-era relic, like the railway itself, whose construction had been menaced by lions. There was a porcelain wash basin and pull-down wooden tray. The journey took about twelve hours.

We woke in the early morning to glorious sights: WaKamba tribal villages; snow-capped Mount Kilimanjaro to the south, giraffes feeding on acacia trees; and the elephant herds of the rolling Tsavo plains. There was a knock on the door and morning tea. Our journey had begun in the crisp, highland air of Nairobi, a mile-high city. Now, opening the windows, we felt the warm, moist air of the Kenya coast. It was—wonderful.

Leaving "my own people" behind on a pathway only three camels wide; moving through shallow water on patterned tiles; moving down a dried-up river that flows only seasonally; moving through the night along tracks that had once been threatened by lions—and always, by these means, arriving at the unanticipated, which can be accompanied by a feeling of facing "confidently what lies over those hills," and which can arrive in many forms, such as "one beautiful room after another"; or waters that heal; or a landscape so full of novelty that when you opened the windows to it, "it was—wonderful." Here, I thought, were several different kinds of clues that could be followed. On the one hand, there were specific pointers to what it is we have to do to take ourselves to the starting point—advice about how to reach the reaching point, so to speak. Beyond that there were the beginnings of descriptions of what it's like to be "beyond the turnstile."

First things first. Maybe we can learn to summon Deep Travel or find our way to it at will, rather than awaiting its pleasure. Putting together pieces from three of these passages (the phrases "It was—wonderful" and "I stood for a few seconds in wonderment at it all" and the idea of following a riverbed through which water no longer flowed) led me to wonder about wonder, a feeling, it's frequently said, that is alive in children but has dried up in adults. There are famous sayings about wonder—Descartes called it "the first of the passions"; Plato celebrated it as "the only beginning of philosophy"; Ralph Waldo Emerson saw it leading to a different passion, in his words, "Men love to wonder, and that is the seed of science." But how do you isolate or amplify the taste of it? A friend suggested looking at a small book on the subject by Rachel Carson, *The Sense of Wonder*. Carson, now revered as a founder of modern environmentalism, brought out only four books in her short lifetime—three about the sea and *Silent Spring,* the famous best seller about the dangers of DDT and other pesticides. She died at the age of fifty-six, and *The Sense of Wonder,* originally a magazine article, "Help Your Child to Wonder," was published posthumously.

Carson agrees with the widespread and almost despairing assumption that wonder is perishable and too easily outgrown:

A child's world is fresh and new and beautiful, full of wonder and excitement. It is our misfortune that for most of us that clear-eyed vision, that true instinct for what is beautiful and awe-inspiring, is dimmed and even lost before we reach adulthood. If I had influence with the good fairy who is supposed to preside over the christening of all children I should ask that her gift to each child in the world be a sense of wonder so indestructible that it would last throughout life, as an unfailing antidote against the boredom and disenchantments of later years, the sterile preoccupation with things that are artificial, the alienation from the sources of our strength.

The hope the book offers is almost a hope against hope—she thinks parents can, in effect, teach their children to stay aloft and, in the process, regain an ability to fly they themselves may already have lost. Buoyancy, she declares, can be both rescued and regained once wonder is focused on the natural world: "If a child is to keep alive his inborn sense of wonder without any such gift from the fairies, he needs the companionship of at least one adult who can share it, rediscovering with him the joy, excitement and mystery of the world we live in." The book has many pleasures, among them a story of her first offering this gift to her twenty-month-old great-nephew, by wrapping him in a blanket and carrying him down to the Maine seashore on a stormy fall night: "Out there, just at the edge of where-we-couldn't-see, big waves were thundering in, dimly seen white shapes that boomed and shouted and threw great handfuls of froth at us. Together we laughed for pure joy—he a baby meeting for the first time the wild tumult of Oceanus, I with the salt of half a lifetime of sea love in me. But I think we felt the same spine-tingling response to the vast, roaring ocean and the wild night."

In *The Sense of Wonder,* there's a quiet lament about neglecting nature, thoughts brought on by walking outside and seeing the stars one summer night in southern Maine. "If this were a sight that could be seen only once in a century or even once in a human generation," Carson writes, "this little headland would be thronged with spectators. But it can be seen many scores of nights in any year, and so the lights burned in the cottages and the inhabitants probably gave not a thought to the beauty overhead; and because they could see it almost any night, perhaps they will never see it."

Here was the entrance I was looking for. It wasn't that the value of the stars had dimmed, or that their supply had in any way diminished. It was that certainty had triumphed over scarcity. What had dried up and disappeared from the mind's riverbed was the flow of attention. Because with certainty can come the complacency of pseudocertainty. It's a matter of confusing some "thats" with a "what." Knowing from repeated experience that we can count on the stars to be there and that their continuing presence is not an immediate threat, we begin to think we can say with the same level of confidence that we know what they are. Attention is withdrawn and moves in a different course. Some people know a great deal about the stars, others next to nothing. There is always more to find out. But habituation—not noticing something that seems unchanging and harmless—can cloak both knowledge and ignorance with the same mantle of indifference: "Oh, yes, the stars." Something we have a word for.

The tiles Louis Palmer walked along on his way to immense and beautiful rooms were decorated with fish and flowers; they could just as easily have been engraved with the reminder, "I don't really know what this is." Bringing this one realization back into your mind, elementary as it is, I've since found, can bring you straightaway into Deep Travel. The "wonder induction," it could be called—a simple matter while you're moving around or looking at a scene or at anything at all, maybe something as humble as a fire hydrant, and saying to yourself that, however many times you've seen it or one like it, you don't know exactly what it is. Or at least that there's a lot you haven't found out so far. Such as how it works, and what it's connected to, and where it came from, and who thought of it, and how many people are responsible for it, and when it might next be used, and why it looks the way it does, and how and when it got there. And having thought such thoughts, attention surges back, and the world opens up again and the immensity of the not-yet-known and the still-to-be-explored returns and beckons. Even after infrequent contact or what feels like a long absence, "wonder" hasn't vanished. It's constantly only a single thought away from making a fresh appearance.

The life of Jean-Henri Casimir Fabre, considered the father of modern entomology, and praised by Darwin as an "incomparable observer," seems to exemplify Emerson's observation about wonder growing into science. Fabre, who died in 1915, at the age of ninety-one, made many of his pioneering nineteenth-century discoveries about bees, wasps, beetles, grasshoppers, and crickets by walking around the two and a half "worthless" acres he owned for thirty-six years in Provence while peering through a magnifying glass. I've kept for twenty-five years in my small "Wonder" file of clippings a short appreciation of this "marvelous old man" by the American essayist Edmund Fuller, who had spent part of a May day wandering though Fabre's small garden, and then quoted from what Fabre had written about his "laboratory in the open fields": "I go the circuit of my enclosure over and over again, by short stages; I stop here and I stop there; patiently, I put questions and, at long intervals, I receive some scrap of a reply. . . . This is what I wished for . . . a bit of land, oh, not so very large . . . an abandoned, barren, sun-scorched bit of land, favored by thistles and by Wasps and Bees. . . . I observe, I experiment, I let the facts speak for themselves."

Fabre's "best instruments," Fuller wrote, "were 'Time and Patience.' In a difficult period, closing the third of his ten volumes, he wrote, 'Dear Insects, my study of you has sustained me in my heaviest trials. I must take my leave of you for today. . . . Shall I be able to speak to you again?' He did, again and again."

Perhaps age-old moral injunctions, such as "pride goeth before a fall," have parallel uses that apply to our access to perceptions. Maybe "pride" is a deadly sin or a vice (the original Latin word means "failing" or "defect"), and maybe—less judgmentally—it's a technical description of a specific kind of fragmentary perception; or should it perhaps be called a restricted information flow, like an artery unable to pump enough blood? This would make it a state people can get stuck in without realizing it—something that, along with, say, anger or greed, can deaden sensations that might otherwise reach you. A tendency to be preoccupied by a "love of one's own excellence"—Saint Augustine's definition of pride—would leave little room for wonder. Whether or not being humble (the "holy virtue" that, according to Dante, acts as an antidote to pride), or at least being more forthright and honest about what you know and don't know, will make you a better person, it can certainly restore a far wider range of awarenesses.

When I told an old friend one day about the "wonder bridge" into Deep Travel, he said, "Oh, there's an even easier way than that. What you're calling Deep Travel brings with it, you say, a remembrance that you don't know nearly what you could about what you're passing through if you open yourself up to it. But what about those times when your ignorance is total, and you don't even know where you are? Those are the off-balance moments when I think everyone is projected head-long into Deep Travel. You slow down; you may stop altogether. You're lost. You've *got* to find, and soon, some way to proceed, and so your senses are wide open and for the time being everything and everyone is a potential source of information. But that's not what I'm suggesting—getting lost. That's the situation behind the idea I use."

This friend works at the Metropolitan Museum of Art, in New York. "I call it the 'Warsaw Induction,'" he said. "All you have to do is look around you"—we were having a sandwich in a crowded coffee shop on Madison Avenue—"and say to yourself, 'What would I notice, what would I want to know more about, what would I find compelling and be fascinated by if we were having lunch in Warsaw right now, instead of New York?' I say 'Warsaw,' of course, just to mean some place I've never been before; if you've been to Warsaw, try Cairo instead, or Cape Town or Ulan Bator.

"Suddenly there is no way of knowing," he went on, "whether what you're seeing has been there for a long time or was only just put there, and you don't know, either, whether what's happening goes on all the time or is something brand-new. Everything around you has a question inside it, and the answer may have something unusual or exceptional to tell you, not just about how to fit yourself into Warsaw patterns but about how to live your life anywhere, although if that's the case, you probably won't know about it until later. Why is there a picture of the Bay of Naples on the wall behind us? Why was there a bowl of pickles on the table before we even sat down? Does the noise in here mean that lunch is a celebration, the high point of a day? Or is it just that things are at their loudest in hours that mark the farthest away from home that people get, the other end of an orbit that's about to swing back?

"I should add that there are a couple of ways to play Warsaw—in 'Warsaw Lite' you assume you speak 'Polish.' Meaning that if you're in New York and can understand the conversations of the people at the next tables, then that's extra information that's available to you to help you figure out where you are and what's going on. In 'Intense Warsaw' you don't know 'Polish,' so you try to ignore the words you're overhearing to let yourself be guided only by the tone of voice or the gestures that accompany it, maybe a stare or a smile or a frown."

One of the things my friend was pointing out was that there are moments when Deep Travel may be mandatory, a kind of automatic safety feature or emergency override whose function is to offer us a third option between fight and flight, a chance to *sit tight* for the time being. Which helps us, before we take any action, to gather our wits, sort things out, find out what we can, reassess, and reevaluate our choices. Deep Travel's automatic intervention in such situations is another suggestion that it may be a constantly active state of mind, at least on a standby basis, even when we're not in motion.

There are other indications along these lines—the times when Deep Travel seemingly just sort of sneaks up on you, or pops in out of nowhere, and then there it is. When I first got interested in learning more about Deep Travel, I started jotting down notes about some of the most unremarkable trips I was taking to see if there was any kind of travel that was so routine it was in effect off-limits to Deep Travel, at least as an unplanned-for and unsummoned guest. These were chores that involved both travel not undertaken for its own sake and destinations part of me didn't even want to reach: a subway ride to a periodic medical checkup; a bus ride to the dentist. Looking over my notes later, I was surprised to find that most of them had given rise to moments where my focus shifted all by itself, I would have said, and that, in addition, there was a pattern to these "extra glimpses." They seemed to arise whenever something unpredictable, rarely encountered, inexplicable, or uncategorizable presented itself. For instance, on a number of New York City subway lines, local tracks and express tracks run parallel to each other. Usually, if you're on a local train, the express overtakes you with a roar and a blur. But occasionally, when the system gets congested at rush hour, something more disconcerting happens, and an express pulls alongside a local between stations and then slows down to the local's pace.

Modern New York subway cars have large picture windows on both sides, which most of the time look out onto darkness, as if their principal function was to be blank screens. Since space inside a subway tunnel is used very sparingly, parallel tracks are only a few feet away from each other. So you can be sitting in a window seat on the left, or express-track, side of a local looking out, and if an express on the track next to you happens to match your speed, then rather than feeling that you've joined a race through the shadows, you'll instead have the sense that both trains have stopped moving altogether and are standing perfectly still. Sometimes, and quite arbitrarily, this virtual motionlessness lines things up so that for a long moment you are immediately adjacent to someone in a window seat in the other train, someone sitting on the right, or local, side of the express—someone you've never seen before and almost certainly after another few seconds will never see again. In the meantime that person is suddenly so close to you (you can even imagine that you might be sharing the same extended bench) that if the two of you could somehow open the windows and lean over, your hands would touch. There is just time for each of you to think, I wonder what chain of events brought that particular person—who is much younger than I am, or so much older, or so familiar-looking, or on the contrary completely unlike anyone I've ever seen before—to this place, if you can call it a place, on this day? Then the local starts to slow down for its next stop, and the express, without changing pace, speeds away.

My wife once made a note of her own, after a Fifth Avenue bus ride home one afternoon, because it struck her so strongly at the time. She says that mostly on the bus she counts streets until she's home, but that "you always do get glimpses of humanity." That day she was sitting just in front of an older couple who began by talking to each another about Republicans and Democrats, which led them to elephants and donkeys. There was a pause, and then this:

> HE: I've never ridden an elephant.
> SHE: You've ridden a camel.
> HE: It's not the same thing.
> SHE: It's bad enough.
> HE: It's a different motion.
> SHE: I rode a camel—it was all right when I got on, but then the camel stood up.
> HE (*after another pause*): Elephants are smarter than camels.

Incidents like these, as they accumulate, unmemorable trips that somehow build lasting memories, have convinced me that most of us are at least dipping in and out of Deep Travel much of the time, although perhaps noticing it only in retrospect. At the time, if we put any name on it, we're likely to think all we've done is continue some ordinary action—such as, for instance, look up from a book to glance out a subway window or happen to overhear a nearby conversation. But something jogged our minds, so certainly some kind of organized mental activity with its own perspective stays active whenever we're moving around. It's closer to consciousness than we might think, because if it weren't it couldn't so readily lean over and take us by the hand at any given instant.

Sometimes Deep Travel finds us, appearing either automatically in an emergency as a precaution and protection or more irregularly in safer situations, in the role of a prompt or a tug at the sleeve or some quick glimpse beyond the preoccupations of the moment. Alternatively, we can find it, largely, as we've seen, by remembering the limits of our own knowledge. We can "simulate ignorance," so to speak, in an as-if, "Warsaw" way, in order to take an instantly fresh look at things passing by we no longer notice; or, using wonder and questioning, we can more slowly remind ourselves that whatever we know at the moment about these things is only a placeholder, a stopgap, a "story-so-far" synopsis ready to be changed the next time we find out more.

Whatever the approach, and whether it's been deliberately sought or is an impromptu meeting or, as sometimes happens, seems more like being enveloped by something advancing inexorably from the other end of the street, the journey at its end feels like one of return. The wider focus available demonstrates that we have just reentered, at least temporarily, the realm of the unknown. For the most part, this is a surprisingly calm and comfortable sensation. It has a buoyant, balanced, unhurried feeling to it. It's like—well, it's an unlikely comparison, I know, but the one setting I can think of where what your body goes through most closely parallels what your mind encounters in Deep Travel is the experience of bobbing along the "lazy river" pool behind the MGM Grand, the five-thousand-room hotel on the Las Vegas Strip.

Have you ever floated down a lazy river? A cross between a shallow swimming pool and a very tame water-park ride, a lazy river is officially, I suppose, a form of transportation. Little kids adore it. The

MGM lazy river—called the Backlot River by the hotel, and widely considered a classic by lazy-river fans—is about three and a half feet deep, six feet wide, and one thousand feet long and follows a windy, twisting oblong course. It looks like a pool, with light blue concrete walls and floor and a row of dark blue tiles just above the water line and just below a flat, sandy-colored concrete lip. What makes it a lazy river is that it has a current. You can swim if you choose, but underwater jets create a flow just strong enough so that if instead of swimming you position yourself inside an oversized rented inner tube—which for some reason comes in a slightly different shade of light blue—you immediately get carried forward, head and chest in the air, hands and feet underwater, out under the pale Vegas sky, while the heat from the intense desert sun presses implacably down from above and glints off the rippling, sparkling surface of the pool.

Who invented this improbable, low-tech delight? It's like the half-finished support infrastructure for a themed water ride that works better than it would have if the ride had ever been completed, outfitted with little pretend pirate ships or spinning teacups. There are no uphills or downhills. You pass pleasant but standard-issue resorty poolside props—rows of towel-covered deck chairs and square canvas umbrellas and some shady clumps of palm trees. Each detail registers. Other people in the pool, for the most part, don't knot together and block your path because they themselves are being swept along. Here and there you pass under or next to some low, gentle waterfalls. Everything moves by at the same measured, steady clip of—three miles an hour. A walker's pace, a poky donkey's pace, you might think looking at it from poolside, but in the water this same tempo feels accelerated, sinuous, energizing, effortless, with the same kind of gliding forward motion you have when flying in a dream. Part of the fascination is that it happens without you doing anything except leaning back and watching it all unfurl. You didn't start it, you can't stop it, and no actions of any kind are needed to sustain it, not even an occasional paddle.

It takes ten minutes or less to make a complete circuit of the pool; if you'd like to take a closer interim look, YouTube, once again, already has in-river videos on file. ("Lazy River MGM Vegas Pool, Part 2," for instance, shot from a floating inner tube and posted in 2007, shows an almost minute-long segment of one loop around the Backlot River.)

It's this topsy-turvy, they'll-never-work-together, but at the same time successful juxtaposition of sensations—of motionlessness and motion; of energy and effortlessness; of vivid impressions that don't interrupt and completely relaxed watchfulness; of feeling both a breeze and a current; of skimming forward without any of the rumblings that accompany even the smoothest ride on land—that suggests something of the altogether distinctive flavor of Deep Travel.

So it turns out to be possible, after some travel and some conversations and consultations and some reading and downloading of videos, to begin to get parts of Deep Travel into clearer focus—at least some ideas about reaching it (or it reaching you) and about how to recognize it and put a name to it when you get there (or when it, in an instant, arises and presents itself). It's also possible to explore this different way of exploring more thoroughly, and as a result be somewhat more precise about what makes Deep Travel such a very different way of encountering the world. Beyond that, some suggestions may pop up about where this inborn ability or capacity may have come from in the first place. I realized, too, that there was yet another "slantwise" way to read travelers' and naturalists' books—and some novels and poems—to extract unexpected information from them.

The first breakthrough came from a friend, Jon Natchez, who was helping me digest a tall stack of travel books that I had assembled by asking other friends to recommend books they often returned to. Natchez, a writer and multi-instrument musician who tours internationally (most recently with Beirut, a Brooklyn-based indie band), had one day dog-eared a page in *Trail of Feathers: In Search of the Birdmen of Peru,* a 2001 book by the Anglo-Afghan writer Tahir Shah. Shah took a long trip through Peru, from Machu Picchu to an Amazon tributary, after running across a haunting, four-hundred-year-old Spanish claim that the Incas "flew over the jungle like birds" without machines. The paragraph Natchez had marked was about Shah's thoughts when he himself flew over the Peruvian jungle for the first time (in a jet):

> Iquitos is the capital of Loreto, by far the largest department in Peru. It's the only city of any size in a state as big as Germany. The flight north-east from Lima slices across the sierra and the barren highlands

of the Cordillera Azul. Peer out of the window again and the mountains are gone, supplanted by a carpet of green. Even from twenty thousand feet you can't help but be struck by its vastness. Millions of trees form a single unbroken canopy. Rivers crawl east and west like colossal serpents, twisting with oxbow lakes. All of it vivid with life, in ten thousand shades of green.

"I just noticed something amazingly obvious," Natchez said. "Which is how *description* is such a huge part of travel writing. There are too many similar strong paragraphs in this book even to mark—each one lingers over details, using rich, evocative language. It never hit me before, because we expect travel books to give us a full account, to take us along with them, to be our eyes and ears, to bring us into the experience of a trip. It's why we read them." This started a discussion. Now that they were jumping off the pages at us, we began to consider these precise, intense, color-saturated, resonant descriptions more closely: where do they appear from, and how do they reach us in such profusion? That got me thinking. Even if the observation-oriented approach travel writers use is an outward focus, as I've always sort of instinctively assumed, something else must be at work here, too, maybe just below the surface. On another level. Have travel writers said this to themselves, I wondered? It came to me that virtually all travel writing—all those great harvests of iridescent sights and sounds that travel writers have been bringing back, down the generations—can be read as a reflection of the heightened perception and awareness that travel itself has already set in motion within these writers' minds. This is not to take anything away from what they do—their care and skill at this accelerated level is remarkable. But they're rarely just sending home facts and conjectures about places and trips. They're recording for us the more radiant information that emerges when they gaze at the world directly through the clarifying lens of Deep Travel.

Some of them here and there, I pointed out, have set down surprisingly candid comments about Deep Travel itself, although perhaps many of them aren't quite aware of what they're up to, because they're instead using their energy to convey the torrents of things they're finding. "Doesn't matter," Natchez said. "Even if they are concentrated on looking *into* the lens, we can use their books to look more closely *at* the lens."

This was a different way of finding further clues and hints about Deep Travel's structure and how it organizes the contents of the mind. I e-mailed Tahir Shah in London (he has since moved to Casablanca) and asked him how much attention he gave while traveling, if any, to things that changed within him along the way. In his case a lot, it turned out. In fact, he wrote back, retuning his perceptions was why he'd set forth in the first place: "For me, the travel is the reason. Yes, I set myself towering goals—to find Solomon's gold mines, a lost city, or the Birdmen of Peru—but these are just catalysts: ways to spark a major journey. There is often little meaning in what one finds, but it is the journey itself that gives meaning to the experience."

First, Shah said, there's what travel does for people: "Travel is about ripping yourself away from your usual habits and habitat, wiping your mental canvas clean, and in that state absorbing everything that hits it." As to how travel produces this effect, he said he'd found out that it's not so much a matter of seeking novelty as it is what encountering the new renews within him:

> During a journey one is bombarded with experiences: it's like going into a *hypertime* for observation. I can sit in a café in London (for example) for days and I won't take in much. But as soon as I get up, and travel through new territory, then I'm knocked down with experiences. I find there are several reasons for this. The first is that we become "blind" to our usual surroundings. And, by simple mathematics, anyone who's moving in one direction is likely to encounter far more people and things than if he were stationary.

There is a sort of sliding scale among travel books, with writers like Shah, who are organized and knowledgeable in their own minds about their approaches to Deep Travel, at one end and writers like Marco Polo, perhaps the most famous traveler in history, at the other. Shah's books are so steeped in Deep Travel it sometimes seems as though the people he runs across have sought him out specifically in order to give him pointers about how to grow into his new state and make better use of it: In *Trail of Feathers,* his American guide through the rain forest tells him, "A man who has trod softly on the jungle floor has the blinkers pulled from his eyes. His lungs breathe purity, and his mind is honed to right and wrong." In *Sorcerer's Apprentice,* set in India, a magician instructs him, "With one eye examine the detail, with the other look at the entire picture." And a retired Yorkshire schoolmaster he meets in Calcutta tells Shah he must learn to see that city more clearly: "Spend more time here, and what at first seemed like utter chaos reveals itself as quite methodical. Calcutta has a way of arranging systems. As they develop, they provide security for those who need it. Open the mind to the wider picture. Scan about for a minute or two, and these systems become visible . . . they're everywhere."

As for Marco Polo, a man whose adventures still dazzle, a man hailed as the Middle Ages' most magnificent observer, a man whose entire life seems like an extended metaphor for Deep Travel . . . well, let's just pause for a moment to say in passing that what he shows readers is the endless number of surprises in this kind of research. I was quite astounded to find that I could wander through *The Travels of Marco Polo,* his globally renowned book, for hours without so much as stubbing my toe on a single outcropping or overtone of what had moved through him as he moved across the world. The outlines of Marco Polo's story remain well known: born into a family of Venetian jewel merchants, he left home for Asia with his father and uncle in 1271, at the age of seventeen. The three of them didn't come back for almost twenty-five years, long after their family and neighbors had given them up for dead. For seventeen years the Polos lived in and around "Cathay" (China), where Marco Polo became a favorite of the great Mongol emperor Kublai Khan, who sent him off repeatedly to report back on some of the far-flung lands within the then suddenly enormous Mongol Empire, which at that point stretched from the Black Sea to the Pacific Ocean.

When, already in his forties and back in Italy, Marco Polo came to write about his quarter century in Asian lands few Europeans of the time had even heard of, he set out to compose what he wanted to be accepted as "the book to end all books on Asia," as a modern Polo admirer, Fosco Maraini, has characterized it. Or a "through-the-lens spectacular," as I began to think of it. The catalog of marvels he compiled was mesmerizing—"equivalent to the discovery of Asia," according to Eileen Power, an early-twentieth-century medievalist, since at one stroke it more than doubled the size of the world that Europeans could reach and do business with. The images of Eastern opulence Polo conjured up were so indelible that, as Power points out, his detailed description of Kublai Khan's "summer palace at Shandu with its woods and gardens, marble palaces and bamboo pavilion, its magicians, and its stud of white mares" five hundred years later haunted an opium dream of Samuel Taylor Coleridge's leading the English poet to write, "In Xanadu did Kubla Khan a stately pleasure dome decree . . ."

Polo's own prose, however, is far flatter than Power's summary of it—reading almost as if he had somehow reached into the future and invented postcard writing. In a nineteenth-century translation, for instance, the chapter called "Concerning the Person of the Great Kaan" begins: "The personal appearance of the Great Kaan, Lord of Lords, whose personal name is Cublay, is such as I shall now tell you. He is of a good stature, neither tall nor short, but of a middle height. He has a becoming amount of flesh, and is very shapely in all his limbs. His complexion is white and red, the eyes black and fine, the nose well formed and set on." In another chapter, after becoming the first European ever to see a yak, he introduces them as follows: "There are wild cattle in that country as big as elephants, splendid creatures, covered everywhere but on the back with shaggy hair a good four palms long. They are partly black, partly white, and really wonderfully fine creatures."

"The panorama," as Fosco Maraini, himself a great Italian adventurer—an anthropologist, photographer, and mountaineer who traveled to Tibet and Japan before World War II—says of the book, "is observed from an impersonal distance with a powerful wide-angle lens," a point of view that, he concedes, "leaves Polo's own personality somewhat elusive." The book was an enormous success right from the start, but readers quickly discarded Polo's title, *Divasament dou monde* (Description of the World), and started calling it by Polo's own nickname, *Il milione* (The Million)—"from his tendency," Maraini says, "to describe the millions of things he saw in the Mongol empire." Scholars of an earlier generation fiercely debated the accuracy of Polo's reports; the more recent consensus is that he faithfully put into words both what he had seen and what he had been told, but that some of what was said to him was inaccurate. As the first eyewitness to both the riches and the fables of the East, he left us an account both compelling and remarkably frustrating and tantalizing, since Polo's "inner million," the myriad thoughts sparked by twenty-five years on horseback and camelback and under sail at the other end of the world, never make it to paper.

We can't say why—perhaps Polo thought his incurious tone made his extraordinary tales more believable; perhaps concealment was a simple act of self-preservation for anyone speaking out in the more dangerously close-minded world of the Middle Ages. (Polo's news could have been considered incendiary if not heretical—he had penetrated to the heart of an empire far more powerful and technically advanced than anything in Christendom.) Reading him today, we can see, as perhaps his original readers couldn't, that he's using both eyes to examine details and neither to convey the whole picture. Keeping his readers' attention firmly fixed "out there"—on what Tahir Shah would call the catalysts or excuses for a trip—Polo presents only the pots of gold he keeps finding at the far end of his long rainbow of travels, and withholds any view of the rainbow itself or of the golden lights within.

Among the travel books in my collection that were not quite Shah-like and not entirely Polo-ish, I discovered, now that I was looking for them, a wide array of insights, some incisive, some more glancing or tossed off in passing, about the shape and effects of the Deep Travel lens and the resulting structure and content of Deep Travel as people move in and out of it. After burrowing through a library treasure house practically next door to my New York apartment—the 3.3 million volumes assembled in New York University's Elmer Holmes Bobst Library on Washington Square Park, in Greenwich Village—I picked up some poems and essays that added more hints and several thoughtful commentaries on travel, one of which, *The Mind of the Traveler: From Gilgamesh to Global Tourism,* an exceptional book by Eric J. Leed, a Florida International University history professor, sent me off in a number of new directions.

I began sifting through these Deep Travel references, looking for commonalities and overlaps or clusters of similar discoveries that might suggest recurring patterns or the outlines of recognizable categories. All these travelers and writers had somehow tapped into something innate, a shared "overdrive" capability that all people bring with them into the world, which made it easier not to get stopped by what initially had seemed dismaying: the hundreds of varying, not to say contradictory, purposes and goals that had launched these trips. So I noted but looked past the catalysts (Shah's word again) and the circumstances of each journey: explorers bent on conquest, wealth, or knowledge; business travelers and pleasure seekers and journalists looking for a story; students on foot with no money in their pockets; and on and on. A dozen or more centuries separated some of these narratives from one another; still, the same glowing current ran through them.

Again, there was the obvious to look at first. All the trips we have written reports of—necessarily, by definition—are part of what could be called the "sedentist record." This is because the ability to write things down didn't develop until after people had settled down. Since sedentists soon became most of the population—the next self-evident thought—most travel after that point was something sedentists were doing. We marvel at the variety of trips collected within the pages of travel books: voyages of discovery in uncharted waters; young eighteenth-century gentlemen and their tutors setting off for the grand tour of Europe; college students today deferring grad school for a "gap year" or a "bridging year" or "overseas experience"—what the Germans call a "wander year." But travel books in their way are an even more concentrated reflection of sedentist activity, since until very recently the ability to read and write was largely confined to settled communities. Because literacy and the books it gave rise to emerged within a specific context, the Holocene rearrangement of humanity, they form a record—though we don't usually notice it—of what, viewed this way, became as it expanded a widespread but rather tightly defined and limited set of travel patterns and options. Here was a new perspective on the general physical parameters of Holocene travel and on some of the assumptions that accompany it; it formed a kind of companion piece for Patricia Mokhtarian's ideas about the mental focus that produces still-back-here and already-there travel.

As to the physical or geographical side of things, most postglacial travel can be recognized as "here-to-here" or "here-to-there-to-here" trips or, less frequently, as "out-and-back" trips. Meaning, by the first phrase, local trips, trips that stay within or close to a single anchored group of people, with the result that familiar conditions never completely disappear. Longer trips begin by leaving some particular fixed-in-place group behind. They proceed for the most part along previously established, shared paths and reach a temporary end by arrival within a second group (or within a sequence of new groups, reached after a series of stages)—thus coming to rest in "theres" that are other people's "heres." Unless people are picking up stakes and transplanting themselves, in the old familiar metaphors—which suggest that a plantlike rooting is almost a requirement for human existence—the final end of such trips is a return to the first "here."

Out-and-back trips, on the other hand, leave both "heres" and "theres" temporarily behind, departing from a specific "here" for an unclaimed, uncharted area—a still "thereless" region, by sedentist standards, although it may shelter unknown or "uncontacted" human groups and may reveal landforms and life forms that emerged long, long before the Holocene. Think of Lewis and Clark's Corps of Discovery, the first organized exploration of the western United States, which set off up the Missouri River in 1804 and reached the Pacific Ocean a year later. ("Ocean in view! O! The joy!," Clark wrote in his journal.) Think of John Wesley Powell's 1869 Geographic Expedition down the rapids of the Colorado River and along the bottom of the mile-deep and never-before-navigated Grand Canyon with nine other men and four boats. The "wilderness areas" and national parks set aside by modern governments exist in part to perpetuate the possibility of reaching "therelessness." Out-and-back trips, like here-to-there-to-here trips, also end with the traveler, like Ulysses, returning home again.

Only nomads—and there are fewer and fewer of them—remain exempt from these travel rules. The world's many "heres" and the fixed routes between them, another sedentist invention, are the organizing magnets of most Holocene travel, a situation that partly explains why, despite humanity's vast and still growing numbers, travel remains confined to such a small percentage of the biosphere. On another level, the parallel realm of sedentist-derived travel expectations, a different kind of pull is also at work. Magnets can draw you away from where you are, but "heres" act as a kind of gravity well, a holding-back force, a default position, an inertia that must be overcome or overridden. Without even thinking about it, most people assume, long before a trip, that travel will demand extra efforts from them, both beforehand and along the way; that the longest trips will end; that return is marked by resuming normal routines and "picking up the threads" again; in short, that not-traveling is the norm. There are crossovers and category blurrers: "extreme" commuters whose two- to three-hour daily home-to-office, here-to-here drives are now as long as some shorter here-to-there-to-here trips; perhaps for them Mokhtarian's still-back-here travel is part of a strategy for making time on the road seem shorter and easier to endure. Frequent fliers for whom airport lounges have become more real than the cities beyond them have the opposite problem, and find themselves marooned in the "There is no there there" limbo identified long ago by Gertrude Stein. But even these newer groups of travelers seem to have wrapped themselves in this—what can we call it, a fifth, or sedentist, skin? They are cocooned within the idea that at its heart there is something faintly daring or exceptional or against-the-grain about travel, something . . . unsettling.

Which makes the persistence of Deep Travel throughout the Holocene even more remarkable, a treasured ability that has never been extinguished, capped, diverted, or completely lost track of. Its continuing plentifulness and ready availability suggest that travelers today may also always be responding to a third kind of pull at their minds. If Francois Valla, the French authority on the Natufians, was right in his guess that people long ago began to spend most of their time in one place to increase life's intensity and vividness, perhaps there are additional dimensions of understanding that this close contact does not by itself evoke, dimensions we still continue to reach for, so that even today Deep Travel can be an avenue to this different sort of "therelessness."

I used Shah's concept of hypertime as a starting point—the idea that there can be an almost automatic link between simply being in motion and habits of not-noticing falling away while the mind readjusts. Attention has a new task, receiving and assimilating a sudden flood of novel impressions. This proved to be one of the easiest associations to trace. Leed, the travel commentator, for example, presents a paragraph from Sinclair Lewis's 1929 novel *Dodsworth* that encapsulates such a connection. Lewis's hero, Samuel Dodsworth, is taking his first trip to Europe in middle age, having just sold his automobile factory. Out on the Atlantic, Dodsworth discovers that the ocean liner carrying him and his wife, their "permanent home for a week," is already "more familiar, thanks to the accelerated sensitiveness which is one of the blessings of travel, than rooms paced for years. Every stippling of soot on the lifeboats, every chair in the smoking-room, every table along one's own aisle in the dining salon, to be noted and recalled, in an exhilarated and heightened observation."

Other writers introduced another factor that also accelerated the resumption of close noticing at the beginning of a trip: the idea of freeing the mind and the body by leaving unwanted thoughts and possessions behind. This at first seemed to be a rather simple piece of detaching from "here"-based thinking, a result of discovering that one could often cast off cares simply by taking off; the cares were less mobile and remained attached to the places where they had arisen. This insight, recorded in a number of places, appears, for instance, in the books of Sir Henry Morton Stanley, the preeminent nineteenth-century African explorer.

A quick note—in advance—about foraging today through Stanley's writings, because it seems to apply to any number of writers from an earlier age: reading Stanley requires peeling back layers of Victorian prejudices to look for truer perceptions underneath. Stanley, a prolific author, unblushingly published books with names that, as catch-phrases and caricatures, became sources of hurt for decades: *Through the Dark Continent* and *In Darkest Africa.* Stanley's exploits, on the other hand, are still marveled at; for instance, Paul Theroux, one of today's indomitable travelers, credits him with "opening the heart of Africa" during a seven-thousand-mile trek across the center of the continent that led him to one of the sources of the Nile and to his still famous encounter on the shores of Lake Tanganyika with the lost Scottish medical missionary David Livingstone ("Dr. Livingstone, I presume?").

Here's Stanley's unclouded glimpse of himself at a moment of departure, recorded in an 1871 dispatch he wrote for the *New York Herald* during the quest for Livingstone:

> My heart, I thought, palpitated much too quickly for the sobriety of a leader. But I could not help it. The enthusiasm of youth still clung to me despite my traveled years, my pulses bounded with the full glow of staple health; behind me were the troubles, which had harassed me for over two months. . . . Loveliness glowed around me as I looked at the fertile fields of manioc, the riant vegetation of the tropics, the beautiful, strange trees and flowers, plants and herbs, and heard the cry of pee-wit and cricket and the noisy sibilance of many insects; methought each and all whispered to me, "At last you are started."

Earlier in the nineteenth century, Samuel Rogers, an English poet who near the end of his life declined the honor of succeeding Wordsworth as poet laureate, had seen a similar change in his own mind when setting off for Switzerland and Italy with his sister in 1814. "When the anchor is heaved," Rogers writes, in *Italy: A Poem* (a work long out of print that I found posted in an online syllabus for a Canadian university course on travel), "for a while at least all effort is over. The old cares are left clustering around the old objects; and at every step, as we proceed, the slightest circumstance amuses and interests. All is new and strange. We surrender ourselves, and feel once again as children."

"Space," says Thomas Mann at the beginning of *The Magic Mountain*, his great novel about the last years before World War I and the transformations about to overtake Europe,

> brings about changes very like those time produces, yet surpassing them in certain ways. Space, like time, gives birth to forgetfulness, but does so by removing an individual from all relationships and placing him in a free and pristine state—indeed, in but a moment it can turn a pedant and philistine into something like a vagabond. Time, they say, is water from the river Lethe, but alien air is a similar drink; and if its effects are less profound, it works all the more quickly.

Hans Castorp, the "ordinary young man" who is the hero of the novel, "experienced much the same thing," Mann tells us immediately. "Hovering between home and the unknown," Castorp is taking a narrow-gauge train through the Swiss Alps, having left the "flatlands" of his home on the German seacoast for a quick summer visit to a cousin who is a patient at a mountain sanatorium. Unlike Rogers, Castorp is surprised when freedom is thrust upon him:

> He had not planned to take this trip particularly seriously, to become deeply involved in it. His intention had been, rather, to put it behind him quickly, simply because that was how things had to be, to return quite the same person he had been at departure, and to pick up his life again where he had been forced to leave it lying for the moment. . . . But now it seemed to him that present circumstances demanded his full attention and that it was inappropriate to shrug them off.

A central irony of the book is that Castorp's three-week visit becomes a seven-year stay at the sanatorium after he himself falls ill; by the time he returns to the flatlands neither he nor they are the same.

For some travelers, escape from a "here" and the thoughts that orbit around it—whether sought after or accidentally met up with—is more laborious, and they have to proceed through a series of "herelike theres" before the ordinary is no longer with them. Alexander Kinglake, for instance, an English barrister who set off for the Middle East in the 1830s within a "herelike" bubble (his small entourage included a friend, a servant, an interpreter, and a few others), didn't feel as though his trip had really begun until he had passed through all of western and central Europe and crossed the Sava River, more than one thousand miles southeast of London, just before it flows into the Danube. The Sava these days, at the point where Kinglake was rowed across it, only separates two neighborhoods in the city of Belgrade, the capital of Serbia, but to Kinglake—even though it was, as he says, "less than a cannon-shot" wide—it seemed a chasm, "as though there were fifty broad provinces that lay in the path between them." The river then served not only as a national and religious boundary but was in addition strictly patrolled by quarantine officers who guarded it as a public-health barrier. On one side was Hungary and "Christendom"; on the other, the Ottoman Empire, Islam, and, it was thought, the plague.

Eothen—the title means "from the east"—the 1844 book Kinglake wrote about his trip, has been in print ever since, much prized for its wit and felicitous writing and its ability to make light of the difficulties travel presents; Guy Lesser, an American essayist who writes about and has taught travel writing, considers *Eothen* the founding volume of a now almost two-hundred-year-old tradition, the English public school style of travel writing, characterized by charm and a "modestly superior air." Certainly Kinglake's bubble stays intact as he makes his way through Turkey, Syria, Palestine, Cyprus, and Egypt: "At every halt," as F. A. Kirkpatrick, a Cambridge historian, notes, "his baggage is unstrapped and his tent is set out 'with books and maps and fragrant tea.'" But what Kinglake records most vividly—it pierces through his self-satisfaction and gently worn snobbery—is how, after crossing the Sava, he sometimes finds himself almost completely at a loss:

At Semlin [now Zemun, on the north bank of the Sava] I still was encompassed by the scenes and the sounds of familiar life; the din of a busy world still vexed and cheered me; the unveiled faces of women still shone in the light of day. Yet, whenever I chose to look southward, I saw the Ottoman's fortress—austere, and darkly impending high over the vale of the Danube—historic Belgrade. I had come, as it were, to the end of this wheel-going Europe, and now my eyes would see the splendor and havoc of the East. . . .

We soon neared the southern bank of the river, but no sounds came down from the blank walls above, and there was no living thing that we could see. . . .

But presently there issued from the postern a group of human beings—beings with immortal souls, and possibly some reasoning faculties; but to me the grand point was this, that they had real, substantial, and incontrovertible turbans. They made for the point towards which we were steering, and when at last I sprang upon the shore, I heard, and saw myself now first surrounded by men of Asiatic blood. . . .

The Moslem quarter of a city is lonely and desolate. . . . You long for some signs of life, and tread the ground more heavily, as though you would wake the sleepers with the heel of your boot; but the foot falls noiseless upon the crumbling soil of an Eastern city, and silence follows you still. Again and again you meet turbans, and faces of men, but they have nothing for you—no welcome—no wonder—no wrath—no scorn—they look upon you as we do upon a December's fall of snow—as a "seasonable," unaccountable, uncomfortable work of God, that may have been sent for some good purpose, to be revealed hereafter.

Kinglake's travels had taken him beyond a certain point, to where he could no longer read the faces of the people he passed among and know what they were thinking or feeling. If "Introductory Deep Travel," so to speak, is marked by a welcome and welcoming sense that neglected information has reappeared and is tugging at you (Rogers's "the slightest circumstance amuses"; Stanley's "At last you are started"), as the "here-ness" of one's surroundings—people, customs, landscapes—recedes and fades, a number of travelers find their next few steps forward somewhat less comfortable and comforting. For some, it's shocking; for others, only something else to get used to. It's as if they are crossing yet another border, or passing through a boundary layer, perhaps akin to the tropopause, the thin layer of air that at the equator hovers about eleven miles above the earth, separating the lower atmosphere from the stratosphere, and recognizable as a region where the air dries out and stops getting colder. What we might call "Intermediate Deep Travel" begins on the far side of this "Travel Pause."

For Cesare Pavese, Italian poet and novelist who fled into the hills during World War II to escape German soldiers, the Travel Pause was almost too demanding. For him, he wrote, "Traveling is a brutality. It forces you to trust strangers and to lose sight of all that familiar comfort of home and friends. You are constantly off balance. Nothing is yours except the essential things—air, sleep, dreams, the sea, the sky—all things tending toward the eternal or what we imagine of it."

Or is this brutality only a prelude? That became the profound belief of Albert Camus, the French Algerian Nobel Prize–winning author, a close contemporary of Pavese's. "What gives value to travel is fear," Camus says in his *Notebooks,* which he started compiling at the age of twenty-two. Leed quotes Camus as follows:

> It is the fact that, at a certain moment, when we are so far from our own country . . . we are seized by a vague fear, and the instinctive desire to go back to the protection of old habits. This is the most obvious benefit of travel. At that moment we are feverish but also porous, so that the slightest touch makes us quiver to the depths of our being. . . . This is why we should not say that we travel for pleasure. There is no pleasure in traveling, and I look upon it as an occasion for spiritual testing. . . . Pleasure takes us away from ourselves in the same way that distraction, in Pascal's use of the word, takes us away from God. Travel, which is like a greater and graver science, brings us back to ourselves.

There are degrees and gradations and variations in all of this, and sometimes actual physical distance from a starting point is not the determining factor. More essential is that as people progress through Deep Travel, at some point or "at a certain moment," in Camus's words, they begin to become more transparent to themselves. They discover that the same Deep Travel lens they've been using to see farther into the world also has a second function, a reverse gear, so to speak, that with the same suddenness lets people turn around and look further within. When awareness gets turned in this direction, a different layer of not-noticing falls away, and several things emerge in front of our inner eye—one close behind the other in what seems, this time, more like a two-step process. When examined more closely, the generally solid sense we have of *who* and *what* and *where,* of who we are and what our knowledge is and where it came from, an attitude we normally have no reason to doubt and rely on as an internal compass that can guide us through a day, begins to waver or wobble, to dim and shrink, to seem increasingly less useful as a universal way finder, to consist of old habits that no longer protect. Seen face to face, as it were, it seems odd, temporary, tentative, and ramshackle, a loose and shifting arrangement of expectations, wishes, memorized instructions, inspired hunches, and wild guesses. Not quite the carefully assembled precision instrument we had thought it to be, more mix than matrix. A kind of mental crusting or rind—is it yet another skin, this one deep inside? More like a screen, maybe, opaque and wall-like until the light hits it the right way, like a theater scrim. Not far behind and beyond or beneath these assumptions, once they get seen through—or thaw out or are cleared away—we can then catch sight of some even more deeply hidden but now no longer shadowed aspects of ourselves.

What's it like when an internal compass, felt but unseen, stops working and no longer provides direction? I can think of an equivalent situation, when an exterior force that silently permeates the world around us and that we take for granted flickered out in an instant, and we had to make our own way for a while without the usual cues and props: the so-called Great Blackout of 2003, which turned fifty million North Americans into Deep Travelers when electric power failed in eight northeastern states and the province of Ontario. All of New York City was within the affected area, which meant that my apartment, too, went dark. I was home when it happened, and it took me a few minutes to realize that almost half of my ordinary "here" had for the time being disappeared. It was the middle of August, and 4:11 in the afternoon; computer screens went blank and air conditioners shut off in the same moment. Looking out the window about a minute later, after the digital clock had failed to click forward to 4:12, I could see that the traffic light on the corner had also blinked out, which made it clear that this wasn't just happening in my apartment. Landline phones were still working at that point. My son, twelve at the time, was taking a summer dance class near Lincoln Center, so I called the dance studio to see what was happening up there. They had no lights either, and since they worked out of a basement, everyone was already being taken up to the sidewalk, where a teacher would stay with the kids until parents arrived.

An old battery-powered transistor radio confirmed that the black-out was at least citywide, which meant the subways weren't available; there was no information about when power would be restored. My wife and I wanted to hurry. We would have to walk, but what made this pickup so different from an ordinary chore was an impulse we had never felt before in New York: we wanted to get ourselves and our son home before dark. We put some PowerBars and water bottles in a backpack—it was ninety degrees outside—and started walking, figuring we would probably just about make it. The sun was still quite high in the sky, and there was about a seven-mile hike ahead of us, round-trip, from Greenwich Village to Lincoln Center and back. It might take no more than three hours.

So far we were meeting an emergency by switching on backup power, so to speak, meaning that we were substituting one familiar pattern of thinking for another—in this case, treating a routine New York errand as if were a sundown hike through the woods. Then we walked outside into an ocean of humanity, and found that the rules New Yorkers usually rely on had been suspended for the duration. When you visit a beach, even a gently sloping one, and walk out into the ocean for a swim, things change right away, as we know—but only sort of, at first, as you step over small waves and feel the chill of the salt water. But soon enough there's a different kind of moment when you can no longer touch bottom while keeping your head above water, and at that point you have truly entered the ocean, and the ocean takes charge.

I don't want to make too much of this, since it wasn't frightening out on the street. It was enormously different in its sights and sounds and in having taken on—during that 4:11 minute that wasn't ending—a sort of inside-out quality, so that the spaces in between buildings had become the culminating achievement of city life, a wellspring, an end point, an open-roofed realm walled by blank-faced, emptying, and now irrelevant structures. It was quieter than usual outside, too—you never notice the grinding roar generated by tens of thousands of surrounding air conditioners until it isn't there. There was also, however, a sense in the street that this was going to be a short-term, relatively benign crisis.

We were immediately engulfed by a tremendous surge of people steadily heading home on foot, some of them momentarily clustered around cars with radios and open windows, cars that were crawling forward far more slowly than the throngs of people who had spilled out into the middle of the street and were pressing around them. The news already being broadcast was that this was not the work of terrorists, not another 9/11, which New Yorkers had lived through less than two years before. This was only an accident, not an attack; a cascade of mechanical failures had started, investigators later discovered, when a tree branch fell on a power line in Ohio, about four hundred miles west of New York. So in Cesare Pavese's terms, most of the people caught up in the 2003 blackout—the largest in American history, as it turned out—had been thrown only somewhat off balance. In addition, for the New Yorkers heading home, certain basic "here"-based rhythms that stabilize our lives were being only minimally disrupted: it was August, a slow time of year; the clocks had stopped less than an hour before quitting time; it was a Thursday afternoon, and so already almost the beginning of the weekend.

But other sureties had vanished. New York in many ways had become a "Warsaw." Every time we reached a street corner on our way uptown, for instance, there was a vague unease. Who was supposed to move and when and in what order? We kept looking at the traffic lights hanging overhead for guidance, but with no colors showing they had become strangely inert pieces of urban sculpture swaying in a slight breeze, looking like—what? piñatas? insect traps? This was something we weren't supposed to have to think about. Instructions on the subject are normally provided every minute of every day, but was this a way for us to program the street grid or for it to program us?

During the blackout there were a few policemen at a few of the big intersections, and some volunteer traffic agents at several others, but otherwise we had all been projected into a kind of Deep Travel "sudden-immersion" situation I had only read about—a city as rearranged by Hans Monderman, celebrated as a counterintuitive Dutch traffic engineer. Monderman, who died recently, believed that streets become more dangerous whenever thought is removed from movement. Traffic signals, he liked to say, "give people the illusion of safety," partly by dulling and misdirecting awareness. Traffic signals in effect perform a kind of circus trick: they train cars and pedestrians to do what they wouldn't otherwise choose to do, which is move in parallel lines that ignore one another, as if tigers and ponies had been made to run around the same ring. But circus tricks are precarious.

Side-by-side streams of people on foot (moving at 3 or 4 miles an hour) and people in vehicles (galloping at ten to fifteen times this speed) can remain in motion next to each other day after day only by suppressing a sense of the dangers so close at hand. Some psychologists think this isn't so hard to do—that cars don't automatically seem ominous enough to most people, even fast-moving nearby cars, because we haven't lived alongside them for millions of years, the way we have with, say, snakes. So perhaps people mistakenly assume that there's some kind of equivalence between walkers wearing a "second skin" and drivers encased within a movement-enhancing "third skin," in this case a tiger skin. Perhaps, too, this complacency is reinforced by the fact that even our first skin offers some real protection—just not enough. The human body, as Ben Hamilton-Baillie, an English architect who has become a Monderman champion, likes to point out, is built to withstand and endure collisions inflicted by anything moving less than approximately 20 to 25 miles an hour. This seems to be self-protection, an innate recuperative capacity that strengthened as our ancestors grew faster. Twenty miles per hour is about the maximum speed of the fastest runners sprinting, which suggests the nature of the impacts they would therefore need to be shielded from, should they themselves be the ones doing the crashing into something not moving, like the ground or a tree.

Monderman's solution was not to heighten fear but to reactivate what he called a "social code," a subtle human skill prized by earlier sedentist communities that modern sedentist traffic engineers suppress or ignore, a pattern of cooperation and give-and-take based on constantly renewed eye contact with other people rather than repeated glances at traffic lights. This way of self-regulating movement through space reasserts itself, he realized, whenever the circus ringmaster's authority is withdrawn. Drivers slow down immediately without being told to because it's the only way they can look closely enough at bicyclists and pedestrians to hope to catch their eyes and discover their intentions. Not-noticing disappears. "The traveler becomes a citizen," as Hamilton-Baillie puts it. A driver has "to use intelligence and engage with his surroundings."

Insights like these have led people to consider Monderman counter-intuitive. The term sometimes serves as a grudging compliment, used by people willing to acknowledge that something works even though they continue to think there is no framework that would suggest why it does. Such a framework perhaps already exists, however. Although Monderman and Hamilton-Baillie use words like "intelligence" and "social code" to describe the kind of expanded mental activity they want to restore to urban streets, rather than "Deep Travel," there is a common denominator: the overlapping ideas that a wide-angle awareness is a basic piece of human equipment; that it is frequently evoked by moving around; that it plays a special part in making a trip; and that people can either activate it or resume contact with it by choosing to. Monderman and Hamilton-Baillie raise several further possibilities, too: that Deep Travel has had a continuous presence throughout the long sedentist period; that it formerly played a larger role in day-to-day trips; and that it can somehow be "swamped" or overridden by inappropriate and un-thought-through changes to established movement patterns.

Monderman found that he could restore the kind of human interactions that had been banished from city traffic flows by redesigning streets and intersections—or perhaps "undesigning" them is closer to it. He advocated stripping away anything that might seem to restrict or subdivide the space or slice it into lines, or that gave orders to the people in it—which meant a permanent blackout on traffic lights, lane markers, warning signs, right-of-way signs, any kind of signs. In a 2001 Dutch newspaper account, written for the popular Amsterdam afternoon daily NRC *Handelsblad,* a reporter, Tys van den Boomen, put Monderman to the test, accompanying him to Drachten, a growing industrial town in northern Holland, to see "an intersection used by 10,000 cars a day" that Monderman had only recently transformed into "a junction where everyone walks, cycles, and drives higgledy-piggledy across in seeming anarchy." "To demonstrate the safety of the new arrangements," van den Boomen noted, "Monderman walks backwards across the junction as we talk. It is unnerving, but illuminating. No shrieking brakes, no horns; cars just drive quietly around us."

Cars drove quietly around New Yorkers, too, during the blackout; it took some getting used to. We stopped short at the intersections closest to home, but we could see, when we looked around as carefully as possible, that others were also looking around. So perhaps their perceptions, too, had changed since 4:11. New York is not Drachten—meeting someone's eye locally sometimes requires trying to see through a tinted windshield or a pair of mirror sunglasses. Still, it was a beginning, and there were glimpses of what happens when people start exchanging glances and use them to make constant small adjustments to their speed and direction. Forward progress continues, but it's based on side steps and wiggle room instead of straight lines or imagining that invisible tubes are somehow sluicing people safely through the streets. At the same time, this was an emergency, not a field trial for the possible future "Mondermanagement" of New York—a long and unexpected trudge home for most of the tide of people around us, carrying with them worries they couldn't set down right away. Pizza parlors with gas ovens that still worked had hot slices to sell; corner ice cream trucks were besieged; and delis, bars, and bodegas had thrown open their doors and were selling everything in their coolers and freezers before it warmed up or went bad, often below cost, giving a kind of "drop holiday" boost to the afternoon. But what was happening at the other end of the road, at home? Most cell phones weren't putting through calls; ATMs were inoperable.

For my part, I kept one eye always fixed on the lengthening shadows thrown by the buildings around me and on the position of the sun in the sky, whenever I caught a glimpse of it at a street corner. With each block, the walk home after picking up my son seemed more and more like something I had never done before. A brilliant sunset with fiery orange clouds burned brighter than any I could remember and then filled half the western sky longer than seemed possible—there was no "skyglow," the dome of radiance thrown upward by nighttime lighting in city streets and buildings, to swallow it up or snuff it out. Skyglow, sometimes called light pollution, luminous fog, or perennial moonlight, is light that gets away, sprayed into the sky by unshaded, high-intensity, pinkish-purplish outdoor lighting fixtures. The squandered light, bouncing off minute dust particles in the air, creates shiny skies that can be seen but not seen through.

Skyglow, which came to us only recently, during a long era of abundance when lighting became as cheap as water, brings about some changes—are they dark holes or blind spots?—in the ease with which people's minds flow or come to rest. For Rachel Carson, writing in the

1950s, the night skies were a source of wonder that her neighbors chose not to look at because these sights were commonplace. Now, more often than not, choice itself has vanished: "two-thirds of Americans," says a 2007 Internet posting by the National Park Service, "can no longer see the Milky Way from their backyard." So for a majority of us, an age-old portal to Deep Travel has been disabled, and the outsides of our houses no longer seem directly connected to the galaxy that formed the earth on which these houses stand. Furthermore, if sedentism has given us an invisible fifth skin, so that we find ourselves layered within a better-stay-put reluctance to travel, skyglow, yet another sedentist invention, although not noticed as such, certainly reinforces this inner holding back. A glowing, pinky-gray opaquing of the air, a lens cap clamped over the far end of Deep Travel's outward reach, skyglow bounces attention as well as light waves back onto the familiar ground of various "heres," suggesting that whatever the "beyond" may contain, it is murkier, more insubstantial, less rewarding, and maybe scarier than might have been suspected—and so perhaps not worth bothering about. In 1989, on the night after the Loma Prieta earthquake cut off power in much of San Francisco, residents called 911 to report a gas cloud in the sky. They were in fact seeing the Milky Way for the first time in years.

Skyglow only cuts sunsets short, rather than extinguishing them—so they are still a recognizable part of what the sky can show, and don't set off alarm signals inside us. On the other hand, on ordinary, non-blackout days, most city sunsets register as a momentary jolt and little else, seen in a glance out a window before a room's lights get switched on and skyglow comes to swallow the display. They're a quick gulp of radiant color, but they're essentially an irrelevance, a nonagenda item, a fluke, barely remembered by bedtime, if at all, something that keeps coming back but now pops up with no more impact on the rest of an evening than an exclamation point that finds its way into the middle of a long and frequently tedious paragraph that must be read to the finish.

By contrast, the lingering blackout sunset arcing overhead on the long walk downtown was a commanding presence, a constant companion for well over an hour. It was a force that seemed to take on greater strength and to speak ever more directly and distinctly and with greater patience even as it slowly pulled away and withdrew from the sky. Every ten minutes or so I would form a markedly different idea about what I was walking through and what I was supposed to do about it, and I kept coming up with new names for it. At first it was a kind of perishable delicacy, celestial but still near at hand, something I had to catch up to and stoke up on and fill buckets with while it lasted, like a hillside of blueberries at the summer's end or a deli counter's melting box of ice cream sandwiches. Then it was a lifeline, a deep-sea diver's air hose, a last link to the oxygen and the tang and taste of the daytime world. Next it became my competitor, something right behind me that was racing me home, something I had to beat to stay safe.

Then, in an almost Mondermanish transformation, these images disappeared and I started to think of the sunset as a companion, gliding by my side into the approaching night, ready to prepare me for what lay ahead, if that was what I needed, to answer questions, even. In the absence of preprogrammed instructions—this was Monderman's advice—look around for other instructors. I remembered, too, Pavese's line that only the sky and other eternal things are available to travelers, and in that moment felt that the sunset's slow unfolding could be read like a handbook, a daily tutorial about meeting darkness on more equal terms. Perhaps I was responding this way because of something older than any social code that was already quite automatically under way within me; my eyes were readjusting to dimming light levels. Skyglow, still a newcomer outdoors, has an indoor counterpart that arrived earlier—"dayshine," we might call it. The abrupt light-dark transitions so frequent in an electrified era (flick a switch in a darkened room and bright light floods back in faster than a genie could summon it) have tricked us into thinking of light in terms that are too either-or, too all-or-nothing—too black and white, perhaps. That's because our eyes can largely readjust to brightness in no more than a minute, but "prolonged exposure to bright light" delays the reverse process, as a 1996 essay by Kevin Fly Hill explains; he developed a type of red-tinted night goggles that help amateur astronomers speed up the reversal. The consequence of the eye's built-in delay, as the International Dark-Sky Association, a nonprofit group set up in 1988 to "stop the adverse effects of light pollution," concurs in an Internet posting, is "poor visibility for a while," or "transient adaptation."

After too much brightness, in other words, we see more darkness than is actually there—a jarring paradox indelibly captured in a famous 1950 surrealist painting that's often reproduced as a poster, *The Empire of Light, II,* by René Magritte. I can still remember how the "wrongness" of this painting of a charming Belgian village stopped me in my tracks one day long ago on a school trip to the Museum of Modern Art in New York. The upper half of the painting is open sky, the lower half a short, quiet street of small, pretty houses. It's a picture of contentment, you would say, serene, hushed, with nothing stirring, except that the sky is pale blue and sun-drenched, and dotted with small, drifting, puffy white clouds—a midmorning summer sky—while it's late at night down on the street, maybe the same season, maybe not; it's hard to tell because the only light comes from a few curtained windows and a single pale streetlamp. The painting makes you squint twice when you look at it, first to soften the glare of the sky, then to try to penetrate beyond what the lamplight is letting you see. The sky has endless depth, but the shadowed street seems no more than a flat surface, impenetrable, unforthcoming. Are there even people within? There are trees between or behind the houses, but it's impossible to say which—only their tops are visible, silhouetted against the sky. Are they concealing anything? Probably not—nothing here seems menacing— but it's impossible to tell. The darkness is unyielding; the street has closed itself off for the night. You've arrived in town so late that, like Alexander Kinglake crossing the Sava River, you can't read the situation. Old information is valueless, and new information is unavailable. This is the sadness of this extraordinary picture. You're a stranger and will have to stay one until dawn somehow arrives. There's more distance between you and the street a few steps in front of you than between you and the faraway sky.

In a blackout when night approaches, midtown New York at street level quickly gets dark in a split-level, Magritte-like way, even while brightness still dominates the sky. The hulking, century-old, fifteen- and twenty-story loft buildings I was passing would have remained unimaginable until electricity arrived to light them inside and out and run their elevators; and along with their bulk came deep, dark shadows that spread outward at daytime hours except high noon. This recurring gloom enfolded me soon after we turned south for home, and for the first half hour, as my thoughts about the sunset kept shifting, the darkness was a growing absence, a force subtracting information I needed and—more echoes of Magritte—turning me into a stranger in my own town. The revelation that finally reached me, as I walked along now-emptying streets where the only lights other than the sunset's glow came from an occasional car headlight or taillight, was that darkness is not the unchanging, alien, off-limits realm that years of prolonged exposure to bright light had made it out to be in my mind. Skyglow and dayshine hold it at bay, when in fact darkness is something we can know and navigate through as it flows in around us. Seen this way, twilight has a thousand gradations, each with its own sensations and flavors. Cocooned in brightness, I had forgotten that the ability to experience the night was already mine—shared by everyone, and older than the power to kindle a fire. All that's needed is a chance to adjust to growing darkness gradually. Whenever this happens, human eyes don't stay stalled in "transient adaptation" but continue through a longer, more complex process called "dark adaptation" that fully restores our citizenship rights in the Kingdom of Dark.

The science of this I learned only after the blackout, when I found Kevin Fly Hill's "Introduction to Dark Adaptation," which explains how dark-induced perceptual dearth and famine can be transformed into a complex alternative simply by not running back into light: "In darkness, after exposure to bright light which bleaches the visual photopigments, there is an initial hundredfold increase in sensitivity, following an exponential time course that reaches a plateau after 5 to 9 minutes. . . . Thereafter, there is a 1000 to 100,000 times increase in sensitivity, following a slower exponential time course that reaches a plateau in 30 to 40 minutes."

It isn't just the stars we've lost contact with; we've also let go of the land at night. Using only half our eyesight, we assume we must head outside as light bearers and congregate in places where we have posted light sentinels, rather than remembering that we are our own dark detectors. As I walked through the blackout with my eyes retuned, one fascinating sight materialized. There was one brigade of people still hard at work: night supers and night watchmen. They were standing or sitting on folding chairs outside the open front door of each of the old loft buildings, keeping their own eyes steadily trained on the street, and it seemed to me I could sense a force field created nightly by caretakers and cleaners, one that renews the strength of city buildings and helps keep them in readiness for another day. There was more to come that night—beginning with some preblackout things to enjoy at home, such as a shower (I live in a walk-up building low enough not to need a rooftop water tank to bring water to my floor), a cooling breeze from a portable battery-operated fan bought for watching Little League games on scorching afternoons, and peanut butter and crackers by candlelight in front of a tiny, battery-operated TV. Later I took a late-night walk—through quiet so deep that I could hear conversations on the other side of the street—to see the stars and an almost-full moon that was unbelievably bright.

The next day, when the air was clearer than on any New York morning I could remember—more than one hundred northeastern and Canadian power plants had been put out of operation—my building's super set up a grill in the backyard at lunchtime and barbecued hamburgers for anyone who wanted them. In the middle of the meal, we heard a sudden loud hum: up and down the block, air conditioners had clicked back on. The Great Blackout of 2003 was over. The "external compass" provided by ordinary circumstances, including traffic lights, skyglow, and dayshine, had returned. For some reason, a line from Tahir Shah's e-mail about travel began running through my head, an idea he'd come to that "anyone who has been on a long, hard journey knows" that "the person who leaves is not the person who returns. You return in a changed state." So had anything changed for me, I wondered while still sitting out in the backyard, now that everything was the same again? It was probably an unfair and misguided question. I'd had an adventure of sorts, but I hadn't been gone long, and I'd had a pretty easy time of it during my involuntary and very local Deep Travel day. Still, were there any differences—had I brought something home with me from the dark, quiet New York with crystalline, mountaintop air, a fleeting city that I might never get to visit again? A few years later, I can say yes; the principal thing that has stayed with me is the sense that I got to touch bedrock more than once during that day. Simple actions—dealing with traffic and moving through slowly fading daylight—had given me a chance to see into several unfamiliar corners of myself, and the tall buildings I pass today still remind me of the glimpse the blackout gave me of New York's nighttime custodians taking up their burden and, like Atlas, carrying the city on their shoulders.

THE SECOND LEAP

Deep Travel, the ability to wake up while already awake, has its own pathway or flow pattern, its own shape and sequence, stages and series of landmarks—a "second traveler" within us, I've called it, a "second vehicle." It can also be described as a "shadow journey" that, once entered into, keeps pace with our motion through space, a parallel force with different propellants that nevertheless stays alongside, like a sailboat that could dart next to a coastal railroad track, or a small future-century spaceship bound for the edge of the solar system that could choose to hover over a highway. If movement and change of scene and the acceleration of perception can set this parallel journey in motion, then a quick reset of awareness so that it becomes more inclusive—the shaking off of not-noticing that so many people have reported—is only the first consequence and the first level of new buoyancy. The certainty that accompanies narrowly focused attention and the ability to exclude from consideration so much readily available information has been cast aside, and a "first gravity," so to speak, the stabilizing pull felt whenever the mind stays closely tethered to what is already known, is no longer operating.

Many Deep Travel forays leave it at that. A further kind of letting go comes only after a "second gravity" has been left behind. A whole range of assumptions and categories of thought about oneself and the world—about what's being observed and who's doing the observing—seem inadequate or no longer apply at all, and fall away like a spent booster rocket. This is when a more powerful internal compass falters, and a carefully built story line that we carry around with us, our shorthand summary of what it is that we know and how we came to know it, is silenced. So there are several shapes that a Deep Travel "shadow trip" can assume. Putting aside one's state of mind, every journey of any sort almost inevitably seems to take on the form of an arc—lifting off from and leaving behind a single fixed point of departure and eventually gliding down to a second point of arrival. (It's a shape that can be flattened by a state of mind—such as "still-back-here" travel, for instance—but holds true nevertheless and remains recognizable.) Moving through Deep Travel is something else again. It always begins by rising up from that first arc into a second curve that springs above the first as soon as not-noticing disappears. The resulting trajectory is what architects would call a "three-foiled cusped arch" or, in more everyday terms, an arch that looks like a three-leaf clover. Sometimes, however, the second, higher travel curve is itself only preliminary to further arcing, and, as assumptions disappear, the traveler leaps upward into yet another loop, or even into a series of further loops, curling and connected semicircles that can extend all the way from launch to landing, from the starting gate to the finish line, creating in passing a so-called multifoil, or scallop-shell, arch of travel.

It's clear from their thinking that this "second jump" within Deep Travel, the more difficult one, is a central concern for a number of contemporary travel writers, even though they use different terms to describe it—talking instead, often enough, about "tourist" versus "traveler." Here, for instance, is Pico Iyer on the subject. A prolific and best-selling travel writer, Iyer is also a novelist and a former foreign correspondent. These comments are from a wide-ranging essay, "Why We Travel," written for Salon.com: "Though it's fashionable nowadays to draw a distinction between the 'tourist' and the 'traveler,' perhaps the real distinction lies between those who leave their assumptions at home, and those who don't. . . . The first lesson we learn on the road, whether we like it or not, is how provisional and provincial are the things we imagine to be universal." Using the same language, Tahir Shah implores readers to take the second leap and abandon fixed conceptions: "Package tourists are not travelers. That's their common misconception. Yes, the ground passes beneath their feet, but they usually see nothing, and have little in the way of experience. I wish such people would spend their time and money sitting on a single street corner somewhere, watching. Their courage would be repaid a thousand times."

When easy explanations fade away and assumed "universals," like it or not, as Pico Iyer says, fall short or no longer even apply—and the mind becomes, in Camus's words, "feverish but also porous"—there's often a sense of peeling off or pulling away from "false selves" or "smaller selves" or "fractional selves," some self-constructed and normally considered reliable, some that have been imposed or pasted on by others and remain fiercely resented. These fragments, once brushed aside, are replaced with . . . what, exactly? Something half-remembered and long since abandoned; something still raw or perhaps only partly forged; something never met up with before? Or is trying to put a name to it reaching too far ahead toward something not yet visible when the second arc opens.

There are times, says the modern American poet and novelist David Wagoner, when acceleration itself is enough, all by itself, and can be used without any added mental effort to shed—however briefly—an ill-fitting, unwanted sense of self. In his poem "Speeding," teenagers in a small town "floor the pedal" at midnight, "roaring through stop signs and blind corners" and

> Into the dark past streetlights rushing our way
> To vault over our heads and show up again
> With nothing new to shine for but another
> Cross street another nothing we didn't want
> To be somewhere we didn't want to be
> Anywhere even sooner than possible
> Or somewhere else ahead to be anything
> Different something here not now but there
> Not then to rocket to break it off

Slowing down at the end of the street and talking about "how good it had been" they find themselves

> Scuffling home now having been somebody
> Who would get us through the night and the slow morning
> And the slower afternoon the regular walking
> Around the sitting the nodding the figuring
> And being agreeable dutiful.

Adults, too, can "abandon themselves," so to speak, in travel, leaving behind and repudiating other people's assumptions about who they are or ought to be. Pico Iyer celebrates this casting off of personalities in his "Why We Travel," an essay with a number of Deep Travel insights: "Abroad we are wonderfully free of caste and job and standing; we are, as Hazlitt puts it, just the 'gentleman in the parlor,' and people cannot put a name or tag to us. And precisely because we are clarified in this way, and freed from essential labels, we have the opportunity to come into contact with more essential parts of ourselves (which may explain why we may feel most alive when not at home)." Iyer probably sees labeling and pigeonholing and stereotyping more acutely than many people, because, as he explains, "I was born, as the son of Indian parents, in England, moved to America at 7 and cannot really call myself an Indian, an American, or an Englishman. I was, in short, a traveler at birth, for whom even a visit to the candy store was a trip through a foreign world where no one I saw quite matched my parents' inheritance or my own."

William Hazlitt, the English essayist cited by Iyer, was a contemporary of Samuel Rogers's who also knew Wordsworth and Coleridge. "On Going a Journey," written in 1822, has the passage that caught Iyer's eye—it's about the pleasures of dining alone in a private room at a country inn: "The *incognito* of an inn is one of its striking privileges—'lord of one's self, uncumber'd with a name.' Oh! it is great to shake off the trammels of the world and of public opinion—to lose our importunate, tormenting, everlasting personal identity in the elements of nature, and become the creature of the moment, clear of all ties—to hold to the universe only by a dish of sweetbreads, and to owe nothing but the score of the evening—and no longer seeking for applause and meeting with contempt, to be known by no other title than *the Gentleman in the parlor!*"

Even earlier, it becomes clear that for Hazlitt, even more passionately than for Iyer, stripping off a too familiar and confining sense of self in the early moments of traveling is only the initial step toward reclaiming contact with a part of himself that seems out of reach whenever he has stayed too long in any one place. So heading outward is actually returning; renunciation is an act of recovery:

> We go a journey chiefly to be free of all impediments and of all inconveniences; to leave ourselves behind, much more to get rid of others. . . .

Give me the clear blue sky over my head, and the green turf beneath my feet, a winding road before me, and a three hours' march to dinner—and then to thinking! It is hard if I cannot start some game on these lone heaths. I laugh, I run, I leap, I sing for joy. From the point of yonder rolling cloud I plunge into my past being, and revel there, as the sun-burnt Indian plunges headlong into the wave that wafts him to his native shore. Then long-forgotten things, like "sunken wrack and sumless treasuries," burst upon my eager sight, and I begin to feel, think, and be myself again.

Discarding selves—molting or sloughing off aspects of "present being"—is a personal quest that not all embark on, and parts of the process may require intense effort. An Ethiopian Tahir Shah encounters on a hunt for lost gold (described in his book *In Search of King Solomon's Mines*) tells Shah that his health, his education, even his conviction that there will be food on his plate that night are like "a layer of fat" around his mind: "You come from a country where people have choices, even though they may be unaware of the fact." In Ethiopia, the man says, people can't yet afford a level of awareness that allows for alternate futures, and instead "live second by second, minute by minute, hour by hour until your time runs out."

Deliberately plunging into the uncertainties of travel is for some the only way to arrange circumstances so that it's no longer a matter of choice, and they have to get closer to fleeting, furtive pieces of a self or selves that remain elusive even after their standard definitions of who they are evaporate or have been left behind. Not surprisingly, both Pico Iyer and Tahir Shah, two "travelers from birth" from similarly nonfixed backgrounds—Anglo-Indian-American, in Iyer's case; Anglo-Afghan in Shah's—take up this subject, too. Iyer, for instance, in "Why We Travel," finds, like Hazlitt, that "the great promise" of traveling is "to return at moments to a younger and more open kind of self." But, unlike Hazlitt, whose joy came from unburdening himself for a time from adult cares and distractions, Iyer's younger self is a self thrown back on its own devices, a self that has "left the first caravan," so to speak. Hazlitt leaping through the countryside near London was still almost in the situation of children playing contentedly in a backyard, knowing what is expected of them and sensing that a benevolent eye is watching. Iyer's younger self, by contrast, no longer has either of these easy assurances, and works much harder than grown-ups usually have to. Iyer has picked up a different thread from the past than Hazlitt, resuming contact with the watchfulness and patience and extra effort that children use when they feel their way through a novel and ambiguous situation, like a serious illness, or while they're still mastering the habits of their home community, as on the first day in a new school.

"Traveling," Iyer says, "is an easy way of surrounding ourselves, as in childhood, with what we cannot understand. Language facilitates this cracking open, for when we go to France, we often migrate to French, and the more childlike self, simple and polite, that speaking a foreign language educes. Even when I'm not speaking pidgin English in Hanoi, I'm simplified in a positive way, and concerned not with expressing myself, but simply with making sense."

Tahir Shah, on the other hand, seems to scour each travel episode for moments when some unfamiliar part of his mind has to accelerate and act in order to handle the untoward or keep him safe—when nothing that's ever happened to him before can offer guidance. A journey, he says in *In Search of King Solomon's Mines,* "is of no merit unless it has tested you. You can stay at home and read of others' experiences, but it's not the same as getting out of trouble yourself." Strategies emerge in tricky situations—but of course he can present only cursory notes about what he's learned at such moments, because by the time he sits down to write about them, the self that emerged is already at one remove, so that as a result his readers, too, are left with something secondhand, a report of another person's experiences, the tracks left behind by something that has already withdrawn itself back into wherever it came from. To get around this difficulty, he directly addresses readers, offering, almost in shorthand, a few hints that blend seemingly clipped advice with some measure of the sharp, electric flavor that accompanies the abrupt, condensed thinking that such an emergency self brings with it. Calmness, he says, for instance, "buys you time," and solutions "present themselves if you give them time." "When you're in a scrape," he notes, ". . . the best thing to do is the unexpected."

An assumption that often remains behind even after conventional selves disappear is that travel will steer us toward something in ourselves that has always been there, bringing us that much closer to what is already ours. "What we find outside ourselves"—this is Iyer again—"has to be inside ourselves for us to find it." Iyer finds the same thought in the writings of the seventeenth-century author and doctor Sir Thomas Browne: "We carry within us the wonders we seek without us. There is Africa and her prodigies in us." "Thus travel," Iyer concludes, "spins us round in two ways at once: It shows us the sights and values and issues we might ordinarily ignore; but it also, and more deeply, shows us all the parts of ourselves that might otherwise grow rusty. For in traveling to a truly foreign place, we inevitably travel to moods and states and hidden inward passages that we'd otherwise seldom have cause to visit."

Iyer is a meticulous observer who, following a course of self-determined studies that has some parallels to the pioneering work of the great Jean-Henri Fabre, trained himself to hold on to what he was finding out by writing about it—instantly and at length. During graduate school in the 1970s, Iyer spent summer vacations as a writer of *Let's Go* books, best-selling budget travel guides produced by Harvard students. This meant "covering 80 towns in 90 days," as Iyer recently told Rolf Potts, an online travel writer often called the "budget wanderer" (Potts has written *Vagabonding: An Uncommon Guide to the Art of Long-Term World Travel*), during an interview for Potts's Web site. Throughout these summer-long Deep Travel expeditions—which brought about what Iyer himself calls an "abroad" state, meaning one where "we live without a past or future" and "where we stay up late, follow impulse, and find ourselves as wide open as when we are in love"—Iyer again and again found himself sitting and writing at great speed: "scribble and scribble and scribble . . . to catch all the experiences and impressions and feelings that are flooding through me." He had no choice in the matter, having discovered early on that an "abroad" encounter with any "place is like a dream, and unless you record it instantly, however tired you feel at the time, it will fade and fade, and you will never be able to recapture it."

What he learned from this apprenticeship, as he reports in "Why We Travel," is that "the most valuable Pacifics we explore will always be the vast expanses within us, and the most important Northwest Crossings the thresholds we cross in our hearts." Decades later, now that he's a veteran traveler, Iyer can relaunch some of his earlier voyages, returning to places that correlate and resonate with previous inner discoveries, and in this way can revisit himself: "I go to Iceland to visit the lunar spaces within me, and, in the uncanny quietude and emptiness of that vast and treeless world, to tap parts of myself generally obscured by chatter and routine."

Occasionally, travel writing conveys a suggestion of something altogether different—the sense that beyond or between, or perhaps it's above or beneath, the Pacific and Arctic Oceans where rusty selves can be reclaimed, there are circumstances that might engineer or at least prepare someone for an encounter with a never-known self. Or even with one that hadn't even existed up until that instant—an "Africa" in us that has only just appeared from the swirling waters. What kind of arc would such a trip inscribe on the mind? Would it even return, in the end, to familiar ground?

Sometimes it's no more than a momentary sensation, but one that's never forgotten. Eric Leed, for example, picks out an almost throwaway passage from *On the Road* in which Jack Kerouac remembers waking up when he was twenty-five in a Des Moines hotel room:

> I woke up as the sun was reddening; and that was the one distinct time in my life, the strangest moment of all, when I didn't know who I was— I was far away from home, haunted and tired with travel, in a cheap room I had never seen, . . . and I looked at the cracked, high ceiling and really didn't know who I was for about fifteen strange seconds. I wasn't scared; I was just somebody else, some stranger, and my whole life was a haunted life, the life of a ghost.

An unsettling passage about a brush with that sort of possibility is, again, almost casually inserted into the middle of Emily Hahn's *China to Me: A Partial Autobiography*, one of fifty-two books by this prolific American journalist; the book was sent to me by an old friend, a writer who in middle age became an Arctic explorer. *China to Me* was considered shocking when it was first published, in 1944, and partly as a result became a best seller. I got to know Hahn slightly many years later when we worked out of the same office; she was by then a rather stooped, quiet, older woman who outwardly had kept from her China days only a certain intense steadiness in the way she looked at you. Before her China trip, Hahn had trained as a mining engineer (unheard of for a woman in the 1920s) and had worked with the Red Cross in what was then the Belgian Congo. She went to China in 1935 and later got caught there by World War II. During her eight years in the country, she was befriended by Madame Chiang Kai-shek, the wife of the Nationalist Chinese leader; lived with a Chinese poet; became an opium addict for a while; and—something that particularly shocked her readers—had a child with Charles Boxer, who ran British intelligence in Hong Kong and was at the time a married man. He and Hahn later married and moved to New York, where she died in 1997, at the age of ninety-two.

The circumstances of Hahn's Deep Travel self-encounter in China already read as impossibly remote, though the experience itself, which describes a connection not quite made, still seems to defy categorization. Hahn had spent an afternoon and evening visiting Madame Chiang, on a hill outside Chungking (now Chongqing), in western China, at the time the provisional capital of the country, and was returning home through a valley in a sedan chair carried by two bearers, or "chair coolies," as they were then known. (Sedan chairs, which by two hundred years ago had already largely become a thing of the past in Europe, remained a relatively common sight in China until well into the 1950s.) "I don't really know," Hahn begins her Chungking story, "why I bother to tell this incident. It has no value as an anecdote. I only want to evoke, if I can, for my own sake, the sensations of that night." She then explains that China had become so much a part of her during her time there—"all her scents and noises and colors"—that she could wake up at midnight in almost any part of the country and know immediately where she was.

On the other hand, "that night in my chair, gliding along the dark road from Madame's house," she says,

was a special moment. It had no familiarity. It was not China, and it was not me. Somehow we, the coolies and I, had become new people in a different universe. We trotted along at the bottom of a deep, dark canyon of blackness and all the exciting pleasures of the afternoon, my talk with Mme. Chiang, the poem we had read, the sunlight on my neck as I crossed the field, the flowers I was carrying even now, in the back of the chair—they were not there. I had it all in my mind, like something I had read in a book, but it was no more real than that. My whole life was just that: a book I was reading. That moment, then, that was the proof. Once and only once, for the first time, I closed the book and laid it aside. I sat back in the chair as it jounced and joggled along to the soft pats of the coolies' feet on the road, and wondered: Now what?

Along the edge of the world which we approached there was the faintest possible glow of rosy light. We padded along in the blackness and the glow grew stronger. I had really forgotten what book I was reading or who I was now that it was closed. I didn't care. I watched, curious in a mild way, as we drew nearer to the glow, and then we topped a rise in the road and we were in a village. It was late. Nobody came out into the road to look at us. We swung along strong and quiet through the dimly lit street. Then all of a sudden, off to the right and behind a hill, there came loud singing. It must have been the music of a Chinese talking picture, one of the many that they make nowadays in the studios of Chungking. It was turned on high, so loud that the world was full of it. Chinese voices sang words that I didn't understand, but the music itself was familiar. They had borrowed a waltz from us. They sang it slowly, chantingly. It was amazingly loud and full of meaning there in that valley between the mountains, and at night.

It came to me with a little shock, not unpleasant, that I had opened my book again. It might have been different. Down in the blackness of the valley I might quite possibly have opened another volume and emerged as a different individual, but no. I was still Emily Hahn, going home to Chungking in a chair, after dark.

Lost selves reclaimed; new selves that, when opened up to, can settle on your hand like a hummingbird, perhaps to stay, perhaps to dart away again. A related Deep Travel tradition raises the possibility of meeting up with selves that are still incomplete when they first emerge and that travel itself can then shape and sculpt. This idea, of travel as refinement, is an ancient one. Eric Leed, the travel historian, links it directly to the *Epic of Gilgamesh,* or *He Who Saw the Deep,* a Sumerian legend of travel and heroism first written down perhaps thirty-nine hundred years ago; it's the story of a young king forced to leave his city, Uruk. In Leed's retelling, Gilgamesh, "too strong for his city, is sent on a journey as a way of decreasing his excessive appetite for labor, soldiers, and women."

His journeys transform him from a predator upon his city into "the shepherd of the city." On his journey, Gilgamesh is, like Odysseus, stripped of his following, of his energies, of his chief companions, and of his ambitions. Ultimately he is brought to the extremity of the world, the Far West, the land of death and immortality. Because he falls asleep during a night in which he must stay awake, Gilgamesh fails to win immortality; and, on the way home, he loses his consolation prize, a rejuvenating plant. But his travels have the desired effect: he is reduced to a level coherent with the precincts of his city, and he is made wise: "This was the man to whom all things were known: this was the king who knew the countries of the world. He was wise, he saw mysteries and knew secret things, he brought us a tale of the days before the flood. He went on a long journey, was weary, worn-out with labor, returning he rested, he engraved on a stone the whole story."

Travel as part of a lifelong process of polishing the still-rough self is a theme that, since Gilgamesh, has never disappeared from view. "Much travel," says an old Middle Eastern proverb, "is needed before the raw man is ripened." More than seven hundred years ago (which is also more than three thousand years after the story of Gilgamesh was first inscribed in stone or clay), Jalaludin Rumi, the thirteenth-century Afghan poet, wrote:

> *Exalted Truth imposes upon us*
> *Heat and cold, grief and pain,*
> *Terror and weakness of wealth and body*
> *Together, so that the coin of our innermost being*
> *Becomes evident.*

Rumi became an involuntary traveler early in life: fifty years before Marco Polo was welcomed by Kublai Khan, Rumi and his family fled west from Balkh, in northern Afghanistan, then considered the "mother of cities," shortly before it was utterly leveled by Mongol armies led by Genghis Khan, Kublai Khan's grandfather. Rumi's family eventually settled in what is now Turkey, where Rumi supposedly turned down a chance to become a king, preferring to teach and write. Among his writings are a book of table talk, *Fihi Ma Fihi* (In It What Is in It), and a book of stories and poems still considered a world classic, the *Mathnavi-i-Maanavi* (Couplets of Inner Meaning), which is more than fifty thousand lines long and took him forty-three years to complete.

Beginning in 1950, a new way of explaining how people perceive the world began to emerge from visual studies being made by J. J. Gibson, an American psychologist who taught at Cornell University for many years and died in 1979. "He upset the applecart," as his admirer and student Edward S. Reed, an American philosopher of science, has said. "And he did so repeatedly, often undercutting his previous most radical pronouncements with still more radical arguments and experiments." Reed, himself a remarkable thinker, died in 1997 at the age of forty-two, two years after completing a trio of books that added further radical arguments to Gibson's. In college in the 1970s, Reed had been bowled over by reading Gibson and spent a year "learning Gibson's theory," as he says at the beginning of *Encountering the World: Toward an Ecological Psychology,* one of his final three books—which, he noted, "meant unlearning everything I thought I had known about psychology."

At the heart of traditional Western psychology, the thinking it took Reed a year to unlearn, is the idea that the mind is something acted upon, a recipient and a processor; it responds to, and tries to make sense of, the many stimuli that reach it from the world outside. In the Gibsonian view, also called ecological psychology, the emphasis is reversed, and the mind itself is the active force, reaching out for information that the world readily provides. Awareness, and not some external agent or force, is the central factor guiding human and animal behavior. For Gibson, awareness becomes one of the defining characteristics of living creatures, an inborn ability or attribute essential to functioning and well-being, and as such one of the qualities that sets us apart from the inanimate world. Because awareness resides within, another consequence of this point of view, as Reed explains in one of his earlier essays on Gibson, is to give new standing to the mind and the role it plays in human life. As a result of the scientific revolution, Reed says,

Mind has had no home in the universe for the past few hundred years. Since Descartes' day, mind has been relegated to whatever area of the cranium is least well understood. As more and more has been learned about the brain, the mind has found itself lodged in depressingly cramped quarters, retreating from one shelter to another or taking refuge in a nonphysical existence. Finally, with ecological psychology, the mind has found a home, not alongside the complex physical relations of the brain, but amidst us, the mental being conceived as our ability to experience the environment . . . and act appropriately in it.

Or as Gibson himself once put it, "Ask not what's inside your head, but what your head's inside of."

Gibson is probably best remembered for putting forward the idea of "affordances"—a concept, in Reed's estimate, that can be "extremely difficult to grasp" in its entirety, although the basic insight behind it is a straightforward one: namely, that the world is intelligible because it has a structure the mind can take in. What the mind notices, in a nutshell, is not abstractions like space or time but the fact that there are some things within the environment that are persistent and others that undergo change more frequently. Using this interplay between persistence and change as a context and background—or maybe it's closer to the mark to say as a set of coordinates—the mind can then pick out things that are meaningful for its purposes. This would include things to approach because they can be used and that, in addition, offer information about how to go about using them; as well as things to avoid. To Gibson, these potential uses as they are discovered are resources or disclosed possibilities or, more poetically, offerings. They are what the environment either affords or withholds. They are specific to the perceiving of a particular animal and its capabilities— "for example," Reed says, "a land turtle perceives that a cliff is dangerous, and affords stoppage of locomotion, whereas an aquatic turtle does not." For a person, he notes, the affordances of an object may come and go, appearing and disappearing as changes overtake persistence: "An apple may be eaten or thrown; it may rot or ferment. It affords eating only once, but it may be thrown several times; if it rots it is so changed as to afford very little, but if it ferments it affords a new form of eating which is intoxicating." As far as the mind is concerned, Reed reminds us, throughout this process it is not apples so much as "it is the affordance of such objects which are seen."

Perhaps part of the appeal of Deep Travel's initial arc is that this first leap opens up to us an entire second range of affordances, one that remains invisible when we are otherwise preoccupied—just as some of the simplest and most ordinary-looking flowers, even dandelions, are transformed and reveal new purposes when looked at under ultraviolet light, which is how their pollinators see them at all times. To birds' eyes or butterflies' eyes, flowers that to our eyes are merely decorative are resources gaudily arrayed to compel attention, blazing near the ground almost like fireworks below a flight path—beckoning the airborne downward with dark stripes laid out like a landing pattern, or pulsing like a target with a brilliant bull's-eye center, or peppered over with pollen grains pinpointed by a contrasting fluorescent glow. Gibsonian principles could also be used to explain some of the "new selves" that appear during the second, scallop-shell arch of Deep Travel. The mind, in Gibson's portrait, detects affordances directly, so if the environment suddenly seems full of novel possibilities, that in itself could be an indication that an unfamiliar aspect of the mind, one we normally have very little contact with, has found its voice and is being listened to. As a result, "asking what your head's inside of," as Gibson advised people to do, could also be a way of finding out more about a particular part of us that, as it surveys the world, is disclosing potentialities that we never before knew were present and available to us.

Some of the Gibsonian insights that Edward Reed arrived at after J. J. Gibson's death and in the last years of his own short life are perhaps even more helpful in understanding underlying Deep Travel processes, since they begin to suggest why the second leap within Deep Travel sometimes seems so troubling and, on occasion, overwhelming. These are the moments when an extra effort of some sort seems to be required to keep the travel trajectory from foundering, and when something must be done other than just redoubling whatever one was doing a moment before. But what? For Reed there is a definite link between the upwelling of fear that Camus felt; the inability to understand or be understood experienced by Iyer's childhood self when it reappears as he travels; and even the sense of being stripped of all energies, companions, and ambitions, as legend tells us Gilgamesh had to endure. A link, and a way forward again.

Encountering the World, Reed's pathfinding exploration through territory in the mind just beyond the realm that Gibson had pioneered, throws light on this problem by bringing to it the questions an ecological psychologist would ask. Reed devotes some pages in the book to contemplating "the daily life of the mind," as he puts it, and how our ordinary mental routines slowly emerge from a highly stylized, intricately structured part of early childhood nurturing that he was among the first to study in depth. Reed sees this web of carefully prompted learnings as a "powerful force in human development"; his own name for it is the "field of promoted action."

The processes of child rearing that he investigates, repeated interactions between parents and other adult caregivers and children of various ages—infants, toddlers, and grade-schoolers—and the gradual acquisition of skills and competence that takes place as a result (the "actions" that are being "promoted"), are familiar in every country; everyone alive has been through this training. It's of course equally well known that the practical results of these years of instruction and encouragement vary from culture to culture. Reed notes: "Some children will learn to collect kindling, whereas others will learn to draw; some will learn to carry water on their heads, whereas others will learn to ride bicycles; some will learn to collect shellfish, others will learn to stay out of the kitchen."

But with this groundwork established, Reed veers away from conventional analysis. Remember that, for a Gibsonian, a principal benefit children pick up from the adults around them is the ability to recognize the affordances that will be of continuing importance to them in their lives. This is, to Reed, the basic human need that led over countless generations to the creation and constant elaboration of each culture's "field of promoted action"—and it also explains why these fields are universally present within human communities. Every child needs to be able to look at an object and decide whether it is sittable (or, in more Gibsonian language, whether it affords an opportunity for sitting). Similarly, every child will need to know whether the objects they might make use of can be kept from tipping over, although only some of them will be concerned about keeping bicycles balanced.

Fields of promoted action, Reed explains, are organized in part to take advantage of one of the first "knowings" that emerges in young children through encouragement and repetition—they get the idea that there is something to be learned even before they have a sense of what they will be learning or how. Reed calls this talent an ability to pick up "unfilled meanings" and says that caregivers look for it. "The child's general assumption of meaningfulness," as he puts it, "often occurs well before the *particular* meanings of a particular situation are understood. . . . As a child begins to act in ways he or she cannot yet quite manage—whether it be walking without falling, holding a book in front of her face and babbling, or swinging a bat nowhere near a ball—this is taken as a signal by caregivers to begin to 'fill in' the meaning. Typically caregivers do this, not by describing the meaning to the child, as one might do to an adult learner, but by carefully orchestrating the child's environment and activities." That's because the "universal tendency for children to engage in actions with 'unfilled' meanings . . . tends to act as a trigger for intense and task-specific scaffolding of the relevant tasks by caregivers." Such "scaffolding" often involves props—some of them objects that have been deliberately and playfully exaggerated to make their affordances more visible and palpable, such as fat, soft, lightweight plastic bats and plump, squishy balls.

But, Reed says—and it turns out to be a very big but—despite its strength and permanence and global reach, and despite its charming moments and the love that powers so much of it, the field of promoted action is in many ways a rough and uneven piece of ground, a flawed instrument of human development that brings about imperfect results. It is oblivious as well as inclusive, harsh as well as tender, and it produces both deficits and capacities, equipping us with blind spots in the midst of clear-eyed vision. In Reed's words: "The field of promoted action includes all the affordances made available to or emphasized for the child by other people and excludes those affordances forbidden to the child by other people." So it's at once a field of promoted action and a field of demoted and distorted and avoided action, and sometimes a field of inaction, too.

Deep Travel, in Pico Iyer's phrase, "spins us around in two ways at once"—changing both our inward view, as it shows us the selves we don't know well, and the view out into the world, putting in front of us "sights and values we might ordinarily ignore." As many travel accounts make abundantly clear, it's this greatly expanded outward view that is often the most riveting, although Reed's "field theory," as it might be called, suggests that it's actually a "semi-outward" view that people find so compelling. Meaning that when we see people in a new place doing something we don't know how to do, we're seeing a "sight" and a "value" at the same time—an affordance that wasn't part of our own training. So noticing actions we don't understand is a way of noticing a hole in our own field of promoted action, and we have a chance to move beyond limitations we've just identified.

The poet John Keats, at the age of twenty-two, went to Scotland for just such a semi-outward purpose, as we know from a letter he wrote home to London: "I should not have consented to myself these four Months tramping in the highlands but that I thought it would give me more experience, rub off more Prejudice," and in that way "strengthen more my reach in Poetry." Paul Theroux, the novelist and traveler writer, who as a college graduate in the 1960s settled in Malawi for two years as a Peace Corps volunteer, decades later looked back and saw a similar strengthening in himself: When "I became a traveler," he writes in *Fresh Air Fiend,* a collection of shorter travel pieces published in 1999, "I was as full of preconceived notions as Columbus or Crusoe—you can't help it, but you can alter such thoughts."

Maybe the field of promoted action that we grew up within is yet another kind of "here" that we carry around with us. Although Deep Travel lets us see the holes in this "here," it's often not lightly abandoned: any number of travel accounts show that it's very common that people encountering strange affordances—customs or creatures or unexpected capacities—at first almost reflexively try to keep their preconceived notions intact. Antonello Gerbi, an Italian historian Eric Leed quotes from, noticed that this tendency had a strong hold on the early post-Columbus European explorers of the New World he was writing about: "Saying that a new—generally animal or plant—species is 'like in Europe' or 'like in Spain' . . . means accepting it within one's mental horizons, appropriating it to the known and familiar world, recognizing that it possesses the normality, traditionality, and rationality of the animals and plants of our own climate."

The mind could perhaps be making an oddly similar kind of mistake—although a much more painful one—when people find themselves overwhelmed or beleaguered in the midst of their travels, at those moments when an internal compass wavers or the loops of Deep Travel's second leap seem to spiral like an eddy that has become disconnected from a steady current now sweeping past it. In the first case, the "like in Spain" case, there are no "new" meanings to be found, only extensions of already assimilated and therefore somehow "more real" meanings. In the second case, it feels as though all meaning is gone, because old meanings have vanished and new meanings have failed to appear. In both cases, the problem is that the mind has been overtrained, so to speak, by its childhood immersion in a field of promoted action—to the point of thinking of it as the only reliable stepping stone to meaning. In both cases, new meanings are already present, but they cannot be appreciated for the time being—because the mind is either clinging to the framework of the field when it no longer needs to, or clinging to its absence. When the known no longer seems to offer guidance, the ache and sense of loss that well up are feelings of having been left behind or cast adrift, cut off from the source, and of being becalmed and rudderless—but all that's really happening is people have moved beyond the orbit of the field they grew up in and have been carrying with them ever since. It's still the world, and it still has people in it. What it doesn't have is any recognizable scaffolding to highlight new meanings as they emerge, and travelers are no longer surrounded by an organized squadron of sympathetic adults eager to start "filling in" even the first glimmers of any meanings that may appear on the horizon.

Paul Theroux, in *Fresh Air Fiend,* says that his way of getting past this situation has been by accepting travel as its own kind of total immersion experience: "Non-travelers often warn the traveler of dangers, and the traveler dismisses such fears, but . . . you have to find out for yourself. Take the leap. Go as far as you can. Try staying out of touch. Become a stranger in a strange land. Acquire humility. Learn the language. Listen to what people are saying. It was as a solitary traveler that I began to discover who I was and what I stood for. When people ask me what they should do to become a writer, I seldom mention books . . . I say, 'You want to become a writer? First leave home.' "

But maybe you don't have to leave everything at home. Edward Reed's advice is to acquire patience; to remember that unfilled meanings, like travel itself, are part of an arc that has a destination; that scaffolding can be reassembled out of scraps. As he says near the end of his chapter on the daily life of the mind:

The idea that people from one culture are barred from understanding people in another culture stems from ignoring the role that unfilled meanings play in much of human learning, especially human learning about cultural practices. If I cannot understand *that* your words and gestures carry *some* meaning without already knowing what the meaning is, then I can never come to learn what it is you mean. But if I can realize that you are doing *something* meaningful, then I can put myself in the position of a child and encourage you to promote both my action and my understanding. Obviously, this is not always an easy matter, but it is not impossible.

After Edward Reed's death, a close colleague, William M. Mace, who's now chairman of the psychology department at Trinity College, in Hartford, wrote, as part of a memorial tribute, about Reed's gift for "helping people discover their own views." "Now," Mace said, "we can only turn to our 'internal Eds' to answer the question 'What would Ed think of this?' " I didn't get to see this directly, since I met Reed only once, at a party in New York celebrating a fellowship he'd received to write *Encountering the World*; he was kind, he was still in his thirties, he was bubbling with ideas. I do know that his books are like a journey of discovery you can return to, and I only recently realized that something he had written was pushing me to think again, and to find as a result that *Encountering the World* has at least one more piece of advice for people who may be encountering bumps along Deep Travel's second trajectory.

Reed, when introducing people to the field of promoted action that helped shaped them, also immediately brings up the limitations of this great teaching tool, pointing out that it can transmit only whatever the community using it allows it to—and, as he says, it "excludes those affordances forbidden to the child." As I was rereading Reed, this passage, already familiar to me, jumped out all over again. This time, for the first time, it brought to mind the idea that people, as they get to know this formative part of their mind, can learn to "wear it lightly," so to speak. By looking *at* the field as well as *through* it—in a fashion similar to getting to know the workings of Deep Travel—we find that it gets easier to see certain assumptions and attitudes that may well have slipped inside us and been absorbed along with the rest of what the field was providing while we were growing up. One of them is a consequence of a natural childish tendency to exaggerate the importance of what came in first and to believe (for a while, at least) that what's known is known because, of all the things that might be known, these are the things that are most worth knowing about. By the same logic, or lack of it, what's been forbidden probably should remain unknown, has less value, and may be confusing or even dangerous. Carried into adulthood, this assumption leaves some traces, among them a feeling that what's known can be trusted and therefore weighs more heavily on the

scales of knowledge than what's unknown, and that the process of finding out new things is one of "rolling back the unknown," putting it to
the test, as if a central pool of light generated by what's known is gradually expanding outward.

Whereas, paradoxically, the opposite is closer to the truth, or as
Lewis Thomas proclaimed several decades ago, "the greatest of all the
accomplishments of twentieth-century science has been the discovery
of human ignorance." Thomas, a doctor who at the time was chancellor
of the Memorial Sloan-Kettering Cancer Center, in New York, and
who had already written *The Lives of a Cell: Notes of a Biology Watcher,* a book
of science essays that, like Rachel Carson's *The Sense of Wonder,* is still
prized for its forceful simplicity of expression, in 1981 was invited to
address a Carnegie Foundation Colloquium on Common Learning
and found himself celebrating the growth of ignorance and the "rolling
back of the known." "We live," Thomas told the assembled educators,
"as never before, in puzzlement about nature, the universe, and ourselves most of all. It is a new experience for the species."

Was his audience astonished? There are no reports, but Thomas was
relentless as he turned the accepted definition of education inside out.
"Now," he said, "for the first time in human history, we are catching
glimpses of our incomprehension." It was a theme that recurred in a
number of his published essays, as well. "We are an ignorant species,"
says one of them, "new to the earth, still juvenile, still in the earliest
stages of inquiry," and "we are nowhere near comprehension." Furthermore, "each time we learn something new and surprising, the astonish-
ment comes with the realization that we were wrong before.... In
truth, whenever we discover a new fact it involves the elimination of
old ones. We are always, as it turns out, fundamentally in error. I cannot think of a single field in biology or medicine in which we can claim
genuine understanding, and it seems to me that the more we learn
about living creatures, especially ourselves, the stranger life becomes."

Speaking a quarter of a century later, at the New York Botanical
Garden, E. O. Wilson, a Harvard biologist and noted author (who has
been awarded the Lewis Thomas Prize for Writing about Science, in
addition to two Pulitzer Prizes), echoed Thomas's words. At a gathering in honor of Carolus Linnaeus, the eighteenth-century Swedish
naturalist celebrated for setting himself the task of finding, naming,
and compiling a master list of the planet's living creatures, Wilson said

that 250 years later, despite enormous progress throughout the world, the process is no more than 10 percent complete: "We live, in short, on a little-known planet. When dealing with the living world, we are mostly flying blind. When we try to diagnose the health of an ecosystem, such as a lake or a forest, in order to save and stabilize it, we are in the position of a doctor trying to treat a patient knowing only ten percent of organs."

Looking back through time at Proto-Indo-European, or PIE, the long-lost but partially reconstructed, early Holocene "mother tongue" from which so many of today's languages derive, Lewis Thomas thought he could see linguistic signs that people had been more forthright about acknowledging human ignorance thousands of years ago. "Human," "humane," and "humble"—three separate perspectives for us—stem from the same root word, he told the Carnegie educators. "It comes as something of a shock," Thomas said, "to realize that the root for words such as 'miracle' and 'marvel' meant, originally, 'to smile,' " and that the full meaning of the single PIE root "*sa* can only be put back together again by blending the now distinct feelings found in three modern words it gave rise to: "satisfied," "satiated," and "sadness."

I keep Thomas's and Wilson's comments in a small file of Deep Travel–related clippings I can't quite find another home for, labeled "The Unknown as a Default Position." (It's not far from my "Wonder" file.) The "Default Position" file primarily has news items that reflect current understanding on a variety of subjects actively being explored—such as, for instance, a report in *Nature* that data from a NASA satellite launched in 2001 to study the faint afterglow of the Big Bang "support the strange theory that we live in a Universe dominated by invisible dark matter and dark energy, a force that drives space to expand" and "relates to nothing we can measure on Earth"; "Largest Cosmic Map Confirms How Little We Know" runs the headline on a parallel piece. "Plenty More Dinosaurs Still in the Ground"—the next article, published in 2006 in *New Scientist*—introduces a story that says that even though "we are currently living in a dinosaur renaissance" (a way of saying that "about as many dinosaurs have been discovered in the past two decades as in all of previous human history, largely because of an explosion of findings in countries such as China and Argentina"), the "good news" is that, according to a mathematical model paleontologists consider reliable, "at least 70 percent of dinosaur genera remain unknown" and "should still be waiting to be found."

A few years ago, when he was seventy-three, E. O. Wilson took a *New York Times* reporter out to the site of Henry David Thoreau's cabin in the woods just beyond Concord, Massachusetts, for a Jean-Henri Fabre–like field trip to demonstrate the nearness of the unknown. Down "on his hands and knees, pawing in the leaf litter near Walden Pond," the reporter noted, Wilson "eases into a half-sitting, half-reclining position and holds out a handful of humus and dirt. 'This,' he says, 'is wilderness.' " Entering this wilderness, Wilson explained, was a matter of what he called "microesthetics," or adjusting one's scale of vision. " 'This ground' he said 'we see it as two-dimensional, because we're gigantic, like Godzilla. When you just go a few centimeters down, then you're in a three-dimensional world where the conditions change dramatically almost millimeter by millimeter. In one square foot of this litter you're looking at the tens of thousands of small creatures that you can still spot with your naked eye.' "

In Deep Travel, the unknown is the inescapable default position. Its presence is immediate, unhidden, and undeniable, closer to us than the nearest dirt outside. As it reappears before the mind's eye we can see within it a whole spectrum of gradations and shadings. In every square foot of our surroundings there are a multitude of possible additional meanings—maybe even ten thousand?—and there no longer seem to be hard and fast boundaries between what's partially known; what could be quickly mastered; what could sink in by our waiting for it; what might get revealed after a lifetime of study; what might more slowly become apparent to successive teams of sympathetic investigators as the generations pass; and what might permanently remain unknowable by people.

I'm still haunted by a 1988 newspaper photograph of Willie B., a gorilla at Zoo Atlanta, as he peers beyond a gate that has just opened and faces the unknown in middle age. Behind him is the concrete cell he had lived in for twenty-seven years, with only a TV set for company. In front of him is the zoo's just-completed, $4.5 million Ford African Rain Forest, a lush, outdoor setting reminiscent of the lowland Cameroon hills where the gorilla had been captured as an infant. The picture shows Willie B. on the brink of abandoning the familiar forever—yearning, troubled, hesitating, torn, pulled outward, but holding back, still hanging on to the meager blessings (any satisfaction? satiation of sorts, mostly sadness) and the seeming certainty of the only existence previously afforded to him.

Willie B., once called the loneliest gorilla in the world, was the centerpiece of a turnaround program at Zoo Atlanta; after it was cited as one of the worst zoos in the country, a new director had dedicated 10 percent of the zoo's land to creating a completely different gorilla habitat—Willie B.'s new home. This was then the revolutionary new idea in zoo design: settings that would restore the affordances of the wild; landscapes in which animals could totally immerse themselves. Slowly, over the course of several days, the gorilla entered and began to explore the multiply complex world beyond the gate. He reached up to touch a low-hanging leaf; he stuck a toe into newly planted grass. It wasn't always easy for him. On the first day, for instance, as Vicki Croke, Animal Beat columnist for the *Boston Globe,* described the scene, "the novel sensation of tiny raindrops drove the massive animal inside."

Whenever the vastness of the unknown becomes too uncomfortable, we can duck back inside ways of thought that are not set up to notice the unknown. Or we can stay in touch with the thoughts of people who have changed their default settings in order to keep the unknown in sight. We can remember—with Thomas and Wilson (and Thoreau)—that all we've done by noticing the unknown is resume contact with a reality that continually surrounds us anyway, whether we feel its presence or not. We can remember—with Reed—that the field of promoted action he made visible is a semipermeable membrane of thought, and that we don't have to think of ourselves as permanently defined by the affordances we already know about. We don't always need to keep thinking about the known, or even see it on the horizon, in order to stay afloat or aloft or on course. Even if it's the nature of travel to keep us permanently off balance, we can actually wobble ahead for a time, or even start to glide, without water wings or training wheels.

A SENSE OF TIME

For a time . . . If Deep Travel were less complex and compelling and didn't involve so many rebalancings, the striking differences in the way time seems to behave when Deep Travel absorbs us might get more of our attention, and sooner. Especially so because, once we register these time changes, it's clear that they're so much at the heart of how we go about extending our perceptions that they're actually part of the initial retuning that makes Deep Travel possible and, as they take effect, become its essential companion. If Deep Travel, as we've said, is a lens that brings us face to face with the world's intensity and variety, the time changes that accompany Deep Travel have a different but complementary function—and their most immediate role is to help us stay attuned to the vividness Deep Travel discloses so it can sink in, and we can make better use of it. What otherwise might have been just fugitive glimpses or quick takes can be explored, savored, evaluated, and held in the mind, becoming fixed and lasting impressions.

Whenever Deep Travel brings us into a larger "here," the time changes that accompany it are its coequal partner. They sustain this voyage by surrounding us with what feels like an extended, a longer "now," a kind of subtle, supple force field that polishes the lens, keeps the lighting bright, adjusts the shutter speed, and buoys our attentiveness to let us take full advantage of what we're finding. In essence, this new "now" is a more durable, less fleeting "present moment." It's at once an acceleration and a slowing of time. Meaning that—in what feels like a unity, not a paradox—things move faster in its embrace but don't end as quickly. And the double shift of this new "now," its ability when it appears both to change the pace of events and keep them open, provides an underpinning for Deep Travel's new thoughts that holds them in place, and then a context for fitting them together.

In Deep Travel, time becomes a stretchable moment. One that, as it unspools, continues to maintain itself entirely within the present tense, instead of—as so often happens—repeatedly breaking apart into separate segments, only one of which, relatively small in size, can be called "the present," until it, too, slips aside and gets attached to that vast territory of "the past."

Time is maybe the most beckoning and yet, curiously, at this point the least explored part of Deep Travel. Yes, at first mention Deep Travel time sounds . . . unlikely. Still, that could be said about many of the statements in this book, since one of the problems that's built into looking around at the mind is that the way any focus of awareness is organized seems foreign, or suspect, or . . . unlikely when it's being evaluated by various other and more familiar forms of awareness. But when it comes to "time thinking" there's even more of a disconnect. Partly I think this is because many of us have acquired a "cover memory" of time, so to speak—meaning that we have fallen into the habit of thinking that there isn't that much there to think about, except for some recurring internal rhythms that have picked up the name of "biological clocks" and a few widely acknowledged variations—as, for instance, that sometimes when we're preoccupied an hour speeds up, though it can slow down when we're bored. The two parts of this daily roller-coaster ride sometimes get lumped together and labeled "lived time." There's also a countercurrent that has been commented on, the fact that the years tend to go by ever more swiftly the older we get. Beyond these are the past, which can seem no more than the nebulous, muffled accumulation of events that bygone years keep joining.

Having thus decided that time is not worth our attention, we withhold further attentiveness, and then draw up a meager report to ourselves, the gist of which is that time is something of a . . . disappointment, even a distraction. Time, from this perspective, feels curiously uniform, inert, abstract, and "over there," as it were, something almost as removed from immediate concerns as the receding past.

This makes time, from one angle, elusive, ethereal, and hard to put into words, and from another a topic hardly worth bringing up, merely "a part of the given," one of the inexplicable local customs that three-dimensional life requires us to adapt to, a stage direction, maybe, or even a sort of annoying, distracting surcharge or extra burden of some kind—one of those odd, unmodifiable circumstances that almost immediately after arrival on earth we find ourselves immersed in and enmeshed by—like, say, gravity. Only, unlike gravity, time doesn't just exert an unvarying pull that holds us so firmly bound to the planet that only a rocket ship has enough force to thrust it aside. Time, by contrast, seems able to flow past us at its own pace while also somehow slowly tugging us along in its wake. Summarized this way, time both resists analysis and, confusingly, fades into the background, becoming easier to use than to come to terms with. In between uses, the implication is, time can be put aside as something that can't or won't do much either for us or to us. As such it has a kind of shadowed limbo existence, remaining something that seems neither to invite nor to require much in the way of serious thought, something that without regret we can let drop below the horizon of interest.

Which is perhaps a backward way of saying that thinking about Deep Travel, and about place and motion, has—quite unexpectedly—shown me the real value of thinking about time and motion. Spending time with all forms of time, which includes looking more closely at and behind and beyond any cover memories, turns out to be . . . time well spent—particularly when you discover that the cover memories don't begin to describe the richness of the reality they conceal, and represent instead a kind of learned disinterest, almost an imposed discouragement. Noticing time in its many day-to-day aspects is in fact easier to do than it may sound. It's a way of gaining a more precise, vigorous, and less pallid "time vocabulary," so to speak, and for present purposes it does a lot to help us get even more out of Deep Travel. Even if this is an area of our lives where not-noticing has hardened somewhat—for the most part without our ever registering the fact—only just beyond where awareness normally focuses, a number of what are actually long-familiar "time sensations" or "time landmarks" are waiting to be rediscovered and reclaimed. Which is why when you begin to explore them, meeting up with them feels far more like getting reacquainted. Refamiliarizing ourselves with some of the more ordinary varieties of time also helps set them apart from Deep Travel time, which is altogether distinctive—a highly unusual sense of the present. It helps organize Deep Travel; can be used to prolong it or to summon it; and serves as a conduit to far longer time frames.

Something else happens, too, when we start reinvestigating a range of time senses—settling into them briefly, or is it more like a taste test, or trying them on for size? We begin to reclaim an underused capacity. Time doesn't just happen to us. In a quiet way, we can intervene in its workings. Within Deep Travel, at least, time becomes something we can handle, take charge of, adapt, alter, extend, reshape.

But maybe that's at the other end of a short road, a side excursion, a journey within a journey. Let's get there first, and then display Deep Travel time as one of a series of special abilities entrusted to us. On the assumption that many people have been finding, as I have, that their time awareness seems somewhat rustier than their place awareness, below, as a start, are a few notes about several of the more general and of the more overlooked aspects of sensing time.

I t turns out to be a good moment to be thinking about time, in part because we can now learn directly from the specialized work of theoretical physicists, who in recent years have been thinking intensively about the meaning of time. One recent survey of the subject—*In Search of Time: The Science of a Curious Dimension* by Dan Falk, a Canadian science writer—points out that "it has never been quite clear which discipline is 'in charge' of studying" time, and that "the struggle to make sense of time has involved not only physics but also psychology, linguistics, anthropology, neuroscience and cognitive science, and of course philosophy." They may not be the designated leaders, but physicists have put forward some of the most provocative current comments about time, perhaps because their field of study is actively trying to determine if it needs to be cast loose from the concept of time.

Although physicists' principal concern is a precise telling of the largest story humanity has so far been able to give its mind to, the nature and history of the universe itself, I've noticed that, for anyone looking for further insights into Deep Travel time, the spillover from their often theoretical and abstruse debates, at least as chronicled in more popular mainstream science books and journals, offers some helpful, early thoughts about how time and human experience mesh. For physicists, one main issue is an ongoing conversation about the

nature of reality. More than three hundred years after Newton proclaimed that time—"absolute, true, and mathematical time"—is a fundamental property of the universe, part of the framework that allows
us to construct explanations for the cosmos and its structure, physicists
have reached a point where many of them find they are no longer sure
whether time even exists. Or, if it does, whether time remains essential
to describing either the birth of the universe or the full reach of the 13.7
billion years of overarching cosmic change and expansion that have
elapsed since that moment.

It's the kind of inquiry people now travel around the world to think
about together. To consider "what exactly time is," for example, and a
growing sense that this has become "perhaps the most fundamental
question of all," the Perimeter Institute for Theoretical Physicists, in
Waterloo, Ontario—an international community of scholars that, after
only a decade of work, has become a Canadian-based counterpart to
the Institute for Advanced Study, in Princeton—in 2008 convened a
high-level assembly of "increasingly argumentative" physicists, mathe-
maticians, and philosophers to "thrash out time's problems," as one
participant, Michael Brooks, later put it. "Everyone involved seems to
have a different idea," Brooks, a quantum physicist and the author of *13
Things That Don't Make Sense: The Most Baffling Scientific Mysteries of Our Time,*
has written. His account of the meeting became a *New Scientist* cover
story. One suggestion, presented, Brooks reported, by Roger Penrose,
an Oxford mathematician, is that time "pops in and out of existence
as the universe matures." But how can we be certain, John Norton, a
University of Pittsburgh philosopher, wondered, that space and time
even exist on their own and are not what Brooks called "convenient
illusions"?

What might that mean—that space and time are illusions? And how
would it affect our lives if it can be shown that they move forward and
unfold in the presence of mere shadows? Dan Falk addresses these
questions, which he finds troubling ("a novel and counterintuitive way
of thinking"), in *In Search of Time,* a book published as the Perimeter
physicists gathered. Falk roots his presentation of time's existence
within a discussion of a better-known phenomenon he calls "illusions
of emergence"—qualities that, though not innate, appear in aggregates
or are partly a product of some shortcoming within human perception.
"Consider the 'wetness' of water," Falk says. "We now know that this

wetness emerges only when we have millions of water molecules together; individual water molecules have no such property. (One might also argue that a sentient observer is needed to *experience* that wetness.) The 'hardness' of matter is a similar illusion: atomic physics has shown us that a rock is mostly empty space, but we are oblivious to the vast tracts of nothingness between the nuclei of atoms. To our macroscopic touch, a rock is—well, rock hard."

But "if the flow of time is an illusion," Falk continues, "it seems more profound than any of these. Physicists may tell us that time 'emerged' at the moment of the big bang—but it seems to be a more confounding emergence than that of water's wetness or a rock's hardness. Taking the 'flow' out of time seems more disturbing than taking the wetness out of water. Without time's flow, what are we left with? Is time still recognizable as . . . *time*?"

If human beings can't touch water without encountering its wetness, or pick up a stone without being aware of its rigidity, does the same hold true for the flow of time? Is time, too, an illusion we're inevitably caught within, or can we somehow "see through" time's web? For James Hartle, a University of California cosmologist cited by Falk, the time illusion is inescapable, a necessary condition of life, a constraint built in long ago and retained because it promotes survival. Hartle, according to another *New Scientist* report, has spent "many years worrying about time" and remains uncertain about whether it should be considered a fundamental component of the universe, since time may be only a force that "emerges gradually from space." The internal human sense of time, he would say, however, is a far more ironclad and unshakable presence: Hartle's idea is that early on in the earth's history another emergent force, evolution, guided this planet's living organisms toward a way of dealing with daily events that as part of its organizational logic and structure carries with it an unstopping sweep of attention that "feels" like time in motion along a one-way path, advancing in a way that does not allow for a return.

An organism's first need, in Hartle's formulation, which combines elements from cognitive science, math, engineering, and evolutionary biology, is to focus at once and without delay on anything that might either prolong or cut short its continued existence. At the most basic level, this quick, strong responsiveness, which applies with equal force to opportunities, such as the presence of food, and to problems, such as the approach of a predator, is what makes an organism effective. But, adds Hartle, its efficiency gets increased if it can also add another layer to its response, so that situations that have already been resolved by rapid actions (eating or running away) can somehow be held on to after circumstances have changed, so they can be reviewed, called on another time, and learned from later on (food that had turned brown made us sick; some predators can't leap well). This power to reconsider actions was gained only after a great variety of organisms among them developed an orderly though quite rigid sequence of internal process-ing operated by means of gradually withdrawn attention. After an action is taken, awareness of it does not disappear but instead gets increasingly diluted, "stepped down," and "deintensified," almost like a room being darkened by a dimmer.

The system works—accumulated experiences are retained and remain available—but it brings with it a consequence that perhaps eventually also becomes a "cost." We wind up, at any rate, mistaking one thing for another, having acquired a kind of undetected squint. This takes the form of an "imposed echo," as it might be called, an inside-out reversal, so that our own rules and sequences seem to be part of the innate structure of the cosmos. Whereas what we're really seeing in the world outside is only a displaced phantom, a distorted reflection of the internal mechanism we use to keep events we've been through parked in orbit within us, so they can't altogether escape.

The motion we sense is real, but it's sweeping through our minds rather than swirling through the world. It isn't time that's flowing; it's our attention, focusing on and then slowly disengaging from events. Interpreting everything through a filter, we construct "time lines"— meaning that, paradoxically, we do something in our minds to explain something else we are already doing in our minds. We move forward convinced that we are caught up in a linear narrative and see time all around us, an unending succession of "befores" and "afters."

It's a framework that persists from generation to generation. It's robust and long-lasting because, as Hartle says, "our powerful sense that there is a 'now' and that time 'flows' from the past, through the present, to the future has survival value. It is the only plausible expla-nation." When Hartle describes how organisms inadvertently conjure up time, he avoids words like "awareness" and instead borrows lan-guage from the more impersonal vocabulary of information theory (brains, for instance are for him "IGUSs," or "information gathering and utilizing systems"). As Falk sets it out, "His idea, to summarize very roughly, is that any entity that gathers and uses information (this would include human brains) initially holds that information in 'input registers,' but then transfers it to 'memory registers' to free up space in the input areas. That passage of information between registers somehow 'feels' like time." Eventually, as memory registers fill up, information may then get moved to a "schema," a simple model of the environment that collates previous experiences. Finally, with no further use to be wrung out of it, information simply gets "dumped."

"It is the passage of images between registers, until they are erased and 'forgotten,' that creates an impression of the flow of time," as Marcus Chown, a radio astronomer and cosmology consultant, who interviewed Hartle for *New Scientist,* notes. But, to reiterate: in Hartle's model, what has actually been in motion throughout this process is not time but the location of our own attention, which at first deals with something directly; next, having moved on to think about something else, holds itself in readiness to recall the initial event or person or circumstance; later still, after further jumps in focus, either retains some part of the first encounter and incorporates it into general noticing— perhaps a face, a taste, some quirk worth bearing in mind, some advice heard, or maybe some startling juxtaposition never previously registered—or dismisses it absolutely, and is then no longer subject to its influence.

Other minds have in recent years also been catching glimpses of attention's interior journey. William Bronk, for instance, an American writer of haunting poems who a decade after his death is beginning to be discovered by a wide audience of readers, traced attention's progress in these lines: "Things of the present reflect the presence's life. When the present is past and dark the light is still."

Hartle's concept—or Bronk's—certainly seems to cover the general run of things. The "flow of time" washes away many events, leaving behind a residue that itself continues to shrink, recede, pale, and grow ever fuzzier. But this is something that we're doing ourselves, that we make happen, not something that just happens or is bound to happen. By creating "time," we are bending the world to our own purposes— bringing an extra awareness with us to each new situation. Which means there is probably a next step. Once we know that we can alter time and the world in this particular way, dividing events into past, present, and future, by implication we can impose other changes as well. "Uniform time flow," powerful as it is, may be only one part of a larger picture, and just one of many abilities we have within us for harnessing and guiding the pace of events.

For starters, we know instinctively that there are some events that have already occurred that actively resist being swept away. They stay with us, undiminished; they keep their original vividness intact, as if they had only just now happened. For instance, although I have no clear sense of what the evening sky near my apartment looked like on December 4, 2008—I know there was a moon, and that's about it—I have an exact, enduring picture in my mind of the same darkening sky three nights earlier. Because on December 1, looking south as sunlight withdrew, I saw something that, according to astronomical projections, which have already been precisely calculated up through the year 2890, I will never get to see again, at least not in such a spectacular fashion. Almost brushing the top of the spotlighted glow of the marble Washington Square Arch was something even brighter, a temporary constellation that was now the dominant object in the sky. Ever more incandescent minute by minute, and slowly arcing toward the western end of the park, a tightly grouped, upside-down isosceles triangle pointing like an arrowhead toward the earth had been created by the three most brilliant objects in the nighttime sky: the moon, still a crescent that night, and the two evening stars that children have always wished on, Venus and Jupiter. (Venus was on the bottom, with Jupiter above and to the right, and the moon above and to the left.) Their planetary and lunar wanderings had brought them into a close conjunction that on that night could be seen around the world, even in light-polluted cities, and in a bunching so tight and bright it will not be repeated for another forty-four years, reappearing for those here then on the night of November 18, 2052.

I'd gone outside to take a look, bringing a digital camera with me. Together, the two planets and the moon filled less of the sky than my outstretched thumb. It was a beautiful, blazingly white, arresting sight, a radiant celestial tiara low in the sky—"a head-turner," as one astronomer called it; something that pulled at the attention even of those "who normally don't bother looking up," said another. There's speculation that the star of Bethlehem that heralded the birth of Jesus might have been a Venus-Jupiter conjunction so close the two planets appeared to shine as a single star. It was certainly easy to see why conjunctions have often seemed to have some compelling purpose and remain formidable symbols, even when they no longer mean what they once did. The "star and crescent" device, for instance, now widely considered an Islamic symbol, since it appears on the flags of twelve mostly Muslim countries, originally commemorated a Greek battle in a long-lost pagan kingdom won under a waxing moon more than twenty-three hundred years ago—and almost a thousand years before the birth of the Prophet Muhammad.

But it wasn't just the beauty of the occasion—or even its extreme unusualness—that caught at me. Or the idea that the heavens were smiling on humanity. For me, sighting the two-stars-and-a-crescent conjunction on December 1 was turning into a different kind of rare occasion. Standing on the sidewalk across from Washington Square Park, I began to feel as though the triangle of lights in the sky I was looking at could unexpectedly be rearranged into another alignment. The sky wasn't a flat screen or just a dome anymore; it had opened out, taken on depth, its boundaries dissolved. What had been only a triangle overhead could now be seen as a pathway leading outward through the sky, with the earth as a fourth coordinate at its terminus. The lines of the old triangle were rearranging and extending themselves, almost as if I were unwinding an immensely long folding yardstick, so that one arm of this new shape ran from the earth to the moon, another connected the moon to Venus, and a third stretched away from Venus until it finally reached Jupiter. The crescent moon and the two dots of the planets were trail markers along the way, lighted buoys bobbing on a dark, receding ocean. As a result, without moving and simply by casting a single glance upward, I had something close to a straight-shot glimpse out across the entire width of the inner solar system. (The inner solar system is often thought of as everything on the near side of Jupiter—so it would include what I was seeing, plus Mercury, Mars, Mars's two moons, and the asteroid belt.)

I'm not sure quite how this new view came about—although I had just been reading a preview of the conjunction event on the Internet ("Spectacular Sky Scene Monday Evening," by Joe Rao, meteorologist and guest lecturer at the Hayden Planetarium, in New York), a piece that mentioned the planetary distances involved, so perhaps I was primed for it. The distances in my head, calculations supplied by Rao, were far more precise than anything I could sense, but it did seem that the moon, only a quarter of a million miles from earth, was the nearby, short-hop, first way station, still semi-suburban, and that then the lengths between the lights became far off in a way I didn't have any comparisons for in my mind—it was another 93 million miles from there to Venus, according to Rao, and then an additional 447 million miles beyond that to Jupiter. Meaning that the other end of this partic-ular line was more than 540 million miles away.

What would you call this? I didn't yet have a name for it. Deepest Travel, I've since thought. The earth seemed suddenly smaller; it, too, had become a heavenly body, but as such was no more than the fore-shore at one end of a vast voyage, and I could feel my feet pressing into and gripping the pavement, in case gravity started to slip away, as it suddenly seemed as though it might. But that wasn't the end of it. I knew that the half-billion-mile-long straight line I could see across, the tube through space that had become my telescope for the evening, was only a momentary lineup. It couldn't last, but in the meantime and for the moment I was in touch not only with the current position of a moon and three planets but also with the swings and loops of rotations and orbits that had brought them for one night into seeming align-ment. It wasn't so much that I was feeling these movements as that I was gaining a sense of participating in them; as far as bodily feeling goes, we respond to changes in motion (acceleration and deceleration) rather than to constant speeds. Similarly, in much the same way that we know that visible light is only a small fraction of the electromagnetic spectrum, we're aware that our motion detectors pick up only a narrow slice of the full range of the motion and speeds exhibited by other objects. But for once, by standing still and keeping my eyes fixed on that outward path through the sky, I could appreciate and—without getting dizzy—even revel in the understanding that the motionlessness I was feeling was another illusion. There was a whirligig around me, sweeping me through space. What I was looking at wasn't two points and a curved sliver of light; it was a combination of eight gigantic, end-less, tumbling, and always silent systems of circular motion. Four heav-enly bodies—the earth, the moon, Venus, Jupiter—rotating on their axes, while one satellite—the moon—circled the earth, and three planets—Venus, Jupiter, and the earth with the moon in tow—revolved around the sun. The voiceless music of the spheres had become a concert anyone could hear.

According to Jeff Kanipe, a science writer and former managing editor of *Astronomy* magazine, I was still thinking small, or perhaps I should say listening somewhat restrictedly. In a recent book, *The Cosmic Connection: How Astronomical Events Impact Life on Earth,* which I started reading only after my glimpse across the solar system, Kanipe talks about a Deepest Travel encounter with the Milky Way, our own galaxy, on a winter night in Australia. "From our vantage point on Earth," Kanipe says, "we can't see the Milky Way as the vast wheel of stars that it is. We see it only as this band of gray, grainy light crossing from north to south—that is, if we see it at all." It's "hardly noticeable" in any area with skyglow, and, even through clear skies—for anyone looking upward through clear skies from the Northern Hemisphere, where 90 percent of humanity lives—it never climbs higher than about a third of the way up the sky.

Not so in the Southern Hemisphere. Seen from a beach near Hawk's Nest, a shoreline weekenders' and vacationers' village in southeastern Australia—where Kanipe was visiting a high school friend who had relocated from southern Texas—the Milky Way "floats high overhead, a distinct bulbous glow mottled by channels of dark interstellar dust. From either side of the bulb extend both segments of the Milky Way, one of which billows down to the southern horizon, the other to the northern horizon and into the Pacific Ocean. To the left, or southeast, of the main band," Kanipe writes,

> I could also make out the patchy Small Magellanic Cloud and, a bit lower, the L-shaped Large Magellanic Cloud, both satellite galaxies of the Milky Way. It was my first time to see them.
>
> Suffice it to say that the vista was a stunner (or, as they say down under, I was gobsmacked), and my friend Gary was amused as I went on and on about the view. With such a celestial panoply laid out before you, it doesn't take a lot of imagination to envision the great arms of the Galaxy sweeping out of the north, passing broadly in front of the central bulb, and trailing southward off in the distance around the far side of the Galaxy. As a science writer, I have spent most of my life intellectual-

izing the Milky Way both in print and vocally as a multiarmed spiral galaxy, just like many other multiarmed disk galaxies in the universe. But from Australia, the Milky Way is something more visceral, entirely other than an abstraction. It isn't just a band of light in the night sky: it is a *wheel*. And, moreover, you realize we are *in* the wheel—and that the wheel, and everything in it, is moving. Such was my epiphany at Hawks Nest!

The other day I looked up some of the actual speeds involved, both the circlings of the inner solar system and the wheelings of the galaxy itself. We are never actually still or at rest. We are always being taken somewhere. For anyone in New York, the earth is in motion around itself at about 795 miles an hour; for those in Hawk's Nest, the speed is closer to 870 miles an hour—speeds increase as you get closer to the equator, since the wider the earth is, the faster it has to turn to keep up with itself. This is one of the few unnoticed motions we can almost see and sense: at sunrise and sundown, providing our eyes are appropriately protected, the sun's path across the horizon becomes apparent. But our tendency is to misinterpret these events, which should more properly be called "landset" and "landup." Meaning that, in this case, it is we who are in motion, not the sun. The earth's spin, for all of us who are its traveling companions, is a constant tilting movement to one side, like an airplane going into a steep, permanent bank. Face north and spread your arms out. Raise your left arm a little while lowering your right arm by the same amount. Land is ascending in the west, declining in the east. With a little practice, we can, if we choose to, change "almost see and sense" into something more accurate. Just before some future sunrise, for instance, try leaning backward a little, as though the entire east in front of you, however level it may seem, is a craggy slope you're clambering down, and then pause and watch as the edge of the earth, down at the bottom of the hill, sinks slightly, slowly, and steadily, taking about three minutes (if you're in New York) to fully reveal the red ball of the sun. Or as a sunset approaches, lean forward and watch as the peak of the westward mountain rises to hide the sun and its light from view.

Meanwhile, all the towns on earth are on a second voyage at a uniform speed, as the whole planet swings around the sun at more than 66,600 miles an hour. Venus and Jupiter, the other trail markers along the cross–solar system pathway that opened up for me the night of the conjunction, have their own and very various motions: Venus rotates extremely slowly, at only about 4 miles an hour, but moves around the sun faster than we do, at about 78,000 miles an hour. Jupiter, on the other hand, has a rotational speed 26 times that of the earth but an orbital speed less than half of ours. Wheeling through space, the Milky Way adds yet another pull to each of the planets: the galaxy, carrying the solar system along with it, revolves around itself, which, computing specifically for our neighborhood, just over halfway out from the galactic core, translates into a speed of about 483,000 miles an hour. The earth, after four and a half billion years of existence, has reached the age of twenty in "galactic years," where one galactic year is the time it takes the Milky Way to make one complete, 225,000,000-year-long cycle.

At the same time, the sun slowly bobs up and down as it makes its way around the galaxy, almost like a phonograph needle playing an old vinyl record. At the moment, the sun and its solar system are moving toward Hercules, a constellation that, for people in the Northern Hemisphere, is almost directly overhead every July. So this is a second celestial motion we could perhaps occasionally feel some connection to—by standing outside on a July night and remembering that there is a force calculated to have a speed of about 37,000 miles an hour that is impelling us (and the ground beneath us) almost straight up.

Finally, we might add a fifth element to this preliminary and selective list of the "out there" velocities to which we are subject, a list that so far includes only those that produce the day, the year, the galactic year, and the vertical oscillations that perhaps fill a "galactic month" or more. This fifth motion is the work of the "Great Attractor," now thought to be an immense supercluster of galaxies, "or something even bigger," as astronomers at NASA's High Energy Astrophysics Science Archive Research Center suggest, which is "pulling the Milky Way in its direction" at a speed in excess of 1.3 million miles an hour. And not just the Milky Way—it's only one small part of what astronomers at the University of Tennessee in Knoxville are calling a "mass migration" of local galaxies, clusters, and superclusters. "As if," they write, "a great river of galaxies (including our own) is flowing with a swift current of 600 km/s [kilometers per second] toward Centaurus."

Meaning that the Great Attractor has been located in the same part of the sky as the constellation Centaurus, full of bright stars and often called the "jewel of the southern sky." Each May, people in the Southern Hemisphere can find Centaurus (the name commemorates Hercules' tutor) high in their sky, near the Southern Cross—giving them, too, a chance to feel themselves in alignment with one of earth's longest journeys.

Many of these overlapping trips, until recently, weren't even known to us. Copernicus demonstrated to the world nearly five hundred years ago that the earth is always in motion, thus recasting the day and the year—which previously had just been recurring events—as voyages that keep us constantly moving. It wasn't until the twentieth century that we began to think, first, that the entire solar system is gliding through a galaxy, and, later, that the galaxy itself is never stationary. But twentieth-century discoveries also expanded the whole concept of what Copernicus had called the "mobility of the earth," by turning attention in a new direction: downward. Earthquakes occur so infrequently that one of our most basic day-to-day assumptions is that there will be solid ground under our feet whenever we move around. Now we know better. Rhythmic pulses are rippling through the earth at every moment. "The planet is a trampoline," a friend of mine, Christopher Meier says. "Or a conveyor belt, an airport slidewalk, a bubbling pot of porridge." The best understood of these subterranean rhythms is the constant motion of the continents—a concept that, after being ridiculed for decades, was accepted by geologists in the 1960s as a fundamental principle. The fact that there are no fixed positions anywhere is hard to handle, because concentrating on it takes us "off the chart" at both ends—our space travels are too fast to think about, and the knocks and bumps and slithers our planet is subject to move too slowly for us to take in.

Except, perhaps, for a couple of them. There are "hurricanes under your feet," according to the title of a news report about upward-spinning currents in the earth's liquid outer core, 1,800 miles beneath us. These we can never notice in any way. But motions nearer to hand are another matter. The eight great continental and oceanic plates that girdle the world are slipping sideways, pushed along by riverlike flows coursing below them through the sticky, viscous, plastic, elastic, soft-solid rocks of the asthenosphere (the word is Greek for "weak" sphere), which is the uppermost part of the earth's mantle. This deep earth layer lies between the crust and the core, in a zone that begins only about sixty miles from us, wherever we are—a straight-down distance shorter than many daily commutes along the surface. Floating on these mantle currents, North America drifts westward by about four inches a year—a speed that happens to intersect with a rhythm embedded within human lives. Just before you clip your fingernails, it has been pointed out, at that moment every week or two when they actually feel as if they're growing, you're paying attention to the growth rate of a hard band of protein that progresses at continental speed, about four inches a year.

Then there's Britain's almost-noticeable "bounce," which was accurately mapped for the first time at the beginning of the twenty-first century. The "bounce" is produced by the tides of the Atlantic Ocean. Twice a day, the weight of each rising tide pushes down on the continental shelf around the British coast, and the whole country sinks a little, rising once more as the tide goes out. The total distance involved, top to bottom, is—again—about four inches: the kind of height you can add on by rising up on your toes. Other countries have their own "bounces," but those haven't yet been as well calibrated. So, says Chris Meier, people in Britain for the moment have an edge on the rest of us. They can, should they choose to, get a simultaneous sense of four otherwise unfathomable journeys that happen to be transporting us as passengers—an odd kind of meditation, admittedly, since it would involve your fingers and toes as well as leaning to one side and feeling a rabbit-ear tug through the top of your head.

A simplified head-and-foot version works just as well, in addition to being a lot less less awkward. Thinking that your feet are being pulled sideways (by a continent) and that your whole body is being tugged upward, headfirst (by the dolphin-like bobs of the solar system in its long swim around the galaxy) gets to the essence of it: whatever else we may be doing, we are also part of a never-halting caravan that proceeds both by inching and by soaring, and the speeds within our middle realm of motion are even now being accelerated both infinitesimally and overwhelmingly by the speeds of the large-scale objects that surround us. It's an unusual sensation, moving at three or more velocities at once, and though hard to sustain it leaves behind a lingering sense of buoyancy and balance.

Something else has stayed with me, too, since I started experimenting with the idea of forging mental links—or perhaps fuzzy approximations is closer to it—that can move through or at least jar loose some of the inner barriers that ordinarily keep Unnoticed Travel completely hidden. Namely, a newly strengthened sense of how ready the mind is, sometimes even without being asked, to override its own default settings and supply us with wider viewpoints than the ones we normally work with. It's often said that nature is economical—that, for instance, any kind of built-in ability to sense something, like the movements of the heavenly spheres, would be an extravagance and even a danger, since a restricted awareness can protect us, so that we can focus exclusively on any suddenly menacing movements springing at us in our own sphere. What we can't know about, by this line of reasoning, can't distract us.

After all, there are innumerable recurring rhythms, patterns, pulses, and cycles of motion in the motions of the planet and the sun—most obviously, the alternations of day and night—that we are cradled by and embedded within and whose effects we are able to deal with (by, for instance, coordinating nighttime and sleeping) long before we learn about what causes them. We can do this because our bodies, along with those of other living creatures, are automatically tuned to these rhythms (or "entrained," as is sometimes said) and, as a result, can respond to them without our having to think about them or plan for them. These reflexive reactions, collectively, are our "biological clocks," so many of which have now been revealed and investigated, particularly over the past half century. (The field of study is now called "chronobiology.") The constant presence in us of these planetary tides, or at least of the apparatus we have installed for monitoring and making use of their ebbs and surges (causing us to get hungry and then sleepy and so forth on such a regular basis), is probably the other principal reason, along with the Hartlerian processing of events, that time normally feels so tangible and undeniable and . . . "real." What the biological clocks register, however, is not so much the onward flow of time but the "eddying of time," where time's motion is circular or cyclical, not linear—and points to the over-and-over nature of events ("There is nothing new under the sun") but also to the predictableness and reliability of renewal, since spring can be trusted to follow winter, year after year.

The most widely known and intensively studied biological clocks, of course, are the circadian rhythms ("circadian" meaning "about a day long"), which govern the full range of our daily day-and-night, sleep-and-wake changes, hormone levels, blood pressure, heart rate, and body temperature, among other things. Perhaps more surprisingly, though, circaseptan rhythms ("about a week long") have also been detected in us. These, too, are innate, and they're reflections of processes around us that are far older than the human invention of the week, whose seven-day form seems to date back about twenty-six centuries; it was adopted by the Jews who had been exiled in Babylon for fifty years during the Babylonian captivity. The common cold, for example, tends to last about seven days; chicken pox has a "doubled-septan" existence, making its appearance about two weeks after exposure. More generally still, a recent discovery at the University of Georgia that at least 25 percent of the genes of bread mold are under the direct control of biological clocks, "points," the scientists involved concluded, "toward the biological clock as a crucial player in the health and well-being of all living things."

But if nature is economical, human beings are also aspirational, and maybe one of the best pieces of evidence for that is the easy availability of states of mind that can extend our awareness in so many directions. It's been more than forty years since Desmond Morris suggested, in *The Naked Ape,* that "neophilia"—meaning a love for the novel and for innovation, and a passionate curiosity—is a trait that developed among primates and has been inherited by humanity. But perhaps neophilia, over the long years since it first became a human characteristic, has acquired a further dimension as well, and now can serve a purpose that goes beyond just "wanting to know more." As the "older" part of neophilia puts us in touch more and more often with novel situations we then have to handle, a new kind of curiosity arises, and we find ourselves "wanting to get better at knowing more," just to keep pace with ourselves. This brings with it, as a different kind of novelty, an "awareness of awareness," so to speak, and, with that, a need to get to know awareness itself better, and to find out whatever we can about the extended viewpoints that have been passed on to us. Is awareness something we're trying to grow, or tame, or refine, or disentangle, or redistribute, or just use more frequently and with greater confidence?

We tend to think of the need to find answers to such awareness questions as a peculiarly modern predicament—one part of what's sometimes called "learning how to learn." Perhaps our own urgency is prompted to some extent by the newest and most disruptive aspect of

Constant Unnoticed Travel, the only one that we ourselves have set in motion: rising sea levels; earlier springs in every northern country; and other changes to the surface of the earth that have been linked to global warming. "Arctic Summers Could Be Ice-Free in 30 Years," "Glaciers Slip Sliding Away," "Polar Bear 'Extinct Within 100 Years,' " "Meltdown: Forget Polar Bears, the Rapid Warming in the Arctic Could Be a Catastrophe for Us All," "Farewell Cool Britannia" (this English story begins, "London will be like Naples"), "Global Warming Could Displace State Birds" (this U.S. story suggests that Maryland's summers may become too hot for nesting Baltimore orioles within twenty years)—when headlines like these tug at our attention, the idea of taking the earth's pulse begins to feel more like a family matter, and one more way of checking on our own health and chances for survival.

But maybe we're not the first generation to find the outer edges of awareness an urgent subject for further investigation. The concern, when you start looking for signs of it, stretches back further than we might think, and was commented on at some length, for instance, by Rumi, the Afghan poet who lived during the Middle Ages. The most important thing to do, Rumi said, was never to stop short and assume you've exhausted the subject. Instead, follow up each discovery about awareness with still more explorations. Writing about perception more than seven hundred years ago, Rumi defined the pressure this way: "Because of necessity, man acquires organs. Therefore, necessitous one, increase your need."

I f one aspect of the "new neophilia" is a continuing thirst for greater awareness, then it's no wonder that I have been unable to forget my Deepest Travel glimpse and glance across the solar system on the night of the conjunction. It also made me think again about other interruptions I've encountered to the smooth "flow of time"—most notably, one where it was no longer either flowing or not flowing. I discovered this ability entirely by accident, or, rather, by having an accident. Without looking or thinking late one summer night several years ago, I stubbed my toe against a door so hard that I was right away pretty sure it was broken, and as a result spent the next several hours in the patients' waiting area at the NYU Medical Center emergency room until the doctor on duty had time to see me. I had brought a travel book with me, one of the series by Sir Patrick Leigh Fermor, and the triage nurse had handed me a pamphlet that explained "how our ER works so you'll know what to expect." The section called "Waiting" invited me to "feel free to read through our assortment of magazines or watch television," pointed out that "vending machines are conveniently located," and cautioned that "the waiting can sometimes seem interminable." It was a quiet night, so people, mostly orderlies and nurses, only occasionally came and went. Aside from the television murmuring in one corner, the few passersby, and a couple of other patients silently awaiting care, there wasn't much to look at or listen to. The room (which has since been remodeled) was relentlessly plain, functional, unornamented, and almost chilly from the air conditioning. All that was okay; I had only one goal: to find out if I had in fact broken my toe. I was maybe a bit lightheaded from shock, a feeling compounded by the sting of having acted so clumsily, but I was willing to suspend judgment on that point, since the break hadn't been confirmed. I wasn't in much pain—which is why I was sitting there: "triage" means that people who are acutely ill or badly hurt get seen to first, and the minor casualties like me spend time in "triage limbo." From its language, even the welcoming pamphlet seemed to assume that the most common responses to having to wait would be anger and frustration. For whatever reason, that wasn't what I was feeling. Actually, sitting in the waiting room meant to me that the treatment system had accepted me into its care, even if it hadn't yet examined me. The message I was focused on was that I had already been assured that, whatever my problem happened to be, it would get fixed.

This state of mind, which was very betwixt and between, may explain what happened next. I curled up with my book, *A Time of Gifts,* one of the most beautifully written books I've ever read, and returned to Patrick Leigh Fermor's haunting, bittersweet memories of the project he undertook almost seventy-five years ago, when he was still eighteen, to walk the length of Europe, from Holland to Istanbul. Occasionally, I looked up and glanced around, and the second or third time I did so, my eye was caught by some sort of motion on the other side of the room that I hadn't noticed before. The waiting area, I realized, was less barren than I had assumed; there was some kind of kinetic, motorized piece of moving metal sculpture attached to the far wall. A small black metal stick, pointed at one end like a conductor's baton, was swiveling in regular, soundless circles around its blunter end. Two other metal sticks were attached to the same point, making slower and equally silent revolutions. The sculpture's smooth, precise rhythms were restful and soothing to look at, almost like a small, abstract, modern version of a planetarium or orrery, one of those elaborate, nineteenth-century devices that show the rotations of the planets in miniature. I wondered who had dreamed it up and had been kind enough to donate it to the ER to be a constant companion and keep patients like me company. I got into the habit of glancing at it at the end of a chapter—Leigh Fermor was at that point trudging happily through what is now the Czech Republic—to see what new positions the sticks had assumed.

It wasn't until the doctor arrived—I don't know how much later, but maybe a couple of hours—to examine me and tell me that, yes, the toe was broken, and explain that he'd been delayed because he'd had to summon a specialist to work on a patient who'd arrived just ahead of me, that the spell I had been under was broken. If that's what it was, a spell. Or perhaps it was the opposite that was happening, and I was now rejoining a more familiar spell that had somehow been only temporarily suspended. At any rate, it was at that moment that I realized, with something of a jolt, that the smooth, clever, wall-mounted sculpture that had given me such pleasure was not a unique art installation but an altogether familiar, mass-produced object: a clock on the wall. Why had I failed to recognize something I've seen dozens of times a day throughout a lifetime? Because we unconsciously assume that clocks are meters, machines that aren't so much driven by springs and motors as they are powered by the passage of time itself. But the flow of time simply disappeared in the waiting room, and so there was nothing left for the clock to measure. What would you make of a water wheel that continued to turn in an empty river? Would it seem merely decorative or entertaining? What about a steam gauge that continued to bob away on the side of a boiler that had no water in it and no heat under it?

Although I've never had another experience quite like this one, I've begun to think that the ability to abandon time—for the time being, at least—is nearer to hand than it might seem and that activating it doesn't require extraordinary circumstances, such as accidentally stubbing your toe in the middle of the night. Just as the point of Charles Lamb's celebrated essay "A Dissertation upon Roast Pig" is that, even if the first roast pig anyone ever ate was an unplanned event, the result of a fire that consumed a home with a pig inside, it isn't necessary to keep burning houses down to get a second helping.

When it comes to time, it may be that "untimed," or time-free, episodes remain within reach because they have uses that are yet to be recorded or studied. One of these might be to set up situations—using no more than a word or a quick phrase—that allow our minds to register patterns they would ordinarily tune out. I've noticed, for instance, that although many surviving folktales and fairy tales begin with "Once..." or "Once upon a time...," lead-ins clearly designed to bump the mind out of its immediate time frame and into another, parallel path where normal expectations and preoccupations may no longer have the same sway, some stories have far more elaborate and deliberately topsy-turvy introductions, perhaps to suggest that sometimes even the entire grid of time must be cast aside rather than become an obstacle to finding the kernel of certain oddly themed stories. I've recently started pulling together some of these more arrestingly odd story openings. One Romany tale whose "subject" is extending awareness in unusual ways begins, "Before the war between cats and mice, which made all cats and mice enemies, and before the Man in the Moon went there, but lived at the bottom of a well, there lived a Romany who was the seventh son of a seventh son." And the first line of an ancient story from Turkistan, called "The Riddles," which is about learning to cast off a deep-seated spell, is "There was a time, and there was not a time, when the sky was green and the earth was a rich stew."

There is perhaps another reason people may shy away from thinking too much or too often about time. Let's call it the "privacy of time," and then we won't have to say a lot about it, since it's the one thing that awaits all of us, a subject that's fully public when presented as a statistic but otherwise remains intensely personal, something each of us will deal with in the quietness of the heart. From the moment of our arrival, all of us have been caught up in a time-that-is-not-a-time, and set down in the middle of an unsolved riddle. The only definite information we have about our own individual circumstances is that our stay here is finite, yet indefinite. This is a different kind of awareness problem, since thinking about it can be suppressed or postponed but never entirely excluded, and it walks on by our side, a silent companion. Many spiritual traditions recommend taking this companion by the hand, as a way of deepening all awarenesses. But the subject often remains painful, as was pointed out during a brief conversation more than thirteen hundred years ago in the Yemeni desert that still gets passed on to each new generation in the Middle East. A man asked Uwais el-Qarni, a solitary, much respected contemplative from the time of the Prophet Muhammad, how he felt. Like someone, Uwais said, who got up in the morning and doesn't know if he will be alive when evening comes. The man, according to one modern translation, said, "But that is the condition of all men." "Yes," said Uwais, "but how many of them feel it?"

The American poet William Bronk found that for him thoughts about time and thoughts about death were almost inextricably entwined. Bronk, a descendant of the family that the Borough of the Bronx, in New York City, takes its name from, lived in upstate New York and spent eighty of his eighty-one years in the house his parents moved to when he was one; he ran his father's coal and lumber business for more than thirty of those years. He never learned to drive and he didn't travel much, but many people continually sought him out—for his poetry and his kindness and his gourmet cooking. In a poem dedicated to one of his Dartmouth teachers, "The Arts and Death: A Fugue for Sidney Cox," he says that

> Death dominates my mind. I
> do not stop thinking about how time will stop,
> how time has stopped, does stop. Those dead—
> their done time. Time does us in.

On the other hand, there have always been those who have been made more buoyant by thinking about their transitoriness. Rummaging through bound volumes of historic newspapers at the Delaware Historical Society, in Wilmington, some years ago while doing research on the early settlements on the eastern shore of Maryland, I was stopped short by the thinking in a short paragraph in the Miscellany column of the *Delaware Gazette and American Watchman* for Tuesday, March 11, 1834. I copied it in my notebook, and have since had to put it in a "Miscellaneous" file of my own, not knowing where else to put it, since it treats ecology, then not even a concept, as a matter of common decency and good manners, like giving up a seat on a crowded bus. (By way of introduction, the population of the world at the time was just over 1 billion people, while in early 2010 it was 6.8 billion; life expectancy in the United States is now just over seventy-eight years.) "The life of man on average," said the anonymous *Gazette* writer, "is little more than 30 years. . . . The population of the earth is on the increase—a consideration which should show us the necessity of preparation for yielding our places to others, and for joining the invisible flight of spirits which are continually leaving the earth, for no one can tell but that the next moment his soul may be called on to become one of the number."

TIME PIONEERS

Remembering these differing reflections, let's walk softly and move forward aware that thinking about time, and about moving through it or away from it, may at unpredictable moments bring with it an extra echo or undertone, a tug, a reminder of what's still in store. Aware, too, that it's the "time thoughts" we have, rather than the "motion thoughts" as such, that tend to forge the links we sometimes sense between the countless trips we make in a lifetime whose endings we can look back on and that other unfinished journey, the one whose conclusion we can't see with clarity and certainty. Or between our individual journey and some longer, larger human procession, such as the "invisible flight" felt by an unknown nineteenth-century writer in Delaware. All of which sets still other questions in motion—such as, if we are part of a continuing procession of some sort, where might it have set off from, and when did it get its start?

Whatever the answer is to that, it would seem that within this lifetime, unusual times are so plentiful they probably should be considered a norm. Accompanying them and organizing them inside us requires a kind of "time sorter." By this I mean an ability to navigate through these states; to move into and out of a sense of time passing by; and, within the swim of time, to modify and readjust the way time seems to flow so as to suit our own purposes. The sheer number of changes that our time sense moves through during the course of a day remains unduced, perhaps because the changes aren't random. Each activity in a day, once we look more closely at its structure, seems yoked to and coordinated by its own customary "time tune," so to speak, which, like any piece of music, carries with it a pace or beat and an overall sense of duration, or length, or extension—an ongoing advance estimate of how much longer we'll need to finish whatever it is we've already started doing.

Because these melodious, rhythmic "time structures" orchestrate our doings and our comings and goings, it isn't surprising to find that Deep Travel, too, has a time structure all its own. Which means that whenever Deep Travel seems to move physical horizons back for us, the widened sense we gain of "*where* we are" and the new understandings we start collecting about "*who* we are" and about what it is we know or don't know and might learn are interwoven with, strengthened through, and illuminated by a parallel stretching in our sense of "*when* we are."

"Can one narrate time—time as such, in and of itself?" Thomas Mann asks toward the end of *The Magic Mountain.* "Most certainly not," he answers, "what a foolish undertaking that would be." Yet there are those who try, fortunately, and over the past century or so a handful of "time pioneers" have stepped forward to investigate, to explain, to validate the reports made by others. Though their efforts remain uncollated, enough of these wayfarers and pathfinders through time had already stepped forward so that, by the early 1980s, Edward T. Hall, even then the grand old man of American anthropology, could declare that an emerging "science of time will assume greater stature in the future" as "an active, important, major field of study." Hall, who was born in 1914 and died in 2009, devoted his exceptionally long life to exploring the previously unexplorable. "What I see," Hall declared in his 1983 book *The Dance of Life: The Other Dimension of Time,* "is a whole new dimension or set of dimensions to be explored," a search that would be slowed only by a condition that almost thirty years later has still not entirely been thrown aside: "the human race is not nearly enough in awe of its own capabilities."

Perhaps time pioneers, as Hall suggests, are actually the advance scouts of approaching knowledge that one day will have become commonplace. Many of the early time scholars have concentrated on finding answers to specific time questions they have found compelling, such as "Why life speeds up as you get older," a question that in 2001 became the title of a book by Douwe Draaisma, a Dutch historian of psychology. The answer Draaisma passes on is one that Paul Janet, a French philosopher, discovered in 1877, when he became the first person to point out that we seem to measure passing years against the accumulated stockpile of our own birthdays, so that at ten a year is an accomplishment all by itself, representing a full tenth of a lifetime, whereas by fifty it has dwindled as a fraction, becoming no more than 2 percent of the total. Or, as Draaisma puts it, "Throughout our lives we continue to apply a yardstick that keeps changing and is therefore no yardstick at all."

Hall's subject in *The Dance of Life* is the "wide discrepancy between time as it is lived and time as it is considered." His own careful observations, which began when he was still a teenager, had early on led him to conclude that "as people do quite different things (write books, play, schedule activities, travel, get hungry, sleep, dream, meditate, and perform ceremonies), they unconsciously and sometimes consciously express and participate in different categories of time." The time has come, Hall thinks, for a more general recognition that

> time is not just an immutable constant, as Newton supposed, but a cluster of concepts, events, and rhythms covering an extremely wide range of phenomena. It is for this reason that classifying time, in the words of the English Africanist E. E. Evans-Pritchard, "bristles with difficulties." At the microlevel of analysis one might say that there are as many different kinds of time as human beings on this earth, but we in the Western world view time as a single entity. This is incorrect, but it is the way we see it.

In his late teens, Ned Hall, as his friends called him, spent several years in the early 1930s working on Hopi and Navajo reservations in northern Arizona as a construction foreman, which made him almost by default the only interface between Anglo engineers sent out from Washington to build roads and bridges and their Hopi and Navajo work crews. From then on he found himself thinking "outside the clock," so to speak:

> I often saw Navajos and Hopis patiently waiting around trading posts at the agency in Keams Canyon, Arizona. . . . I realized that it was not pos-

sible to imagine myself in their shoes. There was a different quality to the Indians' waiting from my own. In this respect I was no different from other white men. We were all impatient, always looking at our watches or the clock on the wall, muttering or fidgeting. Yet an Indian might come into the agency in the morning and still be sitting patiently outside the superintendent's office in the afternoon. Nothing in his bearing or demeanor would change in the intervening hours. How could that be? . . . It was quite evident that my time was not their time. . . .

Earlier in the book Hall says:

I soon learned that I was dealing with at least four different time systems: Hopi time, Navajo time, government bureaucratic time, and the time used by the other white men (mostly Indian traders) who lived on the reservation. . . . And what differences there were among those time systems! There seemed to be no way at all to bring them in line. Even as a somewhat naive youth, I was amazed and puzzled by how little importance was attached to those differences. They were ignored so that everyone could adhere to his own time system.

Hall's later life only added still more time systems to his inventory. He was, for instance, an army engineer during World War II, commanding an African-American regiment, first in Europe and then in the Philippines (by this time he had already picked up a Ph.D. in anthropology). In 1950, as director of the U.S. State Department's Point IV Training Program for foreign service officers about to be posted overseas, he was again a bridge builder, a man in the middle. Only now he was trying to teach "time as a second language," so to speak, introducing junior American diplomats, as it says on Hall's Web site, to deep-seated "attitudes . . . toward time, space, and relationships" held by other cultures that exist at such a primary level they're never spoken aloud, since they're considered self-evident. Hall also taught anthropology at Northwestern and other universities, and turned almost everything he happened to notice wherever he was into a research project. (He became famous, for instance, for coining the word "proxemics," which in part is a careful notation system for describing the measurable amount of space people from different cultures keep between one another in order to stay comfortable; the distances vary widely, as it turns out.) Along the way he had become a new kind of simultaneous translator, helping Americans meet themselves as well as the rest of the world. The books he wrote follow this generous pattern—they read like the reports sent home by the ambassador from some future America.

In *The Dance of Life,* Hall presents what amounts almost to a tasting menu of nine separate time-as-it-is-lived experiences. The cumulative effect of reading about them is to pull time awareness into the forefront of our attention, making it into something that, like proxemics, can be held in the mind, talked about, studied, appreciated. This is a profound public service that reminds me of the sky-awareness campaign that a former Boston TV reporter named Jack Borden launched more than twenty-five years ago. The difference is that Hall never set up a nonprofit to bring his "time appreciation" insights into American grade schools, while Borden's group, For Spacious Skies, has already brought its sky curriculum to more than fifty thousand classrooms. Already middle-aged, Borden began to notice the sky when, waking one day from a nap in a Massachusetts meadow and still flat on his back, for the first time in his life he saw, as he often tells other reporters, the constantly changing "majesties of the sky," which by then had been swirling over his head, ignored, for the past forty-nine years. "I was just so overwhelmed," he says. "How could I have gone so long without seeing it?"

People who, like Borden, take up an interest in sky awareness say it changes their sense of the world's third dimension, by putting a solid floor and bottom under the volume of the sky, so that you feel that its immensity begins right where you already are, stretching upward from your feet, at the point where the air meets the ground, rather than at some incalculable distance high above the rooftops. ("I felt as though I constantly walked in an atmospheric cathedral," the American landscape painter Eric Sloane, a lifelong sky observer, once said about how this sense had affected him.)

But Hall's time-awareness writings are more than just profound scene shifters, and also make me think of the orderly, sharply focused work of an earlier student of the sky, Luke Howard, the "cloud namer," a man honored today as the "father of meteorology." Before Howard, Keith C. Heidorn, an American meteorologist, points out in a recent biographical sketch, clouds were beyond the grasp of scientists—considered "too transient, too changeable, too short-lived to be classified or even analyzed." But Howard, a young English chemist in the late eighteenth century, found a few simple building blocks within the complex patterns overhead, and in 1802 gave them commonplace, comforting and seemingly age-old names. Clouds, he found, tend to assume one of four basic forms: heaps, layers, what look like curls of hair, and about-to-rain (although this last is as much a darkening as it is a shape). There are also hybrid forms, such as heaps-that-are-about-to-rain—these are the huge thunderclouds that can tower high into the atmosphere. Howard then translated these names into Latin (*cumulus, stratus, cirrus,* and *nimbus,* along with some of the common combinations, such as *cumulonimbus*). Then and still now, Latin is a universal scientific language for species names and for categories of matter and the classification of events. With this, the seemingly chaotic resolved itself into a matrix all scientists could accept and work with, the way a blurry eye chart forms recognizable letters once an optometrist exactly clicks the right lens into place during an eye examination. Howard, said Goethe, who admired him, had found a way "to limit and fasten down the indefinite, the intangible and unattainable and give them appropriate names."

Although Hall doesn't discuss Deep Travel directly, thanks to his closely observed descriptions of what he calls "variable time," it's possible to see that Deep Travel time occupies a kind of middle ground in a broad scale of time variations. At one extreme are time changes that occur perhaps once or twice in a lifetime; at the other are several daily arrivals so frequently encountered we often feel we *are* them rather than being prompted by them or living with their assistance. Like Deep Travel time—but unlike either the smooth, measured Hartlerian flow of time or the regular and reliable interruptions to a day set by our biological clocks—these time variations are sudden alterations within the flow. They're arrhythmic, and they're unpredictable: we don't know when they'll arrive or how long they'll last. They reframe our sense of the present moment by resetting what we think of as its "speed" and its "duration." On the one hand, speed refers to its tempo, pace, or gait, which become subject to what can seem jolting accelerations or decelerations. The sense of speed allows us to answer such questions as, How fast do things seem to be happening right now? How quickly do we seem to be moving through them? Duration, on the other hand, refers to the "size of the now" and whether we think it's getting bigger or smaller. Duration is a measure of now's extent and now's boundaries (the distance, for instance, at a given moment between what's still "now" and what we would say has already become a "then"). Duration also includes our sense of the persistence of the present moment—is it fleeting, or does it have some lastingness? It's one part of the answer we can give to the question captured by the haunting Gershwin song, "How Long Has This Been Going On?"

Emergency situations, Hall points out in *The Dance of Life,* can activate "a built-in, variable time sensor" that can save lives. Time can move at lightning speed when, looking ahead, someone feels as if duration has dwindled to an instant and "one thinks one is about to die ('My whole life flashed before my eyes')." Alternatively, if duration is short and finite and its end is imminent, but maybe there's still a chance left to avert disaster, the opposite can happen. The flow of time is slowed, Hall calculates, to about 1/300th of its normal pace, and as a result the time still available seems to expand by 300 percent. If there were a formula for what it feels like, it might be expressed as "Acceleration = Deceleration." Although it's been more often lived through than written about, this kind of emergency "Time Expansion," as Hall calls it, probably deserves recognition as a "third option" that may be possible for us in dangerous and desperate situations, a uniquely human ability that as a behavior seems to sit almost halfway between the two instinctive emergency responses that we share with other animals: *flight* and *fight*. The function of this third choice seems to be to "buy time," almost literally, in this way helping people handle situations, if possible, rather than give up on them, by taking unexpected and novel actions instead of attacking or running away. The solution-finding involved may include such things as *sitting tight* and *getting fright right,* to continue the rhyme scheme.

Hall's principal example of emergency Time Expansion is one he ran across in a 1980 *Washington Post Magazine* article about a navy test pilot. The pilot had just catapulted off from an aircraft carrier when he realized that his Harrier jet was not developing power, which meant that he had a fraction of a minute either to make it fly or to eject before it crashed and disintegrated. What happened over the next eight seconds later took forty-five minutes to describe, since it involved, as Hall points out, a lengthy series of actions. First the pilot had to determine that the engine wouldn't respond; then he had to eject at exactly thirty feet above the water. Each separate move had to be made "at the right time, in the right order, and without panic. If he had been on normal time, none of this would have been possible. If that capacity to expand time . . . had not been built into the human species, it is doubtful that the human race would have survived."

What the pilot himself sensed seemed more like a change in the nature of space than in the nature of time. It wasn't that his mind was moving faster but that things around him had lost all velocity. "I was very surprised by the whole evolution of the thing," he told the *Post* reporter. "Everything went into slow motion." More than two decades later, we might call this the "*Matrix* effect"—Neo, the hero of that movie, can dodge bullets by moving so fast that they seem to be only crawling forward like an airborne millipede. Acceleration = Deceleration. Hall himself once had a similar sensation. Visiting a naturalist one day, he felt something brush against his leg and realized that a caged mountain lion had just escaped into a narrow passageway where he was standing: "As I watched the lion lick a spot of grease next to my toe, time slowed down." Both fight and flight seemed impossible; the thought, "If you are afraid, the animal will sense it and kill you," flashed through his mind. "But what to do? How to get out of this mess? Putting years of experience with animals to work, while I mentally alternately reviewed and rejected a half dozen options and their scenarios, the only workable solution seemed to be to make friends. This mountain lion, I discovered, could be approached, and it even purred like a Model T Ford. Having assured myself that I wasn't going to die just yet, I didn't push the relationship, either. Eventually the mountain lion (his name was Jim) was back in his cage and I departed."

"How many times events of this sort have happened in the history of the species of course is not known," Hall notes. "But having lived an active, outdoor ranch life in the wilds of New Mexico and Arizona as a young man, I do know that emergencies are legion and that this capacity to slow down time in an emergency has saved me more than once." So it's an arousal state clearly still "necessary for survival" for people spending time in the open, and Hall thinks it may already have been adapted and invoked "to confront a new set of dangers, those of urban life," and maybe now protects people "cut off from nature, swaddled in technology and creature comforts." I'm inclined to agree. A few years before *The Dance of Life* was published and gave me a chance to read about Time Expansion, a car I was driving on Sixth Avenue in Manhattan was sideswiped by a car running a red light on Fourteenth Street. Time slowed down just long enough for me to bend away from the impact and somehow maneuver the car, whose engine had been crushed, across three lanes of Saturday morning traffic and over to the curb. Car crushed, but no bones broken. "You're lucky to be alive!" said a bystander. True, and maybe even luckier to have an ability I didn't yet have a name for.

Accounts of Time Expansion incidents in nonemergency situations pop up in many cultures, and sometimes seem to blur the lines between sleeping and waking. Jean-Marie Guyau, a time pioneer cited by Draaisma, was brilliant and prolific, a philosopher, poet, psychologist, and sociologist and the author of an 1890 essay entitled "The Genesis of the Idea of Time." He wrote of "a student who had suddenly fallen into a lethargic sleep but was quickly reawakened by his anxious friends. In the brief interval he dreamt about a visit to Italy. The shifting series of images of towns, people, monuments, and personal experiences during the visit gave him the impression that he had been dreaming for hours." Such stories are perhaps most common in the Middle East and Central Asia, where the tradition of the night journey of the Prophet Muhammad remains a living part of Islamic heritage; the Prophet, according to the tradition, was summoned from his bed one night to heaven, where he held ninety thousand conversations with God. When he was returned to his room, his bed was still warm and a water jug that had been knocked over by his departure still had water in it. A thirteenth-century discussion about the seventh-century night journey that is itself still current in Sufi study circles mentions that Time Expansion is a faculty that by itself "carries no special significance"—because what's important is the use people make of any extended time granted to them. In a story retold by Idries Shah in his *Tales of the Dervishes,* a sultan who has pronounced himself skeptical of the Prophet's experience dunks his head into a bowl of water for a mere instant at the request of a revered teacher and thinks that he has been transported to a distant land where, over the course of seven years, he does nothing but squander a fortune so that he is eventually reduced to seeking work as a porter.

The revered teacher in the story, by the way, Sheikh Shahabudin

Omar Suhrawardi, of Baghdad, held similar views about the possibilities inherent in ordinary travel properly undertaken. It can be the means of gaining a fortune rather than frittering one away. In one of his works, *Gifts of Deep Knowledge* (translated into English as *A Dervish Textbook*), Suhrawardi writes that "being separated from one's native land, from friends and familiar things" and "exercising . . . patience in calamities" can do much toward "softening hard hearts." Addressing himself to "seekers of *hakikat*" (truth) in language familiar to readers of his day, Suhrawardi says that just as "dead skins," after tanning, show "the effects of purity, of softness, and of delicacy of texture; . . . even so, by the tanning of *safar* [the journey—the English word "safari" comes from the same Arabic root], and by the departure of natural corruption and innate roughness, appear the purifying softness of devotion and change from obstinacy to faith."

As for daily time variations, "Is there anyone," Hall asks, "who has not had the experience of time 'crawling' or 'flying'?" Most people will find, if they take the trouble to chronicle these changes, that in the course of any single day they may find themselves swinging back and forth through a toboggan ride of time speeds. These seeming quickenings and slowings of time speed as we move from task to task—tied always to lengthenings and shortenings of time duration—are so universal and inescapable that they long ago became incorporated into proverbs: "A watched pot never boils"; "Time flies when you're having fun." Strung together as a continuous sequence, daily time speeds are in such continuous back-and-forth motion that they might almost be presented as a tune played on an accordion, sometimes squeezed and pushed, sometimes pulled apart. But since we seem to register or catch up to the "time sense" of given moments only at irregular intervals, it's probably more accurate to say that "lived time," as Hall calls it—meaning waking time as we actually experience it and retain it in our minds—for the most part feels episodic and disjointed, something like an interrupted and staticky transmission. When time seems to slow, that is, we can be painfully aware of each moment, but, in between, what we often sense isn't so much time speeding up again but time simply jumping or skipping, faster than a fast-forward button—like a slow stream that hurtles over the steep drop of a waterfall and then resumes its previous pace. The elapsing of time is similar, in this respect, to the instant that seems to have passed between nodding off to sleep at night and waking up again the next morning.

According to William James, who took up the subject of the present moment in *The Principles of Psychology,* his twelve-hundred-page investigation of the human mind that was first published in 1890—it was twelve years in the making and is still considered a cornerstone of modern psychology—the "strict present," or the "sensible present" or the "specious present," as he also called it (meaning by that our immediate, instant-by-instant sense of "the now around us"), is a "vaguely bounded unit" that doesn't last long. It has some duration: "It is no knife-edge, but a saddle-back, with a certain breadth of its own on which we sit perched, and from which we look in two directions into time." Or it could be thought of as a small boat, "with a bow and a stern, as it were—a rearward—and a forward-looking end." We experience this interval, he thinks, at its far end—as something that has already been happening. But only for a very short while, since anything past is quickly shed: "We are constantly conscious of a certain duration—the specious present—varying in length from a few seconds to probably not more than a minute," he says in one place. "Its nucleus," he says in another, "is probably the dozen seconds or less that have just elapsed."

Based on these self-observations, James concludes that "the time-sense" is "a myopic organ," since the eye can see "acres, even miles at a single glance," while the units of time we use require "mental addition": "To 'realize' a quarter of a mile we need only look out of the window and 'feel' its length by an act which . . . seems immediately performed. To realize an hour, we must count 'Now!—Now!—Now!—Now!—' indefinitely." Experiments by Ernst Pöppel, a modern psychologist and brain researcher who's director of the Medical Psychology Institute at the University of Munich, tend to confirm James's findings. "Whatever grabs our attention during a three-second window," *The New York Times* noted in reviewing Pöppel's 1988 book *Mindworks: Time and Conscious Experience,* "our brain integrates into a chunk we call the present." You can prove this to yourself, Pöppel says, by listening to a ticking metronome. "Instinctively," this *Times* summary reported, "we group the featureless progression of sounds into patterns—DA da da, DA da da, DA da da—and these clusters are generally no more than three seconds long. Likewise, . . . poetry and speech tend to be structured in three-second bites."

Nevertheless, despite this fleetingness, which everyone has tasted, most people have an equally strong sense that there are pieces of most days when, under the differently structured rules of variable time, the restrictions of the strict present are relaxed—and not always in ways that are welcomed. Consider, for example, those recurring "watched pot" occasions where time drags, and the duration of the present moment balloons as if time were holding its breath, and "now" starts taking up so much space it seems to be pushing the future back, holding it at bay, delaying its arrival. "Time dragging," Hall says, "is a synonym for not having a good time."

For "pot watchers" the problem is impatience. The focus, like that of Patricia Mokhtarian's "already-there travelers," is on a future state that hasn't arrived yet (boiling water, in this case), and we want it so intensely that we invoke a kind of magical thinking and begin paying exaggerated attention to the pot, the flame, and the water, as if they can somehow thereby hear our pleas or commands and then hurry the process along. The paradoxical result is that boiling seems indefinitely delayed. Why? For Robert Ornstein, a contemporary psychologist who is both a time pioneer and the author of more than twenty books on the mind and the brain, how long something seems to last depends on how much of a moment or a situation is being consumed or retained by the mind—or, in Ornstein's metaphor, based on the language of information processing, on how much "storage space" and "storage size" the mind will need for the information it is reaching out for at any given point. As Ornstein puts it in his first book, *On the Experience of Time*, published in 1969, "expectancy is a situation which leads to increased sensitivity to stimuli," so that "as we continually 'watch' the pot . . . we are more vigilant than usual," leading to "a greater amount of awareness of input, and consequently a lengthening of duration experience." The pot boils eventually, in the usual amount of time—"but it does seem much longer."

The German word for boredom is *langeweile*—literally, "a long while" or "a long time." Boredom is the other commonly arising situation in which duration expands, sometimes alarmingly so. "Not too much," says Hall, "is known technically about the effect of the different emotions on the passage of time," but it is clear that, as with "pot watching," boredom is a time variation triggered in large part when personal feelings and reactions get entangled in some ongoing event or circumstance. With boredom, it isn't so much wanting something to happen, it's wanting whatever's happening already to stop happening. It's a more intense kind of dissatisfaction than "pot watching" because we're not just up against an impervious force of nature, like heat. Our attention has been constrained and redirected and (it may even feel) kidnapped by another person or group of people, and it can't be reclaimed or ransomed until whatever they've started is over and that long anecdote is done; or the school bell rings; or the delayed plane lands. Impatience is overshadowed by powerlessness, and we endure what we're being force-fed and at the same time try to concentrate on anything else in the room just to see us through: a flowerpot, a fly, our shoes, that little cough the speaker uses to emphasize a point. Things are out of our hands, even if we can see how they might be improved. Any future value the occasion might bring is hidden from us. "Now," once more, is, for the moment at least, interminable. "In storage size terms," Ornstein says, more dispassionately, in *On the Experience of Time,* "situations which we label 'boring' are ones in which we are forced to attend to more of the stimulus array than we normally would, like listening to a professor drone on and on. Again, an increase in attention, relative to normal experience, would cause a lengthening of duration experience."

Contrast this with the way time simply disappears when, in a familiar and safe setting, we give ourselves over almost wholly to a task we find worthwhile and rewarding. "Concentration of any sort," Hall says—on "almost anything that is sufficiently involving"—"obliterates time." Meaning both the sense of time passing by and even some of the preliminary urgings and periodic chimings of various biological clocks. Hall talks about the work of a microsurgeon whose team worked nonstop for twenty-four hours and twenty minutes, successfully reattaching four fingers to an eighteen-year-old girl's hand. This doctor later said, "I wasn't conscious of time." A young Swiss filmmaker who works by herself tells Hall that she "experiences the time between meals when she is working as mere minutes. Suddenly she will feel hungry and realize hours have gone by." The same goes for having fun. Hall asks, "Is there anyone who has not had the experience of being deeply involved in a happy transaction and suddenly realized: 'Oh, my goodness! I was having such a good time. I had no idea it was getting so late'?" This is what it means to "lose all sense of time."

Deep Travel time, on the other hand, is time regained—a stepping aside from the complex of time rhythms and scheduling systems, some regular, others more syncopated, some idiosyncratic, and many deep-seated, that we respond to and live by.

And yet—
Before celebrating Deep Travel time, it may help to acknowledge one other "elephant in the brain"—that is, one further reason why it's a subject that almost automatically makes us feel . . . uncomfortable. At least at first, and at least if "us" refers to Americans and northern Europeans. One of Edward Hall's most original contributions to time research is what he calls "time as culture" or sometimes "the language of time," by which he means specific rules about "when"-ness—such as when to do what, and with whom, and in what order. It's a topic he wrote about for over fifty years—in fact, the first chapter of his first book (*The Silent Language*) is called "The Voices of Time" and begins, "Time talks. It speaks more plainly than words. . . . It can shout the truth where words lie." What's being shouted are rules of appropriate behavior. These rules vary from culture to culture, as languages do, but, again like languages, they are universally present and are absorbed at such an early stage of life—becoming part, as Edward Reed would say, of each person's frame of promoted action—that their power becomes almost invisible and impalpable. Cultural time rules, globally, are, as Hall says in *The Dance of Life*, "known to all, obeyed by all," "taken for granted," and each culture's time language, or time culture, is "so thoroughly woven into the fabric of existence that we are hardly aware of the degree to which it determines and coordinates everything we do."

North Americans and northern Europeans—this is another Hall discovery—share the same time language. Both groups are controlled by "the iron hand of M-time," or "Monochronic time." These terms of Hall's basically mean that, despite frequent praise for multitasking, we're trained to do one thing at a time and to coordinate these actions with the time readings displayed on clocks. We then treat this seemingly simple proposition "as though it were the only natural and logical way of organizing life." It has its pluses—for instance, people can pool their talents by scheduling a meeting, which then seals them off from everyone else, "like a room with a closed door ensuring privacy. The only problem is that you must vacate the 'room' at the end of the allotted fifteen minutes."

M-time was originally "industrial time," an eighteenth-century way of making sure that people converged simultaneously to operate machines gathered in one place, such as a factory. In the nineteenth century it expanded to become "railroad time," which coordinated the actions of people and machines that move about; the central element of railroad time is the "time zone," a convenient fiction that synchronizes "noons" across bands of countryside as much as eight hundred miles wide. (All the clocks in the eastern time zone, for example, will say noon at the same moment each day, even though the sun will still be registering 11:30 over the western end of the zone, and will already have advanced to a 12:30 position over the zone's eastern end.) One of the reasons M-time's pervasiveness goes so unnoticed is that it has been so successfully both externalized and internalized. Externally, we are surrounded by clocks. At this moment, at my desk, I'm wearing a wristwatch (these became popular after the First Word War); my living room has three calendars (one in my computer, one sitting on my desk, and another in my appointment book) and seven clocks (one at the bottom of my computer screen, two alarm clocks, a clock on the cable box, an unset clock on the DVD player, and two antiques on the mantelpiece that need to be taken to the watchmaker); the rest of our four-room apartment has eleven clocks.

Internally, M-time's rules have by repeated training been imprinted onto our consciences, which means that they now come accompanied by two stings: anxiety before an infraction; guilt afterward. "I feel anxious," Hall records about himself, "when I see I am going to be late and will do what I can to avoid it, not only because I feel an obligation to be on time but because I want to avoid anxiety." These same stings are used to assert and enforce rank and status. Time flexibility is one of the rewards of success. Whereas a subordinate must arrive on time to be considered reliable and any other conduct would be an insult, a boss has the privilege of inconveniencing others by being late, up to half an hour or a bit more. Maybe it was the inadvertent workings of this unconscious process that unexpectedly produced my time-that-was-not-a-time in a hospital emergency room. It benefitted me, but it doesn't always work that way. "Some physicians and most hospitals," Hall says, are notorious in their violations of the nation's [time] mores. It would not be so bad if it weren't so stressful for the patients. The message comes through, however, that hospital staff is in charge; they are important, the patient isn't (he's lucky to be there). The patient's status, by all applicable nonverbal criteria and measures, has in most instances become reduced to that of a nonperson. It wasn't designed that way; it just happened. But it doesn't have to stay that way.

Southern Europeans and South Americans, on the other hand, who have been raised on "P-time," or "Polychronic time" (two more of Hall's terms), have been trained to be involved in several things at once, and to answer to a different set of obligations. Their consciences tell them that finishing whatever's happening at the moment—a meeting, a conversation—is more important than abandoning these companions in order to assemble on the dot for a meeting that hasn't started yet. Each time culture, M and P, finds the other rude and unreasonable. "For more than twenty-five years," Hall could say more than twenty-five years ago, in *The Dance of Life,* "I have been intimately aware of the difference" between the two time systems. "Not only is one polychronic and oriented to people and the other monochronic, stressing procedures (procedures are fast while people are slow), but . . . neither takes the other seriously."

"Calling the clock of hours, minutes, and seconds 'real' time," says Robert Ornstein, in *On the Experience of Time,* "is like calling American money 'real money.' " But that is the kind of foreshortened perspective that can keep us at arm's length from something as rewarding as Deep Travel time.

To resume—
Deep Travel time, when it arrives, is unstained by ingrained time attitudes, such as M-time. In terms of affinities, it has the clarity of emergency Time Expansion, without the overwhelming urgency. But it's not so much a temporary tourniquet on the flow of time as it is a rearrangement of how past, present, and future move by. So, oddly enough, Deep Travel time's closest relative, at least in the similar ways they both alter speed and duration, is the most disliked of our everyday time visitors, boredom. But Deep Travel time, a giver, not a taker-away, is more like "boredom inside out." Or perhaps boredom is a distortion,

a misconception, a blur, and a smudge—Deep Travel time's reflection as seen in a broken mirror. The most pronounced characteristic of both boredom and Deep Travel time is a "now" that doesn't disappear, but the prolonged sense of the present that spreads around anyone who enters Deep Travel acts as a guardian, not a jailer. This "now" is a flexible tool; that other one feels like being handcuffed. The "indefinite now" of Deep Travel time—a larger, longer "now"; a better-equipped and more durable "now"—emerges and stays with us to give us a better chance of making the most out of every Deep Travel arc we participate in. Perhaps this means finishing a thought or finding a meaning, following through on something that has caught our interest—instead of feeling diverted, forced to turn away too soon, or brought to a premature halt.

In Deep Travel time, the goal is not, as in boredom, to reach the end of it but, instead, to "accelerate in place," as it were, to look around ourselves with even more intensity within the moment so as to make the best use of it while it lasts. Time proceeds, but because it can be renewed and prolonged, and because it doesn't dwindle as it progresses, it feels more like what we usually think of as time out and time off. It's no longer the "strict present" that James defined, because the rules have become less tight. It perhaps can still be thought of as something resembling a saddleback, as James called it, meaning a perch that lets us ride the flow of time while observing it. In this case, however, the reins are, so to speak, in our hands, because we have the ability to choose our own path through the flow. With its wider viewpoint, the "now" of Deep Travel time can't be accused of myopia, since one can easily look back along its full length and know at a glance where it began and what's happened since; likewise, the way forward also seems to stretch out along a continuous path. Maybe this is the time variable that gave rise to the classic Henny Youngman joke about the man who's given six months to live: when the man can't pay the bill, his doctor gives him another six months.

No wonder at all, then, that for some writers, time changes are by far the most important differences that travel makes possible. Thomas Mann, for instance, famously interrupts the telling of *The Magic Mountain* for an "Excursus on the Sense of Time," a short, intense, personal chapter with an urgency and harshness quite foreign to his normally smooth, sonorous, ironic narrative style. Directly addressing his readers, Mann pleads with us all to see to "the refreshment of our sense of time," without delay and before it is too late. Traveling is not easy, Mann says, because it takes work, particularly the "laborious process of getting used to new surroundings." But without this or some other similar stimulus, "something psychological, our very sense of time itself . . . falls asleep, or at least grows dull," and when we become victims of "monotony—uninterrupted uniformity can shrink large spaces of time until the heart falters, terrified to death." There is only one remedy: "If the years of youth are experienced slowly, while the later years of life hurtle past at an ever-increasing speed, it must be habit that causes it. We know full well that the insertion of new habits or the changing of old ones is the only way to preserve life, to renew our sense of time, to rejuvenate, intensify, and retard our experience of time—and thereby renew our sense of life itself. That is the reason for every change of scenery and air," because "interest lends the passage of time breadth, solidity, and weight, so that years rich in events pass much more slowly than do paltry, bare, featherweight years that are blown before the wind and are gone."

What does Deep Travel time feel like? There's a name for one of the things it does, the way it helps us keep a sustained, continuous, even-handed focus on some event or question that may take days or even weeks or more to unfold: *suspending judgment.* We usually, however, consider this an intellectual concept, an aspired-to ideal, rather than something with a broader meaning that includes a set of awarenesses we can actually bring into play and apply to any situation where it's important to postpone reaching too early a conclusion. But there's one area of modern life, as I realized a few months ago, that strongly brings the need to suspend judgment into the forefront of the mind: jury duty. Of all the safeguards built into the jury system, perhaps the most sacred is one of the first instructions jurors receive: *Keep an open mind.* Of course, as soon as you hear this you know it's in some ways an impossibility—since we all have parts of our minds that aren't just closed but that are so closed off from ourselves that we don't even know they're there. Nevertheless, we do what we can to honor the obligation, because another person's freedom is in our hands, and this is only one step away from making a life-and-death decision.

A week as a trial juror in a lower Manhattan courtroom, I found, offers a concentrated course in applied fairness. It isn't just a matter of contending with different versions of what may be the truth; it's that you're immediately confronted with an unusual demand on your attention. You are asked to do something quite out of the normal: namely, to sit in the same spot for hour after hour and, without talking yourself, extend the same close, undivided concentration to a long series of stories other people are telling, as well as to their questions, explanations, and allegations. You have to keep your mind from wandering and your energy from flagging, so you can stay focused on accepting the events of each moment, remembering them, awaiting the next moment, and all the while withholding certainty. Delayed gratification is a skill that takes years to learn in childhood, but jurors have to get good at delayed assessment in no time at all.

It's very difficult for jurors, until you get the knack. I know we all struggled with the assignment at first—on the first day, the juror two chairs down from me asked the judge during a short break if it was okay to keep notes. (It was, as long as they remained in the courtroom overnight.) Something has to give, and what happens is that your sense of time opens up in a way that's parallel to the way Deep Travel time starts to unfurl. The entire task at hand—the duty to reach a true verdict, if possible, along with everything that has to be assembled beforehand to make that possible—becomes a temporary, elongated "now." It's interruptible: you can go home at night and not think about the case, but inside the courtroom, as soon as the trial resumes, the past is what happened before the prosecutor began to present the charges, and the future is what will happen after the judge discharges the jury. It's the sense of this "can't end yet" or "still happening" present moment that for the time being lets you listen with equal emphasis to the often wildly contradictory statements and evidence by each of the lawyers and witnesses, one after another; to the laws as summarized by the judge; and, once the case has been handed to you, to the comments your fellow jurors will make in the jury room from their own store of trial-time observations. Then, perhaps, a true verdict emerges, after a journey of sustained alertness that may have taken days and that has no resting place until that instant. It doesn't always work, a search for the truth supported by movable time boundaries, but that's what's attempted every time a jury is empaneled—and enough people get good enough at it most of the time to have established suspended judgment as a cornerstone of our system of justice.

Within an extended "now"—a "now" that endures for a while; a "strict" present that becomes an almost "unrestricted" present moment—time can act as a container for the content collected by Deep Travel, one that keeps getting bigger as you keep adding to it. This elongated sense of "now" puts several abilities at our disposal, most obviously as a kind of tracking device that follows and records all our expanded noticing. It's also a flow regulator that keeps us from being overwhelmed by our perceptions as they arrive. It serves as a gathering point in the mind for sorting and organizing the new information we're taking in, creating a cleared space in the middle of our thinking that can almost make us feel as if we're stepping out into an open meadow. Or maybe this new central place is more like a portable display case or shelf, a temporary stage that can hold and make available everything we're giving our attention to. Or perhaps it's a table top, one that can seamlessly add an additional leaf or two whenever called upon to do so, so that no new impressions are lost. Instead, they can be cradled and then highlighted. Stretching the moment, in other words, is like gaining the automatic assistance of a support team that steadies our thinking, organizes and clarifies discoveries we're making, and acts as an encourager, by keeping enough of our attention free so we can keep on searching. Or, in the language of Ed Reed, it's as if time itself can function as a field of promoted action. No doubt this is one reason why Deep Travel time changes seem so rewarding. There's a sweetness in their swiftness, a deftness and unobtrusiveness that softens the shock of the accelerating arc of travel.

The new "now" that steals over us when Deep Travel kicks in often gets far less attention than the sights and sounds outside us that we're taking in. But the extended "now" can itself be noticed, like a flower that opens unseen at dusk, bringing with it a fresh scent that wasn't present before. Captivating and lingering, this particular fragrance leaves the mind feeling calmer and less pressured. Sometimes it's this quality of inner easiness in the midst of energetic activity that registers on us as a new development. It's as if we've settled into a comfortable seat in a special kind of theater where both the house lights and the stage lights are brightly aglow as the performance begins, leaving no corner in shadow.

As with the extended "now" that jury duty brings forward, there's also a feeling within Deep Travel time of needing to wait for a while, to hold off, to keep everything open and in play until a further caravan of impressions can arrive. It's a form of patience, but it's patience with a purpose, or a patient expectancy, a sense of being engaged in something that remains incomplete, that can't be hurried or ended abruptly or prematurely. In the same way, a building can't be assessed when only the foundations are in place, and an election can't be called until votes from the outlying precincts have been recorded.

Maybe it's easier to think of Deep Travel time as something that can be recognized more easily by listening for its appearance rather than looking around for it—more like hearing a song drifting in through a window, one you've never heard before and that somehow pulls you up short and stops you in your tracks. You just have to keep listening, because you can't yet tell where it's headed or whether its shape will change, and you can't know what it's saying to you until you've heard it through.

In the search for meaning, we're often on the look out for shortcuts, for cues, clues, tips, and pointers, for pages of notes with the important words already underlined. Deep Travel, as it accelerates noticing, puts a lot of new information at our disposal—and then, through the time changes that accompany it and that act as its partner and enabler, it seems to make more time available as well, giving us an extended chance to respond to all the words on each page of information, including those that were too pale even to make out before. This seems parallel to—but not identical with—the interests of the modern Slow Movement, which among its other objectives urges people to take more time eating (by choosing "slow food," the opposite of "fast food"), so as to savor the taste of locally grown food in the company of friends. "Had you realized," asks a Web site called Slow Travel Europe, "that it is not compulsory to take the fast train? Comb the timetables, and you still find the lazy slowcoach of a train that dawdles from one country station to the next." Deep Travel time, though, is not necessarily about taking more time. It's about making more time by elongating any interval, short or substantial. Spinning straw time into golden time. Time within time. At least up to certain limits. "We travel to slow time down," Pico Iyer says in one of his essays, and then, in a practical aside, doesn't so much qualify his thought as he quantifies it, restating it to reflect the possibilities he has himself encountered. We can, he says, "reverse time, to a small extent and make a day last a year—or at least 45 hours."

Deep Travel, we've said, offers what amounts to an unsuspected form of life extension, by allowing us to reclaim and redeem and get the full worth out of trips we might otherwise write off or hurry through with eyes and attention averted. But here's the second half of this secret-that-is-not-a-secret: with time on our side, we can prolong the present moment of the intensified time we have recovered by plunging into Deep Travel. When you wish someone a long life, you are in effect encouraging them to "live longer" whenever possible.

This sense of having started to live longer and then delighting in it famously intermingle in the Deep Travel time sense that overtakes Hans Castorp, the young hero of Thomas Mann's *The Magic Mountain*, high up in the Alps, within the first few days of what he still thinks will be only a short visit to the Swiss sanatorium where his cousin is a patient. Mann presents Castorp as someone who even as he summarizes what's been happening to him is still struggling to find words that can adequately convey the full meaning of what he's already been through. All he knows for sure is that the time speeds and time durations he's been used to all his life—time definitions that now seem as flat to him as the lowlands he has left behind—have melted and intermingled in ways that are still strange to him:

> After a few days, he said to his cousin (while gazing at him with bloodshot eyes), "I've always found it odd, still do, how time seems to go slowly in a strange place at first. What I mean is, of course there's no question of my being bored here, quite the contrary—I can assure you that I'm amusing myself royally. But when I look back, retrospectively as it were—you know what I mean?—it seems as if I've been up here for who knows how long already, and that it's been an eternity since I first arrived. . . . It has absolutely nothing to do with reason or with measurements of time—it's purely a matter of feeling. Of course it would be absurd to say, 'It's as if I've been here two months already'—that would be pure nonsense. All I can really say is 'a very long time.'"

Therefore, to give yourself more time, do more. This was the solution adopted by Jean-Marie Guyau, the vivid nineteenth-century French writer celebrated by Douwe Draaisma, the modern Dutch historian. Guyau's essay "The Genesis of the Idea of Time" has this advice for all who read it:

> If you want to lengthen the perspective of time, then fill it, if you have the chance, with a thousand new things. Go on an exciting journey, rejuvenate yourself by breathing new life into the world around you. When you look back you will notice that the incidents along the way and the distance you have traveled have heaped up in your imagination, all these fragments of the visible world will form up in a long row, and that, as people say so fittingly, presents you with a long *stretch of time.*

Draaisma, who quotes this passage admiringly in *Why Life Speeds Up as You Get Older,* finds it unconsciously autobiographical and as a result hard to forget—Guyau died of tuberculosis at the age of thirty-three. His essay on time wasn't published until two years later. "Exciting journeys," Draaisma points out, "were no longer granted to him during his last few years, at least not in the geographical sense. You might say that he lived a longer life by renewing his inner world at every turn. His swift, almost obsessive voyage through the most divergent branches of philosophy and psychology must have had as mind-stretching an effect as a genuine voyage."

LONGER "NOWS" AND
LARGER "HERES"

Deep Travel time changes—the "Longer Nows" summoned by
Deep Travel—are adjustable and have their own special uses
and applications. They can be a starting point as well as an
accompaniment, and they are almost an independent variable. Because
when you get the taste of them in your mouth, so to speak, you can use
them as a vehicle within Deep Travel, and steer it in any one of several
directions. The Longer Nows can, for instance, slow down an exceptional moment almost indefinitely—to the point where it leaves an
indelible impression that later becomes a vivid and imperishable
memory. Travel books present many examples of these "Suspended
Moments," as I think of them. One that immediately springs to mind
is the closing scene from the book I had with me during my late-night
stop-time hours in the NYU Medical Center emergency room, *A Time
of Gifts,* by the dazzling modern English writer Patrick Leigh Fermor
("Paddy" to his many friends). The passage, which is almost like a suspension within a pause in the middle of an intermission, recalls an
endless late afternoon Leigh Fermor spent halfway across the Mária
Valéria Bridge over the Danube River between Slovakia (then Czechoslovakia) and Hungary. It was the day before Easter Sunday in 1934.
Leigh Fermor was traversing what amounted to unattended territory
in between jurisdictions, since the five-span iron bridge he was walking
on had been constructed in 1895 by an overarching empire that no
longer existed (Mária Valéria was a nineteenth-century Austrian arch-
duchess). He later wrote, "My passport was stamped at the frontier

post at the Czechoslovakian end of the bridge. The red, white and green barrier at the far end marked the beginning of Hungary. I lingered in the middle of the bridge, meditatively poised in no man's air."

It was, in a way, the opposite of the situation that Alexander Kinglake, crossing the Sava River, had faced ninety years earlier. Instead of leaving behind the comfortable bubble of familiar Christian Europe for what was then unfamiliar Muslim territory, as Kinglake had, Leigh Fermor had, as it were, brought a self-carved, potent bubble pipe with him in his backpack, along with the two books we know he carried, the *Oxford Book of English Verse* and the *Odes* of Horace. For Leigh Fermor, it was not the far shore that would feel unknown, it was the "just now" and the ordinary process of getting across that had already become an unknown and explorable region. The two newly independent successor countries at either end of the Mária Valéria Bridge were peaceful neighbors, and both shared the same Catholic religion. But Leigh Fermor had found a narrow crease, a recently placed stitch across what had been a seamless political fabric, and it was here that he took his stand. And despite the unity of belief in the communities on either bank of the Danube, both were in the grip of the most unstructured day in their calendar, Holy Saturday, or Silent Saturday, a brief time of cessation, the hours between Jesus's death and his rising again. Altars are stripped bare or covered in black cloth; at the end of the day all lights are extinguished and no words are spoken, no music played. Leigh Fermor sensed this ebb as he neared the bridge: "There was a lull in the air" that "cast a spell of catalepsy and suspense. . . . There was not a fisherman on the river, nor a peasant in the fields."

One of Leigh Fermor's subjects in *A Time of Gifts* is the ancient Europe that was about to disappear forever, after first being stripped bare and then largely obliterated by the Nazis, and modern readers feel the weight and touch of several pauses he was not yet aware of when he set forth on his travels: the mid-1930s quiet before the still unimagined horror of the Holocaust, and, for Leigh Fermor himself, the extra breath taken at nineteen at the crest of life's first hill, where childhood lies behind and a wider world is about to open up.

The Mária Valéria Bridge itself, although it has recently been restored and reopened, was a ruin by the time Leigh Fermor sat down to write about it—its middle three spans, including the very spot where Leigh Fermor had stood, were blown up by retreating German troops on Christmas Day in 1944. His book, the first in a projected trilogy about his twelve-hundred-mile walk across Europe as a teenager, wasn't published until 1977, forty-three years after the events it chronicles; *Between the Woods and the Water,* the second volume in this account, which begins in Hungary, on the far side of the Danube, didn't appear in print for another nine years. The concluding volume has yet to be completed, although in 2007, at the age of ninety-two, he stopped writing in longhand and taught himself to type in order to speed the process along. The delay in getting the project done has been entirely unintentional, but the balancings and juxtapositions and puttings-off within the text are wholly deliberate, Leigh Fermor's way of indicating his extra message to his readers, I would say: that even the most seemingly insignificant of moments can be revealed in all its dimensions and fully drawn out and reveled in simply by our marveling in it sufficiently.

It's a celebration that fends off both the future and the past, and, given permission, the Suspended Moment spreads out to cover almost as much ground as the great Danube itself, which at the point where it is spanned by the Mária Valéria Bridge is almost a third of a mile wide. Now that I have steeped myself in them, I think I also understand one of the reasons Leigh Fermor's books take so long to write. They're the only travel books I know of by someone with so much devotion to the places he visits and with such a burning desire to do justice to them and see them shine forth. Although he doesn't have a name for it, I think he closes in on this goal by cultivating and clothing himself in Deep Travel—to the extent that he no longer takes a step without its assistance, and after reaching home again can't record his findings until he has reinvoked it and retuned himself to the moment he's writing about. Which makes his eight books, at least for those who want to consult them as such, something like installments of a still growing encyclopedia of Deep Travel knowledge. They remind us what it is like to swim in wonder, day after day. (Leigh Fermor himself, at one point in *A Time of Gifts,* refers to "those protracted moments of rapture which scatter this journey like asterisks.") His books can also be turned to as users' guides to the many varieties of Longer Nows that Deep Travel time releases to us.

Although long revered in England, many of Leigh Fermor's books have been in and out of print in the United States. Some of his most fervent American admirers are poets who have tried to capture the effects his writing has had on them. "A friend of mine," says one of them, David Mason (in his essay "The Greatest Living Writer"), "who read one of his books, 'Mani,' in Greek translation, reacted to its descriptions of her native region (the middle finger of the southern Peloponnese) by calling them *phantasia,* her face alight as she pronounced the word. She meant 'fantasy' as we know it, but also its root sense, a 'making visible,' as if the author were a sorcerer." "And then there's his prose," writes Ben Downing, managing editor of *Parnassus: Poetry in Review,* in a long appreciation; Downing considers *A Time of Gifts* and *Between the Woods and the Water* "the finest travel books in the language" and "uniquely beautiful and satisfying." "Unmistakable, without obvious antecedents, and fairly leaping off the page, the style of Patrick Leigh Fermor is a thing to make us mere hacks despair," Downing says. "His prose moves to a cantering rhythm all its own," creating "a cumulative magnificence, building up in golden passage after golden passage," and "as he advances into deepening enchantment, so goes the reader headlong with him." "For me," Downing concludes, "he captures uniquely the excitement, meaning, and value of travel; one learns how to travel better by reading him."

On the subject of style, here, for instance, from *Mani,* is a single sentence taken from Leigh Fermor's description of the air in Greece:

The air in Greece is not merely a negative void between solids; the sea itself, the houses and rocks and trees, on which it presses like a jelly mould, are embedded in it; it is alive and positive and volatile and one is as aware of its contact as if it could have pierced hearts scrawled on it with diamond rings or be grasped in handfuls, tapped for electricity, bottled, used for blasting, set fire to, sliced into sparkling cubes and rhomboids with a pair of shears, be timed with a stop watch, strung with pearls, plucked like a lute string or tolled like a bell, swum in, be set with rungs and climbed like a rope ladder or have saints assumed through it in flaming chariots; as though it could be harangued into faction, or eavesdropped, pounded down with pestle and mortar for cocaine, drunk from a ballet shoe, or spun, woven and worn on solemn feasts; or cut into discs for lenses, minted for currency or blown, with infinite care, into globes.

The one problem with seeing Patrick Leigh Fermor clearly is that magical episodes in his life rival the magic called forth by his words. He is, for instance, a decorated war hero. In 1942, when he was twenty-seven—this was eight years after his walk across prewar Europe—Leigh Fermor, by then a major in the British Army's Special Operations Executive, was parachuted into Crete, where, disguised as a shepherd, he spent the next two years living in caves in snow-capped mountains with a small band of English commandos, all of whom had been sent from London to organize resistance to the German occupation. In 1944, he led a party that kidnapped the German commandant Major General Karl Heinrich Kreipe and, after three weeks of mountaintop marches, successfully smuggled him off the island. Several days after capturing the general, according to "Abducting a General," the report on the Kreipe Operation that Leigh Fermor later prepared for the Imperial War Museum, in London,

> We woke up among the rocks, just as a brilliant dawn was breaking over the crest of Mount Ida which we had been struggling across for two days. We were all three lying smoking in silence, when the General, half to himself, slowly said:
>
> > "*Vides ut alta stet nive candidum*
> > *Soracte . . .*"
>
> > ["You see Mount Soracte standing white and deep
> > with snow . . ."]
>
> I was in luck. It is the opening line of one of the few odes of Horace I know by heart (*Ad Thaliarchum*, I. IX). I went on reciting where he had broken off:
>
> > " *. . . Nec iam sustineant onus*
> > *Silvae laborantes, geluque*
> > *Flumina constiterint acuto*"
>
> > [" . . . the woods in trouble, hardly able
> > to carry their burden, and the rivers
> > halted by sharp ice."]

and so on, through the remaining five stanzas to the end.

The General's blue eyes swivelled away from the mountain-top to mine—and when I'd finished, after a long silence, he said: "Ach so, Herr Major!" It was very strange. "Ja, Herr General." As though, for a long moment, the war had ceased to exist. We had both drunk at the same fountains long before; and things were different between us for the rest of our time together.

But I find myself drawn back to Leigh Fermor's earlier Suspended Moment, the one he encountered, or conjured for himself, halfway between Czechoslovakia and Hungary in 1934, and then, many years after the war, chronicled in A *Time of Gifts*. Standing in the center of the Mária Valéria Bridge, he finds he has been transfixed by the scene: "There was much going on: in the air and the sky, on the river, along the banks; almost too much. I was determined to linger, suspended there in a void, and let a few more hundred thousand tons of liquid rush under the girders before stepping across the remaining yards into Hungary." Ahead of him, in Hungary, he sees a crowd of villagers and an honor guard of grandees, still off duty, but already brilliantly garbed in dress uniforms with caps made of bear fur and heron feathers, milling about the base of a steep, green hill crowned by a cathedral, the Esztergom Basilica, the largest church in the country, where Easter services will begin in a few hours. But his attention is caught by the sky: "A number of large and mysterious birds were floating high overhead. . . . There were about a dozen, snow-plumed except for black flight-feathers which ran along the inner edge of their wing like a senatorial stripe of mourning. They were storks! When they circled lower, the long beaks and the legs that trailed in the slipstream showed red as sealing wax. An old shepherd was leaning on the ramp close by and gazing up at them too. When some of the great birds floated lower, the draft of their feathers brushed our upturned faces."
But that wasn't the end of it:

Touching my arm, the shepherd pointed downstream at something in the dark-shadowed east high above the river and just discernible across the failing sky. Ragged and flocculent, fading to grey, scattered with specks of pink from the declining sun, varying in width as random fragments were dropping away and re-cohering and agitated with motion as though its whole length were turning on a single thread, a thick white line of crowding storks stretched from one side of the heavens to the other. Mounting Africa along the Nile, they had followed the coasts of Palestine and Asia Minor and entered Europe over the Bosphorus.

Then, persevering along the Black Sea shore to the delta of the Danube, they had steered their flight along that shining highway until they had come to the great bend a few miles downstream. Defecting from the river, their journey was now following a westerly as well as a northern bias; they were bound for Poland, perhaps, and shedding contingents as they went at hundreds of remembered haunts. We gazed at them in wonder. It was a long time before the rearguard of that great sky-procession had vanished north. Before nightfall the whole armada would subside in a wood or settle all over some Slovakian hamlet—astonishing the villagers and delighting them, for storks are birds of good omen—like a giant snow storm; taking to the air again at first light. . . .

A jade-green radiance had not yet abandoned the sky. The air itself, the branches, the flag-leaves, the willow-herb and the rushes were held for a space, before the unifying shadows should dissolve them, in a vernal and marvelous light like the bloom on a greengage. Low on the flood and almost immaterialized by this luminous moment, a heron sculled upstream, detectable mainly by sound and by the darker and slowly dissolving rings that the tips of its flight-feathers left on the water.

"I found it impossible to tear myself from my station and plunge into Hungary," Leigh Fermor says, summarizing the vista being presented to him. "I feel the same disability now: a momentary reluctance to lay hands on this particular fragment of the future; not out of fear but because, within arm's reach and still intact, this future seemed, and still seems, so full of promised marvels. The river below, meanwhile, was carrying the immediate past downstream and I was hung poised in mid-air between the two."

In a recent essay, E. O. Wilson—who is himself a time pioneer, among his many other accomplishments—writes that human beings have at best "a feeble sense of time" and that we are biologically constrained by the "architectural requirements of thought," which keep us "trapped in a small box of time," one bounded by seconds and decades. We are smart enough, he says, to have learned that we live within an uninterrupted immensity of other time scales but, along with "all animals," we have a built-in time numbness that prevents us from sensing our place along this continuum. Our brains are both too slow and too fast-acting—this is his lament—for us to feel any true kinship with the rhythms of the rest of the "spectrum of conceivable time." At

best, we can only half-know some aspects of time. Through instruments and deduction and experiment, we can *know about* any number of
time's circumstances and dimensions, but we can never *know* them or
fully inhabit them. The human mind, our "quart-sized brain," is unable
to make direct contact with the microtime "quantum-level events of
physics and chemistry" that vanish so rapidly that endless chains and
sequences of them are crowded into the blink of an eye.

Equally, Wilson thinks, we are divorced from sensing our participation in the many long series of macrotime sequences that often require
far more than any single human lifetime for their full unfolding.
Among these, he numbers "ecological time," as he calls it, which "passes
too slowly to be comprehended by direct observation," because you
might have to stand in the same spot from youth to graduate school to
see "organisms come and go across flurries of generations" and "a forest emerging from an abandoned field," as other nearby habitats rise
and fall. Beyond this stands the still longer "evolutionary time" scale,
measured in hundreds and thousands of years, during which "even the
rotation of local ecosystems is an indecipherable blur" and "only the
genes of entire populations (such as red maples, house finches, and
human beings) persist . . . unbroken." Finally, at still another time level,
we can see the outline of even more slow-moving processes than these,
such as "the geological history [still] transforming the planet" or, at the
largest scale of all, the quasi-eternal events that mark "the potentially
infinite duration of the universe."

For all his optimism about the founding of a "science of time" within
the foreseeable future, and about the accelerating approach of a period
when people will awaken to a greater appreciation of their own capabilities, Edward Hall shared Wilson's sense of our inherent limitations
when it comes to grappling with the extremes of time: "The human
sensorium," he says in *The Dance of Life,* "is only able to respond percep-
tually to a small fraction of the visual part of . . . [the electromagnetic]
spectrum. The same applies to time. Mankind's capacity to experience
time frequencies is limited to a tiny fraction of the total our instruments will tell us are present in the universe. Clearly the human
species' time on earth is so short as to make it difficult to imagine when
compared to the total."

I'd be inclined to agree with this learned, logical conclusion, or
would have been, if I'd never run across the books of Patrick Leigh Fermor and been immersed in the time spells they cast. Since then, I've

been alerted to a whole series of ingenious leaps that people have devised over the years that can carry them across time boundaries. It's largely a matter of affiliating ourselves—or maybe it's just aligning ourselves—with "Other Presents" that we discover we can reach out to. Some of these methods are homegrown and spring up again and again in individuals, and as a result are constantly reinvented without being consciously passed along. Some "time alignments" are more successful than others, or have a longer reach, but enough of them exist to make me suspect that we have a built-in urge to span time boundaries and transcend time isolation whenever such opportunities present themselves. This may mean that, with only a quart-sized brain, we have to make do with half-pint solutions, many of them rough and approximate. But it's a beginning. E. O. Wilson some years ago coined the word "biophilia" to express the innate affinity people develop for other forms of life. Perhaps there's also a parallel sense of "chronophilia" at work in us, an urge to link what we know to what we could be learning from taking a longer view.

This emerges spontaneously in children who, particularly if their own circumstances seem constricted, can come to think of a towering tree nearby as almost an older brother or sister, a being whose "present moment" extends back into circumstances that may have been less threatening or confining. "The trees in the streets are old trees, used to living with people," Stephen Vincent Benét wrote in *John Brown's Body*, about this reaching out to an "Other Present." "Family trees that remember your grandfather's name." The most famous example of a tree that might remember more than any person could is the Anne Frankboom, as the Dutch call it—the Anne Frank tree, the old horse chestnut tree behind the Secret Annex, the empty offices in Amsterdam where Anne Frank and her family hid from the Nazis during World War II. The top of the tree, which was then already about ninety years old, could be seen through the one attic window that, because it faced the sky, had not been blacked out to prevent neighbors from looking in. In a famous passage from her diary, Anne describes a morning "visit" to the tree in early 1944 with Peter van Pels, the son of her father's partner, whose family had joined the Franks in hiding:

> This morning (Thursday) when I went to the attic again, Peter was busy clearing up. He was finished very quickly and when I sat down on my favorite spot on the floor, he joined me. Both of us looked at the glo-

rious blue of the sky, the bare chestnut tree on whose branches little raindrops shone, at the seagulls and other birds that looked like silver in the sun and all these things moved and thrilled the two of us so much that we could not speak.

"I believe," she added, "that nature sets all fear at rest for every trouble, even when there are bombs or gunfire."

"How could I have suspected that it meant so much to Anne?" her father asked years later. In 2007, when it was over 150 years old, the tree, partly infected by fungus, was almost cut down. But after international protests, an Amsterdam judge ruled that it was still healthy enough to stand for another ten years or more. It has since been encased in a steel frame, at a cost of $70,000. "Anne's tree" has taken on a new kind of timekeeping role. In the minds of many people around the world, young and old alike, it has become a kind of "surviving sibling." "That tree is not just a tree," says Helga Fassbinder, a woman who can see it from her own apartment and is the founder of a committee to save the tree. "It is one of the last living witnesses to Anne Frank and all that took place here."

The trick of it—what people are reaching for—is establishing or making contact with a continuum across time. In the same way that a tree can bring an earlier time period forward, preserving its "present"-ness for a generation or two, families and communities can hand on eyewitness accounts about notable events that have just slipped beyond living memory—such as, at this point, the day Arizona joined the Union, becoming the last of the forty-eight original, "contiguous" states, on Valentine's Day in 1912. Practically no one who remembers that occasion is still around, but plenty of Arizonans, some of them still quite young, can remember hearing firsthand about what happened that day from those who were there. A number of older Arizonans, on the other hand, can still recall the oversized and quirky personality of the state's first governor, George W. P. Hunt, a bald and walrus-mustached populist who served seven terms, earning the nickname George VII, and lived until 1934. "As a child," according to a 1990s reminiscence of Governor Hunt by Lester Ward "Budge" Ruffner, a Prescott, Arizona, writer, "I remember him when he was a guest in my home, and I sat fascinated as he scooped peas from a plate and placed them in his mouth with his dinner knife. An art I have always admired but never achieved."

My own family started calling this traditional practice of sustaining vivid moments "the great span" shortly after my father and mother, while still in their twenties, met the "Great Dissenter," Supreme Court Justice Oliver Wendell Holmes Jr., then an old man, who had never forgotten that his grandmother had told him that, as a small girl, she had looked out her living room window one morning to see British troops marching up Beacon Hill, in Boston, at the beginning of the American Revolution.

I've been hesitant to say it, because it sounds so incendiary at first, offering a promise that can never be kept, but linking present moments together does constitute a form of time travel. Maybe the only legitimate and substantiated one. Certainly a usable, practical, feet-on-the-ground, anchored-to-the-everyday kind of time travel, since you stay exactly where you are and let other moments rush to join you, the way sparks can leap a gap between two wildfires to make a single wall of flame, or—more coolly—the way beads of mercury brought next to each other can then become a single pool of shining liquid. It is solely based on finding, to the extent possible, a commonality with the elements of a once-present moment that still overlap and resonate with our here and now, rather than on imagining "what it must have been like."

When it comes to connecting with the "intermediate past," as it might be called, meaning either the past century or so or the last three or four human generations, this search doesn't always need to rely on finding a natural "landline" of transmission, like an ancient tree, or even on the presence of a "telephone tree" or "bucket line," an unbroken series of beholders and their testimony. Very unlikely things can happen. I'm thinking, in particular, of an ahead-of-its-time invention devised for a never-achieved purpose that now, many years later, has the power to conjoin our own time to an era assumed to have vanished forever, almost without a trace. Have you ever heard of the Russian photographer Sergei Mikhailovich Prokudin-Gorskii? I never had, until a friend sent me a link to a Library of Congress Web site set up to commemorate a 2001 exhibition of his work (www.loc.gov/exhibits/empire/). Prokudin-Gorskii died in 1944, in exile, at the age of eighty-one. For five years, between 1909 and 1915, he led a kind of fairy-tale life—he was Marco Polo in a Pullman car, traveling around the vast Russian Empire, second in size only to Kublai Khan's thirteenth-century Mongol Empire, as a special representative of the czar. He had been handed two "open sesame" documents allowing him access to any place he cared to see and ordering any official he met to offer him assistance, and he moved about, at government expense, in a private railroad car with its own darkroom. His mission was to record " 'things of interest and significance' in what he called 'natural color,' " as *Photographs for the Tsar,* one of the few books about his work, states.

Color: this is what had brought him to the attention of Nicholas II, last czar of the empire. Prokudin-Gorskii's great invention was an ingenious early system of color photography that created bright emeralds and rubies from dim minerals—or color images from black-and-white photographs taken through different colored filters. This breakthrough was perfected almost four decades before Kodacolor film came to market, but—this was its flaw—it produced slides that were so difficult to project (since three images of the same scene exposed one right after the other on a glass plate had to be precisely superimposed) that no one else ever took up the technique. Nevertheless, it worked well enough in his hands for him to roam northern Russia, the Caucasus Mountains, and the old khanates of central Asia and bring back thirty-five hundred pictures to St. Petersburg and the czar: onion-dome churches; children on a hillside; camels in the snow; a nomad woman in front of her yurt; a stork's nest on a palace in Bukhara; a switch operator on the Trans-Siberian Railway; a melon vendor in Samarkand; the tomb of Tamerlane (Timur the Lame). And on, and on.

Prokudin-Gorskii slipped out of Russia in 1918 with two thousand of his glass plates. After his death in France a quarter of a century later, nineteen hundred were brought to the Library of Congress, where they sat for many years until, in 2000, the librarians began digitizing them in preparation for the 2001 exhibition. The effect these rescued images have on people today is uncanny. They display a world that seems further away than the almost-gone Europe Leigh Fermor sampled twenty years later—everything in Prokudin-Gorskii's photographs is "pre-" something: pre–First World War; pre–Russian Revolution; pre–Russification (the wholesale resettling of ethnic Russians into the lands he'd seen east of the Caucasus); premodernization and pre–massive industrialization and pre-smog. Yet all the scenes look immediate, contemporary, "next-door." How is this possible? Part of it is, simply, the color—the unlikeliness of it as well as its crispness and purity. "I discovered the online exhibit in mid-May" of 2001, an American architecture student named Addison Godel wrote on his own Web site later that month, "and was, frankly, overwhelmed; not to knock the fine art of black and white photography, but I'd always felt that the past was somehow obscured by being viewed solely through a grayscale window. To see places, buildings, and especially *people* in color was to understand, on a very deep level, that they had at one time really, truly existed—that the 'Typical Russian Peasant of Figure 32' was not merely some gaunt presence in the side of a textbook, but a genuine person who, if not for temporal chance, could have been my neighbor or my friend. It was touching."

My own sense, when I look at Prokudin-Gorskii's pictures, is that viewers are also responding to something else he's added to the mix, an aspect of these images that's every bit as special—and as unexpected—as the brilliant color. There's an imposed stillness here that compels a second look. The most awkward "drawback," as Prokudin-Gorskii would have thought of it, of the way he had to work turns out to be, from a time-mingling point of view, an essential element in an alchemy that lets his time, so strange, so remote, seem so remarkably similar to our own—though this was clearly never his intention. It's a matter of the ponderous way in which each "multiple photograph" had to be exposed. As *Photographs for the Tsar,* by Robert H. Allshouse, a Russian scholar, explains: "Using a small folding hand camera...he photographed three exposures of the same subject, made at about one-second intervals on a glass plate... mounted vertically in the camera. The plate dropped to a new position after each exposure.... Because of the need to take the same picture three times, Prokudin-Gorskii was limited to subjects that would make no movement. Thus, much of what he recorded consisted of fixed objects."

Fixed in time, that is, as well as in space. It wasn't so difficult for a railroad bridge or a monastery to remain still for Prokudin-Gorskii, but it was considerably harder for the people who posed for him. How long did it take Prokudin-Gorskii to capture each set of images? There are conflicting accounts. Three seconds by his own reckoning, though on reflection he later thought it had been more like six when he came to take Leo Tolstoy's photo in 1908 (the only known color photo of Tolstoy). From the way the moon inches downward over a small Russian town over the course of a set of three pictures taken in 1909, a recent digital reconstruction of the images has determined that maybe as much as a full minute might sometimes go by before Prokudin-Gorskii had finished and was ready to fold up his camera. That's one slow taking in and letting go of a breath, at least, and perhaps as many as ten or twenty.

The people in the portraits he brought to the czar all had to adjust to this situation when the camera turned their way, and looking at these pictures today, we can watch them making the effort. It's a subtle effect, one that at first may go undetected. We see it in the solemn faces of three peasant girls standing in front of a log cabin with bowls of berries, their traditional offering to visitors, and in the weary frown of the all-powerful emir of Bokhara, seated in front of his palace in an iridescent blue silk robe embroidered with purple-flowering tulips (the colors *are* extraordinary, gaudily so—his gown is encircled by a wide gold belt and he's clasping a gold sword). To accommodate the photographer, they had to focus on immobility, on quiet relaxation and stilled thoughts just long enough so that almost all of them have responded by stepping out of the "strict present" and into a suspended moment. Seeing them do something we do ourselves in our own day and time is what touches me more than anything else, short-circuiting the distance between us and them and helping me realize that in some ways it's only "temporal chance" that separates us from them.

When it comes to associating ourselves with far longer Nows—or should we call these even more extensive lengths of time "Deep Nows"?—Leigh Fermor and an American writer, John Hanson Mitchell, seem to have independently found the same method of approach. The only difference is that Mitchell has actually given it a name, "Ceremonial Time," and has modestly disclaimed authorship, saying that he was tutored in the art by two Native American friends, Tonupasqua and Nompenekit. In the early 1980s, Mitchell had taken on himself the task of studying the complete post–ice age history of his Massachusetts town, Littleton, a farming area almost thirty miles northwest of Boston that is only now rapidly suburbanizing. He could trace the three hundred years—and almost a dozen generations—of European-American settlement easily enough, learning along the way, to his pleasure, that the square mile around his own house had in the nineteenth century been called, less grandly, Scratch Flat.

But tracing things further back, he encountered a profound discontinuity. The original Native American inhabitants of the area, who'd hunted, roamed through, and then settled in the area over the course of more than four hundred generations, had been displaced by the white newcomers very early on, and had withdrawn to Canada. In the book that Mitchell subsequently wrote about his findings, *Ceremonial Time: Fifteen Thousand Years on One Square Mile,* he describes how he filled in the gap after meeting two Pawtucket Indians, members of the tribe that had left Scratch Flat in the late seventeenth century. His new friends not only had much of the information he needed, they refused to let him feel sorry for their "plight," explaining that, to their way of thinking, as long as the land retains the features it had when the first of their forebears arrived, perhaps hundreds of generations earlier, nothing has changed for them. Their tenancy has not been dislodged, and their understanding of what they have always known remains intact, unbroken.

This is Mitchell's introduction to Ceremonial Time, which, in its Pawtucket incarnation, at least, might just as easily be called Holocene Time. That geological name refers to the postglacial epoch that creates the physical context for all of modern life, the era in which the shapes of the hills we can see are the same shapes that emerged when the most recent glaciers receded north and plants and animals and people took their place. During one evening meeting in the book, Nompenekit, speaking with some exasperation, has to spell it all out for a still doubtful Mitchell:

"You know you're always so worried about the past," he said. "What does that matter, you know? What is it anyway? We don't believe that our people have ever gone away. We're right here now, you know what I mean?"

"No," I said, "I don't know what you mean," although I had an idea then of what he was going to say.

"The Indian people, we're all this, you see," he answered, and at this point he lifted his head sharply, indicating the marshes and the dark line of the pines on the hillside beyond. "We're made of this, the marshes here, the trees. No different, see what I mean? You don't understand this because you look on this world as something that is not you. But Indian people believe that we are no different than a squirrel or bear, just a different form. We're all the same, squirrel, bear, me. Okay?"

It is a Deep Now based on persistences. The continuing presence of things around us becomes a kind of present moment, a durability, a steadfastness, a perseverance whose resilience and still continuing lifetime we can attach ourselves to. For Mitchell, even after he gets the hang of it, this kind of time expansion is only flickeringly available at first. Visiting what might once have been an ancient Native American burial ground, he gets "a sense, suddenly, not of the past, not a rollback of time, but of the reality of those late Woodland Indians" from perhaps a thousand or more years ago. "I felt all at once a sudden sense of sharing with these obscure Indians. They were very like us." Eventually, Ceremonial Time becomes a more pervasive reality for him—a Deep Now through which "past, present and future can all be perceived in a single moment."

At the very end of the book, he uses Ceremonial Time to look as far ahead as possible and finds himself at the Holocene's eventual end. Walking home one night, he says, "It seemed to me that all was interlude, the two-thousand-year reign of the Paleo-Indians, the long span of the Archaic peoples, the period of the Woodland Indians, and the brief flash of Western civilization. I was thinking that there will come a day on Scratch Flat when people will remember that somehow the winters were [once] much warmer and the summers were longer and hotter. . . . Finally there will be nothing but winter. Life on Scratch Flat will become intolerable" and people "will migrate south, following the general drift of other tribes and nations." Then "the great ice pack will begin to move south and the place that was Scratch Flat will disappear for another sixty thousand years."

Patrick Leigh Fermor, half a century earlier than Mitchell, when he was inching his way across central Europe in 1934 by following the Danube east on foot, and started meeting up with so many intermingling people and languages and histories—being befriended first by Austrians, then Slovaks, and then Hungarians—came to the realization that this "jigsaw puzzle" of a region, as he called it, could become coherent in his head only if he almost redoubled his receptiveness and threw open even more widely the doors of his mind. He devised and deployed in consequence a combination of the close noticing that Deep Travel had made possible since the evening he'd left London and his own kind of Ceremonial Time: a "long view" in which the almost infinitesimal pace of geological changes to the continent of Europe becomes the constant he can anchor himself to, a Deep Now container or a force field from within which he can watch the relatively rapid scurryings of migrating groups of people—Germanic, Slavic, Magyar (or Hungarian)—that occupy perhaps hundred- or thousand-year units of time. He alternates between these states of mind, these lenses of discovery.

Entering Slovakia, he records, as a close noticer, that "all at once I was surrounded by fresh clues—the moulding on a window, the cut of a beard, overheard syllables, an unfamiliar shape of a horse or a hat, a shift of accent, the taste of a new drink, the occasional unfamiliar lettering." But earlier, while still in northern Austria, he'd "climbed to the ruins of Aggstein," a castle one thousand feet above the Danube where robber barons once dominated the gorgeous Wachau Valley below—it's now a prosperous wine-growing area and a UNESCO World Heritage Site—to set up the internal telescope that was now the complement to his mental microscope. "A falcon," he says, "beating its wings above an unwary heron half-way up this northern bend, would command the same view of the river as mine," and from this perch, once he'd caught his breath after a steep scramble up an almost vertical cliff, he could begin his broader survey and chronicle of the historic wanderings of the prehistoric dispersals that had eventually peopled the center of Europe:

> How vaguely and slowly nations float about! Lonely as clouds, overlap-
> ping and changing places, they waltz and reverse round each other at a
> pace so slow as to be almost stationary or work their expanding way
> across the map as imperceptibly as damp or mildew. What a relief it is
> when some outside event, with an actual date attached to it, jerks the
> whole sluggishly creeping osmotic complex into action!

The same mood and deep-focused vision overtakes him again a few weeks later, when he reaches Bratislava, the chief town of Slovakia (then a provincial backwater, recently severed from its long ties to Vienna; now a national capital). This time he doesn't need the spur of an astonishing vista down the length of the Wachau Valley to gain an even more Olympian perspective on long-ago events. Prowling through the streets of Bratislava, he starts to see the once-upon-a-time movements and migrations of the proto-Europeans into and through the region as something beyond even their conscious control, and more like actions taken under the command of forces emanating from the continent itself—which has shed the role of a backdrop to become the prime actor and shaper of events:

> The shift of mountains and plains and rivers and the evidence of enormous movements of races gave me the feeling of traveling across a relief map where the initiative lay wholly with the mineral world. It evicted with drought and ice, beckoned with water and grazing, decoyed with mirages and tilted and shifted populations . . . steering languages, breaking them up into tribes and dialects, assembling and confronting kingdoms, grouping civilizations, channeling beliefs, guiding armies and blocking the way to philosophies and styles of art and finally giving them a relenting shove through the steeper passes.

Maybe an ability to join Deep Nows around us that are already in progress is something that can grow only in stages, and our "feeble sense of time," as E. O. Wilson calls it, is a faculty in training and still undergoing reconstruction and expansion. After all, the whole idea of "Deep Time," meaning the idea put forward by geologists that the earth itself, if closely examined, can tell us how old it is, is a relatively recent phenomenon. (The name "Deep Time" is even more recent, and was contributed by John McPhee in the 1980s.) Until almost two centuries ago, the Bible—throughout Christian realms, at any rate—remained the accepted chronological authority for calculating natural as well as human history, and well into the twentieth century, as Dan Falk points out in *In Search of Time,* Bibles continued to be printed showing the so-called Young Earth date for the creation of the world that had been arrived at, after careful textual study, by James Ussher, a seventeenth-century Anglican archbishop in Ireland. Ussher, a noted scholar, counted the Bible's "begats" backward, added them up, and, after comparing them to other ancient sources, determined that the "deduced first origins of the world" dated back to precisely 6 p.m. on Saturday, October 22, 4004 B.C.

In contrast, James Hutton, the eighteenth-century Scottish geologist now considered the "father of time," who consulted the rocks he found while roaming through the Scottish Highlands (Hutton was a great walker) and then read the landscape itself backward, as has been said, realized that, judging from their chemistry, the granite boulders he was hiking past had once been molten—and that it must have required enormous quantities of time for such substances to have been extruded from deep in the earth as liquid rock, before cooling and hardening and then weathering at the surface. "The result, therefore, of our present enquiry," Hutton later wrote, in his landmark book, *The Theory of the Earth*, "is that we find no vestige of a beginning and no prospect of an end." It was a difficult concept to grasp, at first—one of Hutton's younger friends, John Playfair, who after Hutton's death became his champion and popularizer, confessed that when off on an expedition with Hutton and looking at the rock formations, whose origins Hutton would start to explain to him, "the mind seemed to grow giddy by looking so far into the abyss of time."

You can't enter a room that you don't think exists. It's now scientific orthodoxy that the earth is something like four and a half billion years old (plus or minus forty-five million years). The Deep Nows reported by Mitchell and Leigh Fermor stretch back only a fraction of this distance, of course—but they leave Archbishop Ussher's boundary wall of time far behind. They're a "here" as well as a "now." They're based on joining a continuum and caravan and on carving out a larger identity, and they're not just formed by a solitary "digging within." They're a kind of collective or collaborative present moment, a shared sense of time, a sense of "we"-ness that embraces and enfolds the others of us who have gone before and will come after and who have met and will meet up with similar circumstances. "We have been here," Tonupasqua, one of Mitchell's Pawtucket friends, a medicine woman, tells him. "And then," he related, "she would drop her words and roll her right hand over and over in a circular pattern, extending her arm outward as she did so. The gesture was time." In Leigh Fermor's case, surveying the Wachau from the crag of Aggstein, it is more of an extended-family feeling. His new friends—German, Slav, and Hungarian—are the ones who "have been here," they and so many rolling generations of their families.

The "here" that binds these different groups together is a "timed here," so to speak. The Scratch Flat people have been responding to the hills revealed by the glaciers; the central Europeans have all threaded their own way through the Carpathians and other mountain chains, either by their own choice or, possibly, as directed by the mountains themselves. Both of these Deep Nows, as we've said, are distinctly

Holocene moments, successions of human events taking place within a contiguous set of physical parameters that are, let's say, "permanent for the time being," at any rate. But how flexible are the diameters of these "heres"? Can they still gather our thoughts into a whole if they express "movable continuities," as we well might call them? Meaning features of the planet that predate the Holocene but relocate themselves periodically in space, and may appear on more than one continent at a time.

For instance, when I was writing an earlier book, *The Experience of Place,* some years ago, I ran across a grass expert, John H. Falk, an ecologist, who had become fascinated by the fact that Americans had planted so many front lawns and back lawns that if you put them all together they would cover as much ground as the state of Indiana. That led him to undertake landscape-preference studies around the world, showing people photographs of every kind of setting, from rain forests to deserts, and writing down their reactions. After a while it became plain that, in addition to liking the places they'd grown up in, people shared what he called "a deep, innate preference for a grass landscape"—even those who'd never personally grown up in, or even visited, a grassland setting.

Falk was one of the first of a generation of evolutionary psychologists and biologists who have thought this preference can be traced all the way back through human history and represents a genetically transmitted liking for a setting that was a cradle of the species: the tropical, tree-dotted, open savannas of East Africa, where many human traits evolved and which later became the setting-off point for all of humanity's subsequent travels. "So much of what defines humanness relates to that savanna," Falk said at the time. He also thought this kind of retained liking was commonplace in the animal kingdom: "Every vertebrate has a genetically transmitted habitat preference. Knowing what constitutes home has good survival value, so it's hard-wired—that means the animal doesn't have to think about it." People today may not need this understanding in order to keep going from day to day, but it stays with us even now, both "as a guide to behavior," as Falk puts it, and as a kind of dashboard fuel gauge of the kinds of environmental stimulation we instinctively seek out to be at our best. "Full" in this case means full of complexity and pattern; frequent alternation of light and shade; the ability to see some considerable distance without obstruction, if not clear to the horizon.

Also implicit in Falk's way of thinking is an ever-present potential shared by small backyards, medium-sized city parks, and wide-open prairies to evoke a Very Deep Now, a "greatest span," and a homecoming of sorts. A "We have been here" feeling still latent in all of us over the last two hundred thousand generations or so, ever since modern human beings who had most of our own capabilities began to leave Africa about fifty thousand years ago and, during the course of the next forty thousand years, peopled the globe. As if we who are here today, the ripples still spreading outward from the center of the pond, have kept our direct connection with that initial eruption. Maybe this is too much of a stretch. My own Deep Now contacts have been contained within the standard Ceremonial Time range. A few years ago, while researching H2O: *Highlands to Ocean,* the book I wrote about the surviving strength of the original landscape of the New York metropolitan area—a still vibrant force despite four hundred years of development, though now largely hidden and therefore often unsuspected—I spent an afternoon in the Dismal Swamp, in Edison, New Jersey, a big, busy suburban town with a hundred thousand inhabitants only about six miles west of New York City.

The "Diz," as it's known locally, is a large wooded wetland that has never been built on. You can still find beavers and muskrats at the Diz, along with clear, pure springs filled with watercress, bog turtles, box turtles, snapping turtles, 165 kinds of birds, and a wealth of frogs, including green frogs and spring peepers. On a spring evening, the peepers are almost deafening, and when an ambulance drives by at night it helps you locate the resident coyote packs, because a siren sets them to howling.

But what pervades the place is an overwhelming sense of *still the same.* Native Americans set up winter camps here almost twelve thousand years ago, shortly after the glaciers left, and, alone in these woods late in the afternoon and hearing a growing chorus of frogs, and nothing else except a sigh of wind in the trees, I kept thinking, Well, the sounds haven't changed. Stooping for a quick drink from a bubbling spring, the water cool and sweet in my hand, I thought, It tastes exactly as it did when the spring first bubbled forth. I can't say I had John Hanson Mitchell's feeling that I was in the presence of Indians from back then;

it was more like an edge-of-sight sense that the Diz, too, was listening for their footsteps. So they might've just left; or maybe they were still in the neighborhood—after all, their appearances had always been only seasonal. What was clear was that they would be welcome at any time, and were even, perhaps, expected. The point of H2O, the book I was writing, was that the New York area still has so much of its natural heritage that the 16 million people who live there can all lay claim to having two addresses, a street address and a place within the larger landscape. But I could just as easily have been presenting the area's timescapes, and writing about how New Yorkers and New Jerseyans still have access on a daily basis to a regional Deep Now all their own, as well as to the more familiar time variants that arise in every place, hour after hour.

Still, Falk's landscape work raises some questions that have yet to be answered. If a sense of "being at home" is an essential thread that must run through every part of any Deep Now experience, how much "home" do we need to get started? How many familiar sights and sounds have to be within reach for us to say not necessarily that we "were here," but that we "could have been here"? That there was enough "at-home"-ness around us so that we could have staked in the ground one of the tent pegs that support the airy pavilion of a Deep Now and give it structure? What are the outer limits of these encounters, and what is the "Deepest Now" we might attain and settle into and consider a comfortable fit once we got used to it—a frontier outpost beyond which our minds would tend to hyperventilate, growing giddy within the abyss of time? Admittedly, we can for the moment only speculate. But it's worth noting, for instance, that grasses preceded humanity, appearing about 50 million years ago, near the beginning of the current Cenozoic (or "New Animal," which is to say post-dinosaur) era, and becoming more prominent 25 million years later, as the climate cooled, at the beginning of the Miocene (or "Less Recent") epoch, now considered the "golden age of apes." So maybe we aren't entirely bound by our own beginnings.

I had got this far with my thoughts when I happened across a poem of Rumi's, called "Evolution," which six hundred years before Darwin's *On the Origin of Species,* shows life proceeding in specific stages, moving through mineral, plant, and animal phases to humanity's "present reasoning, knowledgable, robust state" (itself a way station, Rumi says, preceding "a thousand other forms of Mind"). In Rumi's formulation, each new level is accompanied by a letting go and forgetting of earlier forms of intelligence—except for a small residue of learnings and likings that are transportable and can be carried forward. For example, once a creature is at the animal state, there is no longer "any memory of his being vegetable—except for his attraction to Spring and to blossoms."

If we've carried an inherited liking for flowers around with us somewhere inside ever since, this might be the piece of us that could resonate to a time considerably preceding the one that became the heyday of the grasses. The first flowers appeared on earth perhaps 130 million years ago, about two-thirds of the way through the Mesozoic ("Middle Life" or "Middle Animal") era—with the dominant "middle animal" being the dinosaur. There was little, if any, "at-home"-ness on earth prior to this, even though life had emerged onto land more than 300 million years earlier. The Carboniferous (or "Coal-Bearing") Period, the time when coal deposits were laid down 300 million years ago, has, for instance, been characterized—in *The Emerald Planet: How Plants Changed Earth's History,* by David Beerling, an English paleoclimatologist—as a "lost world of giants," dominated by dragonflies with wingspans more than two feet wide and fernlike "scale trees" that towered as tall as a thirteen-story building. The first true flowers were no more than dots of color in the gloom, growing and glowing on small understory trees in tropical forests.

But then came the "big bang" of flowering plants, and within the next few million years they began spreading to all parts of the planet, meanwhile diversifying rapidly and producing 99 percent of the ancestors of today's flowers, such as roses and sunflowers; flowering vines, such as tomatoes; and flowering trees, such as oaks and apples. No one knows why this profusion occurred so quickly—Darwin called it an "abominable mystery"—but it produced what Michael Novacek, provost for science at the American Museum of Natural History, in New York, has called "a garden of delights," becoming, along the way, as Novacek sets forth in a 2007 book, *Terra: Our 100-Million-Year-Old Ecosystem—and the Threats That Now Put It at Risk,* "the foundation of our modern ecosystem" and "the cornucopia of life" sustaining the world we know.

The "great matrix of the modern land ecosystem," as Novacek calls it, represent a "now" that's almost nine thousand times older than the Holocene. Perhaps the not-yet-explained triumph of the flowers will prove to be strongest candidate for the Deepest Now we can easily embrace. After all, the earliest oceans, billions of years ago, were a yellowish green, and later turned red for a couple of hundred million years. The land itself began to turn green with plant life only about 400 million years ago. The "now" that Michael Novacek describes is based, as he says, on an "extraordinary act of cooperation between two different kingdoms of life," more specifically, an "intimate interconnection between flowers and insects":

> When angiosperms [flowering plants—the scientific word literally means "enclosed seeds"] arrived, they neither threw their pollen to the wind nor dropped it to the ground or in the water. Instead, they relied on animals, mostly insects, to pick up, transport, and drop it off. Inducing this laborious assistance from animals required temptations and, usually, rewards, and an infinitely varied palette of color, a complex bouquet of aroma, sweet nectar, and endless ingenuity in flower architecture, in modes of attraction and deception. As for the insect visitors, the system selected for equally spectacular innovations, including elongated probes, acute color vision, hairy appendages for pollen collection, and, in the case of the remarkable bees, the complex language of the dance. This system brings together all the ingenuity that can be mustered by two of the most dominant groups of organisms on Earth. It is difficult to imagine a more radical evolutionary development, a more extraordinary retooling of reproductive strategy, and a more wholesale resculpturing of life on land.

It may be that now that we're getting better at establishing contact with the various Deep Nows available to us, we're also beginning to see their possible practical applications. A 1983 book, *The People of the Secret,* by Ernest Scott (the name is a pseudonym used by Edward Campbell, a former literary editor of the London *Evening News*) was one of the first to suggest how opening up to Deep Nows can lead to a different way of assessing human achievements. "To the individual man," he says, "whose present moment at maximum is his own lifetime," humanity's progress may seem no more than the whim of chance and accident. But "if the whole of humanity is an organism on another time-scale," and if an individual's "present moment could be greatly extended and if, from this viewpoint, he could see some sort of Ego-continuity outside a single life, his relationship to 'fate' would be wholly transformed."

"Sweet are the uses of adversity," says Shakespeare in *As You Like It,* "Which, like the toad, ugly and venomous, / Wears yet a precious jewel in his head." Campbell offers a different kind of analogy to make a similar point, and to try to make such considerations seem less "remote and impersonal":

> Suppose a young child has a thorn deeply embedded in a finger. The mother sees the situation in terms of a present moment vastly greater than the child's. She sees her baby's life as a whole, its well-being, growth, maturity. She takes a needle, digs it under the thorn and removes it. . . .
>
> In terms of the child's present moment . . . [this is] a deliberate infliction of needless suffering. The child does not understand, and cannot, that the mother's action arises from concern for its own ultimate good.
>
> To appreciate this, the child would need access to a present moment which it does not possess and, at its stage of development, cannot possess.

Campbell, who died in 2006, at the age of ninety, was for many years absorbed by the question of what life is trying to tell us, and prepare us for. In a 1971 monograph, *Some Unusual Aspects of Communication,* he speculated about another kind of outcome that may await us, writing, "Suppose man's final destiny requires that in future time he should encounter other intelligences in the universe. It seems unlikely that with the means at present available to him he would be able to communicate. Some new technique, some radically different grammar of communication would be necessary." Campbell himself, as a young newspaper reporter in Glasgow, spent several months shortly before World War II training a lion, two lionesses, and a brown bear to do circus tricks, using only "patience, perseverance, and kindness," as one of his obituaries noted. "I wanted to see," Campbell said, "if the allegations of the anti-circus societies—that no wild animal act could be trained to professional standard without cruelty—had any basis in fact." The allegations were incorrect, and one lioness learned how to walk a double tightrope sixteen feet long. Perhaps mastering the use of Deep Nows is simply one more aspect of studying a more advanced "grammar of communication" with our surroundings and circumstances, one that has to do with learning different ways of conjugating time, which we can practice by combining past and present and future into new tenses. Maybe Deep Nows are the "Plupresent"—or would it be or the "Perfect Present"?—of such an approaching grammar.

On Christmas Eve 1968—this was seven months before Neil Armstrong became the first person to set foot on the moon— one of the three American astronauts on a preparatory mission that orbited the moon but didn't land on it suddenly started shouting. "Oh my God!" he said, according to the National Aeronautics and Space Administration's transcripts of the *Apollo 8* mission. "Look at the picture over there! Here's the earth coming up!" The astronauts had spent the day with their only windows facing the moon—they were the first people ever to circle the moon, and their job was to take high-resolution images both of the "dark side," which faces away from the earth, and of places on the near side that might make the best future landing sites. Finally, on their fourth orbit, they turned their lunar orbiter the other way; they needed to see the moon's horizon to take a navigational fix with a sextant. A few minutes later, "a blue-and-white fuzzy blob," as it seemed, peeped over the horizon: the earth. One of the astronauts, Bill Anders, rushed to take a color picture, an image now known as "Earthrise," or sometimes "Earth in the Rearview Mirror," or simply "that photograph," the first photograph of the earth ever taken from beyond the planet.

"It was," Frank Borman, the mission commander, later said, "the most beautiful, heart-catching sight of my life, one that sent a torrent of nostalgia, of sheer homesickness, surging through me. It was the only thing in space that had any color in it. Everything else was either black or white. But not the earth."

Many of the details of these moments emerged in a fortieth-anniversary commemorative essay, "The Mission That Changed Everything," by Robin McKie, the science and technology editor of the London *Observer*; it appeared in that newspaper near the end of 2008. McKie's piece argued that Anders's photograph, and not the six subsequent landings on the moon, in 1969, 1971, and 1972, may in the end be remembered as "the most important legacy of the *Apollo* space program"—because, "thanks to this image, humans could see, for the first time, their planet, not as continents or oceans, but as a world that was 'whole and round and beautiful and small,' as the poet Archibald MacLeish put it."

Nineteenth-century technology played a part in this, according to McKie. McKie flew to Chicago to interview Jim Lovell, the third astronaut on board, in a restaurant Lovell owns. There, Lovell told McKie that Anders had the only camera on hand with color film and a telephoto lens (a device perfected in 1891). "That is what makes the picture," Lovell still thinks. "Earth is about the size of a thumbnail when seen with the naked eye from the moon. The telephoto lens makes it seem bigger and gives the picture that special quality."

"Earthrise" appeared as a U.S. postage stamp the year after it was taken, and *Life* magazine later called it one of the "100 photographs that changed the world." How? This "epiphany in space," as Robert Poole, a British space historian, called "Earthrise" when he was interviewed by McKie, led directly to what Poole in his own recent book about the photograph has called an "eco-renaissance": a generation of environmental activism and landmark laws, including, in the United States, the Clean Air Act, in 1970, and the Clean Water Act, in 1972. "Suddenly"—this is how Stewart Brand, creator of *The Whole Earth Catalog*, explains the onrush of the environmental movement—"humans had a planet to tend to"—one that "looked tiny, fragile, and rare." In a special edition of *Time* magazine celebrating the thirtieth anniversary of Earth Day, in 2000, Brand, discussing "Earthrise," wrote, "It is no accident of history that the first Earth Day, in April 1970, came so soon after." "Planet-scale perspective on atmospheric health, ocean health, and stable climate made strictly national approaches obsolete. Environmental non-governmental organizations bloomed."

In retrospect, Poole is inclined to think, this "larger here" point of view was what the space program was aiming at all along—the "unofficial space program," he calls it in his book, *Earthrise: How Man First Saw the Earth*. "Humans," Robin McKie says, "had spent billions in an attempt to explore another world and in the end rediscovered their own." In this case, the voyage home turned out to be the justification for the voyage outward. Because while "the moon, was 'dead as an old bone,' " as Poole quotes Lewis Thomas as having said about the *Apollo 8* trip, 'the earth was 'the only exuberant thing in this part of the cosmos.' "

But, according to Stewart Brand, the most startling part of the subsequent impact of "Earthrise"—and this begins to mesh very closely with the kind of observations Edward Campbell was making—is that it has compelled us to start learning a new time language, and to become, in effect, at least "bitemporal" and, preferably "multitemporal." It's one thing to start seeing the earth as a "larger here," a place whose "whole earth" needs have to be addressed in a unified way—that's the *what* of the matter. But the *how* of it, finding actions that can, say, prevent the projected extinction of five hundred species of birds and more than that number of mammals over the next fifty years, can happen only when we also begin adopting the perspectives offered by "Longer Nows," such as "the domains of deep, slow change," as Brand calls them, and, in particular, the rhythms of "biosphere time." Otherwise solutions remain theoretical, intellectual, and tantalizingly out of reach.

"Environmentalism," Brand says, "teaches patience"—which he considers "a core competency of a healthy civilization." Everyday life is woven out of several different time strands, he has realized, "operating at a number of different paces at the same time. Fashion and commerce change quickly, as they should. Nature and culture change slowly, as they should. Infrastructure and governance move along at middling rates of change." Before this sank in, he notes, "Governments limited to next-election thinking had no way to grasp environmental issues. Corporations limited to next-quarter perspectives were similarly blinded," because "such issues as climate, biodiversity, and population could only be dealt with in terms of multiple decades, even multiple centuries."

"A new time perspective," then, was the other big post-"Earthrise" breakthrough. We didn't just need more tools and more people using them to deal with the planetary nature of environmental threats; we needed tools shaped to various time sizes and "the differing paces of change." This is because "lag times and lead times" in atmospheric and climate changes prove to be "decades long," and the continuing health of forests, oceans, and aquifers, since they involve "multigeneration equity," will need a new kind of bucket brigade, one where the same level of concern is passed along from fathers and mothers to sons and daughters, again and again and again. Previously, Brand says, "ecological problems were thought unsolvable simply because they could not be solved in a year or two." Whereas "it turns out that environmental problems *are* solvable. It's just that it takes focused effort over a decade or three to move toward solutions, and the solutions take centuries."

Brand's interest in promoting "long-term foresight"—"where 'long-term' is measured at least in centuries"—has led him to suggest that we need a more capacious term of reference for describing our own time; he proposes that we stop thinking about living in *the twenty-first century* or the *the new millennium,* and instead start thinking of ourselves as having arrived on earth in the middle of a twenty-thousand-year time period that's remarkably similar to John Hanson Mitchell's Ceremonial Time—since they both started at the end of the last ice age—and that Brand calls "the Long Now." He and some friends set up the Long Now Foundation to popularize the term and to create some external reminders of this internal expansion. They're not pointing to the enduring shape of the hills, as Mitchell does, but they have bought land in Nevada for an eighty-foot-high Millennial Clock, or Clock of the Long Now. According to Dan Falk, who's visited the clock's smaller prototype, now on display at the Time Measurement Gallery of London's Science Museum, it " 'ticks' twice a day" (although it's currently awaiting a replacement part), and at midnight on January 31, 1999, it "started the third millennium with two rings of its one-thousand-year chime." The foundation also adds an extra zero when writing dates, so that 1999, for instance, becomes 01999.

Ceremonial Time and the Long Now are both "time umbrella concepts," as I think of them, or "time envelopes," as Brand calls them, meaning that both of them make room for time gone by and time yet to come within their shelter and embrace. Or call them "two-way telescopes," since they bring both past and future closer. Mitchell, who at the outset of his explorations thought of himself as a historian, someone primarily focused on the story so far, early on hooked into a preexisting, pre-Columbian Deep Now, a specific present moment originally launched by North America's first inhabitants soon after their branch of humanity had finally made it from Africa to the previously isolated New World. It was only after Mitchell began to feel at home inside this fascinating time sense, which stretched behind him as a result of continuing and unbroken transmissions, that eventually, through the good offices of his two Pawtucket Indian friends, he began to see Ceremonial Time's forward thrust and realized that it would also let him see ahead as far as the next glacier's advance, something we can expect—when? Geophysicists think of this as a somewhat open-ended date, one that could come about in the next few thousand years or might instead be pushed back indefinitely by global warming. They're reasonably sure, however, that the next "glacial period," as they call it, will be at its height in another eighty thousand years. (You can't ask them when the next ice age will begin, because as they measure such events we're still in the unrelinquished grip of a million-year-long ice age, so that the entirety of Holocene Time, by their reckoning, is no more than an unusually placid warm spell, a breather and something of a quirk, or, as they say, more neutrally, an "interglacial.")

Unlike Ceremonial Time, Brand's Long Now has a predetermined and definite end date. This is partly because, unlike Mitchell, Brand arrived at his idea by deduction, not instruction, extrapolating from time senses already widely familiar to modern Americans. William James's saddleback-shaped "strict present"—that most immediate of "nows," the small perch "from which we look in two directions into time"—can be unfolded several times and still retain a shape we recognize. Used more loosely, as Brand says, the word "now" conjures up a compact neighborhood of days, the clustered trio of yesterday-today-tomorrow, a close-in and movable frontier of time awareness that we reset each morning by moving it forward by one notch. We have been carrying this notion around with us ever since learning these Post-It-like, permanent-but-transferable day-names in early childhood. (It's only later that we learn that days also have a separate set of names, such as Sunday, Monday, and Tuesday, that always stay in one place and don't slide around, so that they can accompany us as we move on from one day to the next.) Similarly, for Brand, the word "nowadays," learned later on, tends to spread out to cover a thirty-year interval, the almost eleven thousand days that add up to three bundled-together decades. This progression also needs resetting periodically, but it somehow stays sewn together in the mind; it's a unit of time that extends from the start of the decade before the current one and terminates at the far end of the decade just ahead.

It takes a bigger jump to get there, but by further extension of the same process Brand arrives at the Long Now, which has the same shape as the previous "nows" but a different size, since it's basically "the Holocene epoch times two," so to speak. The "before" of this Doubled Holocene is a thousand decades long, and, retaining symmetry, so is its "after." The beginnings of Ceremonial Time and the Long Now are coterminous because the most recent retreat of the glaciers set two events in motion: on the American continent, a Deep Now that John Hanson Mitchell was eventually able to contact and, farther to the east, in the Old World, the long sequence of increasingly complicated and energetic cultures whose advances came to include sedentism, agriculture, cities, writing, and, along the way, further development of the human intellect. Most people have learned in school how to "think back" (however hazily) through this list of milestone accomplishments and see in them the forward march of "civilization," so it seemed reasonable to Brand, as he says in his book on the subject, *The Clock of the Long Now: Time and Responsibility—the Ideas Behind the World's Slowest Computer,* to suggest that "we should develop an equal perspective into the future." This would give us a way of pointing up the contrasts between a period when actions were taken without much thought for their impact on the future and a comparable period when people would instead be thinking ahead. During this time, long-term thinking might become "automatic and common instead of difficult and rare" and "the taking of long-term responsibility inevitable"—with the result, perhaps, that the people who will eventually become the earth's inhabitants at the end of this Long Now, after another millennium of decades, won't be saddled by the dismay that faces those of us here today.

All of this suggests that there may be some practical, previously unanticipated, near-term "foresight" uses for dips into Ceremonial Time during our own nowadays—if we think of our time, in Stewart Brand's terms, as no more than a meantime or, more precisely, as the exact middle, the fulcrum at the center of the current postglacial (or is it merely an interglacial?) "now." Maybe periodic jumps into and out of Ceremonial Time will take their place as part of a self-taught starter course in what Brand calls "getting people accustomed to the slower pace of biological time." For instance, because of the pressure of "slow crisis" or "biotime" events, the century ahead—a mere ten decades long, one of them already expired—will, according to E. O. Wilson and many other biologists and ecologists, be a time of tremendous readjustment for humanity. Wilson calls these approaching difficulties "the bottleneck." The image is one of squeezing through a narrow passageway—in this case, that means an unprecedented situation in which over nine billion people (the projected world population by the middle of the twenty-first century—an increase of almost 2.5 billion over today's numbers) will have to find adequate room and food and water for themselves without completely usurping the room, food, and water used by the rest of species with whom we share the planet. How many other species are there? Maybe three and a half million, maybe more than 100 million—so many, at any rate, that even after more than 275 years of organized scientific counting and assigning Latin names to species, we're still making crude estimates about exactly how much variety surrounds us.

What we do know is that the continued survival of this overwhelming variety is now intertwined with the continuing arrival of more and more people—that's because in 2000, when there were only six billion people, we were already appropriating for our own use 40 percent of the nutrition produced by all the plants in the world; nine billion people would consume 60 percent. It's as if Noah had gathered all the world's creatures onto the ark but had, during the boarding, moved his own family into two of the ship's five decks—and had then, even while setting sail, started to cast his eye on a third deck as well. As Wilson calculates the risks, we can decide right now, or very shortly, to keep half the land on the planet unsettled and off-limits to human use (while also keeping away from 20 to 30 percent of the ocean)—or face the loss of a quarter of the other species within fifty years, and half of them by the turn of the next century.

"There is no way to weasel out of this choice," Wilson says (in *The Creation: An Appeal to Save Life on Earth*). What's more, the wrong choice may endanger the ark itself, because it, too, as it happens, is alive. "Earth," Wilson suggests (in *The Future of Life*), "unlike the other solar planets, is not in physical equilibrium. It depends on its living shell to create the special conditions on which life is sustainable." This is the biosphere, "a stupendously complex layer of living creatures," which "creates our special world anew every day, every minute, and holds it in a unique, shimmering physical disequilibrium. On that disequilibrium the human species is in total thrall. When we alter the biosphere in any direction, we move the environment away from the delicate dance of biology. When we destroy ecosystems and extinguish species, we degrade the greatest heritage this planet has to offer and thereby threaten our own existence."

The bottleneck that Wilson foresees may turn out to be a much longer tube than he has been anticipating. Wilson assumes that human numbers will decline in the twenty-second century—but the United Nations Population Division, which agrees with this estimate, also predicts resumed population increases in the twenty-third century. As a result, the UNPD says, there will once again be nine billion people here by 2400. Or 02400, as the year would display on Stewart Brand's clock.

These are early days," says Brand. "Thinking in ten-thousand-year terms is new to us." On the other hand, we are starting to take actions—such as making plans to bury nuclear wastes—that will still be affecting the world more than ten Long Nows from now. According to a *New York Times* report, for instance, a 1999 study by the U.S. Department of Energy predicted that "the peak period of radioactive releases from the waste will be so far in the future—200,000 years or more—that man-made features, like corrosion-resistant canisters, will not be reliable. . . . The time scale is so long that it probably includes climatic changes including ice ages."

Leaping across time in the mind in order to threaten or inspire the present has a long history in books and tracts, such as the nineteenth-century million-copy best seller *Looking Backward: 2000–1887,* by Edward Bellamy, a still-powerful 1888 novel in which a young Bostonian falls asleep for more than a century to find, when he wakes up in the year 2000, that the United States has in the meantime been transformed into a Christian socialist paradise. "With a tear for the dark past"—this is Bellamy's cry of triumph—"turn we then to the dazzling future, and, veiling our eyes, press forward. The long and weary winter of the race is ended. Its summer has begun. Humanity has burst the chrysalis. The heavens are before it." *Looking Backward* immediately inspired many imitators, rebuttals, and variants, including *Looking Further Backward, Looking Forward, Looking Further Forward, Looking Beyond,* and *Looking Within.* But while visions of the future can be hard to sustain—the "Nationalist" clubs that had sprung up to support Bellamy's views were already in decline by the time of his premature death in 1898—"visions within the present" may prove to have more staying power. This is doable, I've found, by starting slow and thinking nearish-term—only to the other end of the Wilsonian bottleneck, say—while letting a kind of directed, or specifically focused, Deep Now take hold.

Let's say, for instance, that E. O. Wilson's sense of the timing of the narrowest constriction of the big squeeze that lies ahead of us is accurate, and that world population pressures will ease in another hundred years or so. Let's also say that for the moment our interest is concentrated on achieving the primary goal he's put forward—the "half an earth" challenge, to give it a name. Making sure, that is, that human communities throughout the next century, even as our numbers swell, limit ourselves, year after year, to consuming no more than half the provisions provided by the planet and to occupying at most two and a half decks on the five-deck global ark. The aim is more modest than Edward Bellamy's: not to change human nature or revolutionize human society but only to steer a steady course; to move the preexisting forward; to shore up and sustain the very arrangement of the world we were ourselves brought up within and know so well; to protect and celebrate and restrengthen the intricate balance of the biosphere.

It can feel like a discouraging prospect—if what you bring to the job is a sense of constantly intensifying pressure. Consulting the Ceremonial Time perspective turns things around. Taking this off-ramp onto the slower lane of biotime, it feels as though the momentum for getting this task done—for seeing it through—was generated long ago and is still the strongest force on the field. In the postglacial northeastern part of the United States, where I live, four hundred generations before the one active today have looked out and seen and cherished the same hills, woods, and flowers that appear to us. (Other areas of the planet clearly have much longer trains of transmission—ongoing human awareness in Australia, for instance, as codified by the sacred "dreamtime" experiences of the indigenous Aboriginal people, may stretch back perhaps forty thousand years, or sixteen hundred generations.) Joining hands—or is it glances?—with all four hundred of the Ceremonial Time generations within my part of the world to form a kind of "continuing viewshed" of the hills that don't change, and at the same time conjuring an imminent link to come with the next few generations that will follow ours, lets people in my area become more than the end point or receivers of experiencing. Instead, we are merely the four hundredth in a line of, say, 404 successive dwellers within this particular spread of time, the "Deep Now at Hand." Just as we can by extension feel ourselves looking through the eyes of the first generation of the region's tenants, we can as easily expand the service area of this current of continuity so that it takes in the "404s" to come—and then start looking out through their eyes, as well. Which allows us to realize that they, too, will be seeing the same hills, and that—if we do our share of the work, a mere fraction of an age-long task—at least half of those hills will still be forested and will have been left to themselves by then, and placed under their own management.

Although we still have only a shadowy sense of the "1s"—the first generation of people to see these hills after mile-high glaciers were no longer pushing them around or hiding them from view—we've recently learned a little more about the route their ancestors took to get here. The starting-off point was the lost land of Beringia, wide grasslands that were flooded by what is now the Bering Strait after the glaciers melted but before that had formed a land bridge between Siberia and Alaska, temporarily uniting the Old World and the New into a single supercontinent. At the height of the ice age, a wall of North American glaciers had prevented further travel, and during this "Beringian standstill," as anthropologists call it, a small isolated group of people that had gathered there from Siberia persisted in place for several thousand years—certainly more than long enough to generate a pre-Holocene Ceremonial Time sense of their own, one they had to put aside when times changed and they were able to move on again. Newly discovered genetic evidence suggests that when the Beringians eventually dispersed, cousins of the "1s" traveled almost due south along the west coast of first North America and then South America, arriving in the end in Tierra del Fuego, the subpolar islands at the southern tip of Chile. Whereas the direct forebears of the "1s" went only a little way south—but, having reached the long east-west line marking what was then the southern edge of the still-retreating glacier, "took a sharp left turn," as Meredith F. Small, a Cornell anthropologist puts it, and began spreading out over inland North America.

We don't yet know, as Small points out, whether this was a journey being made by people who felt themselves being pushed from behind (perhaps by a changing and less friendly climate) or pulled from somewhere in front (perhaps by herds of animals they had been hunting that were also on the move). "Or maybe," as Small says, in a recent Internet article called "Why Did Humans Migrate to the Americas?" "they came because they could"—and it's all as simple as that.

We share more than just the hills with the "1s," according to Joe Rao, the Hayden Planetarium lecturer, who also writes the Skywatching column for Space.com. At night, when we look skyward, we're also—through the skyglow—still seeing what they saw, both here and even further back, during their grandparents' days in Beringia. Most of the night sky constellations that we point to are patterns invented in the early cities of the Middle East 3,000 or more years ago and later picked up by the Greeks. But one of those constellations, the Great Bear, the sprawling group of stars high in the northern sky that includes the Big Dipper, was a picture independently arrived at, as Rao recounts in one of his columns, at least 8,000 to 12,000 years ago, during "the estimated era of the last migration from Siberia to North America across the Bering Strait."

Seen from within the continuing perceptions of Ceremonial Time—a long corridor through clock time, but a much shorter interval of biotime—the large-scale idea that E. O. Wilson and others are putting forward of using the twenty-first century to assemble a protection plan for the biosphere seems less formidable and unprecedented and more like something we long ago committed ourselves to and that a long line of people have been working on ever since. Which shrinks it down a bit, so it becomes more ordinary. Almost like a maintenance job, or one of the region's household chores. One of those tasks we can take in stride. And from the biotime perspective, we're almost there. These are no more than the last few laps—for now, at any rate, until some new challenges present themselves. Furthermore, it's encouraging to understand that "inevitable" and "irresistible" are words that don't necessarily refer to change. Shoring up the region has been accumulating its own kind of unstoppable momentum since shortly after the fall of Beringia.

I've also tried "Bellamyizing" this same time-encompassing process, which involves engaging in almost the same sort of "Directed Deep Now" but giving it a slightly different *Looking Backward*–inspired emphasis and tilt. I start off in exactly the same way, by looking at or thinking about some nearby hills in the New York City—or "H2O"—area that even in this landscape of generally undramatic changes in elevation are spectacular enough to anchor the region. An immediate choice would be the cliffs of the Palisades, which years ago became a well-defined compass point in my own mental map of my town and its surroundings. Most of Manhattan's hills have been sacrificed to development, but just across the Hudson River the great almost twenty-mile-long expanse of the Palisades north of the George Washington Bridge became public property a century ago. These giant tree-topped, jagged, gray-brown columns of rock, which have sheer, near-vertical drop-offs more than three hundred feet tall, are far older than the Holocene—but the beginning of the Holocene is, from all that is known, when these cliffs first became an ongoing presence in human awareness. That's when the "grandfather" people, as local Native Americans, the Lenape, call their forebears, are thought to have arrived in the area. So invoking the continually reinforced gazing at these rippling curtains of rock that have been accumulating across so many generations begins with the completed lifetimes of the ancient grandfathers, sweeps through the not-yet-complete lifetimes we enjoy, and comes to rest in the not-yet-launched lifetimes of people who might someday be our own great-grandchildren.

This, as before, adds up to the subtotal of the generations of the "hereabouts people"—locals and visitors—who have seen, are seeing, and will see the Palisades from the beginning of a Brandian Long Now until shortly past its midpoint. Except that in the *Looking Backward* scenario, it is the "404s," those people who will one day replace us, who seem already to have taken on a more active role, and who—as instigators and guides—are calling back to us with instructions and encouragement to keep making sure that the two views of the hills, the one we know and the one they will come to know, can be superimposed without any blurring or loss of vividness. It's as if both groups have only just come to understand their vulnerability and partialness; they need our energy and we can use their advice and guidance, the way sailors on the bridge of a ship will signal final course corrections down to the engine room crew when approaching port. Or perhaps it can be likened to a time-lapse partnership between the recipient of a package and its sender, an unusual kind of arrangement in which unwrapping the box after it gets there helps you specify new special-handling precautions to take before sending it off. So that the cliffs, the woods, the wetlands of the H2O Area—or any other area—can get carefully inspected and leave the here and now intact and full of life, rather than tattered and ailing and shopworn, and are properly wrapped and cushioned so they can arrive in the "here and then" undamaged and undented, and not semisquashed or stretched to the breaking point. In this way the common heritage in the making—theirs and ours—will find its way through another century undiminished in resilience, intricacy, and beauty.

Relying on the thinking of more than one generation at a time may become more commonplace as the Holocene continues to unfold. People in the H2O Area around New York today have, in a sense, already been born into such an arrangement—since it was the work of the area's "397s," the generation in residence at the turn of the last century, that saved the Palisades from being mined for trap rock that could be pulverized to pave the streets of Manhattan. The task ahead, meanwhile, keeps getting more complex. The shape of the hills has been retained—but the shape of the shorelines will be changing, as global warming and climate change that are also the result of earlier human actions bring higher sea levels and new warmth: summers in New York by 2080 are expected to be as hot as those Atlanta already gets. So the challenge has become one of finding actions that will deliver a local landscape undiminished in species richness and abundance rather than one that will have retained exactly the same species mix, since some of the plants and animals that need colder weather will have drifted northward, opening up room for subtropical replacements.

Those plants and animals of the next century will all need unbroken corridors of natural land for their south-to-north journeys, a pattern we can see and hold steady in our own minds as soon as we reenter the unbroken time corridor that has room for us as well as those who went before and those who will come later.

Edward Bellamy's hero, Julian West, looks backward with disdain mingled with horror. The Boston of the year 2000 he has awakened to is a city where inequalities have been erased. It's adorned with, West notes, "public buildings of a colossal size and architectural grandeur unparalleled in my day," and, having cast off "self-serving," its citizens have gained "faces unmarred by arrogance or servility, by envy or greed, by anxious care or feverish ambition." Interestingly, the natural setting of this perfected future is unchanged—the "green islets" of Boston harbor look exactly as West remembers them, and the city's keen east winds are still "marked by the same penetrating quality." (The other thing that hasn't changed are Victorian patterns of speech. "Oh, Mr. West!" the book's heroine exclaims. "You don't know, you can't think, how it makes me feel to see you so forlorn. I can't have it so.") To Julian West, the people he has left behind seem almost like "beasts of prey," whereas in the Deep Now I like to visit the abilities people can call on in themselves haven't changed between now and then—and the shining future has not yet been fully determined, which is why our generation is being commissioned to take a hand. Deputized, as it almost seems. Signed up and sworn in.

Bellamy, in *Looking Backward,* wants us to see the present through the eyes of the future, but he assumes this can only increase our dissatisfaction with the world as it is. This is what happens to Julian West, who on a brief return to the Boston of 1887, near the end of the book, can see around him only "squalor and malodorousness . . . facts I had never before observed." The focus, as in already-there travel, is on the "golden century" at the end of the journey, and the present's only value is as a goad or spur, something to accelerate through and put behind us as soon as possible. The effect is quite different if we step outside while thinking of ourselves as delegated agents of the future and look at the present through the eyes of the 404ers ahead of us. Then, even deep in Manhattan—although especially in the late spring—instead of feeling scared and troubled, we can still draw a deep breath of satisfaction. What luck! It's not too late—we got here in time. We didn't let it get away; it's all still here. The air—still feels soft on the skin in a breeze, and still smells fresh after storms pass. There is still the play of light on gathering thunderclouds; the blue of the sky on cloudless days; the depth of green in even the leaves of the small trees pushing unasked out of the ground with so much strength and force in vacant lots. We are almost oversupplied with chances and choices that will celebrate and safeguard the surrounding H_2O landscape, for planting and protecting and reconnecting it, for bringing it back and showing it off. It's almost too easy. Now—where to start? Which actions of ours will give those young 404s a sense of a job well done?

THE "OTHER POINTS"
OF TRAVEL

In addition to everything else it opens up for us, the extended present of Deep Travel time also alters the way a trip can accumulate and take on a recognizable shape in the mind. As a result, we often bring home unlikely, intangible, and even unclassifiable trophies and souvenirs—that string of things that stays fresh for us, the people or moments we otherwise might never have encountered or been able to notice. This modifies, and sometimes transforms, the "point" of the trip. Almost every trip has a preset "point," as we know, even if it's only to be aimless. This is more than just a destination, because it includes, even before we set forth, a projected trajectory and a budget of expectations, such as the predetermined calculations we make about the amount of energy and attention we'll need to see it through, so to speak—which is almost, although we don't quite put it this way, like thinking about how much extra stamina we should be stuffing into a carry-on bag. Added together in this ordinary arithmetic, the known goal and the already-looked-for constitute the original "point" of any journey, business or pleasure or simple errand—and a way of deciding afterward whether it was worth taking.

Less ordinary, but not uncommon, is another idea that also precedes a trip, the thought—sometimes only a hope—that it might later on, after the fact, turn out to have had a "second point," as well. Something unplanned and unplannable, and most clearly visible only when looked back at. Meaning the feeling you get ahead of time that somewhere along the way, in addition to all the many things that won't turn out as they had been expected to, you might be overtaken by a "never before" moment of sufficient force that it then stays with you as a kind of "ever after" revelation or disclosure, because you find it's grown into you and become a part of your understanding of things. It can be small, and can take any number of forms—and it can't be guaranteed in advance. But it could be worth keeping an eye out for. Just in case. As a practical example, I have had the word "Scheveningen" lodged in my head ever since I was teenager and friends of my parents', the Blumenthals, explained how it had, many years before, become the "second point" of their honeymoon and one of their best ways of avoiding future mistakes. Scheveningen is a popular, Victorian-era seaside resort town in Holland that in more recent decades has been swallowed up by The Hague, the nearby big city. The Blumenthals had spent a miserable day in Scheveningen—realizing only after they left town that this had been because he'd gone there assuming this would please her, and she'd gone there just to please him, when in fact neither one of them had ever wanted to go there.

Some "second points," even in retrospect, still seem unlikely, a long shot, an improbable jackpot, a payoff that could easily have been passed by. I can remember, for instance, an incredibly hot night my family spent a few years ago at the bottom of the Grand Canyon. Just being there is of course a special circumstance for almost anyone, because only about four hundred people live in Supai, the little Havasupai village that is the canyon's one permanent settlement (and is a town so hard to reach that mail has to be carried in by mule). We'd spent a day afloat, running rapids on the Colorado River in "baloney boats" (they look like big inflatable sausages) while staring up at the immensities around us: the canyon is 277 miles long, up to eighteen miles wide, over a mile deep, and at least six million years old, although, according to a new theory, a "proto–Grand Canyon" began forming sixteen or seventeen million years ago. The long stripes of ancient red, yellow, gray, and black rock in the canyon's sheer walls were so bright they seemed almost like two endless mile-high rainbows standing up on either side of a river. Once we'd put in for the night, the silence that wrapped everything was broken only by the murmur of the river. At the end of this long day, I was keyed up, excited, and at the same time hungry for sleep. And not sure what to do next, because sleep was impossible. Long after dark, the 1.8-billion-year-old black rocks next to my sleeping bag still seemed almost molten from all the sunlight they'd soaked up throughout a cloudless August day. Vishnu schist, as these rocks are called, was named after the "all-pervading" Hindu deity to honor their antiquity. They're the "basement rocks" of the canyon, almost half as old as the earth itself, and are visible in only a few places, because it can take an extraordinary event—like a river capable of cutting through a full mile of younger rocks—to expose them to the sun.

Since sleep was impossible, I went for a walk—easy enough, as the moon was up. Everything was silver, except for the still-black Vishnu schist. An hour later, Jupiter rose behind the canyon walls, blazingly white, emerging, I saw, at the same spot as the moon had, just to the right of a particular and eye-catching jagged rock formation. After another hour, Saturn, fainter but just as white, appeared, again from behind precisely this dip in the rocks at the top of the canyon. Everything felt stripped down to a few basic, ancient, silent essentials, in which almost the only visible objects were elemental, three planets and one moon, now displayed in single file, and where the only discernible movement was their own tireless, coordinated, concentric whirling. I felt myself in the presence of something close to the Deepest Now, far older, anyway, than the Now of the Flowers suggested by Michael Novacek, a time rhythm measured by a pace so slow and deliberate and so preorganic and prebiological I had never thought it might be possible to contact it directly or personally sample it.

From my unique vantage point at the bottom of the canyon, staring upward at the piece of the sky revealed by the towering walls, I seemed to be looking outward through a kind of porthole that manifested only occasionally but had somehow opened up deep within the earth on the night of my visit. Further, I seemed to be peering through an unusual sort of a lens that might be made out of what the Northern Irish science-fiction writer Bob Shaw once called "slow glass," an imagined state of matter that because it could tame the speed of light allowed people to see past events as if they were still unfolding. Only the Grand Canyon's Vishnu schist porthole was more of a time tamer, one that might have been expressly designed to display events that were, and still are, taking place in Solar System Time—a single celestial moment that began as these planets and subplanets came into being almost 4.5 billion years ago and since then has recorded every turn in their long circle dance. What we see now is maybe fifty million years younger than the original system—assuming that the "giant impact hypothesis" is correct and the moon formed only when Theia, a lost planet as big as Mars, collided with the proto-earth and pieces of our planet were cast off and quickly coalesced to form our satellite sphere. There are currents and possibilities here we are still only beginning to explore: maybe other "moonlets," called Trojans, came into being at the same time and then circled the earth for a hundred million or even a billion years. Maybe Venus and Jupiter are even today tugging at the moon from far away, pulling it into a more oval orbit than it would otherwise assume. But even with these added fluxes and eddies and reconfigurations, the orderly rotation of the sun's system, if considered as a single moment, is an event about a third as old as the universe itself, and it will end—when?

With current astronomical knowledge, precise calculations of the solar system's motions can be calculated for only the next twenty to thirty million years. There seems, nevertheless, to be a slight chance—maybe one in one hundred—that three and a half billion years from now the motions of the planets will become disrupted (and an even smaller chance, on the order of one in twenty-five hundred, that as a consequence the earth might collide with either Mars or Venus). But if that doesn't happen, and if current projections of what astronomers call the "life cycle" of the sun are anywhere close to correct, then the particular celestial cycle that made itself known at a temporary viewing platform at the bottom of the Grand Canyon may now be nearing its midpoint, and will in all likelihood outlast any life on earth. "Life's life span," meaning the future of terrestrial plants and animals and microbes, may have only another 500 million years or so to run. On the other hand, the planet itself—"sterile earth," as its postlife state has been called—will spin on, and it may be another 5 billion years before the dying sun, having entered its red-giant phase, swells to several hundred million times its current size and either swallows the earth or flings its charred cinder into a new and more distant orbit.

For those of us now alive on earth, an ordinary "strict present" moment, of the kind William James defined as the shortest naturally occurring unit of human attention, fills our awareness for at most just a little longer than the time needed to take a couple of deep, slow breaths. So, operating in its own time, one that both predates life and will outlast it, perhaps the solar system has at least one more good, long breath still ahead of it before something else gets started.

Now, admittedly, trips that prove in the end to have been conceal-ing notable or even life-changing "second points" are an excep-tion. But perhaps their scarcity makes it easier to see another extra that the prolonged present of Deep Travel time brings our way on a more regular basis. Whenever we enter Deep Travel and, in this "larger awareness," attune ourselves to a greater sample of the changing possi-bilities around us, surprising bits of information we might not ordinar-ily register flow into the mind. Then, once having appeared, they stay with us, embedded within the continuing moment, even if we can't make immediate sense of them or fit them into any known pattern. After that, as they assemble in our minds, we start to carry along with us on any trip an ever-lengthening list of provisional observations and tentative conclusions, fragments of experience with their own pulse. They may never jell into anything substantial, since they seem to be awaiting confirmation or at least a second appearance or to be asking for a follow-up investigation we may never get around to.

On the other hand, there they are.

For example, walking down Greene Street in Manhattan near dusk not long ago, I happened to glance left when crossing Houston Street, at the foot of Greenwich Village, and was startled to see that—from this one angle, at least—the dominant object on the horizon, standing seemingly at the foot of this truck-crowded, eight-lane, lower Manhat-tan crosstown traffic artery, was a towering tree, an enormous, dark sil-houette with a perfect Christmas-tree shape, perhaps 110 feet high, making it taller than any of the buildings or billboards near it. Imagine, a New York highway-sized thoroughfare dwarfed by a single tree!

Now, New York is like a concert hall with strange acoustics—the music reaching many of the seats is muffled but gets amplified at oth-ers, ringing out like a trumpet call at a few seemingly random locations. Too often, there's no chance to find out more about something you happen to notice, or overhear, in this way, but in this case, I had time to change course and walk east along Houston until I got the full story— and to realize, too, that, more than at any other spot, the Greene-and-Houston corner showcases the great tree, not that anyone planned it this way, because there's a steep, two-block-long hill rising just east of Greene Street, which, down at the bottom, gives the effect of elevating the tree even higher, putting it up on a podium or, in this case, a huge Christmas-tree stand.

The tree in question, as becomes clear as you draw near and it takes on depth and is no longer just an outline, is a real tree, not a logo, or a billboard, or a stunt. It's a metasequoia, or dawn redwood, meaning a tree from the dawn of time, a species thought to have died out at least five to ten million years ago, until a small remnant stand was found along a remote stream valley in Sichuan, China, during World War II. Now propagated around the world, the metasequoia grows with great rapidity. The Houston Street dawn redwood is part of the Liz Christy Community Garden, New York's first greened-up empty lot, an abandoned, rubble-filled space reclaimed entirely by volunteers, and was planted thirty-five years ago, during the garden's first year, by Christy, a Lower East Side artist, and a group of friends and neighbors who had organized themselves as the Green Guerrillas. This was a time when the city almost went bankrupt, and the community garden movement, which went on to replant hundreds of properties that over the years people had just walked away from, became and remains one of the most visible signs of the city's resilience.

Deep Travel glimpses like these are not exactly the "point" of anything, except that once we've spotted them, they've joined the realm of the . . . well, perhaps not the known and the undeniable, but at least the provisional and the pending. Things we would recognize should they recur. As these little outliers and extensions of the everyday pile up or drift together in our awareness during any single journey, they give each trip—every trip, if we let this happen—its own unique, distinctive flavor. It doesn't matter that, even taken together, they may never amount to a definitive statement, let alone a revelation, or emerge as anything as organized or as purposeful as a melody. But they are notes that have joined the scale of sounds, and have perhaps enriched the future. The next time around, if we ever hear them again, they could become part of some tune that for now remains unwritten. Sometimes, in passing, I make a few quick jottings about these new notes, to serve as quick reminders of the poetry created by the extended present, the extra bits that proceed in parallel with the prose of travel—the shopping lists and schedules and boarding passes. Two different kinds of raw ingredients, side by side. Are they equally essential? All I know is that the regular facts, the solid parts of a trip, are over and done with as soon as a trip is complete, while the harder-to-categorize occurrences, since they remain unfinished business, are less easily cast aside.

I found the first page of one of these "keep looking" jottings the other day about a trip to Las Vegas—an odd set of scraps as they seem now, unsorted, disconnected, taking up more syllables than a haiku but with nothing like the meaning. A bouquet of buds, not blossoms. No hints of anything that might have bloomed to become the indelible "second point" of that trip. Yet worth hanging on to just the same, if only because maybe the "third point" of a trip is to remember not to unpack our minds when we unpack our bags. In the long run, some meanings may come to us more easily by being gathered than by being hunted down. Even if they don't arrive, the "over" after a trip is only a short pause, and while at rest we are still being beckoned forward, sometimes by "might yet" encounters, and perhaps sometimes even by things we may personally never meet up with. "MTK," as journalists of my generation have traditionally slugged their stories in progress: "more to come." Or, as William James more memorably says, in his *Varieties of Religious Experience,* writing about "potential forms of consciousness" from which we are normally parted by "the flimsiest of screens," such awarenesses and understandings can never be disregarded and may already be helping us even if we never master them: "They may determine attitudes, though they cannot furnish formulas; and open a region though they fail to give a map. At any rate, they forbid our premature closing of accounts with reality."

What I had written down about the Las Vegas trip was:

NY–LV 7/19/04

I. E TRAIN	I. PREACHER W/O A CONGREGATION
II. AIR TRAIN	2. ROLLING PUMPKIN SUN
III. JETBLUE	3. "LEFT TURN IN ALBUQUERQUE"

Deciphered, what this referred to was the first hours of a family summer trip in 2004. The "prose" or "first point" part of this trip was in Roman numerals—and had to do with deciding to try the then-new "AirTrain," an automated monorail out to Kennedy Airport, before climbing on an evening flight. We wanted to see if this latest addition to New York's mass transit system would save time and money at rush hour and save us from having to spring for a taxi—even though it would also mean tacking on a subway ride from our apartment to a commuter train station in Jamaica, Queens, because that's as close as the AirTrain ever gets to Manhattan. Reading the left side of the list, I remembered—not that much. The price had been good; the time it had taken to get to the airport had seemed reasonable. There'd been a good deal of extra schlepping involved, since we'd had to walk our bags to the subway, up from the subway to the elevated AirTrain, and then from the AirTrain over to the JetBlue terminal. In addition, I remembered that I'd been impressed by the AirTrain's big picture windows—remembering, too, that often there's not much to see from them except the tops of cars, since much of the train's route runs along and directly above the median of the jam-packed, multilane Van Wyck Expressway.

Rereading the right side of this short list was like adding a Dolby stereo soundtrack to the flattened facts of memory. Now I remembered feelings, colors, moment-to-moment events, intimate details, but also things that had happened more than six feet beyond wherever I had been sitting or walking, and things that to this day are still only questions in my mind. The subway car had been so crowded with people heading home from Manhattan it seemed impossible for even one more standee to squeeze in. Yet one more had, a large man with a Bible in his hand. For fifteen minutes, while no one looked at him, and many raised their newspapers higher so they couldn't see him or dialed the volume on their iPods way up so they couldn't hear him, he preached loudly in Spanish about salvation and the world to come. Would he sleep well that night? What did he think he had been accomplishing?

The Jamaica AirTrain station is connected to the Long Island Rail Road's old headquarters station by a long, sleek steel-and-plate-glass corridor, whose only purpose is to be scurried through, since the platforms of the original station and the platforms of the new one are farther apart than passengers would like. But just as we reached this corridor, hurrying like everyone else, the setting midsummer sun, bright orange, had just lightly touched down on the line of rooftops across the street, and as we moved forward, the sun, as it does in such situations, seemed to change directions, shifting to the left now rather than descending, and in this way joining us and exactly matching our pace, rolling along at eye level, unhindered, as plump as a pumpkin, like a beach ball skimming along a swimming pool. This now movable sunset lasted the full length of the corridor, and came to rest only when we stopped in the AirTrain station itself, waiting for the next train to pull in. It was only then, in fact, that the sun seemed to resume setting and slowly disappeared from view. Are the angles of construction and the corridor's sight lines arranged so that this seems to happen only on long summer evenings? Had any of the terminal's designers ever noticed that they had incorporated this animated, kinetic reimagining of a Stonehenge sun celebration into their work?

Every seat on a JetBlue plane has a small TV screen in front of it. For some reason, though I hadn't selected it, there was a Bugs Bunny cartoon on the screen at my seat just at takeoff. As we roared down the runway, Bugs popped his head up out of a sand dune in the middle of the Sahara Desert, explaining that he had been tunneling in search of Miami Beach—"I knew I should've made that left turn in Albuquerque"—one of his celebrated and frequently repeated lines. I remembered that Chuck Jones, the director of many classic Bugs cartoons, had defined one of them as a "corner" picture—meaning that watching it was similar to "turning a corner in a strange city," where the next scene would "reveal new and enchanting vistas." Well, here was a travel question that comes up over and over again, although usually not at the precise moment when giant jet engines are accelerating down a mile-long runway in order to lift you thirty-five thousand feet above sea level: How much do we stand to lose or gain whenever we get deflected from some of our original purposes or destinations? Maybe the only answer to a question like this is to stay in touch with it over time—to roll along beside it, like a pumpkin on the rooftops, rather than expecting to hear an answer shouted at you in a language you know only a few words of. Also, we can keep track of the gains without too much trouble, since they're roughly equal to the sum total of the "original points," "second points," and "third points" of our traveling to-date.

One form of Deep Travel time is an entirely modern invention: jet lag. Before jet airliners began flying across the Atlantic Ocean, in 1958 (which also happened to be the same year that for the first time more people crossed the Atlantic in planes than on ocean liners), it was impossible for travelers moving east or west to "outrun the sun"—or, at any rate, to cross more than two time zones while still awake. (So this was also the moment, as has become even more clear in retrospect, when nineteenth-century railroad time, which gave rise to the idea of time zones, was superceded by twentieth-century airline time, which is no longer bound by them.) As we have since discovered, arriving somewhere at (let's say) sunset, local time, after only enough clock time has elapsed for it to be approaching lunchtime at the jumping-off point disrupts people's internally recording biological clocks, and often leads to headaches, to eating or digestion or sleep problems, and to changes in the way people feel. These changes, according to one online chart, manifest as "disorientation, grogginess, irritability, mild depression." Why is this? Neurobiologists at the University of Washington, according to a recent BBC News report, think this is because "we have two timekeeping centers in our brains—one sticks to the clock, the other is influenced by cues such as sunrise and nightfall." Problems arise when the two groups of brain cells devoted to the two clocks—they exist separately but are linked—start receiving contradictory information and no longer act in sync. Working together as they normally do, they seem to regulate the ordinary sequence of sleep states. The daylight-sensitive clock center coordinates the appearance and timing of non-dreaming deep sleep (or quiet sleep) periods that, it's now thought, counter the effects of physical fatigue, while the daylight-ignoring clock center seems keyed to the intervals of dreaming sleep (also called active sleep or REM—rapid eye movement—sleep), which usually follow deep sleep, and which have more complex uses and purposes.

Considering our origins, says Stephen LaBerge, the great exponent of lucid dreaming (in the book *Lucid Dreaming*, which summarizes his findings), you might logically expect to find two different sleep-related clocks in our brains, since quiet sleep emerged with the earliest mammals 180 million years ago and helped keep them inactive at night and safe from predators—a protective feature the reptiles who preceded them hadn't needed. As cold-blooded creatures dependent on the warmth of their surroundings, reptiles automatically slowed down whenever the sun set; nighttime itself was their sleep clock. Whereas active sleep developed 50 million years later, at a time when more advanced mammals first started bearing live young that were altogether helpless at birth. Active sleep and dreams, by helping stimulate the growth and refinement of their not yet fully formed nervous systems, were part of preparing these little ones to protect themselves from predators. For the next 130 million years, coordinating these two forms of sleep never needed to take into account the possibility that any mammals might someday need to protect themselves from the effects of too many time zones at any one time. But after simulating the light changes associated with a Paris–to–New York flight, according to Horacio de la Iglesia, one of the leaders of the University of Washington study, his team found that "REM sleep needed six to eight days to catch up with non-REM, or deep sleep." Or, in other words, it can take a week for your dreams to find you again and resume their proper place in the sleep sequence.

Many travel writers of our time leave jet lag out of their stories, treating it either as an occupational hazard, like malaria, or, as Pico Iyer suggests, in Jet Lagged, a holiday-time travel blog he wrote a few winters ago for *The New York Times,* as a distraction they can with practice learn to ignore or silence, like a public speaker handling a heckler. "Jet lag," Iyer says, "remains one of the great unmentionables of long-distance travel, as if not to speak of it is to help it go away." Iyer, on the other hand, not only acknowledges jet lag, he celebrates it—not surprisingly, perhaps, for a writer for whom the "first point" of travel is always to "slip through the curtain of the ordinary," as he says in one of his books, *Sun After Dark: Flights into the Foreign.* For Iyer, time in jet lag is a trip to "a deeply foreign country . . . more mysterious in its way than India or Morocco." Although Iyer doesn't quite say this, perhaps the "disorientation" reported by jet lag sufferers is itself a novel and adaptive emergency override response that, like Deep Travel, now kicks in when the mind, left without inner time certainty, abandons ordinary assumptions, filters, and self-censorship in order to find a new footing and balance point as quickly as possible. What Iyer does specifically say is that, when a traveler is jet-lagged, "something deeper is dissolved," and that he has come to realize that he can trust whatever he notices in this "nowhere state": "It's not quite a dream state, but it's certainly not wakefulness, and though it seems as if we're visiting another continent, there are no maps or guidebooks to this other world. There are not even any clocks."

Jet lag doesn't always show you what you want to see—which may help explain why "irritability" and "mild depression" are listed as symptoms. On the other hand, Iyer says, once you learn how to peer past the headaches, queasiness, and "grogginess," jet lag "can open up the world," furnishing a kind of unsought but prolonged "second point" to a trip: "I use the sleeplessness to try to see a world, a self, I would never see otherwise." Because *Sun After Dark* is, he says, devoted to "journeys that left me shaking in some way" (and because Iyer estimates that he spends about eight weeks a year jet-lagged), he sets out at some length what may be the first formal attempt to detail the effects that jet lag has on a person's thinking capacity. "I feel, when lagged," as he says, for instance, "as if I'm seeing the whole world through tears, or squinting; everything gets through to me, but with the wrong weight or meaning." Most memorable to me from this book is his description of a haunting jet-lag-aided discovery about modern America he made almost immediately after a nonstop flight across eight time zones from his home in rural Japan back to California for a visit with his mother:

> The next day, trying to pick up the pieces of my life, I go to the post office, the bank, and all I can see is a desperate loneliness in the faces in the California street; they seem plaintive, unclaimed somehow, as if they were issuing a cry for help. For someone who has just stepped off the plane from Japan, where people wear masks of cheerfulness as they go from one place to the next, it looks abject.
>
> The next day, though, I have begun to settle into the world around me; I hardly notice the lonely faces. Four, five days later, if you were to remind me of what I'd said before, I'd say: "What are you talking about? Everything's normal. These people are just the way they're supposed to be."

"TELL ME WHERE IT IS GONE"

*F*ading... The one drawback to Deep Travel that some people have pointed to is its impermanence. Because it's not a preset default position in the mind, it's not something you can count on being able to "return home to" every day, and even when it appears, it can be hard to hold on to and seems to slip away, following some schedule of its own. This dismay, perhaps not surprisingly, has been most poignantly presented by Thomas Mann, who, toward the end of his "Excursus on the Sense of Time" in *The Magic Mountain,* presents its disappearance as emblematic of his greater subject, the many acute and irreparable losses that everyone is condemned to endure over the course of a lifetime:

> The first few days in a new place have a youthful swing to them, a kind of sturdy, long stride—that lasts for about six to eight days. Then, to the extent that we "settle in," the gradual shortening becomes noticeable. Whoever clings to life, or better, wants to cling to life, may realize to his horror that the days have begun to grow light again and are scurrying past; and the last week—of, let us say, four—is uncanny in its fleeting transience. To be sure, this refreshment of our sense of time extends beyond the interlude; its effect is noticeable again when we return to our daily routine. The first few days at home after a change of scene are likewise experienced in a new, broad, more youthful fashion—but only a very few, for we are quicker to grow accustomed to the old rules than to their abrogation. And if our sense of time has grown weary with age or was never all that strongly developed—a sign of an inborn lack of

vitality—it very soon falls asleep again, and within twenty-four hours it is as if we were never gone and our journey were merely last night's dream.

Why would this be? According to an ancient short poem by the eighth-century Muslim scholar Hasan of Basra (Basra, the name of a city in southern Iraq, also means "seeing everything" in Arabic), the disappearance of something can be fully explained only by understanding its origins and purposes and how it operates—"seeing everything" by observing it from within a far longer present moment or Deep Now:

> *I saw a child carrying a light.*
> *I asked him where he had brought it from.*
> *He put it out, and said:*
> *"Now you tell me where it is gone."*

But maybe we can work backward, and start with the stark contrast between what Mann calls Deep Travel's "youthful swing" and the empty follow-up feeling that nothing really happened and that "we were never gone"—and that "everything's normal," as Iyer puts it. The first thing to recognize, I think, is that the question applies specifically only to "involuntary" or "naturally occurring" Deep Travel, the kind that just presents itself or steals over you, in contrast to deliberately invoked or freely chosen and therefore easily sustained and quickly renewed Deep Travel. (The two stand in roughly the same relationship to each other as the tie that unites ordinary dreaming and lucid dreaming, except that dreaming is of course an everyday activity, while unplanned, unexpected plunges into Deep Travel are far more infrequent. Also, the ability to change unaware traveling into "Lucid Deep Travel" seems to various people I've talked with to be much simpler to reach out for and contact than lucid dreaming and, once having been summoned, to last longer and to be more easily retrieved and resumed.) So we are talking here solely about the end or the tailing off of something that has appeared by chance, rather than by choice.

One person I felt it important to consult was Dana Raphael, a medical anthropologist, writer, and teacher, after hearing that years ago she had independently compressed Thomas Mann's "new place" insight into travel advice that seemed so urgent and unforgettable that one of her former students had to interrupt himself to tell it to me when I met him at a recent New York party. I happened to mention that I was writing about travel and time. The man now runs a public relations firm, and he can still recite almost word for word what Raphael told him more than twenty-five years ago, when he was about to leave America for the first time: "The first forty-eight hours in a place are so critical they're almost the only time you really have there." "The best warning I've ever been given," he told me. "It was seriously said, almost like a safety tip. She was telling me to guard my time in any new place every bit as carefully as my money or my watch." Raphael, when I called her at her Connecticut office, said that the "Two-Day Rule" was something she had herself gradually figured out and started to live by during many years of travel, much of it as the founder of a now-worldwide network of doula programs (so called after a Greek word for "woman of service"). These organizations pair families with women in a community who can "mother a new mother," first before and during birth and then throughout what Raphael sometimes refers to as the "tenth month of pregnancy."

Raphael says she looks forward to the first forty-eight hours in a place because this is the only period when she's almost compelled to notice things she's never seen before and, in many cases, finds herself totally unprepared for. "It's more than just a 'learning moment,'" she said, "because it's practically inescapable. All you have to do is leave your hotel room and you get the full impact of whatever's there. Well, maybe that's not entirely true for Americans, because it helps to be a bit quiet, and we talk so loudly, and have to say everything we're thinking as soon as we think it." Echoing Pico Iyer (and his sense of the need to "scribble and scribble and scribble" to "catch all the experiences and impressions and feelings" that flood through him as soon as he arrives somewhere), Raphael says that "to capture it, to fix it firmly, to keep it, you really want to write and write and write throughout the first forty-eight hours"—and then ideally, she thinks, not look again at what you've written until you get home, because these words are in effect a message from a place you are about to leave. Or at least are about to drift away from, and soon won't even quite recognize anymore. The writing, she finds, is a self-protective act, although with an unusual twist—as if she were a castaway and had an advance sense that she ought to seal a note in a bottle and throw it into the sea just before getting picked up by a passing ship and being reunited with friendly faces, realizing that otherwise she would be "rescued" from her own innermost thoughts and might never find her way back to them again.

"Inevitably," Raphael says, "after a couple of days, or even sooner, someone is going to, as they think, throw you a lifeline. Maybe by showing you how to do something the way it's done by people in that community—some simple little action, some sort of reaching out—and at that point you start to feel welcomed and included, even if only provisionally. Or you will see people assuming roles that are familiar to you from any other group—with some who are angry, while others are helpful, and still others stay aloof—and then they take form as recognizable individuals, and once they're not so mysterious, you're more comfortable." While you're still in overdrive, the condition, as she says, of the first two days, one part of you is reaching out for the wholly unknown (and this is what you write down), but another part of you is already eagerly searching for the familiar, even if that means pieces of the unknown that begin to reappear or repeat themselves and thereby become more predictable. "The result of that," she says,

is that once you get used to certain things, you start taking them for granted. And you no longer notice them. Some of this return to a more normal condition of avoiding available information is probably good for you and keeps you from being overwhelmed—if you no longer smell the incense in the marketplace, you can also walk through India without being devastated by the sight of the beggar children. It's possible that this very withdrawal of interest is part of a long-term survival mechanism; we've moved around as a species so often since we left Africa, many of us may need this kind of protection or cloak so that we can keep moving on when necessary. At any rate, after the first two days in a place have passed, and noticing is no longer purely automatic anymore, then the next phase of a journey has begun. And at that point it's up to you to take the process over, and to start to think carefully about what it is that's going on around you that you want to try to keep alive to, and what on the other hand you may want to dissociate from.

The implication here is that Deep Travel's function is to feed or soothe or help reorient a specific part of the mind, an embedded set of skills sometimes called our "social intelligence," in an attempt to group together into a single concept all the many abilities we have that let us function as part of various ongoing groups. The term was first coined in 1976 by Nicholas Humphrey, a British evolutionary psychologist, who suggested that, for instance, an innate capacity to predict the behavior of others—a talent so hugely important for maintaining any kind of social cohesion that it's also referred to as "Machiavellian intelligence"—might well have emerged as long as 10 million years ago among the higher primates who lived in groups and bands and families in the African forests. (According to subsequent thinking in evolutionary psychology, modern humans come preequipped with a variety of "specialized mentalities"—or, in the field's jargon, "multiple, content-rich, domain-specific mental modules.")

A truly early date can be pointed to for social intelligence because there are strong signs of a similar capacity among contemporary great apes (detailed, for example, in *Chimpanzee Politics: Power and Sex Among Apes,* a book written after a six-year study of bluffs, reconciliations, power grabs, and coalition building within the world's largest captive chimpanzee population, in the Arnhem Zoo, in the Netherlands, by the Dutch primatologist Frans de Waal). It's also thought that all four of today's surviving hominid (or "humanlike") species—gorillas, chimpanzees, bonobos, and humans—began to diverge from a common, and presumably already socially intelligent, ancestor about eight million years ago. Since then, Humphrey suggests, this ancient thinking capacity has proved so continuously useful that it was selected for and retained by any number of in-between species before ultimately becoming the common inheritance of both humanity and our three fellow hominids.

So Dana Raphael's Two-Day Rule could be a way of taking note of a process in which a part of the mind—the various talents and traits that, taken collectively, constitute our social intelligence—finds itself temporarily overwhelmed or out of its depth and no longer able to evaluate the information being received, and as a result moves into overdrive and turns for assistance to the larger awareness of Deep Travel as a way of casting a far wider net. Going on "full alert" would mean opening all the floodgates of perception and overriding blocks regulating every internal "intake valve" until something familiar appears and normal operations can be resumed.

Or maybe another drive that's closely associated with social intelligence, the ebb and flow of a more personal desire to get and give and exchange attention from and to and with other people, is at work in some Deep Travel situations, commandeering and deploying a larger awareness and then withdrawing from it when attention demands, the equivalent of a daily meal, have been met. In an essay on this aspect of attention theory by Idries Shah, "Characteristics of Attention and Observation," he suggests that "attention-hunger" is awakened in infancy and immediately gets connected to the need to be fed and protected but often remains unrecognized and undifferentiated from other demands, with the result, he says, that even as grown-ups most people frequently, if unnecessarily, find themselves "attention-deprived." "This is one reason," Shah reports, "why new friends, or circumstances, for instance, may be preferred to old ones." The glow of Deep Travel can quickly fade once someone is no longer "attention-starved"—the way food starts to look ordinary again, or even distasteful, after the conclusion of a feast.

An entirely different set of interior forces—or mental modules, if you like—whose focus is the "search for a stable geography," as I sometimes think of it, could also be pulling us away from Deep Travel. Animals, in general, are travelers (motion is at the heart of a number of the root words for "animal," such as the Greek *anemos,* or "wind"). Only a very few animals, like barnacles, are limited by the fixed immobility that we associate with plants, a condition biologists call "sessility," which means "fitted for sitting." "Motility," or spontaneous motion, the opposite of sessility, confers innumerable benefits: it takes animals to feeding grounds, to breeding grounds, to safe havens, and to many other places.

But it has a cost: it uses energy. Some early marine animals, maybe half a billion and maybe as much as a billion years ago—no one is yet quite sure of the dating—initially solved this problem by letting the ocean currents decide where they would end up. But passive drift makes finding food (new energy) and safety a matter of mere chance, and over the hundreds of millions of years since then, more recent and more complex animals have devised a series of movement strategies that, by automatically guiding and shaping their many travels, convey yet another advantage: letting any animal stay concentrated on the urgent purposes of each trip, such as spotting a meal while avoiding becoming one. Since animals' independent, self-propelled motion has been connected almost from the start with staying alive, and since animals began to move around long before they became sociable, these inward and self-protective "guidance traits" are probably one of the most fundamental underpinnings of an animal's mental capacities.

Over the eons, as these inner traits, or "movement mini-minds," as they might be called, have coevolved in collaboration with a wealth of new outward, body-changing, physical "guidance equipment," like fins and feet and feathers, and while animals in consequence have spread across the world, the story of animal movements has become almost inexplicably intricate and varied, since they now encompass an earthworm's inchings, day-to-day forays by both predators and prey, and seasonal migrations that take some species vast distances every year. Millions of sooty shearwaters, for example, grayish brown-and-white oceanic birds with a three-and-a-half-foot wingspan, leave islands off New Zealand each summer on zigzagging and often figure-eight trips that take them across the entire Pacific Basin. (Keep in mind that the Pacific is the world's largest ocean, bigger than the landmass of all the continents put together.) The shearwaters first head east across the southern Pacific to near Chile, then travel north and west to one of several northern Pacific feeding grounds (some choose a gigantic zone east of Japan; others prefer either a smaller area near Alaska or a medium-sized one off the coast of California), before returning home in late autumn, after two hundred days of traveling and feeding that—round-trip—add up to almost forty thousand miles of flying.

A great deal of information about long-distance animal movements has only recently become available. The flight paths of the shearwaters, for instance, were not discovered until 2005, after the advent of a new and sufficiently tiny generation of miniaturized transmitters, tags, and data recorders. The endurance and the acrobatics of these epic annual journeys are dazzling (the tags on the shearwaters also showed that they can dive two hundred feet down into the ocean when hunting for fish or squid) and are made even more compelling by the fact that we're only now getting to know about them, filling in a picture that had always been obscure for us, of things that happen away from our own pathways, particularly those that take place at sea, over the horizon and far beyond the land's edge. British biologists, for instance, working in South Georgia, a remote subantarctic island in the South Atlantic

Ocean, east of Tierra del Fuego, have tagged gray-headed albatrosses, oceangoing birds much larger than shearwaters, to find where they mysteriously disappear to for up to eighteen months between breeding seasons. Their discovery: some of the albatrosses spend this time flying twice around the globe. A French ornithologist, Henri Weimerskirch, working almost simultaneously from the Crozet Islands, an even more remote subantarctic archipelago in the Indian Ocean southeast of Africa, a breeding ground for wandering albatrosses, seabirds with wingspans of up to eleven and a half feet, has "pierced the veil of obscurity," as he's written, "and tracked albatrosses on their amazing foraging journeys." During a single food-gathering trip of ten to fifteen days, Weimerskirch reported in a 2004 article for *Natural History* magazine, "the birds flew more than 1,800 miles from their nests and covered as much as 9,300 miles"—"as if," he says, trying to put his discovery into a more recognizable perspective, "birds nesting in New York City flew to the shores of Italy to forage and then returned to their nests."

Migrations in general—to give the whole phenomenon a bit more context—can be marveled at as pulses of animal movement tracing a series of ever-renewed "life tracks," as zoologists call them, above and through oceans and across continents. Most humpback whales, for example—animals that weigh eighty thousand pounds apiece—swim ten thousand miles a year from the equator to the Arctic Circle and back; and each October, at the outset of the most celebrated migration of all, Africa's spectacular cataract of mammals, two million wildebeests, zebras, gazelles, and other grass-eating animals, march south across the Serengeti Plain in Tanzania and Kenya. Migrations, it now appears, are an ancient and still useful food-gathering device that can be traced back to the initial appearance of flying insects—species that resembled today's dragonflies and damselflies—some 350 million years ago. The strategy, first put into play by these insects, is based on "flying to stay in the same place," as is sometimes said, which means following the rainfall and the seasons as they shift position so that a familiar and abundant food supply is always within reach. Adapting by moving on. (Dragonflies still make prodigious journeys. It has only just been discovered that clouds of modern globe skimmer dragonflies—yellow, thin-winged insects also known as wandering gliders—leave India each year after the monsoons and fly across the open Indian Ocean, reaching eastern Africa in time for the rainy season there, before returning to India. It's a round-trip of over eleven thousand miles, more than twice as long as the annual American migration of monarch butterflies from southern Canada to Mexico and back.)

But, widening the context yet again, these epic and age-old exploits can be looked at another way as well: from below and beforehand, so to speak, instead of from above and after the fact. They can thus be celebrated as extraordinary elaborations of an even more impressive, older, and (to-date, at least) permanently successful accomplishment— namely, a steadily available ability lodged in motile animals and passed on to their descendants that lets them, while in motion, keep track of where they are in at least some minimal way and use this information as a constantly moving point along a connected thread that links them both back to where they've come from and ahead to where they're going. It's an ability that they (and we, among them) take for granted, and indeed that's its whole point—by operating automatically, it allows them to focus more intently on what they're searching for. In its most glittering and extravagant form it guides wildebeests and whales year after year, but it also functions moment to moment and day by day, for short forays and small errands.

Such navigating is a matter of finding fixed points amid the flux. We don't yet know enough about how it's done—we can't say, for example, which aspects of the Pacific Ocean shearwaters find reliable enough to depend on during their flights, though there's speculation that they may be responding to large-scale wind currents, such as the trade winds and the prevailing westerlies. We have learned a great deal about the extraordinarily varied array of environmental components, or affordances, that successive waves of species have found it possible to respond to and rely on: some animals take their cues from the place of the sun, the moon, or the stars in the sky or from the angle of the light; some from air or water currents; and others from scents (salmon, after years at sea, can smell their spawning grounds when they get near, and green turtles nearing Ascension Island begin "sniffing the air" while still more than thirty miles from land). Still other species seem able to respond to the earth's magnetic fields; marine biologists at the University of North Carolina at Chapel Hill, for instance, theorize that some baby sea turtles can imprint on "the unique 'magnetic address' of their birthplace," enabling them to return home years later.

So sensory information—much of it from senses that people are not gifted with and have no experience of—seems to be the foundation stone across the animal kingdom for any creature's "reliable geography," the ability, that is, to anchor movement to durable features of the environment you can count on and not have to think about as you move through them. We now know a substantial amount about how these disparate reference points get mortared together within various animal minds to construct flexible "guidance traits" that will be retained from generation to generation, as well. Recent university-led "spatial cognition" and "way-finding" studies have both picked apart the workings of these travel strategies and shown that many of them appear in human beings as well. Two-year-old children being observed by Elizabeth Spelke, a cognitive psychologist now at Harvard, rely solely on "contour navigation," as it's called, when moving through a room and looking for an object that has been hidden from them, meaning that they use only the shape of the walls to tell them where they are and how to go, and ignore any other feature that might catch the eye of a grown-up, such as the color of the walls or the placement of any objects around the room. This is the very same technique, according to a comprehensive *New York Times* Science Times report by Natalie Angier on way finding and Spelke's work, that rodents (such as rats and hamsters) rely on when seeking food rewards placed inside a box. Perhaps contour navigation is the first navigation strategy to emerge in people because it combines two senses, the tactile and the visual, thus providing built-in backup information to children still somewhat unsteady on their feet.

Later in childhood, as Angier discusses in her article, we awaken to other movement behaviors that are even more widespread throughout the animal kingdom—most notably "piloting," which is used when a final destination is hidden at the outset. It's a way of breaking a trip down into a sequence of achievable steps, each one of which has certainty preattached to it, and does this by setting up a series of intermediate goal posts that can't be lost sight of. Piloting requires someone to steer first toward a prominent landmark located part of the way along a route, and then, having reached it, to aim either for another memorable feature of the terrain in the farther distance or for the end point itself, if it has by now swung into view. Just as walking, when mastered, becomes a secure means of locomotion—even though, as motion experts have pointed out, it's actually a form of "controlled falling" (since one foot is always off the ground)—piloting may be a logical development from contour navigation that people get comfortable with at a point when they're ready to abandon the security of following a physical wall and substitute for that a "virtual wall" composed of otherwise disconnected landscape features they themselves choose and link together into a reliable chain. At any rate, piloting knowledge, as someone gets to know a place, seems to proceed from zero-dimensional to one-dimensional to two-dimensional understanding—or in spatial cognition terms, it moves from landmark knowledge (singling out recognizable points: a tower, a hill, a central square) to route knowledge (stringing enough points together to form a retraceable path) to survey knowledge (gathering enough separate but intersecting paths to create a remembered layout, otherwise known as an internalized, or cognitive, map). At this stage, people feel free to cut across known paths to take shortcuts. Or we could say that certainty about where we are begins as a single spark or lamp, becomes a beam of light, and encompasses finally a constellation of floodlights that illumines a whole area.

Full certainty isn't always possible when one is under way. Angier mentions that "path integration," also known as dead reckoning, another guidance system shared by humans and many other animals (including, for instance, desert ants), often comes into play on such occasions—out on open water, say, at those moments when both the harbor being aimed at is still invisible and there are no detectable landmarks between a boat and its next mooring, and no sun or stars to steer by. In such a situation, the immediate past is all you have to go by, and you move forward with only a memory of certainty, proceeding under the reasonable assumption that your speed and direction and the distance you're covering are an approximate continuation of the course that was set at your last known bearing. (Ants, it's thought, do this by somehow "counting their steps.")

Furthermore, adding yet another layer of complexity to the story of human moving around, our species, in addition to incorporating several dependable navigational methods that originated in other animals, seems to have added on early in our own development some deep-seated travel preferences that are unique to us. Interestingly, their main purpose seems to be to provide us with a doubt suppressor. That is, they reinforce a feeling of certainty without necessarily making the process of way finding any more accurate. "For example," as Angier writes in her way finding report after interviewing Reginald Golledge, a cognitive geographer at the University of California at Santa Barbara who has collected much of this information, "people like to head off in the direction of their destination. If their endpoint is east, they hate to start off by going west, even when an initial jog westward may deliver them to a more efficient route. Another preferred strategy is called 'longest leg first.' When conceptualizing a route, Dr. Golledge said, people try to start off going the longest and straightest distance possible before making the first turn.' "

German cognitive psychologists have studied still another human travel preference: if a choice of directions unexpectedly presents itself, we generally prefer to take a path leading off to the right. Reading about these superimposed preferences, I began to see them as a kind of backup device or navigational substrategy specifically designed to strengthen the urge to get going, to keep going, and to pause as seldom as possible along the way. To the extent that these preferences work at all, they would have the effect of shortening a journey. Wondering if this interpretation would make sense to Golledge—I'd noticed that his Web site mentions his "longtime interest in finding the primitives on which spatial understanding is based"—I called him at his office, and got a qualified yes. "We don't actually know," he said, "if these impulses are innate. We do know that people aren't conscious of them, and that they nevertheless pop up often as part of people's travel behavior—most notably, that desire to start off by facing your destination, which appears time and time and time again. If the preferences do date back to cultural prehistory, then most probably they were part of an effort to find the shortest way home. Taking the longest, or most direct, part of a trip first, and only after that making a more local search or course correction, once you've reached somewhat more familiar surroundings, might often serve this purpose well. The internalized instruction could've been something as simple as 'First head for the hills.' "

What does all this have to do with Deep Travel and its appearance or disappearance within us? Since the question's only just come up, there's no direct evidence as yet from any dedicated research studies. But remember what Thomas Mann said about the foreshortening of Deep Travel time: that it begins to falter only to the extent that we "settle in" to a new place, after six to eight days of exploration. (Which is approximately the amount of time it takes to find a basic set of land-marks, rough out a few paths to places worth returning to, and get at least a sketchy sense of the whole. Isn't that what "settling in" means?) Remember, too, that the fundamental "cost" of animal motility—the need to find new food before existing energy supplies have run out—places an inherent time limit on all travel, and makes urgency every bit as much as efficiency and safety one of the preconditions for any suc-cessful guidance trait that might be operating in us. Keep in mind as well that additional human travel preferences, however odd they may seem, may, if they are in fact inborn, have arisen as an attempt to shave a few more minutes off any journey home.

To me what all this suggests is that the "worst" thing that can happen—from the point of view of any inherited travel strategy—is to lose touch with where you are; with where you're going; or with the path in between, the route from "here" to "there." The worst, thus, includes those moments when geography itself has become unstable, unreliable, and seems to have forsaken you. When there are no identi-fiable landmarks and no discernible paths or beckoning guide ways, when no encompassing, explanatory map is available. When certainty is no more, when abidingness has moved away, leaving seemingly no trace behind. When, quite literally, you don't know which way to turn. Or when, more succinctly, you're lost. "The uncertainty of being 'lost,' " as Golledge writes in one of his books, *Wayfinding Behavior: Cognitive Mapping and Other Spatial Processes,* is the state that "occurs when the way-finding process being used to guide travel fails in some way."

This is the deep distress, made even more urgent by near starvation, that to me lies at the heart of one of the world's best-loved folktales, known in the German version collected in the early nineteenth century by the Brothers Grimm as "Hänsel and Gretel." Although this tale about two children lost in the woods became, like many other fairy sto-ries, the subject of intense psychological scrutiny some years ago—Bruno Bettelheim, for instance, in *The Uses of Enchantment: The Meaning and Importance of Fairy Tales,* sees it as a narrative based on the fear of abandonment—after my talk with Golledge it occurred to me to reread the story, which I had of course grown up on. I found that it offers con-siderably different and unexpected insights if approached as a classic of way-finding literature. Viewed as a representative of this genre—a cat-egory that, frankly, had never before defined itself for me, and that I now think of as a specialized branch of travel writing—the story becomes almost a primer about losing your way and then finding it again. If this is the practical impulse the story stems from—if, that is, it originally sprang into being sometime during the early days of human storytelling (and no one knows exactly how old it is) as a way of recording and sending forward some of the conscious understanding by then available about how navigational skills work and the critical importance of keeping them in good repair—we might have at least part of an explanation for the story's ongoing ability to speak to people who live far away from the German forest, in remarkably different circumstances.

Maybe way finding, like the fear of abandonment, is only one element in the continuing power of "Hänsel and Gretel"—since stories from the oral tradition, as Idries Shah points out in the introduction of his own collection of them, *World Tales: The Extraordinary Coincidence of Stories Told in All Times, in All Places,* have "an almost uncanny persistence and durability." They live on "when nations, languages, and faiths have long since died," an ability that, he says, "cannot be accounted for in the present state of knowledge." Without claiming to have exhausted the meaning of "Hänsel and Gretel," what we can say is that the great calamity at the heart of the story is the complete disappearance of the stable geography that all motile animals rely on to lead them to food and their other needs. The story focuses on a couple of imperatives: Don't get lost. If you do, don't stay lost.

Famine is the setting of the tale, and it's in order to save food that the wicked stepmother, who wants the children dead, cleverly plots to conceal her crime. Rather than simply killing them, she will strip Hänsel and Gretel of their navigational skills so that they will be unable to find their way to food and shelter. The first time she abandons the children in the forest, they get home safely again that same night, because Hänsel's emergency piloting system works perfectly—he has quietly left white pebbles at intervals along the way, which after dark "shone like newly-coined silver pieces in the moonlight." The second time, this strategy is thwarted—Hänsel is only able to scatter bread crumbs behind them, because the stepmother locked both of them inside the previous night, cutting off their access to the pebbles out in the front yard. It is his makeshift, secondary strategy that fails; the new trail, as everyone who knows the story remembers, is edible,

not indelible. The carefully placed markers, which might, like the pebbles, have been visible by moonlight, are equally visible by day and vanish because "the many thousands of birds which fly about in the woods
and fields had pecked them all up."

Even without the bread crumbs to guide them, Hänsel, according to
the Brothers Grimm's first edition of the story (D. L. Ashliman, a folk-
lore researcher, has posted comparative versions on the Web),
"thought that he would still be able to find the way home, but they
soon became lost in the great wilderness." Only when they are truly
lost, and forced first to pause and then to wander aimlessly, does the
forest, their homeland, become a great wilderness—an unreadable
landscape. Even though they're still less than a day's walk from home,
the children, without a sense of direction, have suddenly become vulnerable and defenseless. They soon fall prey to the old witch, who, as
we learn, has specifically built her bread house ("gingerbread," it turns
out, is a later interpolation) to lure lost children. Interestingly, she at
first gains power over them by pretending to be kind (in this way trick-
ing their social intelligence, we might say, a faculty that itself, the story
seems to be telling us, becomes less trustworthy when we are lost and
maybe even gets swamped by the urgency of such a calamity). It takes a
month for the imprisoned children to outsmart her—partly by themselves feeding her false information (each day Hänsel lets her feel a
small bone instead of his own finger, so she'll think she's been unable to
fatten him up). Afterward, they are shown the way home by a white
bird—a dove in some variants, a duck in others.

This white duck or duckling, described as a "good animal," makes
only a brief appearance in the story (and only in the final Grimms' version, at that). It can carry them across a wide lake if they ask it to, but
only, as Gretel realizes, one at a time. (On the way home, she's the more
creative and discerning reader of the landscape's affordances.) One
message embedded here may be that in extreme situations we need all
our wits about us to regain our bearings (which in this case means
pooling the awareness and the inventiveness belonging to both brother
and sister). What would you do if you were facing an unfordable,
unswimmable, unbridgeable lake that had to be crossed? The story has
a suggestion: if disorientation ever brings travel to such a standstill that
moving forward, retreating, and even detouring around an obstacle
have all become impossible, the best recourse—and maybe the ultimate

fail-safe mechanism—is to reevoke the mind's "larger awareness." So all senses can scan for previously undetectable or overlooked or discarded or not easily categorized signposts, or for the information that with practice we can develop into brand-new and perhaps more reliable and versatile guidance systems.

This sudden reemergence within travelers of their more extensive awareness is actually a familiar enough sight, though generally it lasts no more than a few seconds and thus gets easily missed by onlookers. We see it when tourists freeze on a street corner, if their guidebooks have run out of hints about what to do next. We see it in ourselves when we park a car on an unknown street or get off a bus at an unfamiliar stop, and have to pause and look around. In the uncertainty, and without our consciously invoking it, Deep Travel kicks in, and for a moment, at any rate, everything we see or hear has to be noticed and evaluated because it just might be the one thing we came for. Then we spot what we knew we were looking for, and the "first point" of our trip reasserts itself. So unless we intervene to prolong the interval, awareness narrows or shrinks again or withdraws itself, having accomplished the limited, fail-safe, jump-start purpose for which it was summoned.

This is not to say that Deep Travel has no further role in way finding. A prime example of what it can spectacularly accomplish would have to be the age-old piloting skills of the Polynesian navigators. Between about A.D. 300 and 1000, at a time when European sailors out on open water were still dependent on dead reckoning or kept an eye on shorelines that would allow them to use contour navigation, these explorers led settlers east across the Pacific Ocean to a thousand or more islands spread thousands of miles apart, including Hawaii and Easter Island, crossing the seemingly featureless seas without instruments in oceangoing canoes. It took years to become a *palu,* an accredited navigator who could "read the ocean" after learning multiple techniques for tracking stars' paths, the ocean's swells, birds' flights, and clouds' reflections, among other subtly repeating patterns. European explorers, when they eventually reached these same islands in the eighteenth century, at first refused to believe that such awareness-derived seafaring techniques were even possible, and assumed that the Polynesians' ancestors had originally made landfall only by being blown off course or by drifting helplessly. The traditional skills, however, outlived the doubters. Now they not only survive among a few

Polynesian practitioners but in recent decades have earned the respect of a wide international audience, thanks in large part to the fact that one of the handful of post–World War II apprentices of the craft was a New Zealand doctor, adventurer, and author named David H. Lewis. In 1972 he wrote a book about what he'd learned, *We the Navigators: The Ancient Art of Landfinding in the Pacific,* which remains in print nearly forty years later.

Within twenty-four hours" of the end of a vacation—according to Thomas Mann's lament—"it is as if we were never gone and our journey were merely last night's dream." There's a passage with much the same thought in Robert Ornstein's *On the Experience of Time:* "When one leaves a familiar situation and goes away for a while (as in leaving the office routine and going on vacation), when he is about to return it seems as if he had been away for a 'long' time. Yet, on return (to the office) it suddenly seems not to have been 'long' at all. Duration collapses. If you have ever had this type of experience you will know that it is a striking one."

It's a sample of what he calls an "after-interval experience"—meaning what you're left with when something is over. Ornstein explains the long-into-short discrepancy using information-theory terms—the "central metaphor" of his book, as he says, sets up an analogy between the way the mind files memories and the storage techniques that get built into a computer, thus making the extra space a computer needs for information a not easily labeled equivalent to the greater-duration "space" or "size" or "length" the mind creates for displaying things it notices but can't easily categorize. (In my own more basic, preelectronic metaphor, I've likened the extended time Deep Travel provides to a table top that expands to include a leaf.) But maybe there's a hidden image here as well, one that again links Deep Travel to way finding, only in this case to a kind of shadow, just-in-case, automatic mental monitoring of events thoughout a journey. During a trip, Ornstein suggests, "when one is involved in an experience, one codes it complexly and notes all sorts of possible outcomes." But "when the experience is over (when one returns to the office) the whole (vacation) interval becomes coded, chunked over. One remembers, 'We went on vacation,' instead of 'We had a fire, and then went to the beach and . . .' "

Until you've successfully arrived home, in other words, your mind is tracking everything that's happening because it just might prove useful should something unexpected come up that would require you to find an alternate way home. But once you're home again, all this information gathered en route becomes extraneous and can be recoded into a single space-saving "No Longer Necessary" or "For Vacations Only" file. (Or, reverting to my more elementary image, it's information that at that point gets swept off the table top and into one or two desk drawers.) The implication here is that, as far as the workings of this mental mechanism are concerned, the only real point of any "third point" insights that someone may have picked up while traveling is to serve as a kind of security guard escorting a trip's "first point"—a force that gets dismissed, disbanded, or dissolved at the end of a journey. The result is that all the new knowings that have been carefully collected get—what? Discarded, shredded, erased? Or is it that, having been refiled, they're still there, somewhere, but harder to come back to, and not nearly as close as something that's hovering on the tip of one's tongue?

This, to me, is the question and the fear at the heart of the "after-interval" problem: How retrievable are the delights and learnings of Deep Travel? In retrospect, what's still available? It's a different kind of being lost—in this case, the apprehension isn't that you'll never reach a goal; it's that, having reached it, you're not sure if you'll be allowed to hold on to it. How many, if any, of the noticings that unlocked so many understandings can be brought back into the front of the mind, and under what conditions? What's the "open sesame" that makes this happen? Is this a "domain specific" kind of situation, with each kind of awareness having its own memory and retrieval system? Has what's happened to us in Deep Travel been folded away, and is it temporarily trapped like something inside a rolled-up rug? Is it still at work within us, even when we can't remember it? Would the whole atmosphere of the original occasion have to be unrolled or reevoked or somehow reinflated before we could pick out and reclaim a single item?

I'd say the situation is actually a workable one—but that confusion and apprehension at first are almost inevitable, because we grow up knowing about only one change in our condition where everything being presented to our senses is swept away in a single instant. It happens every morning when we wake up. So naturally we would tend to assume that there's some sort of commonality between Deep Travel and dreaming—and by the same token we would find ourselves wondering whether what happens in Deep Travel is "even real." This is certainly the dismay that haunts Mann: maybe his journey never really happened, at least in terms of any lasting traces it might have left on his life.

According to Stephen LaBerge's short history of sleep, in his book *Lucid Dreaming*, and how it has developed through the many stages of animal life, when mammals initiated the act of dreaming fifty million years ago, this new talent arrived unaccompanied by any built-in, automatic "dream capture" module—an absence that by itself serves as an protective device. Indeed, LaBarge goes further and suggests we're far more likely to have instead incorporated one or more "dream-delete" buttons:

> Animals have no way to tell each other how to distinguish dreams from reality.... Thus, dream recall would seem to be a bad thing for cats, dogs, and all the rest of the mammalian dreamers except humans. This could explain why dreams are difficult to recall.... We and our ancestors might have been protected from dangerous confusion by the evolution of mechanisms that made forgetting dreams the normal course of affairs.

The idea that human dreams form only to vanish is itself an ancient one, perhaps best captured in lines from the much loved early-eighteenth-century Protestant hymn, "O God, Our Help in Ages Past," by Isaac Watts, in a verse that links dreams to the unrecapturable flight of time's arrow:

> *Time, like an ever rolling stream*
> *Bears all its sons away;*
> *They fly, forgotten, as a dream*
> *Dies at the opening day.*

Yet we've all had the experience that, while dreams can't be recaptured by grabbing at them, they will sometimes reappear—of their own volition, it would seem—at various relaxed moments, like a bird that keeps its distance but may, if you're patient, come and perch on your outstretched hand. This in itself would indicate that dreams don't melt away after all, but simply go into hiding at some undisclosed location. I've also noticed that sometimes there's a logic to the sudden, flashing resurgence of a dream: they return as abruptly as they withdraw and, by the way, present themselves a second time complete with visuals and sound, rather than as just a thought or some words in the mind. I'll be walking up a staircase, say, and while doing so remember a dream about climbing a never-ending set of stairs. Maybe the dream was recent, but not necessarily. If they can be retriggered this way, the question then becomes, Where were they filed, and can we begin to construct and then keep handy a list of the file names the mind immediately turns to? (In my case, for instance, what was I being reminded of: Things that happen when you climb? Or the feelings associated with an endless task?)

We also all know that with practice we can train ourselves to remember dreams, or pieces of them, consciously—a process that usually involves writing down a title for a dream or one or two details from it as soon as we get up. Which is our way of adding a second set of tags to them, a recall device that gives us quicker access and is less easily misplaced.

Just knowing that dreams stay with us and that they can be retrieved, however imperfectly, suggests that if Deep Travel and dreaming do have affinities, maybe they're positive ones. We've already seen that "third-point note taking"—jotting down notes at the time about small and unexpected Deep Travel events, like my short trip to Kennedy Airport, in New York—has the same effect later on in jogging the mind that giving a dream a written title does. Like dreams, Deep Travel events, whenever I bring them back to mind, return as a whole, so that now when I start thinking again about that subway ride during which we were preached at, I'm also reimmersed once more in everything else that was happening that afternoon: how crowded and overheated the train was, and how the subway car kept jouncing, and the way its brakes had what sounded like an extra screech. The completeness of Deep Travel memories makes them "whole sensorium" traces, which might suggest either that they're housed in some "special collection area" or that they're not stored in any single internal organizing system but have been distributed across several different categories of retained events, including "Unfinished Business." This, in turn, could help

explain why they're not necessarily instantly on call at all times, unlike
memories with fewer ambiguities and more defined edges or "sharper
corners," so to speak, facts and images that can be paged through a
broad-gauge, omnibus mental finding aid—and will pop up in profusion simply by saying to oneself something like, "Everything about
Mystic, Connecticut, please."

We also know that even if former Deep Travel events are locked
away in some kind of separate library or specialized card catalog, we
have a passkey that gets us at least into the building, and can reenter it
at will through any one of several doors. Meaning that if access to Deep
Travel understandings is in some way linked to resuming a state of
Deep Travel, we can get there by crossing the "wonder bridge"
(remembering to wonder again about what lies just beyond what we
think we know). Or by invoking the "Warsaw Induction" (remembering to ask ourselves what we would think about anything right in front
of us if we had never seen it before). Or by reinvoking a Deep Travel
extended present—and remembering that in this context things that
once happened are still happening, in the sense that even now they're
still waiting for an explanation.

Not that even this leads to any surefire search procedures, even
though redonning the cloak of Deep Travel is a lot easier than trying to
recapture a dream fragment by falling back asleep—since that may
mean passing first through the strange, flickering, fleeting visions conjured up by the transitional, semisleep condition of *hypnagogia* (Greek
for "leading in to sleep"), which occurs at the very edge of wakefulness,
and then perhaps a renewed period of quiet sleep. When active sleep
resumes, new dreams crowd in, so generally only a lucid dream would
give us any chance of revisiting a former dream. But, as I say, returning
to Deep Travel is only a first step. Once we're there, overly broad categories, whether conceptual or geographical, are—I've found—still not
much help. Saying, "Transformations" to myself, for instance, doesn't
bring up much, nor does "Summer in Vermont or New Hampshire,"
despite many years of such summers. "Fog" and "Chill" are less vague—
but not any more evocative. On the other hand, playing with these last
two and combining them into "Sudden fog and chill" puts me on board
a rackety wooden railroad car, huddled next to my family for support
while we chug and rumble barely at walking speed up the steeply
inclined Mount Washington Cog Railway. This mid-Victorian con-

traption, which has been ascending the highest mountain in the northeastern United States since 1869, had already wreathed us in curls of sweet and sooty coal smoke when, above the tree line but just below the summit, out of a seemingly sunny sky a dark band of cold fog wrapped itself in a single instant around the entire train and we couldn't see either the track in front of us or the engine puffing away behind us. For the next ten minutes we could have been heading anywhere at all, or nowhere.

On the other hand, sometimes being specific brings precise, if unpredictable, results. "Fireflies," for example, calls up a short July evening walk I haven't thought about in years, one that took me through the Arthur Ross Pinetum in Central Park, in New York, a playground and picnic area surrounded by fifteen species of pine trees. This always quiet and shaded, rather closed-in piece of the park is particularly empty and still after dark, when the little kids who use it have gone home. But they should have run back to the park that night, because it was incandescent with the cool, greenish-yellowish flickerings and swoopings through the lower air of thousands of fireflies, opening deep vistas into what had a moment before looked like impenetrable woods, covering the picnic tables with shimmering strings of miniature lanterns, and turning all the smaller pines into living Christmas trees. Christmas in July!

Perhaps our larger awareness arises and recedes frequently, as part of a self-regulating (or deliberately induced) effort by the mind to reduce its own exhaustion—rather than just being an occasional visitor, a seldom-encountered point of view that ordinarily hovers somewhere on a standby basis, or can be quickly reassembled, subject to its being summoned in an emergency as . . . what? A technician of some sort—a rewirer, a pilot, a salvage expert? A kind of special capacity that can solve or soothe or cure or move beyond a crisis or an obstacle or a disconnect in the functioning of, say, our social intelligence or our spatial cognition? Some recent work by Rachel and Stephen Kaplan, married researchers who have spent decades collaborating on environmental psychology investigations at the University of Michigan, puts forward the idea that we periodically move between "two kinds of attention" and that we need to because "directed attention"—their term for the narrowly focused, shut-the-world-out awareness that is so familiar to all of us and that we rely on for close concentration—is "fragile" in the sense that it is effortful to use and as a result can tire out before the body does. In its impaired state, "directed attention" imposes "pervasive costs" that "undermine an individual's competence in many ways," leading to a condition the Kaplans call "Directed Attention Fatigue," or DAF, and consider widespread. A 2002 paper by Stephen Kaplan, "Some Hidden Benefits of the Urban Forest," mentions in its summary of possible DAF symptoms that "individuals with DAF are readily *distracted,*" "*planning impaired,*" and show both "an inclination to be *impulsive*" and "the inclination to be *irritable*" (symptoms which sound remarkably similar to those brought on by jet lag).

"Attention Restoration Theory," or ART, the remedy for DAF the Kaplans have developed, proposes that directed attention can be refreshed if, as "Some Hidden Benefits" says, the mind can "find an alternative basis for maintaining one's focus." "Fascination," their name for "the other form of attention," resists fatigue and is effortless, because it moves by itself without deliberate guidance or manipulation or goading—almost like the difference between a horse that takes you where it pleases and one that must be kept in check by reins and spurs. But how do you change horses? The Kaplans believe "fascination" feels most at home in certain surroundings. It can in this way be evoked or elicited by a number of "sources," among them natural settings (such as urban forests) and other "restorative environments" that have accumulated or developed a sufficient complexity and richness of detail so that they seem to constitute a "whole other world." "Restorative environments work best," Stephen Kaplan thinks, "when one can settle into them, when they provide enough to see, experience, and think about so they take up the available room in one's head." (Parallel research at the University of Michigan and at the University of Essex, in England, links "green spaces" and "green exercise"—hiking and biking in the countryside—to physical health improvements, such as lower blood pressure.)

Although the language and many of the details are different, there's enough overlap here to make me think that the Kaplans and their associates are talking about finding ways to bring people to places where the larger awareness that I've been calling Deep Travel will almost automatically step to the forefront of their minds, without having to be coaxed or conjured. ("If you can find an environment where the attention is automatic," as Stephen Kaplan told an interviewer, "you allow directed attention to rest. And that means an environment that's strong on fascination.") ART writings aren't specific about how long the restoration process may take, but presumably fascination will, unless it is inadvertently interrupted or otherwise dislodged, remain dominant until directed attention has been fully refreshed and recharged and is ready to resume its work, and then withdraw. The concept sounds almost like a sleep-wake cycle that takes place while one is already fully awake.

Reviewing the Kaplans' findings and the other evidence I've been able to piece together about the comings and goings of our larger awareness, I began to form a picture of a clever, useful, largely unacknowledged talent that is kept in the background and seldom publicly seen and for the most part is forced to support or complete the tasks of various other mental modules or forms of awareness and to operate at one's beck and call. *Almost sounds like—a Cinderella story,* I said to myself. That thought came more clearly into focus when shortly afterward I was rereading the final pages of *The Head Trip: Adventures on the Wheel of Consciousness,* a 2007 book by Jeff Warren, a Canadian Broadcasting Corporation radio producer who spent several years assembling and understanding the most up-to-date scientific conclusions, from psychologists and neuroscientists and others, that—however tentative—add to existing knowledge about recognized configurations of consciousness. While summing up his research and trying to use it to draw a new map of how consciousness is organized, Warren realizes there's no longer any place on this chart for what for years had been considered one of the few recognizable islands in an ocean of uncertainty—namely, the "normal" condition of being awake, or "regular waking consciousness," as it is often called by writers of mind and brain studies. For one thing, Warren says, the term doesn't work because there are no "rigidly demarcated *states* of consciousness" per se, since what manifests in us strongly enough to become identifiable is something closer to "extreme *tendencies* of consciousness." But, more specifically than that,

the reason there is no regular waking consciousness on this [new] map is because *there is no such thing as regular waking consciousness*—consciousness is literally all over the map. Waking consciousness is constantly in flux. It's

a mixture of alert mindfulness, absorbed action, and distracted rumination, sometimes plunging deep into one of these tendencies but more
often an overlapping combination of all three.

Different language again: "alert mindfulness" and (elsewhere in the
book) the "SMR," or "sensorimotor rhythm," are terms that in *The
Head Trip* stand for a larger awareness that, as Warren experiences it
and reports on it, could easily also be called Deep Travel. As, for
instance, his account of how this awareness appeared in his mind one
afternoon at a clinic near Toronto, during a neurofeedback (or brain-
wave) "attention training" session he was undergoing as part of his
research. Increased production of the SMR, a "very distinct spindle-
like wave" emitted by the sensory-motor strip, a part of the cortex
associated with physical movement, seems to help people with ADD,
attention deficit disorder, relax and become both alert and still, and in
this way achieve better focus. An SMR-trained music student Warren
had read about described the SMR experience as a tension between
the expectation he felt before a performance and the relaxation afterward: "Somehow," Warren observed, "these two points merged into a
single expanded moment, which allowed, [in] the student's words, 'the
mind [to] breathe.' " When Warren asked one clinic graduate, a forty-
year-old woman, what she'd done "to really get the SMR pumping,"
she told him, "Well, it sounds so simple, but basically I would just try to
experience the moment positively, everything about it. I would *luxuriate*
in the moment."

For both of them, in an instant, or within an instant, more time had
become available. Now it was Warren's turn to try. His earlier attempts
had been inconclusive, although on several occasions, when "something seemed to click," boredom or sleepiness or even anticipation
would disappear, and "suddenly there would be a shift in perspective
and I would no longer be looking at the computer screen but observing
a much larger moment—seeing the whole room in my peripheral
vision, hearing the hum of the hard drive, feeling the breath in my
lungs. At these times no sensual detail seemed more important than
any other; they were all equally fascinating and textured and calming,
even the computer's beeping."

On the afternoon of Warren's breakthrough, he had again been
hooked up to an EEG (electroencephalogram) machine so that his

brain-wave activity could be monitored. This time it showed a sudden spike in his SMR. But the machine could not record what Warren had done to make this happen, or what he felt like as it happened. As he writes in *The Head Trip*:

> I purposely didn't focus on any one thing, but panned back the camera of my awareness to include the whole 360-degree spread of the room and myself within it. The fan belt on the computer would hum and I would smile and think, *This is the sound a moment makes.* What would the next moment bring? I realized that I didn't know for sure, and—as cheesy as it may sound—for longer and longer stretches of time I found this secretly thrilling. I was relaxed, and I was alert, but, most important, I was *accepting.* My SMR slowly crept up. . . . It was working. *This is it,* I thought, *this clarity is what they're talking about.* It was so *simple,* and yet it felt qualitatively different from my normal, surface-skipping mode of operation.
>
> The feeling lasted all the way home. When I stepped out of the office into the cold night the sound of the traffic was very loud. Around each streetlamp the halos of light refracted into bright rainbow prisms. I felt giddy with the vividness of everything, and thought of Aldous Huxley's famous mescaline-fueled observation: "This is how one ought to see, how things really are."

If Warren's "SMR" is a way of describing a larger awareness, his "absorbed action" represents focused concentration, while his "distracted rumination" is another name for daydreaming. (Sometimes Warren will say "mindfulness," a term borrowed from the Buddhist tradition, instead of "SMR"; that's because, after studying the practices of meditation, he concludes, "Mindfulness is just like the SMR; they seem, in fact, like different words for the exact same thing.")

The three states—three *tendencies*—are clearly closely related and tightly connected, appearing to be offshoots of, or aspects of, the same force or source. Might this translate, in the shorthand but practical imagery used by traditional myths and tales, into a story about three sisters living under the same roof? Even more striking is the situation that surrounds the way these tendencies are deployed by people. Two of the three, concentration and daydreaming, leave the house daily, so to speak—meaning that we easily recognize their presence in ourselves and in people around us—while the third is more hidden. Moreover, the first two are so well known to the contemporary world that it long ago reached fixed conclusions about their value, praising one and condemning the other. Indeed, one way of looking at the thirteen years of primary and secondary schooling we now require of children is to see it as a process set up to reshape and train these two mental tendencies, systematically suppressing and denigrating "woolly-mindedness" (daydreaming), while carefully instilling and rewarding habits of concentration. The child thus gradually, grade by grade, learns how to sustain this pinpoint focus over longer and longer periods of time and apply it to a host of useful pursuits. Meanwhile, the third awareness is so little known and still so neglected throughout our upbringing that it might easily be mistaken for the stepchild or the half-sister of the family.

If it was your task to display this set of understandings allegorically so that it could survive intact for many generations, even among people with no technical expertise, what kind of narrative might you devise? Many traditional tales feature three sisters or three brothers, but there is only one story I know of with this kind of intense, two-against-one ill feeling and ill treatment among the three siblings. I began to wonder if, like "Hänsel and Gretel," "Cinderella" might on closer reading prove to be another early Deep Travel story, in this case a message sent forward by some of our forebears about the true nature of an (even by their time) undervalued awareness, one that had already been dislodged as a favorite and, scorned by the favored members of its family, had at some point been consigned to menial work. My research had its intital disappointments. While the story in its Brothers Grimm version does seem to be a plea to *take another look* at this different way of seeing the world, it's not at all forthcoming about the unique qualities in Cinderella that so powerfully attract the king's son's attention to her and not her sisters. Her attributes are listed almost blandly and generically, as if she were still being observed from a considerable distance; she is "good" and "pious" and "beautiful," though to its credit the story does expand on one of Cinderella's attributes, pointing out that she moves easily through the natural world and can speak the languages of the birds and the trees.

In the Algonquin version of the tale, on the other hand—a Native American variant collected by Idries Shah for his *World Tales*; Shah calls Cinderella "one of the most enduring of all tales"—both the maiden and the prince have taken on far greater dimensions and capacities that relate to some of the deepest of Deep Nows. The king's son is now "the Invisible One," a being who lives quietly among humanity with his sister at the edge of a large lakeside village of Micmac Indians—"and everyone knew that any girl who could see him might marry him." The villagers include (as we were sure they would) "an old man, who was a widower, and his three daughters." The two oldest daughters are not alone in not being able to see the Invisible One, because almost every girl in the settlement has at one time or another tried her hand at "the test of sight": "They could be sure he was a real person, for when he took off his moccasins they became visible, and his sister hung them up. But beyond this they saw nothing of him." Nevertheless, most of them pretend that they have seen him when he returns to the lake at night from hunting and even, when asked, describe what they imagine he must be wearing or carrying, such as a rawhide shoulder strap.

When the youngest sister, little Oochigeaskw, or the Rough-Faced Girl, presents herself one evening, the Invisible One's sister is kind to her—"of course, because this noble lady understood far more about things than simply the mere outside which all the rest of the world knows." Then her brother nears home:

> "Do you see him?" the Invisible One's sister asked.
> "I do indeed—and he is wonderful!" said Oochigeaskw.
> The sister asked:
> "And what is his sled-string?"
> The little girl said:
> "It is the Rainbow."
> "And, my sister, what is his bow-string?"
> "It is The Spirit's Road—the Milky Way."
> "So you *have* seen him," said his sister.

And when the Invisible One himself comes in, "terrible and beautiful, he smiled and said: 'So we are found out.' "

FROM LUCY TO THE MOON

Daydreaming has in the last decade been rediscovered by brain researchers, and is perhaps about to be rescued from the contempt it, too, has had to endure. (Eric Klinger, now an emeritus professor of psychology at the University of Minnesota–Morris, points out that as recently as the 1950s psychologists were warning parents that daydreaming could lead to "neurosis and even psychosis.") Called the "stream of consciousness" by William James, and also known as "undirected, unintended thought," or mind wandering or following a train of thought, daydreaming shares a basic attribute with its "sister" awareness, focused concentration: both are disconnected from whatever is taking place externally. According to several estimates, daydreaming takes up as much as 30 to 40 percent of our waking time, popping up so frequently that one psychologist, Malia Mason, from the Columbia Business School, has recently suggested that it be considered as the dominant daytime state—although one that "is routinely interrupted by periods of goal-directed thoughts."

The most startling news came from two neuroscientists at Washington University in St. Louis, Marcus Raichle and Gordon Shulman, who've been studying the brain activity associated with daydreaming, and who announced in a 2001 paper that the "resting brain," as they had always thought of it, is actually associated with "a huge amount of activity" in "a constellation of brain areas" that fades as soon as someone starts concentrating. "There was this neural network that had not previously been described," Shulman has said. They've named it the brain's "default mode." A *New Scientist* feature story about this newly recognized "neural dynamo of daydreaming" calls it "a major system within the brain, an organ within an organ, that hid for decades right before our eyes." Giulio Tononi, a neuroscientist colleague of Raichle and Shulman's at the University of Wisconsin–Madison, finds their work of the first importance: "It's not very frequent that a new functional system is identified in the brain, in fact it hasn't happened for I don't know how many years. It's like finding a new continent."

But what is this continent's purpose and use? That's not yet known, though possibly daydreaming is not just a process that depends on imagination and invention but involves a recurring period when the mind sorts through impressions previously received and decides which to remember and incorporate into understanding. Maybe, says Mason, it's an opportunity for "a kind of spontaneous mental time travel" that "lends a sense of coherence to one's past, present, and future experiences," since "we are not stuck in the here and now." "Whatever it does," writes Douglas Fox of *New Scientist,* "it fires up whenever the brain is otherwise unoccupied and burns white hot, guzzling more oxygen, gram for gram, than your beating heart."

But what of Cinderella herself? If "Cinderella" and "mindfulness" and the "SMR" give us some additional names for Deep Travel, do they also get us any closer to understanding either the origins of this larger awareness or its continuing neglect? The fact that the SMR was first observed in cats, rather than in people—during a 1965 experiment by Maurice B. Sterman, now an emeritus professor of neurobiology at UCLA—would indicate that our human capacity derives from a well-established and now-ancient mammalian precursor. (The last common ancestor of humans and carnivores such as dogs and cats lived sixty million years ago, according to one estimate.) Barry Sterman, as he is known, was a sleep researcher who had hypothesized that asking cats to perform too stressful a task might make them fall asleep; the task was one of making cats wait for a reward—they wouldn't get chicken soup until they pushed a lever only after a tone was no longer sounding. "Except," as Warren tells the story in *The Head Trip,*

> the cats didn't fall asleep. Instead, they stayed stock-still—expectant, alert—waiting for the tone to end. ... To Sterman's surprise, this state of expectancy was accompanied by an EEG signal he had never seen

before in this context: a very specific rhythmic spindle . . . concentrated over the cat's sensory-motor cortex, just under where the EEG leads attached to the cats' skulls. "It was fascinating," recalls Sterman. "We had never encountered this EEG rhythm before, and it didn't exist in the literature." He named it sensorimotor rhythm, or SMR.

Jim Robbins, a science journalist who's written a book about neuro-feedback and Sterman's work (*A Symphony in the Brain: The Evolution of the New Brain Wave Biofeedback*) that Warner cites, calls the cats' alertness "the same state a house cat waits in, feigning heavy-lidded indifference, as a bird makes its way near enough to be pounced on." Sterman, when interviewed by Warren, called this mixture of stillness and alertness "a standby state for the motor system"—a kind of "pause button." Warren himself—when I phoned him recently in Toronto—said he sees his own SMR experiences as corresponding to moments when an unusual kind of "presentness to possibilities" emerges "and you're perfectly poised to make an assessment about what to do next. You could think of it as a fermata inserted into a day—one of those time-stopping musical notes that interrupts the rhythm of a piece and gets held far longer than any of the notes around it, or allows a singer to take a breath."

It seems clear to me that if the SMR represents a mental capacity—or tendency—that our ancestral predator mammals had mastered and that since that time has been handed down through tens of millions of years and is now lodged in both cats and people, it's a trait that human-ity, or humanity's direct progenitors, somewhere along the way adapted so as to be able to extract a number of very different possibilities from some so far "incomplete" situations. For cats, the SMR is a pause in the middle of a pursuit, a kind of delayed gratification that makes their hunting more efficient—so its presence both reinforces the "first point" of their trips (such as pouncing on a bird) and increases their chances of attaining that goal. Whereas people, as we've seen, can, on occasion, use this same pause—or fermata or expanded moment—to achieve such a wide range of understandings. Sometimes they reach the insights of an Oochigeaskw. At other times they find a "second point" in their traveling. Or, if necessary, they're able to change the outcome of a moment by choosing a "third option" that is neither fight nor flight but, instead, something that's never been tried before. Something that wasn't even on a mental list of things known about but not yet tried. Something that, if it works, may in retrospect turn out to have been the *right* or at least the *bright enough* thing to have done under the circumstances.

I can remember, for instance, one of the few times I felt truly vulnerable in New York. I was walking down a still-busy, not quite deserted, long, narrow midtown side street late one winter night. Then, halfway from the corner, I noticed that one of the people coming the other way, a huge, wild-looking man, was silently brandishing what seemed like an even huger piece of wood over his head—at least a two-by-six plank, from the looks of it. Fighting would have been foolish, but flight, too, seemed foolhardy; there were no open shops or doorways to duck into, and I didn't want to call attention to myself by bolting across the street or by turning around and running, although I felt that if I could only make it back to the corner behind me, all would be well. (Maybe there would be a policeman or a taxi back there on the wider avenue, a main thoroughfare; there was definitely a subway entrance.) What followed were a few moments of furious thought that seemed to take forever. No one was looking at anyone, so my first thought was that there was no one I could turn to for help. But then, oddly, when I started to notice the flow of people around me on the sidewalk, rather than just particular individuals, I found the solution I was looking for: one of these people could help me, without even knowing about it, by cloaking me with temporary invisibility. By the time I realized this, I was at a point where there were still several people walking toward me in front of (and themselves seemingly unaware of) the huge man. As soon as I came abreast with the next one of these people, a man huddled in an overcoat, I about-faced, turning on my heel quicker than I had known I could, and walked next to him, matching his speed and stride, while looking over at him intently as if the two of us had always been there and I had been absorbed for the last ten minutes or more by some story he was telling. I had found a way of joining a convoy, a temporary caravan of people. I'd merged with the preexisting pattern of the street without attracting the attention of the huge man. We reached the corner in safety, and I jumped into a passing cab.

There is a lot more to explore here about this expanded use of the SMR pause—as there is about so many of the areas we're discussing.

Briefly, and as a starting point, here are a couple of what I've labeled SMR-related observations that over the years have caught my eye. They both suggest to me that flight and fight are at least in some cases not easily separated but have to be considered as part of a larger whole, one that includes both hunting and being hunted. The first was written by a psychologist, Al Siebert, an expert on resilience, who while still a college student at the end of the Korean War learned survival skills from veterans of an airborne infantry combat unit that had lost ninety of its men during its missions (from Siebert's book *The Survivor Personality: Why Some People Are Stronger, Smarter, and More Skillful at Handling Life's Difficulties . . . and How You Can Be, Too*):

> During our training I noticed that combat survivors have a type of personal radar always on "scan." Anything that happens, or any noise draws a quick, brief look. They have a relaxed awareness. I began to realize that it wasn't just luck or fate that these were the few who came back alive. *Something about them as people had tipped the scales in their favor.*

The other reflection is from *Meditations on Hunting,* by the Spanish philosopher José Ortega y Gasset; this passage was later incorporated into *The Tender Carnivore and the Sacred Game,* a book by the environmentalist Paul Shepard about the habits of sedentism as an artificial constraint on human nature. Hunters become successful fighters, Ortega seems to be saying, only by anticipating a shifting balance of fight and flight, both in themselves and on the part of the prey they are seeking:

> The hunter knows that he does not know what is going to happen. . . . Thus he needs to prepare an attention of a different and superior style—an attention which does not consist in riveting itself on the presumed but consists precisely in not presuming anything and avoiding inattentiveness. It is a "universal" attention, which does not inscribe itself on any point and tries to be on all points. There is a magnificent term for this, one that still conserves all its zest of vivacity and imminence: alertness. The hunter is the alert man.

In any event, *somewhere along the way* the possibilities associated with the sensorimotor rhythm changed and grew. This is what sticks in my mind. At some point after the emergence of the SMR as a new hunting technique that added stillness to relentlessness, it went through a kind of metamorphosis and emerged as a winged creature— becoming the larger awareness that's such a distinct and unusual feature of modern human minds. Can we say where or when or what happened with any specificity? Was there a particular milestone in this long journey that marked either a turning point or a no-turning-back point when what is now Deep Travel assumed a form we would immediately recognize and accept as familiar, when its workings became a continuous part of the minds of successive generations? When it took on, that is to say, a "part of us" or "already ours" feeling and became a lasting interior presence with a sweep and an extent similar to the exterior and outward lastingness that various Deep Nows allow us to sense in the world around us, such as the Now of the Flowers that Michael Novacek writes about in *Terra*?

Can we, in short, take up the challenge of the "child carrying a light" in Hasan of Basra's poem and reach a conclusion, however preliminary and provisional, and just-for-now, about the moment when this particular aspect of our minds first "became human," so to speak?

My strong hunch is that we can, because in this case the "light" itself can show us a direct if largely untraveled route back to the starting point of this transformed and relaunched capacity. An alternate reading of the poem's message—one I hadn't considered when I first came across it—is that sometimes questions about some inner characteristic's appearance and disappearance can be resolved simply by looking steadily into the essence and nature of this quality, and not, as would at first seem logical, by letting too much of your focus become fixated on its comings and goings. But beyond the abstract satisfaction of unlocking one of a poem's meanings, there's a practical and unexpected suggestion here for some further exploration into our human origins—maybe it's couched as a hint, or maybe it's a directive, but that depends on how it catches your ear. Namely, that the same "alert mindfulness" we're investigating can tell us its own story, or a great deal of that story, if we follow its glow. This is partly because this larger awareness is a force within us, closer to us than our own fingers. But it's also because, now that we know it better, we've caught its particular tang and savor, its immediacy and intensity and expectancy, the high alertness involved, as well as the surge of feelings and the pattern of sensations it uniquely evokes. As a result, there's an unmistakable taste to it, as distinct as tea or coffee, one that reappears in the mind even if Deep Travel is only fleetingly present. One we can readily identify whenever and wherever we meet up with it.

I got the first clue about how to use a "larger awareness detector" or "taste test" as a way of tackling the subject of "retrospective awareness"—the tracking down of possible early appearances, however fugitive, of our expanded awareness—one afternoon a few years ago on a wander through the old Hall of Human Biology and Evolution, a cavernous room half the length of a football field in the American Museum of Natural History in New York. (It since then has been extensively redesigned and has now been reopened as the Anne and Bernard Spitzer Hall of Human Origins.) I realized (and it was almost exactly like catching the full impact of the Houston Street dawn redwood) that there was one spot I could stand in—and in this case there was only one; Houston Street is more elastic—where I could without stooping peer directly into the eyes of, and seemingly exchange glances with, a full-scale model of a small prehuman figure (this one had lived more than 3.5 million years ago) on display in one of the museum's famous dioramas, those haunting, three-dimensional, time-capsule assemblages and reconstructions (behind plate glass) of lost or vanishing habitats and ecosystems. The AMNH first perfected this exhibiting technique more than a century ago, when dioramas replaced an earlier generation of glass-fronted cabinets stacked haphazardly with stuffed animals and other curiosities that had been popular with Victorian museum curators. In retrospect, as the AMNH's president, Ellen V. Futter, noted in a *New York Times* interview, dioramas can be recognized as "the earliest forays into virtual reality."

A diorama takes the form of half a snow globe, meaning that what you're looking into is a half slice of a dome—or a quadri-sphere, as I guess this shape would be called. It's a small room with a raised floor, not so different from the one you're standing on, but with a single, curved back wall that merges into a ceiling and that has been so cunningly painted with exactly the right lines of perspective that it seems to be an open-air, indefinitely deep, to-the-horizon extension of the surroundings of the figures displayed in the foreground—in this case only two, sculpted representatives of *Australopithecus afarensis,* male and female, from a long-extinct species. The female was the one I could look at head-on, because her head was craned around to the left and thus outward toward museum visitors; the male was gazing in the other direction, toward the back of the exhibit.

Dioramas, older than a Model T Ford, are still effective, as a 2003 piece by Glenn Collins in *The New York Times*. ("Rescuing the Diorama from the Fate of the Dodo") pointed out, and museums like the AMNH still spend millions of dollars building and repairing them, even in a digital, hologram age. That's because they invite participation; they entice. Though themselves fixed and static, they tempt minds to move. These bright glimpses into suddenly deep vistas of lost or endangered "larger heres" and Longer Nows are like colors and patterns being broadcast to us on wavelengths that only our Deep Travel tendencies can properly register and record. Or you could instead say that they're like little oxygen pumps reinvigorating the air in a stale room. They're ready to retune our awareness, tugging at us like the tiny tendrils of a climbing plant; reengaging an eagerness for the novel and unknown the way whiffs of a sauce simmering in the kitchen can sharpen the appetite at dinnertime. They're journey starters, scene shifters, ignition points. At their best, such as with the "Earliest Human Ancestors" diorama that had caught and held my attention, you feel as though you've at least momentarily moved in next door and are no longer just a passerby, as if you've entered an interlocking quadri-sphere of your own, one that, while it lasts, only you can see or feel.

On the other hand, this capacity that the AMNH and other museums work so hard to burnish exists on something of a standby basis. There are no signs calling attention to it or marked-off zones in front of these displays, so most of the visitors who know about it have stumbled across it at some point in their lives. (It's an understanding that at any rate has seeped into generations of New York City schoolchildren who, like myself, were trooped through the Museum of Natural History on field trips; a memorable scene in J. D. Salinger's *The Catcher in the Rye*, first published in 1951, when he was thirty-two, draws on his own still vivid, pre–World War II grade-school memories of dioramas that featured deer drinking at a water hole and an ice-fishing Eskimo who had cut a hole in a frozen lake.)

Perhaps the museum's silence about the dynamism built into its dioramas is inadvertent; perhaps it is an unnoticed outcropping of lingering "stepsisterish" attitudes, an indication that even when we go out of our way to address messages to our larger awareness and cajole it into showing itself, we remain reluctant to formally acknowledge just what we're up to. More probably it's a complicated eddy of knowings and urges, not yet fully sorted through, and the areas in front of dioramas are specially weighted mingling points within what Jeff Warren calls the constant flux of waking consciousness. Dioramas, after all, are also meticulously prepared compilations of the best available scientific information on a subject, and many of the accumulated facts and conjectures they present can be assimilated in almost a single burst by someone who approaches these displays in a state of focused concentration. Or who, daydreaming, snaps into a state of focused concentration and then moves briskly onward.

All this is by way of introduction. I want to acknowledge that the subtle and attention-shifting force field that dioramas emit, something that as a former New York schoolkid I grew up knowing about and moving in and out of many years before I could describe it or put a name to it, is a part of what was operating in me that afternoon in the Hall of Human Biology, and prompting me to redirect my thinking. It needs singling out because it might otherwise get overshadowed by the special power of the attention-expanding discovery being displayed in the particular diorama I'd stopped in front of. It produced an amalgam of many different feelings, foremost among them, probably, a breath-catching, rearview mirror, "story-so-far" sense that I was both just in time to watch a baby's first steps and simultaneously at the far end of a Deep Now continuum that stretched back almost to the very beginnings of humanity's longest journey, the one that led from very clever animalness to today's distinctive if unfinished humanness.

The diorama (then off to one side, and since then moved to a central position in the new Hall of Human Origins) was (and is) a depiction of one of the most spectacular paleontological finds of modern times: the careful uncovering out on the plains of East Africa of thousands of ancient hoofprints and tracks left by more than twenty kinds of animals (many now long since extinct) on a single day or hour in prehistory and, among them, moving north in an almost straight line, fifty-four unmistakably human-looking footprints. It all happened remarkably quickly, and it all took place about 3.6 million years ago, at a place called Laetoli (the word means "red lily grass" in a Masai dialect), in Tanzania. Antelopes, elephants, and zebras roam there now.

The sequence of events back then was this: Sadiman, a nearby volcano, belched powdery gray ash; a sudden rainfall slicked down the ash, turning it to the consistency of wet cement; animals and birds of all sizes (such as guinea fowl, millipedes, some giraffes, antelopes, an earlier elephant species, an early kind of horse and her foal) happened by and walked across the suddenly sloppy ground, which also recorded the impression of some of the raindrops; the sun dried the prints and drops and then a second cloud of ash descended, so quickly that further rain never had a chance to wash the tracks away and before other creatures could trample on them and blot them out or blur them. This unpredictable pattern of ash bursts, sudden, gentle showers, sauntering animals, and hot sunshine repeated itself several times over the next month or so, forming several layers of intact and covered prints. Underground, all the layers turned to stone and sat there, unobliterated and unchanging but unavailable and unsuspected, until erosion in the 1970s brought some of them to the surface again. Whereupon the first of the humanlike prints was noticed one evening by members of an expedition led by Mary Leakey who were amusing themselves after work by throwing chunks of dried elephant dung at one another. (These cannonball-sized leavings are considered by some to be the snowballs of East Africa.) Dazzling and not fully anticipated finds of spectacular traces of long-ago life that got unintentionally left behind, like the ones at Laetoli (Mary Leakey, already a famous paleoanthropologist, had gone to Laetoli in search of early stone tools), were known for years among paleontologists as the "Leakey luck."

The human-looking footprints, slightly squishy in appearance but nevertheless unmistakably not apelike, caused a sensation and produced newspaper headlines around the world; "Prehistoric Footprints of Man-Like Creatures Found," said *The New York Times.* The prints show big and deep heel marks (ape heels are much smaller), a rounded arch (apes have flat feet), and a big toe on each foot parallel to the other four toes on that foot (while the big toes of apes stick out to one side, like human thumbs, and can be used for climbing and grasping and thus for largely vertical scrambling through trees, since they can curl around in front of the other toes to form a "foot fist," so to speak). These footprints record a different kind of accomplishment: smooth, straight ahead, horizontally flowing, initiated from an upright position, two-legged and two-footed—or, as biologists would say, bipedal—motion at an effortless, constant pace across long stretches of open country. Or, put more succinctly, *walking*. Something people now start getting good at when they're about a year old and after that take for granted. Something, equally, that apes never get very good at at any age, though they can and do walk bipedally for short distances in a sort of awkward, rolling gait. They are, however, very good at various other forms of locomotion wholly or partially denied to us, including leaping, swinging, and clinging, as well as climbing and—in the case of chimpanzees and gorillas—knuckle walking, a slightly higher-off-the-ground version of four-legged, or quadrupedal, walking, where the knuckles of the partially clenched front "hands," not the flat palms, touch the ground.

But the still unglimpsed beings that left the two-legged footprints at Laetoli—we know that there were either two or three of these Laetoli walkers, but there are no bones near the prints—didn't toddle or waddle or roll from side to side. "Make no mistake about it," noted Tim White, University of California, Berkeley, paleoanthropologist who was part of the Leakey expedition, "they are like modern footprints. If one were left in the sand of a beach in California today, and a four-year-old were asked what it was, he would instantly say that somebody had walked there. He wouldn't be able to tell it from a hundred other prints on the beach, nor would you."

So the Laetoli walkers; whatever their other characteristics may have been, manlike or not, were doing something apes couldn't and can't do. As a result they must, in common with us, have become "no longer quite apes," a condition that within the last few years has been encapsulated in a new technical term coined to try to clarify the way prehistory can be classified: "hominins." It's a sifting-through and paring-down kind of word. It separates out chimpanzees and gorillas as separate strands (they are "hominids") and at the same time distinguishes them from the more distantly related orangutans and gibbons (a larger cluster called "hominoids"). Then, having narrowed the focus, "hominins" specifically gathers together as a single unit only humanity's most immediate family, a group that as currently constituted includes us, meaning *Homo sapiens,* a species that took on its present, instantly recognizable physical form about 200,000 years ago. (Subsequent changes in human behaviors and capacities have taken place within this outwardly unchanging anatomy.)

Arrayed around us or before us or beside us in the hominin class portrait stands or crouches a still growing assembly of known-about and guessed-at species of human forebears, the most famous of whom are probably Lucy, a 3.2-million-year-old, three-foot-eight, upright and bipedal hominin found in Ethiopia in 1974 (more formally, *Australopithecus afarensis*—the Beatles' "Lucy in the Sky with Diamonds" was playing on a tape recorder in the anthropologists' camp the night after she was found), and the "hobbits" (*Homo floresiensis*), miniature bipedal but flat-footed hominins whose bones were found in 2004, and who survived on an isolated Indonesian island until only 18,000 years ago—or almost until the beginning of the Holocene. Modern humanity is the only Holocene hominin, but, like us, all the rest of the hominins arose and flourished at various points during the 6- or 7-million-year-long period that began once the hominin line had diverged from the hominid line that led on to today's tree-climbing, knuckle-walking chimpanzees and bonobos, two species that (in common with other hominoids) also occasionally, sporadically, and unpredictably become bipedal when covering short distances.

A few words also need to be said about another component of the AMNH's Laetoli diorama that exerts its own magic—namely, the way footprints made in passing can pull compellingly at our minds, with a power that seems only to increase with their age. This doesn't apply just to human footprints, either, but to all kinds of trails and trackways that record the shadows left behind by animals' movements. Like the opening up of a Deep Now, looking at footprints, and sometimes just seeing pictures of footprints, can act as a kind of time portal, but this is a different kind of manifestation of a larger awareness because footprints have a suddenness about the way they seem able to bump us across even vast spans of time that is uniquely their own. Rather than lengthening the present to connect a past age to our own along a single continuous stretch, footprints can fuse time, short-circuiting our sense of time passing and almost dissolving it. I think they're able to make this kind of super-fast connection because—contrary to what the Victorian poet Henry Wadsworth Longfellow preached so confidently about how to create imperishable traces

("Lives of great men all remind us / We can make our lives sublime / And, departing, leave behind us / Footprints in the sands of time")— footprints and tracks seem so transient to us that we unconsciously grow up assigning them to the realm of the nebulous and the will-o'-the-wisp, along with steam and clouds and mist, or smoke drifting upward from a fire, phenomena that are "all half-life," so to speak, subject to prompt decay and quick obliteration.

So a well-preserved footprint, whatever its age, instinctively has the feel of something that appeared on earth only a moment ago—and that also suggests to us, maybe with something of a start, that we are not alone. When something in front of us looks freshly imprinted and is still real enough to touch, we somehow expect the rest of our senses to kick in as well and almost find ourselves straining to hear or catch a whiff of whatever it was that came this way. Which further defines the moment—the footprint seems to have been left behind by something that only just passed out of earshot. If William James was right about the duration and extent of what we ordinarily take to be the present moment—he defined it, we've said earlier, as a unit of time that lasts no more than a minute; that has the shape of a small boat "with a bow and a stern"; and whose core or nucleus "is probably the dozen seconds or less that have just elapsed"—then a fresh-looking footprint is as recent and as close behind us as the wake just churned up by a small boat. Traces and trackways began to be deposited as soon as animals emerged onto land half a billion years ago; an Ontario quarry, for instance, preserves the scrabblings of inch-long, insectlike, hard-bodied creatures with at least eight pairs of legs.

Other prints and trackways give rare, close-up glimpses of once-upon-a-time instants that extend our awareness toward events that seem vivid and bizarre in equal measure—such as the casual springing into the water of an unknown swimming dinosaur about the size of an ostrich, whose tracks show it launching itself and pushing off from a sandy shore along the long-lost, shallow Sundance Sea, which 165 million years ago covered Wyoming and Colorado. (In the prints the dinosaur left you see—in a line—first a whole, three-toed foot, then the front half of a foot, and finally only the toes and then just the claws as the creature starts to float away.) Or the passing by of a *Hibbertopterus*, a five-foot-long, three-foot-wide, six-legged water scorpion, a distant relative of the horseshoe crab—"as big as a kitchen table," according to one reporter—dragging its posterior and moving in what its discoverer called "a lumbering, jerky motion" across twenty feet of sand in a Scottish valley 330 million years ago. (*Hibbertopterus* has been extinct for 250 million years.) Often the uncoverers and revealers of these somehow never-extinguished strolls and slitherings and passings-by seem particularly struck by the uncanny, tantalizing "next doorness" of the "almost encounters" across the ages that our larger awareness lends to the relics they have been finding, creating an unforgettable blend of immediacy and unlikeliness.

Teresa Manera de Bianco, for example, an Argentine paleontologist, has worked since 1986 to protect a mile-and-a-half long, hundred-foot-wide siltstone shelf at the edge of the Atlantic Ocean that she and her family were the first to see. This flat slab records thousands of 12,000-year-old footprints by twenty-five kinds of mammals and birds made 5,000 years before humans reached this area: horses; flamingos; mastodons; three-foot-long prints left by a *Megatherium* ("great beast"), an elephant-sized, four-ton ground sloth; and the only known footprint ever seen of a glyptodont, a heavily armored armadillo as big as a car. (Mastodons and these last two species all went extinct just before the beginning of the Holocene.) The prints are threatened by rising sea levels and by development; they were exposed after a storm and are visible only twice a day, at low tide. "It was very emotional," Manera said a few years ago, remembering her first sight of the intersecting tracks. "The ocean was still very rough after the storm, and the waves had washed the sand off the beach, leaving the platform of dull-red rock, crisscrossed by footprints. My husband, daughters, and I were the only witnesses to these wonders."

David Braun, an archeologist at the University of Cape Town, who more recently helped find the second-oldest hominin footprints—four short, 1.5-million-year-old *Homo erectus* trails discovered near Lake Turkana, in Kenya—had a similar sense. "It was kind of creepy," he told a Reuters reporter, "excavating these things to see all of a sudden something that looks so dramatically like something you yourself could have made 20 minutes earlier."

Certainly Mary Leakey felt this extraordinary nearby-ness when she talked and wrote over the years about the Laetoli footprints—noting, on several occasions, for instance, how toward the end of the tracks one of the walkers, the smaller one, appears to have stopped momentarily, "as if she saw something or heard something over to her left and turned to have a close look." "This motion," Leakey once wrote, "so intensely human, transcends time. A remote ancestor—just as you or I—experienced a moment of doubt."

But the Laetoli footprints, ever since their discovery was announced to the world in 1978, have also had yet another kind of resonance superimposed on the way we think about them. Nine years earlier, and on live television, the most famous footprints in history, ribbed impressions left by thirteen-inch-long human-made space boots, had been stamped into the powdery, gray dust on the surface of the moon—footprints immediately immortalized by Neil Armstrong, the man who made them, the first man on the moon, as "one small step for a man, one giant leap for mankind." Footprints that are not yet deteriorating because there is no wind or rainfall on the moon to corrode them. Footprints separated from the Laetoli prints by 250,000 miles and 3.6 million years. Footprints that, once the Laetoli prints were uncovered, immediately seemed to bracket the story of mankind, from its first steps on earth to its first steps off earth.

It was this entire journey that seemed to hover before me the first time I saw the Laetoli diorama. Somewhere in there, presumably, as the tread of footsteps continued, the light of our larger awareness began to burn with a brighter intensity. Although since the diorama was built these two bookends no longer fit quite so neatly. Beginning in 2004, two six-wheeled, motorcycle-sized robotic rovers, *Spirit* and *Opportunity*, launched the previous year by the National Aeronautics and Space Administration, have been leaving reddish tire marks on Mars, tens of millions of miles away, and sending home high-resolution, full-color photos—some in three dimensions—of their slow, careful explorations across the Martian surface. In their first five years, the two robots, which landed on opposite sides of the planet, traveled all told about thirteen miles before one of the rovers got stuck in some sand. When mobile the robots can move forward at a top speed of about one-ninth of a mile per hour, but they stop every ten seconds for a twenty-second pause to assess their progress.

Humans have yet to walk on Mars, but we have sent ahead several "awareness-feeding" (and "Deep Travel–inducing") human capabilities, including binocular vision ("the best pair of eyes that had ever been flown into outer space," according to Jim Bell, a Cornell astronomer leading the *Spirit* and *Opportunity* imaging programs) and motion. Jim Bell's 2008 book *Mars 3-D: A Rover's-Eye View of the Red Planet,* has red-and-blue 3-D glasses built into the binding, allowing me, for instance, to sit in my living room and squint out at such sights as two miles of low sand dunes rippling out across the Meridiani Planum, a plain near the Martian equator, before they disappear over the horizon beneath an orange-gray sky; or tire tracks approaching a rounded, low, empty hilltop within a hundred-mile-wide crater, where one of the rovers spent an entire winter. "Because the Sun gets so low in the Martian sky in winter," Bell writes, "there wasn't enough power to drive routinely, so the rover had to park on a hillside, tilting its solar panels into the weak winter sunlight just to stay alive."

These snapshots bring with them an entirely new dimension of solitude beyond anything human beings have encountered before, and the taste of entering a world so far beyond the familiar that Alexander Kinglake's wrenching crossing of the narrow Sava River, with Christian Europe on one side and Muslim Belgrade on the other, seems more like crossing a room to sit in a different chair. In this case there are so few carry-overs, similarities, and reference points that can bridge or provide continuity between the experiences available on both planets. Geology and astronomy offer the only common languages: sand, hills, sky, nighttime, gravity, wind. Even some of these remaining interplanetary "constants" need recalibrating, too, since the sun looks smaller in the Martian sky and a "sol," or Martian day, lasts twenty-four hours and forty minutes, as measured by earth's clocks. As far as the technology of "Virtual Deep Travel" goes, Bell's book seems approximately as advanced in its ability to convey wonder as the stereopticon slide shows of the far reaches of the Russian Empire that Sergei Prokudin-Gorskii prepared for the czar a hundred years ago. Bell's pictures are less carefully composed, perhaps, and they have far fewer swirling colors to record and no human expressions to convey, but they are far more portable and widely available.

Human expressions—that's what kept me returning to the museum's Laetoli diorama, time after time. One plausible interpretation of the two adjacent, parallel trails of hominin footprints at Laetoli is that two individuals, a male and a female, were walking side by side—since one set of prints was made by bigger feet than the other, yet the prints match each other stride for stride. The prints also show that the two hominins were walking close enough to touch. At the suggestion of Ian Tattersall, curator of the AMNH's Department of Anthropology, who helped assemble both the Hall of Human Biology and its successor, the Hall of Human Origins, and who's also the author of more than a dozen books on hominins and primates, this is exactly what the diorama shows: the tracks are in the process of being laid down by a three-foot, five-inch female hominin and a four-and-a-half-foot-tall male walking next to her on her right, with his left arm around her shoulders. (Almost inevitably, even though it's a complete jumble of postwar cultural references, they have been nicknamed Lucy and Desi by the museum staff; the diorama assumes that the original Lucy's species, A. *afarensis,* left these tracks, but they were perhaps created by an older though more recently discovered hominin, A. *amanensis.* Nobody really knows.) Both of the diorama's hominins are sort of semifurry with brown skin underneath. Their feet are human, their heads more hominoid, with flat noses, projecting muzzles, and bony eyebrow ridges. Their eyes are large, liquid, and brown. She's looking off to her left, he to his right. Each is open-mouthed and wide-eyed with sharply raised eyebrows, displaying expressions that are charged with strong feelings and—as Mary Leakey would say—"intensely human."

But what exactly do these expressions convey? Perhaps they represent the "moment of doubt" that Leakey thought she saw in the footprints themselves. Ian Tattersall, who worked closely with the English sculptor who created the two figures, thinks they look "worried," and that this would have been the most appropriate response to their circumstances. "Life," as he's put it in one of his books, *Becoming Human: Evolution and Human Uniqueness,* "would have been dangerous away from the forest for small-bodied, relatively slow-moving creatures such as these." They're crossing "hostile grasslands" separating them from "more congenial habitat," territory that has just become even more dismaying and mysterious because it is now an altogether unknown and alien landscape, camouflaged by an unexpected coating of gray volcanic ash. Tattersall's interpretation is echoed by Neville Agnew and Martha Demas, the last people to actually see the footprints. They led a team from the Getty Conservation Institute in Los Angeles, that in the

1990s decided that the only way to protect the long-buried prints from erosion or tree roots was by carefully reburying them. (So now their only presence is in displays and photographs.) "Looking at the myriad animal tracks at Laetoli," Agnew and Demas have written, "one gets the impression that hominids were not frequently encountered on that landscape—their tracks are too few." "These creatures," they conclude, "must have belonged to an insignificant species," and as a result their "wistful trail . . . is both humbling and stirring."

A girl about to graduate from New York's High School of Fashion Industries who happened to be standing next to me the first time I stopped to look at Lucy and Desi said, "I think they were in love. Even before time, they had feelings." I agreed. Affection and mutual support—and fear—are present in the diorama, and all three are deep-seated primate and therefore hominin traits. But standing where I could look Lucy directly in the eye, I thought I was picking up the clue to something else as well. Perhaps, to be fair, I was responding to all the wider awareness cues at hand: the Deep Now lure that all dioramas exert; the just-around-the-corner-nature of footprints in general; the specific resonance set in motion by seeing the first known hominin footsteps; the further reverberations linked to Neil Armstrong's first footsteps into the cosmos. Or perhaps John Holmes, the diorama's sculptor, had needed to reach deeper into himself than he realized in order to convey the feelings once evoked by an upright walk through sticky ash. Unlike Desi, who to me looked puzzled and almost over-whelmed by his situation, on Lucy's face I was seeing, in addition to fear, a wide range of responses—including surprise, amazement, and even growing wonder—that perhaps can fully register on the mind only with the awakening of a larger awareness of the sights and sounds available in the world.

In other words, it immediately seemed to me that an exhibit designed to evoke a larger awareness (although it's not described as such) had planted a hint (though maybe only inadvertently) about the birth of wonder and the deep origins of Deep Travel. Clearly this thought was either too convoluted or it might lead to something. But I remembered that, just as ordinary flowers when seen under ultraviolet light look like neon signs for hungry bees, our larger awareness can show us patterns that are ordinarily invisible. In this case what I was seeing was still only the suggestion or the faint outline of a pointer, but it raised possibilities that—with some generous expert assistance—I've been looking at closely and can now invite you to view within yourself. Standing in the diorama's glow—admittedly an unusual point of departure for an inquiry—I set off on a backward journey with the hunch that recent discoveries about human origins can be the reasonably precise guidelines for pinpointing a "start date" for humanity's Deep Travel awareness. Another early thought was that this search, if it progressed, would turn out to be closely intertwined with the story of early human walking. Any conclusions are so far tentative at best, but maybe we'll soon be able to say that these two very human abilities, one physical and one mental, though in many ways the products of different chains of circumstances, can nevertheless be considered fraternal twins that shared the same dawn and gained strength at similar rates.

ORIGIN OF THE WANDERING APE

To begin with the physical anthropology, it's because of the Leakeys, among numerous other scientific explorers, that a word like "hominin" has become a necessary, useful, and illuminating term. Since the early 1930s, three generations of this "centrally pivotal family," as the Leakeys have been called, have devoted themselves to searching East Africa for human ancestors. It's been said that they "brought science" to the quest for human origins. As a 1984 tribute to them in *The New York Times* ("The Leakeys: A Towering Reputation"), for instance, notes, the "the pace of exploration quickened" and "the work became more scientific"—more carefully excavated and cataloged—after Mary Leakey's 1959 discovery of a hitherto unknown, bipedal 1.8-million-year-old hominin with huge jaws (*Paranthropus boisei,* or "Nutcracker Man"). One result was the emergence of a modern, multidisciplinary approach to paleoanthropology, now a collaborative effort that welcomes anatomists and geologists and biologists and climate researchers, and "not just bone hunters."

But, perhaps even more importantly, the Leakeys and those they've brought into the field, along with the recruits who've followed them in turn, have among themselves in recent decades brought about what can be thought of as a "second transformation" in the telling of the story of where and when our humanness came from. In the first and traditional, or pre-Darwinian, telling, humanness—our intelligence and capabilities—is a collection of traits that appeared with us and has adhered to us since our arrival in the world, the gift of creation or of a

Creator. (What we've done since then with the qualities entrusted to us at the outset got told as a second story—one that began with the end of the golden age, the Fall of man, or the expulsion from the Garden of Eden, depending on which culture originally shaped this prologue and its account of a diminution or lessening of humanity whose consequences are still being worked out, immersing us in age after age of striving and setbacks and gradual accomplishment.)

In the second telling, a sort of early modern, post-Darwinian, but pre-Leakeyan formulation that flourished before World War II, the focus shifted to the prestory—the getting to humanness. Informed by science, it became a chronicle of change, growth, and evolution that now seems, looking back at it almost a century later, an odd hybrid— scripture in a lab coat, so to speak. Nature (with a capital "N") has replaced the Creator. "The vast continents of Africa and Asia," Sir Grafton Elliot Smith, an Australian surgeon who became the principal neuroanatomist of his time, wrote in *The Evolution of Man* (1924), served as "the laboratory in which, for untold ages, Nature was making her great experiments to achieve the transmutation of the base substance of some brutal Ape into the divine form of man." It was a do-it-yourself story, and it had a happy ending: humankind was self-invented, and humanness a goal first glimpsed, then pursued, and finally attained.

Although no one seemed to notice it at the time, this interim explanation of humanity, as we would now call it, arrived in a form, as Misia Landau, a paleoanthropologist and science writer at Harvard Medical School for more than a decade, explained in an eye-opening 1991 book, *Narratives of Human Evolution,* that was more familiar to novelists and other storytellers than to scientists. It had, she pointed out, the hallmarks, the twists and turns, the echoes, the crescendos, and the plot line of a heroic myth. It was—in structure, if not in content—a folktale and a fairy tale. Specifically, it was a quest story, a journey story; it incorporated themes of exile and, as she said, of adversity in "a new realm," as well as the encountering and mastering of a "series of tests" designed "to bring out the human in the hero," followed eventually by "the hero's final triumph." Ironically, this revised vision of creation retained both Eden and the Fall from the long-cherished explanation it was supplanting. (Eden was now the preexisting primate condition of "a relatively safe and untroubled existence, usually in the trees"; the Fall was the subsequent descent from the forest.) But the Fall had been moved back to the start of the prestory, becoming a prehuman event, and in the process lost its sting and stain and instead could be remembered with thanks as a welcome stimulus, a much-needed wake-up call.

So there came a time, according to Smith, when in the group of apes who would eventually become human ancestors,

> the distinctively Primate process of growth and specialization of the brain, which had been going on . . . for many thousands, even millions of years, reached a stage where the more venturesome members of the group—stimulated perhaps by some local failure of the customary food, or maybe led forth by a curiosity bred of their growing realization of the possibilities of the unknown world beyond the trees, which had hitherto been their home—were impelled to issue forth from their forests, and seek new sources of food and new surroundings on hill and plain.

Meanwhile, two other groups of apes—"unenterprising relatives of Man"—remained deaf to these possibilities, and

> perhaps because they happened to be more favorably situated or attuned to their surroundings, living in a land of plenty, which encouraged indolence in habit and stagnation of efforts and growth, were free from this glorious unrest, and remained apes. . . . While Man was evolved amidst the strife with adverse conditions, the ancestors of the Gorilla and the Chimpanzee gave up the struggle for mental supremacy because they were satisfied with their circumstances.

Why did trained scientists like Grafton Elliot Smith, members of a generation that thought of itself as having thrown off superstition, turn to hero tales to tell the story of humanity? Perhaps, Landau suggests, they had no choice—since literary scholars would argue that it's "storytelling that makes us human" and "scientists have acknowledged that storytelling may have a biological basis." Clearly one reason for casting human evolution as an adventure tale is that the form is almost a blueprint for reports of prevailing over hardships. But I suspect another part of the explanation can be seen by taking this remarkable analysis one step further and adding one more dimension to the variables being considered. Folktales, as we've seen, can among their other capacities be a vehicle for subtly commenting on a larger awareness in a way that slips between other states of awareness and goes almost unnoticed by them (making them "awareness tales" that are able to remain, in effect, partially out of awareness). The brain and its "steady development"—particularly what Smith called "an enormous expansion of the powers of discrimination"—is, as Landau demonstrates, often the hidden hero in many of the narratives by these first-generation Darwinists about "the conversion from ape to man," as she refers to it. This seems to hold true even when the narrators disagree profoundly about what happened when. (Sir Arthur Keith, for instance, a Scottish anatomist and Smith's great rival, maintained that upright posture and walking preceded the advent of larger brains, rather than following it.)

But I think these early evolutionists, as proud products of the universities of their day, had—even if they weren't altogether conscious of the impulse—another, "school-based" message to impart as well. So if, as Landau suggests, it makes sense to accept books such as Smith's *The Evolution of Man* or Keith's *The Antiquity of Man* as latter-day additions to an ancient tale-telling genre, then these long and learned books can also be read not just as histories and not just as hero stories but as an ongoing part of an odd, whispered, faintly echoing metadialogue designed to convey hints about the mind—even though their ostensible subject is the physical transformation of the brain and the nervous system. Looked at this way, the books are also projecting a kind of "modern" countermyth (modern for its time, at least), a didactic "awareness tale" whose moral or warning is that the accounts of a larger awareness and its uses in "Cinderella" and "Hänsel and Gretel" that the nineteenth century's interest in folktalks had brought back into wider circulation, should be discounted and treated warily. That long-told stories reveal themselves, when a fresh view is taken of them, as dated and frivolous, outworn garments that can now finally be set aside.

In this countermyth, it isn't just today's human beings and their brains or even their overall intelligence who are the evolutionary victors. Rather, it's the focused concentration that contemporary minds have at their disposal that is brought forward as the true hero and guide. Where did this capacity come from? The books aren't quite sure, but at some point after the Fall, it found its way onto, as Landau notes, the "battlefields" of the mind, where it was tested and strengthened and then took charge, and because, uniquely, it was able to impose "order, control, and harmony," it became the ultimate agent of human triumph. Although, as the books also point out more ominously, the story isn't over yet; continuing vigilance is necessary, and the current generation must play its own part by persisting in efforts to improve its own powers of concentration.

The countermyth is almost, you might say, the stepsister's revenge. Here, for example, is Laudau's summary of Keith's hymn to "reason," presented as evolution's quiet, great accomplishment, which in his book appears surrounded by the glow of science and enshrined as the only reliable safeguard of humanity:

> With the appearance of reason the transformation to humanity occurs. Though upright and tribal, until they acquire reason man's ancestors are, like the apes, "slaves to their instincts, feelings, and emotions—the wolves and jackals which occupy the kennels of the inner apartment of their low mentality. Reason has not yet appeared in the subconscious vaults of the brain to tame its wild denizens." ...
> Reason ... has been the hero's greatest tool in his struggle to become human. "Nor should there be any doubt as to the battlefield wherein man has won, and is winning, his victories. The battle is being fought within himself; reason has been struggling for dominion in the fields of his consciousness."

So there was no place for Deep Travel or any accounting of a larger awareness in the first "scientific telling" of humanity's story. What about now? "There's room enough—if the case can be made," says William E. H. Harcourt-Smith, a young English paleoanthropologist in the AMNH's Department of Vertebrate Paleontology, who several years ago agreed to discuss these issues with me and to participate in and monitor my informal investigation.

"So far," he said the first time I brought up the subject,

it hasn't been factored in, since we've been too busy looking at other evidence. But the framework could support it, so let's see how far we can get—starting with what's known or at least guessed at in ways that make sense. We've fundamentally changed our rationale since the 1930s. The older version was a heroic saga, an epic that really comes not from science but from the same victory-lap approach to storytelling—with just a little bit of gloating in it—that Virgil used, and before him the Sumerians who put together the life story of Gilgamesh, or *He Who Saw the Deep,* as they called it, the compelling legend of a king bored with the peaceful life who sets out to make an imperishable name for himself. It's great storytelling, and it's wonderfully romantic and seductive, and unfortunately it's also nuts, and it sure ain't science. Of course, then and now, the audience knows in advance how the story will come out—after all, we're here, and we are the end of the story. So the challenge is to tell it without forethought, remembering that the hominins who took part in it never had an aim, except a moment-to-moment one of staying alive. So the end was never a goal or a grail to follow, since at each point along the way there was never any "reading ahead" or knowing what would happen next.

The new telling of humanity's story, the "second transformation" of this tale of ourselves and where we came from, though still far from complete, has already taken on challenges the heroic version was blind to. It tries, for one thing, to incorporate a great deal more information—since thanks to the Leakeys and many others, some twenty species of hominins are now known to have existed at some time during the last six to seven million years. (Smith and Keith were weaving together a story based on only a handful of then-known protohuman species.) "This has made the story a lot 'bushier,' " Will Harcourt-Smith says. "That's a word we like to use. Our ancestry can't be thought of as a simple 'family tree' anymore, because some of these species clearly coexisted with each other, rather than simply preceding one another in an orderly fashion. The old straight line leading from 'them' to 'us' has been obliterated; we've had to move beyond the 'begats.' "

Partly because it now has so much more to make sense of, paleoanthropology has also opened itself up to new ways of examining the evidence at hand—strengthening itself, as Harcourt-Smith points out, by becoming "less pure, and drawing upon a lot of disciplines, many of which didn't even exist in the grand old days of Elliot Smith." What began as a search for "stones and bones," as the old paleoanthropological in-joke for the early tools and fossils being recovered at various digs put it, has most famously in recent decades become a triumvirate of concerns—stones and bones and chromosomes, as I've come to think of it, meaning the work being done by molecular biologists to trace the migrations of different species and their interrelatedness by identifying and dating the few genetic mutations in their DNA that set them apart from one another. But the field could just as easily now be thought of as stones, bones, chromosomes, tones, and ecotones, since paleoanthropology has also grown to include psycholinguists studying the origins of language and paleoclimate researchers, not to mention evolutionary psychologists, developmental psychologists, primatologists, zoologists, geologists, and physiologists interested in the mechanics of motion. Among others.

Not everything brought forward by the early evolutionists has disappeared from the story. Grafton Elliot Smith's outline of the "pre-prestory," for instance, is still generally accepted—the idea that the ancestors of the apes who eventually came down from the trees were tiny, shrew-sized creatures who left the ground and resettled along the branches and limbs of the world's forests as long as eighty million years ago, as is now thought, perhaps in order to take advantage of what flowering plants had brought with them: fruits, nuts, nectar, and the insects who pollinated the flowers. Tens of millions of years of above-ground changes among these early primates eventually led to monkeys and then apes. One of the first changes had to do with a new food source. Insects weren't always that easy to catch, so eyesight replaced smell as the primary sense, and front paws got better at snatching at things. "Our ancestors' moving into the trees was very important," as the conservation biologist Paul R. Ehrlich has summarized this part of the pre-descent story (in his book *Human Natures: Genes, Cultures, and the Human Prospect*). "We owe our binocular vision and adept hands to their arboreal, bug-catching habits. But their departure from the trees was also critical (think how non-dominant squirrel and monkey civilizations are today)."

At the same time, Arthur Keith's insight that walking upright came before either tool use or bigger brains has been confirmed—and the 3.6-million-year-old Laetoli footprints are considered to have clinched the case—"proof positive" in Mary Leakey's own words. The earliest recorded use of stone tools coincides with the emergence of the genus *Homo*—our genus—2.5 million years ago, or almost a million years later. So the Stone Age, to use the old term popularized by nineteenth-century researchers, cannot have begun until then. Similarly, *Homo habilis* brains—the name is Latin for "the handy human" or "the skillful human," a species that appears several hundred years later—were twice as large as australopithecine brains, though only half the size of ours. Laetoli, again, as Mary Leakey wrote when announcing her find in *Nature* magazine in 1979, "indicates that bipedalism outstripped enlargement of the brain." Or as Harcourt-Smith puts it, "You've got well over a million years of seemingly not a lot going on."

We can in some ways now be far more precise than Keith, who said only that "man, by what means we know not, became adapted to plantigrade progression," and that this probably happened about "two or three millions of years ago." Although *why* we stood upright has yet to receive a definitive answer, there is something close to general agreement at this point about *when,* and as now perceived it had its own complexity, since it was a transformation in stages, a process that can be subdivided into distinct periods, each roughly two million years long and each with its own approach to walking. Hominin species, for example, that flourished during the first period after the divergence from chimpanzee ancestors six to seven million years ago are considered "occasional bipeds," beings for whom it was somewhat easier to stand upright than it is for chimps, but who did so only episodically and to cover short distances, and for whom walking was perhaps still a somewhat uncomfortable and off-balance action. At the same time, the infrequent walks of "occasionally bipedal" hominins form a clear and emergent "kind of walking" that can be distinguished both from the once-in-a-while and more effortful walking of their closely related modern primates and from the once-in-a-blue-moon or only-in-an-emergency walking sometimes displayed by several "rarely bipedal" species, such as bears or—more spectacularly—two recently discovered species of tropical octopuses from Indonesia, which evade predators by lifting six arms over their bodies while gliding backward on the remaining two (or "moonwalking," as some biologists call it).

The beginnings of occasional bipedalism keep getting pushed back by new discoveries. *Orrorin tugenensis,* about the size of a chimpanzee and found in Kenya by a French team in 2000, may be 6.1 million years old; *Sahelanthropus tchadensis,* found a year later in Chad by a joint French and Canadian team—and nicknamed Toumai, or "Hope of Life" in a local Chad language, may possibly date back to seven million years ago.

A second group of hominin species, the "habitual bipeds" (the group that takes in the Laetoli walkers), traces back to about four million years ago. Walking had by this time become common, and walkers could cover considerable distances, but it was still only an option, not a commitment. The Laetoli tracks demonstrate that this was a skill that had been mastered, something that could be done purposefully, keeping to a single direction without drifting aimlessly or tiring easily, but, like the "occasional bipeds" of the previous period, the "habitual biped" species probably continued to retreat to the trees at night. Which meant that an above-the-ground setting still functioned as a preferred home base and as a haven. Their days therefore probably had an ultimate destination—someplace that served as an all-night center to their lives, even if its exact location shifted around from one evening to the next. The evidence is still suggestive, not conclusive.

On the one hand, chimpanzees, as Craig Stanford, codirector of the Jane Goodall Research Center at the University of Southern California, notes in his book *Upright: The Evolutionary Key to Becoming Human,* though they usually make a brand-new nest every night, have "favored places to sleep" and "sometimes return again and again to the same nest tree or grove of trees." On the other hand, the distribution of these sites across the landscape, he points out, looks remarkably similar—as Jeanne Sept, an Indiana University archaeologist, was the first to notice—to the locations of scattered stashes of tools left behind by *Homo habilis.* Though *H. habilis* used tools and scientifically has a "human" name, its members were probably themselves habitual bipeds. Sept's idea is that the stashes they created may remain as indicators of their stopping-off points and sleep-over spots. So perhaps a daily pattern of *travel and return* preceded bipedalism and then accompanied it, and was a habit that got disturbed or displaced by the more efficient posture and motion of the habitual walkers.

As for the actual range of the daily travel they could undertake as they foraged for food, habitual bipeds had short legs, which restricted them to a forward walking speed no faster than about two miles an hour. This might have allowed them to cover as much as ten miles in a day, a distance Craig Stanford says is not beyond the reach of knuckle-walking chimpanzees on a "big travel day," if these hominid cousins can once again serve as a reference point. (On the other hand, maybe modern chimpanzees were able to make better time than four-million-year-old habitual walkers could—or modern humans can. Stanford, who has walked behind chimpanzees on research treks through Gombe National Park, in Tanzania, reports that he had a tough time keeping up with them as they headed for a stand of fast-ripening wild loquat trees on a high ridge: "The chimps knuckle-walk at about the same pace that I walk behind them. The difference is that they don't change their pace on achingly steep hills, whereas I slow to a crawl," and, as a result, "by the time that we reach the ridge, I am hyperventilating, praying that they stop to rest.")

Another point worth hanging on to about the era of habitual bipedalism, as it's currently understood, was its fluidity. Now that the human lineage is thought to be "bushier" and less obviously jointed or tree-like, with an understanding that not every older species directly gave rise to species that arose more recently, we can consider that there may have been successive "waves of bipedalism" during this period. Meaning that, since the propensity for habitual walking was not necessarily inherited and thus automatically available to a new species, it may have been independently acquired, or perhaps reinvented from its "occasionally bipedal" rudiments, on at least several occasions. "If this seems unlikely," Will Harcourt-Smith says, "please remember that flying foxes (one of the names used for fruit bats) and flying fish, two groups of species that have nothing whatever to do with each other, can both move through the air."

Approximately two million years ago, with the appearance of *Homo ergaster* ("the working human") and *Homo erectus* ("the upright human")—the two names may refer to only a single species—smooth and fluid walking almost identical to the daily walking modern humans are so good at that they hardly notice it as a separate activity became for the first time an everyday part of the life of human ancestors. They were tall and slender and graceful, with a narrow frame and long legs, which gave them a longer stride, doubling their walking speed and letting them leap or lope or sprint, and they could also jog or run over long distances. When they ran, at least some of them were as fast, it's been estimated, as a modern Olympian marathoner. We know all this because of widespread discoveries of *H. erectus* sites, and because one nearly complete fossilized skeleton of a juvenile has been recovered. This remarkable skeleton, nicknamed Turkana Boy, was found by the Leakeys in Kenya in 1984; 108 bones have been carefully reassembled (the human body has 206 bones). Basically only the boy's hands and feet are missing. He was twelve at the time of his death, 1.5 million years ago, and would have reached a height of about six foot one had he grown to maturity. His face was somewhat flatter than those of habitual bipeds from the preceding period, and his teeth were smaller than theirs—though like them he had large eyebrow ridges, a sloping forehead, and no chin. "But we always joke," according to Harcourt-Smith's insider's take, "that he was human from the neck down."

To achieve all these ways of moving around, the bodies of the new walkers and runners had also given something up—namely, the ability to retreat to the heights at night. Their feet had lost any remaining grasping power, becoming instead a propulsive platform with an elegant design and arched in multiple directions that allowed them to spring forward on the ground. But only on the ground. Adults couldn't grip tree trunks with their feet, and their infants could no longer cling with their feet to their mothers' backs. "This was the second shift within hominin bipedalism," Harcourt-Smith explains, "and by far the more fundamental one. You do get reversals in evolution, but it's clear there's no going back to the trees. Once you come downstairs, you're kind of stuck on the ground, and the more two-dimensional layout of this 'flatland' world, divorced from the overhead canopy of boughs and branches, becomes your new reality. Which is why we call these hominins 'obligate bipeds.' Walking and upright posture is no longer, as it had been, either a souped-up add-on sometimes tried on an experimental basis or a long-familiar choice frequently turned to. Instead, it's all that's left, the only possible way of getting from one place to another."

The word "obligation" implies constraint, with perhaps a hint of regret or remorse. So perhaps "committed" or "enrolled bipeds" or even "eager bipeds" would convey a better sense of what this shift made possible. Because they acted as if a restraint had been lifted and they had been freed to fully engage with the world. *H. erectus* had other advantages beyond their swift feet and legs, such as a bigger brain than *H. habilis,* and they also over time developed symmetrically shaped stone hand axes that were easier to use and had a better edge than the more roughly formed stone choppers and scrapers of the earlier species. But it was their feet that took them almost to the ends of the earth.

This was the moment when long-distance travel began for hominins: they diffused throughout Africa, and by 1.8 million years ago groups of them had left the home continent and spread out across a great swath of southern Asia, reaching the Caucasus Mountains, 1,000 miles away, within perhaps a few thousand years, and after that both China (5,000 miles away) and Java (5,500 miles away), within another 100,000 years or so. They avoided the mountains and the arctic winters of the north, staying for the most part below the 40th parallel, the line of latitude running through Beijing and Madrid and Philadelphia. Roaming and ranging became the norm for the next 2 million years—first for them and later for the species that followed them (the first *H. sapiens* left Africa for what is now Israel sometime between 90,000 and 120,000 years ago). This involved both longer daily traveling and the more gradual generation-after-generation repositioning that extended the presence of "eager bipeds" through previously unexplored lands, bringing *H. erectus* to the shores of the Pacific Ocean, and later allowing *H. sapiens* to become a truly global species that moved into almost every corner of Eurasia, including Scandinavia and Siberia in the far north, and on to Australia and (most recently) North and South America. Sedentism, the replacement for roaming and ranging, became a viable alternative to almost continuous movement only about 10,000 years ago—or during the last one-half of 1 percent of this period.

In the decades since World War II and the abandonment of the heroic explanation of human origins, humanity has given itself a series of unprecedentedly humble nicknames that instead of just assuming and then reasserting our uniqueness takes a more wide-angle or group-shot approach and presents us as an unusual and sometimes highly idiosyncratic member of a larger clan, the primate or hominoid family. The most famous of these redefining terms—and the one most likely to stick long-term—is "the naked ape," a term popularized by Desmond Morris's 1967 best seller, a book translated into twenty-three languages over the next forty years. In that book Morris proposed several additional terms, including "the hunting ape" and "the killer ape," and since then other writers, partly in admiration and partly in rebuttal, have countered with "the moral ape" and "the empathetic ape" and "the territorial ape." (One writer has even turned the image upside down, celebrating the high intelligence shown by some birds by calling them "feathered apes.") At the same time, another part of our own substance hasn't yet been caught and distilled in any catchphrase, a quality whose distinctiveness deserves its own recognition as a hominoid achievement. So let's give it a name—and say that 2 million years ago, we emerged as the only "wandering ape," a transformation that also let us become, uniquely, "the traveling ape."

Part of an idea that Sir Grafton Elliot Smith came up with but never fully sketched out—his thought that human ancestors may have left the trees because they had to, "stimulated perhaps," he wrote, "by some local failure of the customary food"—now seems prescient. The other part of the same idea of his looked inward, and imagined that the descent to the ground had been more of a spontaneous awakening, or else an inner attunement, a beckoning, a response to an irresistible lure, rather than a crisis to be met. A pull, not a push, in other words, with Smith speculating that "maybe" the humans-to-be had been "led forth by a curiosity bred of their growing realization of the possibilities of the unknown world beyond the trees." But the two parts of the idea got entangled and abbreviated in the writing out. It was almost as if he had heard in his head a long and haunting melody, but when he rushed to set it down on paper had been able to remember only the first few and last few notes rather than the whole tune. So the "inner" and "outer" parts of this thought remained juxtaposed side by side but were never properly fused.

Royhan and Nahid Gani, married geologists at the University of Utah who met during their college years in Bangladesh, have recently proposed—building on what is now a whole generation of work by many teams of investigators—that the human prestory is actually a Deep Time story that began more than fifteen hundred miles below the tree roots and soil of Africa about 45 million years ago. That was when a hot "superplume" of the earth's underlying rock mantle about a fifth as big as the moon began to rise toward the surface of the planet like a slow fountain, one that for the most part moved upward at a rate of only about two to four inches a year. Superplumes are thought to be the mechanism behind the congealing and breaking apart of the continents every few hundred million years. (In our time there are only two superplumes within the earth; the other lies beneath the Pacific Ocean.) About 30 million years ago, the African superplume began to drive a wedge between the tectonic plates that Africa and Arabia sit on, sundering Africa from Eurasia by creating the Red Sea—which may someday become an ocean—and at the same time, within Africa itself, opening the Great Rift Valley down the eastern length of the continent. The Ganis calculate—they use both measurements taken on the ground by field surveys and images created hundreds of miles above the earth by instruments carried aboard the space shuttle—that between 2 and 7 million years ago the continuing pressure of the superplume began to change the landscape of Africa even more dramatically.

The so-called Wall of Africa, a nearly 3,700-mile-long, north-to-south chain of volcanoes and uplands that bisects East Africa next to the Rift Valley, rose in several spurts of uplift to its current height of two to three miles above sea level. The Wall of Africa, which extends down as far as the Republic of South Africa, begins at the "Roof of Africa," as the Ethiopian plateau is known, and includes Africa's tallest peak, glacier-capped Mount Kilimanjaro in Tanzania, and Sadiman, the now-extinct volcano near Laetoli. As the ground rose and the Wall took shape, what had been unbroken rain forest, or "near-flat forestland," as the Ganis call it, was changed so as to become almost unrecognizable, reappearing as a remarkably varied landscape characterized by a "vegetation patchwork ranging from closed woodland to desert grassland."

Like the Rocky Mountains in North America, the Wall of Africa casts a rain shadow across the continent. Meaning that both sets of mountains are tall enough to intercept and block the inland movement of moisture-laden, ocean-weather clouds—those moving east to reach the United States from the Pacific Ocean and those approaching Africa from the opposite direction, arriving from the Indian Ocean. A critical time period, as the Ganis reconstruct events, came between 3 and 6 million years ago—that's when the Ethiopian plateau, for instance, grew in height by one kilometer (three-fifths of a mile). Which is almost precisely the exact vertical distance that prevents rainfall. "Reduction of East African present-day topography by just one kilometer," the Ganis wrote in "Tectonic Hypotheses of Human

Evolution," an article summarizing their work published in *Geotimes* in 2008, "would permit moist air to circulate across the region, increasing rainfall. The currently dry and grass-dominated landscape would thus transform into one of tree-dominated vegetation."

It has taken a remarkable amount of knowledge entirely unavailable to Sir Grafton Elliot Smith to assemble this hypothesis—mantle plumes were first proposed by geologists in 1971, superplumes in 1991; and the first space shuttle was launched in 1981. The implication of all this converging information is that there's a cause-and-effect link between the timetable of the long-term replanting of the East African landscape, particularly the gradual withdrawal of the rain forests and their replacement by habitats in which grasses had a prominent place, and the hominin timetable that saw a long, slow shift from occasional to habitual and finally to obligate walking. Eighty-five years after it came to him, Smith's old hunch linking the descent from the trees to "some local failure of the customary food"—mostly tree-grown fruit, at that point—has undergone considerable refinement. In the first place, it's not so much about hominins leaving the trees as it is about the trees leaving them, by dispersing and moving apart from the great clumps and endless stands of earlier days. In the process, food didn't disappear or fail, but instead got redistributed and repositioned. So for the hominins to stay fed, the spatial dimensions of each day had to become very much elongated. Eating required traveling.

But can we say with any certainty that the dispersal of food explains why upright walking became first a habit for hominins and then a necessity? Well, not exactly. Or at least not yet. It's part of the incompleteness of the new telling of humanity's story that even though the *how* and the *when* of walking's beginnings can now be described with some exactitude, students of human origins are still far from agreeing on the *why* of it. That's partly because the two *whens* involved, landscape change and locomotion change, can't at this point be shown as a series of precisely correlated shifts. As the Ganis acknowledge, "It all happened within the right time period. Now we need to nail it down."

"Although," Will Harcourt-Smith says, "the general outlines of change are already plain, and are certainly roughly parallel. Occasional bipeds lived in unbroken forests. By the time habitual bipedalism arose, the look of East Africa was more fragmented—foresty and wooded in places, with thickety clumps of trees. There were long, narrow lines of forests along rivers, but deep, uninterrupted rain forest was a thing of the past. Around the time of the second big shift—to obligate bipedalism—grasslands opened up, vast savannas like the ones we know today."

The *why* of walking has been explained in more than a dozen different ways in recent decades—some of which pay little or no attention to climate change. For that matter, there is still controversy about the underlying *why* of the climate changes that hominins had to contend with. It's a question, as the Ganis acknowledge, of separating out the influence of what they call "the global climate drumbeat," from, in their phrase, "the tectonic rocking of local climates" brought about by the African superplume. Milutin Milanković, a Serbian mathematician, discovered early in the twentieth century that periodic wobbles in the earth's spin (repeated every 41,000 years) and longer alterations to the shape of its path around the sun—a 100,000-year cycle affected by the pull of Jupiter's gravity that moves our planet between almost circular orbits and slightly oval ones—profoundly affect conditions on the surface of the earth, producing, for instance, in recent ages, a 15-million-year-long period of global cooling and drying and, more particularly, over the last million years, a series of intense ice ages, including the one that just preceded the Holocene. So was the gradual fading of the East African forests in some ways a celestial event as well as a deep earth one? The Ganis say that the timing of events in East Africa, where forest changes came later than in other parts of the world, points to the decisive influence of the African superplume. But as careful scientists they point out that "we are still at a preliminary stage of untangling local climatic signals from global noises."

Rebecca Solnit's *Wanderlust: A History of Walking* has a memorably succinct summary of the wide range of current theories about the *why* of walking's arrival, as surveyed and named at the 1991 Paris Conference on the Origins of Bipedalism by Russell Tuttle, a University of Chicago paleoanthropologist who also coined the term "knuckle walking." Landscape variability, for instance, Tuttle noted, had nothing to do with the "schlepp hypothesis" (which proposes that walking came about in order to free the hands to carry food or babies—an idea that was actually first advanced by Charles Darwin); or the "trench coat hypothesis" (walking came about to make hominins more visible and allow females to evaluate potential mates); or the "all-wet hypothesis" (walking came about to make wading and swimming possible). On the other hand, several other theories strongly suggest that in this instance two *whens* combine to make a *why*. Intriguingly, these theories also add another element to the *why* of it: change dictated by an effort to change as little as possible in order to keep things almost the same.

Specifically, the "two feet are better than four hypothesis" (as Tuttle called it) describes habitual walking as an adaptation that allowed hominins to keep eating the same amount of the familiar tree-provided fruit they liked day after day, even if this fruit was no longer close to hand, by increasingly relying on a two-legged way of getting around that, as it developed, used no more energy for covering longer distances than they had previously needed for scrambling around on all fours over short distances. The "efficient walker theory," another name for this hypothesis, reframed the point of walking, presenting it not as moving around to get somewhere but as traveling in order to stay in what felt like the same place. Or, as its proponents (Peter Rodman and Henry McHenry, anthropologists at the University of California at Davis) have said, habitual walking was "an ape's way of living where an ape could not live." It was a change that warded off change, one in which a hominin "evolved potentialities as a ground walker so that he could [continue to] live successfully in the trees."

In a similar fashion, the "hot-to-trot hypothesis" (Tuttle's name for it) explains later, obligate walking as a "conservative innovation," in this case a former forest creature's way of staying cool after food sources had become even more widely separated, with perhaps five hundred yards or up to a couple of miles of sun-baked grasslands in between surviving copses of trees. "It's really hot on the savanna," Will Harcourt-Smith says. "And in grasses you've got humidity. But when you're standing upright, 60 percent less of your body is exposed to the sun, and you can dramatically reduce heat loss and keep going on the same amount of water and food that would sustain you in the shade."

As for the question of why we stood up, Harcourt-Smith has his own thoughts:

My instinct and training is always to keep things as simple as possible. For a change to last, it has to confer "adaptive significance"—create an evolutionary advantage—that makes it easier for a creature to meet immediate, pressing needs. And since the further back in time you go the more strictly biological you have to be, these needs in my mind are in this case powerfully related to getting food. So doing more of something that was already possible—walking—to maintain access to the same diet without exhausting yourself has a strong appeal as an uncomplicated explanation that doesn't try to reach beyond any particular hominin's "present moment" and day-to-day circumstances. And the cooling effects that walking upright brings with it are another strong argument, since they helped later hominins, who by then were also venturing into the savanna to scavenge for meat, stay out in the sun.

In evaluating theories we try hard not to confuse causes and consequences. If, for instance, we first stood up in order to free our hands—the "schlepp hypothesis"—you'd expect to see tool use and bigger brains, the results of sudden schlepping and manipulating, right away instead of so very much later. For this reason that idea now sounds to some of us more like a "Just So" story, one of Rudyard Kipling's animal tales for children where the outcome is the motor that moves the story along. So the leopard one day added spots to its tawny hide to become an invisible hunter in the forest. And the elephant child got his trunk because his "satiable curtiosity" led him into a tug-of-war with a crocodile. Sometimes—we have to keep telling ourselves this—things happen not because anyone wanted them to, but simply because something else happened first. For unrelated reasons.

By the way, Will Harcourt-Smith's presence at the AMNH can perhaps be read as one indication of how very many different kinds of evidence and expertise have in recent years become important to the current, "second transformation" retelling of humanity's story. In another era he might never have wound up working on human origins, since he originally thought of becoming a physician. Instead he found another way of thinking about how human bodies function. Harcourt-Smith is a "postcranial" paleoanthropologist, meaning someone primarily interested in the body from the neck down—in his case, hominin and human feet—and there still aren't very many such people; it's historically been a "craniocentric" field. This is partly because of the nature of teeth, which have to be so hard to stand up to wear and tear on the job that they stay strong indefinitely and are not easily decomposed, so there are far more of them in the fossil record than there are, say, shoulders and pelvises, both of which are thin. But it also has to do with who takes an interest in bones, such as the hyenas that lived in Africa millions of years ago, since—then as now—hyenas are bone crunchers that love to gnaw on and then drag off and scatter foot bones.

"In addition to that," Harcourt-Smith says,

there's still some cultural baggage to shed. The Victorians were obsessed by skulls, in an "Alas, poor Yorick!" kind of way—you feel such a direct connection to a skull, and other bones are more abstract. Even today there's a distinguished professor who tells his students that *the whole point of a body is to carry a head around.* This is changing now that upright walking is being looked at as the earliest human trait to have appeared. The feet, when we can find them, have so much to tell us. Ape hands and human hands are very similar—it's how we use them that's changed. Whereas the foot has radically changed in both anatomy and function, starting as something almost like "another hand at the back" and becoming instead what it is now, a unique propulsive platform with a really elegant design. And once you start to think that, in terms of major changes, the foot came "ahead of the head," you open yourself up to considering other changes that may have played their own part in the story.

THE FIRST HUMAN GIFT

Could remodeled feet have helped reconstruct the head? If so, how? Listening to Will Harcourt-Smith talk about the distinction between causes and consequences brought back to mind an arresting passage about hominin perception in the reading Harcourt-Smith had been encouraging me to take on that suggested a possible pathway or mechanism. It was a before-and-after portrait—before and after habitual walking, that is—a detailed sketch of what the author, Jonathan Kingdon, an Oxford zoologist, thinks of as the concentric "circles of alertness" that organized the hominin approach to the world. (Kingdon's book is called *Lowly Origin: Where, When, and Why Our Ancestors First Stood Up.*) Prewalking, Kingdon thinks, much of a hominin's attention stayed focused within the tightest of these circles, "arm's length," as he calls it, with a radius of no more than about a yard—since as "typical, close-up, intensive foragers," hominins "would have collected and processed much of their food within a perceptual field narrowed to the reach of their arms."

Surrounding this small and intensely experienced area where smell and touch acted as the "foremost" senses was a second circle, the occasional walker's "larger here," as we might say, a broader "zone of immediate action" (to use Kingdon's phrase) that was roughly twenty-five to thirty feet across and where seeing and hearing predominated. Because this larger expanse of ground extended out only to take in anything at the edge of eyesight and earshot, it was like an extension of the inner arm's-length circle, two blended places that stayed within "mental reach," so to speak. The general layout of the outer zone would be well known, and it could be constantly checked for signs of movement by animals or by fellow hominins. It served, Kingdon thinks, as "the main realm for social life," and in its scope and shape it remains a domain familiar to all zoologists—"the ambit in which many open-country mammals and birds spend the greater part of their time."

Habitual and obligate walking added something new, a third and greatly expanded circle of alertness. The "distant ambit," as Kingdon calls it, defining this circle as an almost infinite one, since it extended "beyond the radius of immediate action to the horizon":

> Of all the senses, only vision and the reception and transmission of very loud calls would have been relevant to the perception and use of distant space. Thunder and the scent of rain . . . also could have galvanized early *Homo* into action. . . . The act of scanning would have mainly concerned perceiving the movements of distant con-specifics, enemies, prey, or patterns made by attractive vegetation types, fires, rain clouds, and the sun's cycle. Judgments would have centered on assessments of direction, relative distance, and an awareness of events such as the comings or goings of rain, smoke, dust, or dusk. Because the act of long-distance scanning was relatively slow, passive, and did not involve the need for immediate action, there would have been a potential for reflection and planning.

With its emphasis on "long-distance scanning," on the combined noticing of sights, sounds, and scents, and on an ability to detect hitherto hidden patterns in the land and the sky, this immediately sounds like a description of our larger awareness's moment of arrival—and also clearly like something that appeared as a response to a new way of moving around, something that had been summoned into being by standing upright. Making it a case of the feet (and legs) directly influencing and rearranging the mind. In addition, from Kingdon's account of it, our wider awareness seems—like the Greek goddess Athena—to have been born already fully grown. A fortunate circumstance, since it was almost instantly put to use, as walking hominins "moved out into more exposed situations." "There is nothing in the evolution of primates," Kingdon stresses, "to prepare them for life in such a milieu" of "multidimensional challenges." Without access to a larger awareness, "a feeble and short-sighted primate" might have found itself restricted by what he calls "foraging myopia," and even with its assistance:

A lack of preadaptation in this "lateral expansion" ... may have put them at a substantial disadvantage with many of the animals they encountered away from safely wooded riverbanks. These species may have been predators, potential prey, or competitors; but many of them, especially those with long "lineage-tenancies" in open country would have been in possession of faculties that were superior to those of the hominins in very many respects.

To reiterate and expand slightly on this proposed sequence of events: walking (itself perhaps caused, as we've said, by a scattering of food that was ultimately a delayed outcome of deep subterranean forces) brought with it both a restored access to food gathering, as had been intended, and an unsought access to an enriched, inner impression-gathering device—our previously undeveloped, multisensory, wide-angle awareness. So here was a profound change, walking, with a variety of results, one of which, the purposeful one, was all about continuing to eat fruit. It was thus, as we've noted, a change in the service of no change at all for the time being ("an ape's way of living where an ape could not live"). The other, the by-product that has left no traces in the fossil record, was the enduring, novel, distinctive ability to participate in the landscape, a talent that has long since outlived the original, limited aim of walking. By contrast, this was, as we might say, *an ape's way of no longer being an ape.*

Looked at as part of the history of motion, these two yoked capacities, walking and a larger awareness—one visible, one only sensed—could perhaps be jointly proclaimed as the first distinguishably human "vehicles" and "transportation systems," since upright walking on feet that were no longer paws or extra hands solved the hominin problem of "forest sprawl" by shortening the amount of time that needed to be spent in motion on a regular basis, and along the way introduced the pattern of a daily commute between a home base and the new job of finding meals that were no longer already within reach. A suddenly wider awareness helped hominins embrace and open themselves up to and find reliable paths through the almost immeasurably wider world that upright hominins at that point began to inhabit, a world whose outside edges, now that they stretched to a far horizon, were often thirty or more miles distant, rather than only twenty to thirty feet away. Thus was inaugurated humanity's twin travel inheritance, an inseparable mind-body continuum that's still with us, one that's both a complex physical matter of bodies in motion, along with their acceleration and deceleration and comfort and safety, and at the same time a constantly updated internal process that has an adjustable focus and whose unending concern is assessing, appreciating, and absorbing the information and impressions that motion brings to us.

M ost biological consequences are not so instantly elaborate, nor do they assume such a prominent role from the outset. So perhaps "consequence," though it accurately defines what happened— since our wider awareness, at least as originally conjured into existence by circumstance, was manifestly an effect, not a cause—is in this case too confining a term. Since it later became a springboard for other parts of what it means to be human, including advances within our intelligence, and since it remains an essential part of our makeup, I prefer to think of it as *the first human gift,* something bestowed and conferred on us by life rather than something earned or learned or gained by struggle or problem solving or competition. A present, not a prize.

Logically, a wider awareness must have been assembled from precursor elements that were already present in hominin minds but had never before been stirred together into a lasting mixture. So many questions. Is there some way to identify the individual components? Is there some way to evaluate how well they support each other and whether, having been evoked, they would almost effortlessly jell or bake or bind to each other, forming something seamless and permanent? Would the resulting structure have enough strength and flexibility to be a useful guide to hominins facing the "multidimensional challenges," as Kingdon has called them, of life away from "the shelter of riverine forests"? Kingdon himself thinks that hominins needed more than just a new awareness to see them through this next phase of their existence, and that the "major breakthrough" that ensured their survival was beginning to develop "a more systematic and regular use of tools." Reading Kingdon, I could see that my inclination is to think that right here he overshoots his target and marches on past the landmark he's seeking. What I wanted to say in reply was that the real "breakthrough" had been the inadvertent and yet inevitable acquisition of our new mental tool, the expanded awareness that was now already in place. But what evidence could I possibly bring to the table?

I decided it might be possible to try a kind of "gedankenexperiment," as the Germans call it—the equivalent English expression is "thought experiment." This often refers to calculations that have to be undertaken in "the laboratory of the mind" (the phrase comes from James Robert Brown, a Canadian philosopher of science) because, as he says, they're "impossible to implement as real experiments either because we lack the relevant technology or because they are simply impossible in principle." In my case, though, the mind *was* the relevant technology, or at least the mind plus the body was. My idea was to try to reproduce as nearly as possible from a modern vantage point the changes in perception brought about by becoming bipedal. It was maybe a little silly, but it wouldn't take long, and no one else was home, and I was only echoing something that actually happened millions of years ago.

In my living room, near my desk, I got down on my hands and knees and looked straight ahead, in my approximation of a quadrupedal posture. Getting up again to take out a tape measure, I could see that the spot on the wall I had been staring at was only two feet and an inch above the floor. Getting back down on all fours, I this time tried rising up on the knuckles of my hands, thus assuming what I hoped was closer to the posture of a knuckle-walker. This raised my eye level five inches higher off the floor. Standing up, I'm about five-foot-eleven, which makes my "eye height" about five feet, seven inches. In other words, with upright posture a hominin my size looks out at the world from an eye level approximately two and a quarter times higher than it would be if I were a knuckle-walker, and about two and two-thirds times more elevated than it would be if I were a flat-footed quadruped.

The African savanna grasses that established themselves two million years ago, Will Harcourt-Smith had previously confirmed, grew and still grow to a height of three or four feet, so my rough tape-measure calculations seemed to show that the far horizon of a "distant ambit" would certainly have become part of the everyday experience of obligate bipeds (or at least of the adolescents and adults among them—the twelve-year-old Turkana Boy, after all, was already five-foot-three). By the same reasoning, in the days before the savannas, shorter, Lucy-sized habitual bipeds could probably have peered over the tops of the shorter, less lush grasses growing within the intermittent clearings throughout the increasingly fragmentary forests of an earlier era. That finding thus seemed to confirm one of Kingdon's basic contentions— namely, that it was the act of standing tall in a changing landscape that vastly increased the amount of the planet that was thereafter "real" for hominins. Without, that is to say, directly altering the size and shape of their habitat—defining "habitat" quite narrowly as the places they actually visited and returned to each day, or every few days—it gave that habitat an entirely new context, or "surround."

Now, as we've already seen, the physical amount of space needed for survival was itself already far larger even for habitual bipeds than the "food next door," forest-based requirements of their precursors, the occasional bipeds that arose during the period just after the chimpanzee/hominin split. But what standing, and moving while standing, made truly immense for the first time (by hominin standards, at any rate) was the fraction of the world that was within constant reach of their senses. In a closed setting, what eyes and ears have to tell us is comparable—and perhaps ears even have a slight edge, because their stereophonic qualities make it possible to pinpoint the location of a noise coming from someplace behind that we can't see. But as soon as a creature with eyesight as powerful as a primate's vison stands taller than the "grass curtain" in the near distance, those eyes assume almost telescopic powers, at least in comparison to the reach of any of other senses.

All of this also seemed to sustain another Kingdon assertion: that the opportunity for "long-distance scanning" and other aspects of a larger awareness arose as soon as hominins themselves rose up from all fours. But were they yet in a position—internally—to take advantage of that opportunity in a way that might have "galvanized" their thinking and understanding (to use Kingdon's word), or did something else, as Kingdon himself assumes, have to happen first?

I decided to repeat my "embodied thought" experiment to see if I might have missed any clues the first time around. Granted, I don't have any savanna grass in my living room, but I do have a windowsill three feet, eleven inches above the floor, with a view beyond to rooftops and the sky and, more near at hand, some old crab apple trees in the garden out back, as well as (a more recent addition) a mourning dove's nest on a ledge next to an air conditioner. Granted, too, all I was doing was slowly standing up from a crawling position in the safety of my own home in New York. Granted, further, I had seen the look—the carefully crafted look, as I knew full well—in Lucy's and Desi's eyes in the AMNH diorama uptown. Even so, remembering this, I really expected that nothing much would or could happen. So I was not prepared for what did happen: standing up brought with it an uprush of feelings.

More specifically, there was a quick intensification of several feelings. The abrupt widening and deepening and "filling in" of the visual field was the most obvious difference. I was, of course, only gazing once again at a familiar backyard scene, but the contrast between looking at nothing more than a wall and a radiator, as I had had to down on the floor, and the wealth of information flooding in through the window seemed, as Kingdon says, to invite scanning—and further exploration. Everything I could see seemed to promise that there was more to find out if I moved closer. The world beckoned. This upwelling feeling—which I didn't have to summon; it just appeared—was one of anticipation, eagerness.

But it wasn't the only unannounced feeling that seemed to be almost inextricably associated with standing up. Another sense, I discovered, arrived equally automatically—a remote but pervasive wariness I'd never quite been conscious of before. This was not something I could see, but it affected the way I saw everything. It seemed to strengthen as I rose to my feet and my body unfolded. So it was a response to information coming from our kinesthetic sense, which is sometimes called our "bodily intelligence," meaning, among other things, our innate, ongoing sense of where our body is in space. Part of this, I realized, was that when former quadrupeds stand up, it doesn't just more than double their height. It also dramatically compresses their length. Previously, we were basically just an arm's length high: from shoulder to wrist, and then add a few inches for the head and neck to curve up from and in front of the shoulders. As a biped, our height is from hip to foot (longer than an arm's length by itself), plus from hip to shoulder (the length of our trunk), with then the full length of our now mostly straight neck and head above that. But, meanwhile, while this rearrangement in space is taking place, we're also less than a third as long as we used to be, give or take. A quadruped's length is measured from shoulder to rump, plus neck and head, whereas humans—or upright hominins—are only as long as the distance between their chest and their back.

Another part of it has to do with what happens to the formerly carefully arranged anatomy that we share with other vertebrates when we uncurl. For at least the last 310 to 320 million years, when reptiles appeared on earth during the Carboniferous period, toward the end of the Paleozoic (or "Old Life") era, the dominant body plan for land animals has been a horizontal spinal column, a kind of pup-tent pole stretching from stem to stern, with two legs at either end—and with a digestive tract and other internal organs slung below the pole, supported and partially enclosed by a ring of bones, the rib cage, which springs out from the vertebra, the flexible line of bones that encases the spinal column (and gives us vertebrates our name). Together, these interconnected bones offer built-in protection from any assaults from above or from the side, and because the whole organism is relatively low-slung, there's usually not much danger of an attack from below. (At the same time, attacks from behind are inherently less likely, because there are further bones at the tail end, and that is also where a creature is narrowest and presents the smallest target, and potential attacks from in front can be seen and anticipated.)

Thus, if you think of a typical land-based creature for a moment in crude and reductionistic terms as nothing more than a moving, six-sided, rectangular box, its so-called soft underbelly, the one side that could be most easily injured by accident or intent, is relatively well guarded by both innate body construction and by the posture this three-dimensional form imposes—and daily behavior then reinforces this advantage. Reptiles and mammals therefore rarely expose this less shielded bottom layer as they move about. (It is a sign of trust and relaxation that delights pet owners when a dog or a cat lies down on its back and lets you pat its belly.)

All this changes as soon as we stand up on our hind legs. Now we're perpendicular to the earth instead of parallel to it, and the entire length of our physically most vulnerable side has been lifted away from the ground and is facing the world without any extra protection except what our wits can provide. Yes, we can see farther than ever before, but hand in hand with—or is it moving in step with?—this new ability comes a need for urgently reinforced watchfulness and carefulness. So what's opening up before our eyes is something far more shadowed, nuanced, and layered in the meanings it can convey, more double-edged, if you will, than is suggested by words like "panorama" or "vista"—at least as they're usually used. Twined around the already enticing question of *what could we now start doing in this enormously expanded landscape in front of us?* is the equally urgent question of *what could it do to us?* Or in other words, the larger "circle of alertness" even from the very first time we look through it has a kind of "filter of vigilance" imposed over it—or perhaps it would be more accurate to say fused into the lens of long-distance awareness that standing up grants us. We don't just see ourselves as moving through space, or as about to, or as a force acting on and reshaping a space. We also see ourselves as a force being acted on by that space—as one small object within an immensity that extends even beyond the newly extended horizon.

This was maybe the most astonishing finding of my little experiment: that just standing up one day, more than six and a half decades after I'd first done it—and approximately four million years after it became a habitual act for hominins, and two million years after it became the only way early humans could move around—would reactivate such strong feelings inside, and even give rise to a slight internal tension. Although it was equally unexpected to find that a kinesthetic sense of where my body was in relation to the earth, which I'd always thought of as a sort of altimeter, just a gauge or readout or reminder of information that might or might not be useful at any given moment, could at times color my whole thinking and have an impact at least as powerful as what my eyes were showing me.

Why had I never noticed this before? Perhaps because the two feelings—of eagerness and vigilance—balance each other so perfectly and blend together so well that they almost draw a cloak over themselves and may deflect or even short-circuit our ability either to detect this combination or to single out just one from the pair. Without looking for it, here was another way of accessing a larger awareness that could stand with the Wonder method and the Warsaw method, a quick and easy way of inducing a state of mind that had exactly the same qualities of immediacy, of time slowing and extending, of increased sensitivity to how much was happening at every moment and of its value and weight, and of a returning sense that the not-yet-known and the wholly unknown were shining through even the most familiar of the sights around me. But I had never before thought of this taste as

being a confection made from more than just a single principal ingredient. I was learning something I'd never seen referenced anywhere
about the structure or composition of our larger awareness—as well as
having finally pinpointed, if I was right, the moment of its origin
within us. (So in this case searching for the *when* of something had also
proved to be a way of learning considerably more about the *what* of it.)

By standing upright and redistributing our weight onto two feet, we
were remixing our perception as well, so that it incorporated into its
workings two feelings that between them could buoy us and extend our
reach, and in this way carry or impel or launch us across a hitherto hidden "threshold of inquisitiveness." This new, "doubly heightened" state
created for the first time an exploratory context with a strong emotional involvement, in the process endowing our minds with a new
evaluative mechanism that I sometimes think of as our "bipedal perceptual platform."

According to the late Robert Plutchik, a prolific theorist about the
origins and function of emotions (you can find a short summary of his
life's thinking in "The Nature of Emotions," an article he wrote for
American Scientist in 2001), feelings are an ancient phenomenon that
predate humanity by many millions of years—as Darwin recognized
when he wrote that "even insects express anger, terror, jealousy, and
love by their stridulations." According to the psychoevolutionary theory of emotions that Plutchik himself developed over the course of
four decades, emotions arise as a kind of internal nudge or shove that
can steer an organism to the actions it can take that will resolve a crisis:
"Emotions are activated . . . when issues of survival are raised," and "the
function of emotion is to restore the individual to a state of equilibrium when unexpected or unusual events create disequilibrium."

In Plutchik's model, responding to an emotion and doing something
(classically, moving closer to or farther away from something—
"approach" and "avoidance") to solve a problem, whether social or
food-related or in order to escape danger, would bring a return to a
preexisting state of comparative rest. But what Plutchik didn't address
was the possibility of a situation where all traces of the way back to
an original rest state of, let's say, four-leggedness, had completely
disappeared—as became the case for hominins once obligate bipedalism had been set in place by anatomical changes to the feet. In "Hänsel
and Gretel" terms, the bread crumbs had disappeared. Once there was

no way of falling back into what had been, the only solution available was to "fall forward" into a situation where "balance" had to be redefined, and became a matter of juxtaposing and weaving together and giving equal weight to emotional forces that were not going to subside again, and of finding what it was that a combination of vigilance and eagerness, of vulnerability and opportunity might reveal for creatures who had binocular vision, bipedal motion—and a uniquely enhanced "bi-emotional" awareness.

All human emotions, in Robert Plutchik's theory, are derivatives and combinations of eight basic emotions, which he displayed, using a color chart as his model, as a wheel composed of paired opposites. Three of these are instantly recognizable as the frequent accompaniments of many experiences: rage/anger versus terror/fear; ecstasy/joy versus grief/sadness; and—as a way of assessing social encounters—admiration/trust versus loathing/disgust. Maybe the emergence of wider awareness for the first time in our development brought Plutchik's fourth pair of emotions into prominence, the one pair we still tend to think of as more elusive and less central to our everyday existence: vigilance/anticipation/interest versus amazement/surprise/distraction.

Thinking about the benefits and uses of the bipedal perceptual platform, I was reminded of an almost chance remark I'd once run across, an offhand comment by Cesare Emiliani, a twentieth-century geologist and paleontologist with wide-ranging interests who's best remembered as the "father of paleoceanography," the study of deep-sea sediments for information about how they were created and the life in them in long-past eras. "Because vertical posture," Emiliani had said, "entails a colossal disadvantage—it exposes to attack and injury the most delicate parts of the body—it must have been overshadowed by an even more colossal advantage." I put this together in my mind with an observation Ian Tattersall had once made about *H. erectus*: that it was a species that displayed "a typically insatiable human wanderlust." There's of necessity some kind of "fear/explore" balance in every species, with fear having the upper hand in prey animals, and "find out more" predominating in predators. But maybe a uniquely evenhanded kind of curiosity—not the elephant child's "satiable curiosity," but something more measured, a tempered urge and yet an unquenchable one—is the hallmark of the bipedal perceptual platform. Maybe standing upright was the means of adding a distinctively human imprint and graft to an older outlook on the world, specifically one we've already looked at: the SMR, the mammalian sensorimotor reflex that had already long since become highly developed and devoted to hunting purposes in cats.

Experience, awareness, curiosity—the semantic history of these words offers some support for the idea that people from various earlier times and places have known about or suspected the presence of intermingled impulses within the capacities that have been passed down to them. "Experience," for instance, is traced back both to an Old High German word for "ambush" and to a Greek word that principally means "to try or attempt" but also, in a variant usage, stands for "peril." "Awareness," another cross-language product, derives in part from an Old English word for "careful" or "wary"; in part from an Old High German word for "attentive"; from a Latin word for "to fear"; and also from a Greek word for "to see." "Curiosity"—and also the word "accurate"—comes from a single Latin word with multiple meanings that range from problems faced to solutions found and include "careful" (meaning "taking care") but also "full of care" (meaning full of pain and suffering) and "anxious about" (and thus "inquisitive"), and, at the same time, both "medical care" and a "cure"—either for a physical ailment or for an ailing soul.

Of course, curiosity—of the kind that killed the cat—is sometimes presented as a dangerous impulse, or as a kind of inappropriate snooping. But these uses, to me, sound like definitions coined "from the outside," almost as if they came from the imaginings of another form of awareness, one that somehow felt threatened by the strength of an inexplicably expanded capacity. "Curiosity" in the sense that we're using it here, describing it "from within," meaning as it appears to us when it is at work within us, represents "an awakened interest" and embraces both care and cure. It's very much a three-dimensional sense, partly because it's a way of keeping track of a larger and potentially more dangerous "playing field," one that stretches in all directions as far as the eye can see.

But, more than that, it isn't just the size of the *here* that has to be taken into account that has changed, it's the different sense of *now* that this new situation imposes that has a truly transformative impact, because being an obligate biped is a nonstop matter, a full-time affair.

There's no longer a place of ultimate safety—the trees—to withdraw to, so there are no longer any "time-outs" from full awareness. This curiosity is based on opening up to a realization that opportunity and misfortune can arise both everywhere and at every moment. Awareness itself—the need for hominins to "keep their wits about them"—under these circumstances became a first line of preparedness and protection, a "home base" that existed within their own perceptions, an alertness that had to be maintained at least to some degree even when a group was bedded down for the night. Once hominins entered into the complexities and uncertainties of this enlarged setting for life, "wanderlust" may, after close examination, have turned out to have been not so much a thirsting for travel as it was an ongoing need for motion. We may come to think of "wanderlust" as a shorthand way of acknowledging the "unanchoring" of hominin life at this time, as walking ushered in a period when travel became an almost permanent, slow condition after there were no longer any sanctuaries to retreat to. Even stopping places, in this reading, were no more than temporary halts, just another part of the business of moving on. Eden—meaning a place of safety—was behind us. But maybe we didn't need it anymore.

Recent work by two neuroscientists, Irving Biederman of the University of Southern California and Edward A. Vessel of New York University, about how the brain processes visual information doesn't address the question of when or how our larger awareness arose but does show us another aspect of its staying power, once it had become a part of us. Namely, that, like any of the great human drives—say, for food or reproduction—it's intrinsically pleasurably and rewarding. Biederman and Vessel describe humans are "infovores," meaning we crave information (thus establishing us, in more Desmond Morris–like terms, as "the informed ape"). "They claim," according to a 2006 *New Scientist* report, "that the neural pathways through which we learn about the world tap into the same pleasure networks in the brain as are activated by drugs like heroin. They say that, for humans, only the basic urges of hunger, harm avoidance and the need to find a mate can distract us from this info-craving."

There's more than one surprise here. It's been widely known for some time that the brain rewards itself (after exercise, for instance) by generating its own opioids (also called endorphins and endomorphins), but it's new to think that visual areas of the brain are also equipped with "opioid receptors" of their own. Even more startling is the discovery, as a 2006 article by Biederman and Vessel in *American Scientist* ("Perceptual Pleasure and the Brain") sets forth, that these receptors "are sparse in the early stages" of the "ventral visual pathway," "where an image is processed as local bits of contour, color, and texture," but "grow increasingly dense in later stages." Specifically, there are greater numbers of receptors in an "intermediate area" devoted to the detection of surfaces, objects, places, and people, and even thicker clusters in an area of the brain "where visual information engages our memories."

"So," Biederman and Vessel sum up, "our hypothesis proposes that the rate of endomorphin release ... determines at least partially, the human preference for experiences that are both novel ... and richly interpretable (because such patterns would initially activate an abundant set of associations in brain areas that manifest dense opioid receptors)." Under the terms of this analysis, any awareness state would have its rewards, since an open eye is always processing some measure of visual information. But only the widest awareness would bring the greatest pleasure, since its specific function is to be alert for new meanings that may reveal themselves through intricate and unexpected sights of the sort that Biederman and Vessel call "novel ... and richly interpretable."

A few brief facts about oceans: Oceans cover 71 percent of the earth and yet remain 95 percent unexplored (which means that, even now, while there are almost seven billion people on the planet, two-thirds of it is virtually unknown). The oceans are only seven miles deep at their deepest—about the distance between New York City's two new baseball stadiums, Yankee Stadium and Citi Field—but because they're so inaccessible (at least this is what I've always thought), we tend to measure this third-dimensional distance in feet rather than miles, in order to have in our heads numbers large enough to indicate the immense difficulties (no light, no air, crushing pressures) involved in underwater travel. "More than 1,500 people have climbed Mount Everest," Randolph E. Schmid, of the Associated Press, reported a few years ago, "some 300 have journeyed into space, twelve had walked on the moon, but only two—Jacques Piccard and Donald Walsh—have ever visited the deepest part of the ocean." (Piccard and Walsh descended 35,761 feet to the bottom of the Challenger Deep, part of a trench east of the Philippines, in January 1960, in a unique spherical submersible boat called a bathyscaphe. They spent twenty minutes on the bottom, eating chocolate bars to keep warm, and saw several small bottom fish that looked like flounder.)

More modern submersibles can't reach these depths but find plenty to keep them busy closer to the surface, such as repeated sightings of a hitherto unknown "mystery squid," as they're called, twenty-three feet long, with fins like elephant ears and ten jointed tentacles that have a sort of umbrella-frame shape. In the last decade, mystery squid have been seen all over the world, usually at a depth of 6,000 to 10,000 feet (or—in less impressive dry-land, horizontal terms—at a little more than a mile to a little less than two miles). Dr. Michael Vecchione of the National Marine Fisheries Service, who has been investigating them, says such finds are not unusual. "I think there are a lot of really strange things down there," he told a Reuters reporter in 2001. "Every time someone goes down there and looks they find something really strange. It's Eureka time."

But if "the world's oceans are like an alien world," as *The New York Times* reported in July 2009, "the mysteries do not start a mile below the surface of the sea. They start with the surface itself. Scientists are now discovering that the top five-hundredth-inch of the ocean is somewhat like a sheet of jelly. And this odd habitat, thinner than a human hair, is home to an unusual menagerie of microbes." The ocean, the article notes, is the storage bin for much of the global-warming greenhouse gases humanity produces, but the microlayer is where these gases get absorbed. "It's the ocean breathing through its skin," said one marine biologist. "It's actually sucking the carbon dioxide down into the water column."

All this is by way of highlighting some further information about the sea-surface microlayer that particularly registered with me. "When scientists began studying the surface in the mid-20th century," the *Times* reporter, Carl Zimmer, wrote,

> they found it vexing. A scientist cannot just dunk a bucket into the ocean without dredging up deeper water as well. "Even defining the surface is hard, since it's moving up and down," said Peter Liss, a professor of environmental sciences at the University of East Anglia in England. . . . Dr. Liss said the microlayer was "clearly important, because it's where the ocean and the atmosphere interact."

"But it's difficult to study," he added, "so it hasn't received as much attention as it ought to."

I sometimes find it helpful to think of awareness as a microlayer—far thinner than a human hair—stretched across the surface of the human mind. ("Attention," one of the few words describing mental experience that does not have ambiguous roots, comes directly from a Latin word that means "to stretch toward.") Many parts of the mind, despite tremendous advances, remain largely unexamined and unsifted—a situation that Jeff Warren, after two years of interviewing brain and consciousness researchers for *The Head Trip,* says he senses may be about to change. "This is going to sound hyberbolic," he told an interviewer in 2008, "but I really believe we are at the dawn of a new age of scientific exploration. The external world is mapped; now the explorers are turning inward. They're approaching a huge, mysterious continent. They won't be the first to arrive. There are paths already cut in the forest, where shamans and monks and others have set up outposts and launched their own expeditions into the interior. It's a thrilling story, a lurid epic in the making, and yet almost no one has any idea it's happening."

"It's fraught with peril," Warren also said recently on the subject, because the mind "can be looked at through so many lenses—philosophical, neurological, psychological, phenomenological. Here everything is in flux. It's a rowdy scrimmage of vague experiments, stirring anecdotes, wild speculation, emotional ego wars, new theories, old evidence, new evidence, old theories, and looming over all the dreaded 'paradigm.' "

Studying awareness presents its own difficulties—and perhaps hasn't received as much attention as it ought to simply because, like the sea-surface microlayer, it keeps bobbing up and down. Yet, again like the microlayer, it is "clearly important" as an interface, in this case between the world and the rest of the mind. Some years ago, a New York psychotherapist I know, Gene Yellin, who's president of the board of the Metropolitan Institute for Training in Psychoanalytic Psychotherapy, pointed out that many people would assume I was talking about an uphill climb. According to the prevailing paradigm about how the mind works, he said, such an investigation starts off at an inherent disadvantage. "A fundamental tenet of what we learned in school," Yellin said, "was that, beginning in infancy, attention for survival purposes is for the most part directed outward. You'll find out whatever it is you'll find out, of course, but the lesson we were being taught was that we're none of us naturally sensitive to observing our own states of mind."

Certainly the whole idea of "introspection" (or "looking within") as a royal road for "discovering the laws that govern the mind," got a bad name in the early twentieth century, as a process that was subject to "errors of observation," and the word then took on the added burden of meaning "brooding" and "self-absorbed." But the practice of looking inward survived under other names, reemerging most recently, in the 1990s, as "neurophenomenology." This hybrid technique for investigating the mind combines neuroscience (or "third-person science," as neurophenomenologists refer to classic lab work) with personal experience (now considered potential evidence, and referred to as "first-person science"). *The Embodied Mind,* a 1991 book cited by Warren and cowritten by Francisco Varela, a Chilean biologist; Evan Thompson, a University of Toronto philosopher; and Eleanor Rosch, a University of California, Berkeley, psychologist, sets forth the rationale for attempting to synthesize these two approaches to knowledge:

> To deny the truth of our own experience in the scientific study of ourselves is not only unsatisfactory; it is to render the scientific study of ourselves without a subject matter. But to suppose that science cannot contribute to an understanding of our experience may be to abandon, within the modern context, the task of self-understanding. Experience and scientific understanding are like two legs without which we cannot walk.

Jeff Warren himself puts the matter slightly differently, telling his 2008 interviewer that "If your subject is the mind—and not just behavioral or brain activity—then you have to rely on first-person reports. There's no other way. The question is how to do it rigorously."

A cornerstone of "third-person science"—of the traditional scientific method, that is—is replicability, the idea that an experiment's findings will be considered more reliable if the experiment when repeated can produce the same results. One of the premises of this book is "second-person science," as you might say. My idea, as I've said, is that the larger awareness we've been discussing is an integral part of the equipment entrusted to us by our ancestry, and that, in consequence, awareness experiences very similar to the ones I've been writing about—similar at their core, at any rate, if not in all their particulars—are already a part of everyone's waking day, even if they often pass by unremarked and unremembered. In addition, and equally importantly, contact with this old form of awareness is available, practically at will, to anyone who wants to make further use of it— by choice, and not just by happenstance. In this way, readers of the book are part of the validation process of the concepts it expresses. Every experience and account here can be field-tested in the laboratory of your own mind. My experiences are no more remarkable than the ones freely available to all. But if the Deep Travel moments I've been recording and reporting on—my own and those I've gathered from friends and books and old tales—ring true in terms of what you've kept with you from your own Deep Travel memories, then there's already some common ground. I'm also thinking that you can notice in yourself—maybe just by standing up slowly, or maybe by saying "Warsaw" to yourself (or by entering one of the other doors to Deep Travel we've looked at)—the "axis of feelings," that balance of eagerness and vigilance that seems to me to form the underpinnings of the structure, the bipedal perceptual platform, that gives Deep Travel both its sweep and its urgency.

Another part of the validation process, I've thought, would be to see if the idea that our larger awareness developed as a force and capacity within us as one consequence of our becoming bipedal can fit comfortably within, or maybe even add further clarity to, the twenty-first-century telling of the story of where human beings came from. Corroboration of this sort would depend on whether such a hypothesis, sketchy as it still is, might be welcomed even in a preliminary way by "third-person scientists" who specialize in human origins. I decided to share my very informal findings with Will Harcourt-Smith. I had in my head a warning that had recently been issued by Richard Lewontin, the evolutionary biologist whose long 1972 bus ride through Indiana had helped disprove the notion that there were major genetic differences between human beings with different skin colors. Lewontin, now at Harvard, electrified a 2008 audience at the annual meeting of the American Association for the Advancement of Science, *Science* magazine reported, "when he led off a session titled 'The Mind of a Toolmaker' by announcing that scientists know next to nothing about how humans got so smart. 'We are missing the fossil record of human cognition,' Lewontin said at the meeting. 'So we make up stories.' "

It's a variant of the "Just So" charge and caution. This condition had already been partly met, I thought, since wider awareness seemed to be a spin-off, an unsought outgrowth and offshoot of bipedalism— walking's "leave behind," so to speak. If this was the sequence of events, then, by implication, every time we make use of our wider awareness, we're tapping into a two-million-year-old "now." Meaning that we have—again without asking for it—direct access into a part of our own past that's even more immediate than the sight of a footprint, and better preserved, since the talent has existed within us essentially unchanged ever since. What it does for us now, it began to do then for our forebears. With its acquisition, the mind opened wide, and information flooded in both in quantities and at a rate that would previously have been impossible. Its presence changed the cognitive and "feeling" content of daily motion and, as a result, the learning content as well. Each step was—in its tiny way—a transforming act, a constantly renewed leap across a Rubicon, a river of no return. Over time, its accumulated effects may have proved to be a stimulus essential for further mind enlargement and brain building, which led in an infinitely gradual way to better toolmaking and the strengthening of several "intelligences," sometimes called "technical intelligence" (know-how) and "natural history intelligence" (the ability to respond to and understand the landscape), that in modern humans rival the reach of our social intelligence.

What, more specifically, is "natural history intelligence"? The best description I've run across is in *The Prehistory of the Mind: The Cognitive Origins of Art and Science,* by Steven Mithen, the English archaeologist and "early prehistorian" who's also, as previously noted, written (in *After the Ice*) about the rise of sedentism. In *The Prehistory of the Mind,* Mithen defines natural history intelligence as

an amalgam of at least three sub-domains of thought: that about animals, that about plants, and that about the geography of the landscape, such as the distribution of water sources and caves. As a whole it is about

understanding the geography of the landscape, the rhythms of the seasons, and the habits of potential game. It is about using current observations of the natural world to predict the future: the meaning of cloud
formations, of animal footprints, of the arrival and departure of birds in
the spring and autumn.

Which sounds a lot like the eventual result of Jonathan Kingdon's
third circle of alertness: "patterns made by attractive vegetation types,
fires, rain clouds, and the sun's cycle," and "an awareness of events such
as the comings and goings of rain, smoke, dust, or dusk."

Brains and intelligences grow very slowly, over tens of thousands of
generations, but perhaps we today can activate and use a corresponding awareness to observe firsthand how the shocks and nutrients the
world brings reached the minds of those on the way to becoming
human, once the broad, inclusive filter of wider awareness became permanently available. In this way it became both a fully developed instrument of the mind and an inescapable mental component for 99.5
percent of the last 2 million years—until it was obscured by the ways of
sedentism approximately ten thousand years ago.

If this kind of first-person science proves fruitful and leads to a
careful examination of our past possibilities from within, we'd have
another tool with which to investigate human origins, supplementing
what stones, bones, and chromosomes can tell us with what we can
learn from the awareness that arose as a result of our beginning to
roam. (I'm leaving out climate history and language history, as well as
brain studies, which have already been accepted as research paths that
lead to the same goal.)

Is there any further "third-person science" data to support the quick
post-bipedal emergence of wider awareness? Yes, though it's cir-
cumstantial. One corroborative argument that could be made would
focus on post-bipedal hominin circumstances and look at how
hominins' "need to know" had changed as a result of standing up. In
other words, what information could they no longer afford to be
deprived of if they were going to survive? Lynne Isbell, a University of
California anthropologist, in 2006 asked this question about the pre-
hominin primates of an earlier period, and proposed that the appearance on earth of venomous snakes 60 million years ago had led to what

she called an "evolutionary arms race." Many mammals responded by developing some degree of immunity to snake bites; a particular group of primates, on the other hand—the "catarrhines," or Old World monkeys, which later gave rise to apes (and later still to hominins)—answered the challenge by developing both binocular and color vision so they could see snakes better; by embracing daytime living (or "diurnality") so that they would be awake when snakes were awake; by eating a "sugar-rich diet" (primarily fruit) so their brains could work faster; and by strengthening the connections in their minds to a "fear module," or early-warning network, that their own ancestors had developed 40 million years before to give them advance notice of constrictor snakes, which evolved before venomous snakes and instead of biting squeeze their prey to death.

Though snakes and other reptiles were still part of the 4-million-year-old African landscapes that habitual bipeds such as *A. afarensis* had to make their way through, according to *Man the Hunted: Primates, Predators, and Human Evolution,* a 2008 book by two anthropologists, Donna L. Hart, of the University of Missouri–St. Louis, and Robert W. Sussman, of Washington University in St. Louis, these upright hominins also had to evade species whose agility, size, and numbers made them even more fearsome—such as the still abdundant African crowned eagle, a forest bird with a wingspan of up to seven feet, and now-extinct hyenas as big as bears. (The megapredators of the time were both enormous and ten times as numerous as Africa's surviving carnivores. One such bird with a ten-foot wingspan, Harst's eagle, survived on the other side of the world, in New Zealand, until only five hundred years ago. It had talons the size of tiger claws and is still remembered in Maori legends as a bird that "raced the hawk to the heavens.") Australopithecines, by contrast, were small and without either tools or fire. Studying their remains, Sussman discovered that about 6 to 10 percent of the known hominin bones of the era show tooth or talon marks—almost precisely the same predation rate found today among African prey species such as savanna antelopes and ground-living monkeys. Hence "man the hunted": "He wasn't hunting" anything that could have caught him, Sussman told an interviewer when the book came out. "He was avoiding them at all costs."

Cooperation and group living were useful defenses, according to Sussman and Hart—and equally, to my mind, so would have been an expanded awareness filter that balanced vigilance (the successor to Isbell's proposed primate "fear module") with opportunity and anticipation. Bruce Chatwin, in *The Songlines,* wrote feelingly about "the beast," as he called it, *Dinofelis* (meaning "terrible cat"—just as "dinosaur" means "terrible lizard"), a forest-preferring, saber-toothed cat the size of a jaguar that survived until 1.2 million years ago, and so would have hunted obligate bipeds as well as their predecessors. Perhaps *Dinofelis* even sought them out. Chatwin quotes from *The Hunters or the Hunted?* a book by C. K. ("Bob") Brain, a South African paleontologist who during his career has unearthed more than 240,000 fossils:

> Could it be, Brain asks, that *Dinofelis* was a specialist predator on the primates?
>
> "A combination of robust jaws," he writes, "and a well developed component in the dentition would have allowed *Dinofelis* to eat all parts of a primate skeleton except the skull. The hypothesis that *Dinofelis* was a specialist killer of the primates is persuasive."
>
> •
>
> Could it be, one is tempted to ask, that *Dinofelis* was Our Beast? A Beast set aside from all the other Avatars of Hell? The Arch-Enemy who stalked us, stealthily and cunningly, wherever we went? But whom, in the end, we got the better of?

Some paleontologists attribute the disappearance of *Dinofelis* to the gradual shrinking of the African forests, but Chatwin chooses to give hominins the credit. "Compared to this victory," he concludes, "the rest of our achievements may be seen as so many frills. You could say we are a species on holiday."

On holiday. It's a phrase I'd prefer to reserve for human life after sedentism, a period where—by and large—the feeling of safety comes not from alertness but from being able to detach from general alertness and have more time for tasks and pursuits that concentrate attention to a pinpoint focus—and obliterate the sense of time passing.

NOTES FOR "A SHORT HISTORY"

There's additional "third-person science" data that might help us zero in on the idea that our walking and our wider awareness can be considered a coordinated pair, much of it intriguing, but it remains scattered, since the book I keep reaching for and long to thumb through, *A Short History of Awareness,* has yet to be written. Or perhaps it should be called *A Prehistory of Awareness,* to make clear that it would serve as a companion volume and supplement to Steven Mithen's *The Prehistory of the Mind.* Because at that point we would have reference books both about the "front end of smartness"—awareness and attention as the portals of the mind—and the "back end," the various "intelligences" that assimilate and structure what the mind has absorbed.

All we can hope for at the moment is a preview of *The Prehistory of Awareness.* But there's already more information available than you might think. Just as we found earlier that Deep Travel accounts were a central feature in many travel books if you started to read them "slantwise," so to speak, so, too, even though there are as yet no endowed "professors of awareness" within the scientific and academic community, interest in awareness is often an unannounced subset of many fields of study—more and more so, in recent years—as I've found by looking at books that as cataloged by their predominant themes would seem to be biology books, or paleobiology books, or books whose focus is physiology, or primatology, or natural history, or psychology (including ecological psychology, environmental, social, and research psychology, sleep research, and visual systems analysis).

A survey book about awareness would have to begin by looking as far back in time as possible. For instance, in the definition developed by ecological psychologists like Ed Reed, awareness of at least a rudimentary sort is an ancient phenomenon, because animals can't live without it. "For ecological psychology," Reed points out in *Encountering the World*, "behavior is not 'just behavior.' *Behavior is inseparable from awareness.*" Animals, in this conception, actively seek out the things they can use or need to avoid in an environment (the resources or "affordances" of a place), and successful exploration "requires at least some awareness of that affordance" and the information it contains about its possible uses or dangers. Since the so-called Cambrian explosion, the initial rapid spread throughout the world of complex animals, took place around 530 million years ago (during the Cambrian period, the earliest part of the Paleozoic, or "Old Life," era), we can cautiously peg the birth of some kind of rough-and-ready awareness to that moment—and set aside for another occasion the question of awareness in single-celled animals, even though, as Reed says, "There is no magic line above which animals become aware or intelligent. There is not even a slippery slope along which one might measure awareness or intelligence."

If half a billion years ago, even though it's already a pared-down number, sounds like an improbable overestimate for the cumulative age of awareness, the *Short History*'s future author could, temporarily and even more conservatively, estimate a shorter life span for this core capacity—say, just under a quarter of a billion years. This lower figure would be keyed to studies Charles Darwin made in his later years that, among other findings, displayed the discriminatory powers that characterize the "lowly" earthworm, as he called it, a creature thought to have become part of earth's landscape about 225 million years ago, during the Mesozoic, or "Middle Life," era. In his final book, *The Formation of Vegetable Mould Through the Action of Worms, with Observations on Their Habits*, published in 1881, a year before his death—and twenty-two years after *On the Origin of Species*—Darwin reported the "surprising" fact that earthworms have "mental powers" and "exhibit some degree of intelligence instead of a mere blind instinctive impulse."

The immediate practical result of Darwin's experiments with earthworms, which he conducted in the grounds around Down House, his home in the London suburbs, was to demonstrate that earthworms, then considered a pest, help turn the soil and make it more fertile, and in doing so actually create new soil—about two inches' worth every decade. The "awareness implications" of his work, which have been recognized more slowly, stem from his findings, recounted by Reed, that the linings of earthworm burrows are neither random assemblages nor automatic and repetitious patterns. For instance, earthworms search around a burrow for bits of material they can glue into the walls of a wider, "basket-shaped" opening near the top, and Darwin deliberately scattered Scotch pine needles—long, sharp on one end, and not found in the south of England, and so therefore a shape never encountered by the worms before—on the ground nearby. The earthworms used the needles, and as they did so invariably drew them in by their blunt ends but then turned them around so that by the end of their work, as Darwin noted, "the sharp points had been pressed into the lining" of the nest. "Had this not been effectually done," Darwin said,

> the sharp points would have prevented the retreat of the worms into their burrows; and these structures would have resembled traps armed with converging points of wire, rendering the ingress of an animal easy and its egress difficult or impossible. The skill of these worms is noteworthy.

There's a moral here, Reed says: "It is easy to convince oneself falsely that a behavior is purely 'instinctive' or 'automatically triggered' by a certain stimulus because we humans are often unfamiliar with the kinds of variation found by the animal in its environment. Almost any other scientist would have interpreted the worms' behavior as due to some kind of mechanistic instinct."

Further: A previously unobserved, quiescent (or "sleeplike") state, called "lethargus," has recently been found in a different kind of worm, a tiny nematode less than 1/25th of an inch long, *Caenorhabditis elegans,* which, like earthworms, lives in the ground. Sleep has been recorded in fish, amphibians, reptiles, and all mammals, as well as in fruit flies, but has never been thought to occur in worms. Reporting on the discovery in *Nature,* neurologists from the University of Pennsylvania School of Medicine's Division of Sleep Medicine note that "sleeplike states are evolutionarily ancient." Perhaps awareness and the interruption to awareness that sleep represents both became presences in animal life very early on.

If, as Reed would argue, "exploratory activity" and the "information pickup" it makes possible are "tantamount to awareness," then perhaps awareness itself had started to play a larger role in animals shortly before the arrival of earthworms or nematodes. The "Great Dying," otherwise known as the Permian-Triassic extinction event, killed off perhaps 90 percent of all marine species 250 million years ago, and is considered the dividing line between the Paleozoic and the Mesozoic— between "Old Life" and "Middle Life," that is. The immediate cause seems to have been the eruption in what's now Siberia of what sounds like a "lava glacier"—its technical name is a "flood basalt deposition"— which in this case meant a lava flow a mile high and so massive it covered more than 2.5 million square miles of land. This extraordinary calamity also, in the end, became a "Great Beginning" of sorts, since it unleashed exploratory activity in the oceans. Many of the Old Life forms that died out—as three paleobiologists explain in a recent *Natural History* article ("The Search for Evidence of Mass Extinction," by Scott Lidgard, Peter J. Wagner, and Matthew A. Kosnik)—had been characterized as "filter-feeding, sedentary animals that lived on the sea bottom," whereas many of their Middle Life replacements were

> highly mobile, shell-crushing or shell-boring predators [that] underwent dramatic radiations. Their descendants included many arthropods such as lobsters and crabs, neogastropods [sea snails], marine reptiles, and ray-finned fishes. At the same time many prey animals evolved greater skeletal defenses. The product of that evolutionary arms race is widely known as the "Mesozoic Marine Revolution."

Or maybe we could, in addition, think of the Mesozoic as a series of dramatic "awareness radiations," first in the seas and then on land, a large-scale "unanchoring" of what had predominantly been "sessile" (unmoving and permanently attached) life-forms in favor of "motile" (freely and actively moving) successor animals whose awareness, as it expanded, now included not only things to eat and things to avoid but a reliable sense, as we've already said, of where they are and how to navigate through their surroundings. Lidgard, Wagner, and Kosnik call the Permian-Triassic extinction a "game changer," since it led eventually to "an increased richness and abundance of organisms" exploiting new resources. It took millions of years for these newer life-forms to develop, but perhaps it's not fanciful to think of a game-changing parallel between the oceanic Mesozoic motility-awareness link and the much later and far more closely connected walking-bipedal perceptual platform connection.

This next consideration takes us back into the Paleozoic again, and introduces a different strand (as well as an earlier launch point for awareness—obviously there are still other time lines in the history of awareness that need to be coordinated and reconciled). According to *The Emotional Lives of Animals: A Leading Scientist Explores Animal Joy, Sorrow, and Empathy—and Why They Matter,* a recent book by Marc Bekoff, a biologist at the University of Colorado, research in the 1990s by Michel Cabanac, a physiologist at Laval University, in Quebec, suggests that "the ability to have an emotional life emerged between the time of amphibians and early reptiles"—a very rough date, sometime in the 60 million years between about 315 and 375 million years ago. What Cabanac discovered was that modern-day "reptiles, such as iguanas, maximize sensory pleasure," meaning they "prefer to stay warm rather than venture out into the cold to get food, whereas amphibians, such as frogs, don't show such behavior. Neither do fish."

More specifically, Cabanac was brought to this realization by noticing that "iguanas experience what is called 'emotional fever' (a rise in body temperature) and tachycardia (increased heart rate), physiological responses that are associated with pleasure in other vertebrates, including humans." This led Cabanac to conclude that "the first mental event to emerge into consciousness was the ability of an individual to experience the sensations of pleasure and displeasure." "Consciousness," like "attention," is a word with a seemingly straightforward history; like "science," "conscience," and "nice," it comes from a Latin word that means "to know," although the same word had previously had different shadings, with the connotations of "to distinguish, separate, or cleave." So maybe when feelings were joined to awareness, the result was a clearer sense of which objects and actions were worth pursuing, and in what order.

When it comes to understanding what it is we actually know about awareness and the mind, we're at one of those odd betwixt-and-between moments that often occur in the early stages of studying anything. Information is flooding in about certain traits—for instance, laughter. Primatologists at the University of Portsmouth in

England, according to a 2009 report by Malcolm Ritter, an Associated Press science writer, have demonstrated that laughter is a hominoidal trait, because "people and great apes inherited laughter from a shared ancestor that lived more than ten million years ago." Their experimental method? "Tickling three human babies, and 21 orangutans, gorillas, chimps, and bonobos," and then making more than eight hundred recordings of the sounds that were produced. These cross-species vocalizations show little similarity when people listen to them—"ape laughter doesn't sound like the human version," Ritter explains. "It may be rapid panting, or slower noisy breathing, or a short series of grunts."

But mapped on the graph, various fragments within the sounds showed remarkable affinities—"distinctive features," Ritter reported, that "could well have arisen from ancestral traits." Since orangutan laughs shared some of these characteristics (though fewer), and since orangs were the first of the great apes to split off from the other hominoids, perhaps 14 million years ago, this gives us a tentative date for the origin of laughter. It's a date that makes sense to Frans de Waal, a Dutch-born primatologist who directs the Living Links Center at the Yerkes National Primate Research Center at Emory University, in Atlanta (and whom *Time* magazine thinks of as one of the world's one hundred most influential people). In *The Age of Empathy: Nature's Lessons for a Kinder Society*, a book summarizing recent research by many primatologists and other zoologists, de Waal presents the findings of a fellow countryman, Jan A. R. A. M. van Hooff, of Utrecht University, who thinks ape laughter can be explained by placing it within a wider hominoidal context of accomplishments—and by linking it to the fact that great apes had already developed (and we later inherited) what van Hooff calls a "playful attitude." So ape laughter, as de Waal explains, is "often a reaction to surprise or incongruity—as when a tiny infant chimp chases the group's top male, who runs away 'scared,' laughing all the while. The connection with surprise is still visible in children's games such as peek-a-boo, or jokes marred by unexpected turns, which we save until the very end and appropriately call 'punch lines.' "

But there's lingering obscurity within laughter studies, too. Jaak Panksepp, an Estonian-born psychologist at Washington State University, whose field is "affective neuroscience," meaning looking into how emotions move through animal brains, has learned how to listen to the rats in his lab by introducing a "translator," a machine that can transform ultrahigh-frequency rat chirps into sounds that human ears can hear. Young rats produce these chirps, he noticed, when he tickled them. "When he momentarily stops the tickling," *Psychology Today* reported in 2006, "they run to his hand, seeking more." "We studied these sounds for a couple of years," Panksepp told the magazine, "without understanding they might be laughter." If they are, laughter would be a mammalian trait far older than anything that emerged within the hominoids—since the last common ancestor of humanity, rats, and mice lived 80 million years ago. "It's time," according to Panksepp, "for humans to rejoin the rest of the animal kingdom."

But at this point, much of our "awareness of awareness" is tantalizingly incomplete, and information coming to light serves to remind us how many gaps there are in our knowledge and how much there is left to learn. We know, for one thing, that there are parts of our awareness that we can't switch on or off—they're just there. Take, for instance, the "life detector," a mental tracking system that Niko Troje, a psychologist and the director of the Biomotion Lab at Queen's University in Kingston, Ontario, found in people (and rabbits) after his little daughter asked him why she always got closer to the rabbits near their house when she was on a bicycle than when she was walking. "I didn't have an answer for her then," Troje told an interviewer in 2006. "Now I think I have one."

The answer is that people, animals, and birds seem to have a built-in motion detector that focuses on up-and-down patterns, especially those that are near the ground and getting closer by the moment. This automatic "visual filter" signals even to their peripheral vision the approach of another animal, whether predator or prey, by specifically focusing attention on that animal's feet—or, rather, on the flowing patterns that feet make during forward motion through space as they're lifted and then fall again under "the force of gravity." Rabbits ran away when they saw Troje's daughter walking toward them, but because wheels in motion stay in the same vertical plane, they didn't interpret spinning bicycle tires as a sign of danger. Since the same ability also seems to be present in baby chicks, this suggests that the "life detector"—Troje coined the name for this mental warning module—is hardwired and has a long evolutionary history that might stretch as far back as the amniotes, cold-blooded, four-legged, lizardlike creatures thought to be the common ancestors of birds and mammals; amniotes appeared on earth more than 300 million years ago.

The continuing presence of this early-warning device in so many species would certainly explain, Troje says, why "it is relatively easy to get close to wild animals in a car, a canoe," or any vehicle not obviously propelled by feet. He also thinks that other animal behaviors, such as the slow creep of a cat on the hunt, might have developed more recently to serve as a kind of "life detector" inhibitor or defuser, disguising the fact that feet are in motion. There might also be something of a connection to Lynne Isbell's ideas about the coevolution of primate awareness and snakes, since, Troje notes, "seemingly irrational phobias" persist "toward animals that don't fit the ballistic pattern of a proposed 'life detector.' Snakes, insects and spiders, or birds can generate pathological reactions not observed in response to 'normal' animals."

Awareness or the lack of it has no impact on other seemingly built-in impulses. They simply enact themselves. Timothy D. Wilson, a University of Virginia psychologist (and the author of *Strangers to Ourselves*), and his research partner, Richard Nisbett, a University of Michigan social psychologist (and the author of *The Geography of Thought*), have designed experiments based on the known fact that, as a *New Scientist* report puts it, "people tend to subconsciously prefer the rightmost object in a sequence if given no other choice criteria." Shown five pieces of clothing laid out randomly in a line, four out of five people *did* choose the one on the right—but "nobody gave position as a reason. It was always about the fineness of the weave, richer color, or superior texture." Similarly, Paco Underhill, an environmental psychologist and a consultant to store owners about the "selling environment" (he's the author of *Why We Buy: The Science of Shopping* and *Call of the Mall: The Geography of Shopping*), has learned to rely on "the tendency of shoppers to turn right on entering a store." Why do we have these preferences? As far as we know, we just do.

It's so much easier—comparatively—to see and say where body parts come from, and when, and how they re-formed over time. Consider the words of Neil Shubin, a paleontologist, the provost of Chicago's Field Museum of Natural History, and the codiscoverer (in 2004) of the fossilized "fishopod" *Tiktaalik,* part fish and partly an amphibian tetrapod (or "four-legger"), a find that was almost immediately hailed as one of the most spectacular transitional fossils, or "missing links," ever brought to light, ranking with *Archaeopteryx* (the dinosaur-like "original bird" first unearthed in 1861). This passage comes from Shubin's 2008 book *Your Inner Fish: A Journey into the 3.5-Billion-Year History of the Human Body*:

> Looking back through billions of years of change, we see that everything innovative or apparently unique in the history of life is really just old stuff that has been recycled, repurposed, or otherwise modified for new uses. Human hands are a modified version of mammalian ones, which are ultimately modified fish fins. Bones in our ears originally helped ancient sharks and reptiles chew. The genes that control all of this structure were originally used to build the bodies of ancient worms, flies, and fish. Every part of us tells this story: our sense organs, our heads, even our entire body plan.

Or here's a short part of a *New Scientist* review of Gary F. Marcus's 2008 *Kluge: The Haphazard Construction of the Human Mind*. Marcus is a research psychologist and directs New York University's Infant Language Center; "kluge," which rhymes with "stooge," is an engineering term for a piece of equipment cobbled together out of whatever's around to be scrounged:

> Marcus compares human brains—where the rational parts are grafted onto the primitive, "reptilian" ones—to a power plant he once visited. There, beneath a veneer of high-tech computers, archaic vacuum tubes did the real work.
>
> Like the power plant, evolution never had a chance to "go offline" and install better brains; its only choice was to adapt the imperfect design of previous generations.

For me, a critical chapter of *A Short History of Awareness,* when it finally appears, would be put together from information that, like the meticulous tracking of physical changes from era to era and species to species, already has some solid grounding in post–World War II fieldwork. Its subject would be the marked differences in what have been called the "awareness structures" within groups of baboons and groups of chimpanzees. These recorded differences anticipate recent observations of a "playful attitude" among chimps but, more than that, describe the arrival of conditions that made it possible for our expanded awareness to become the "first unintended consequence" of bipedalism.

The principal investigator of primate attention structures was an English primatologist from the University of Birmingham, Michael R. A. Chance, who first began publishing his results in 1967 (in "Attention Structure as the Basis for Primate Rank Orders," an article he wrote for *Man*, a journal then being published by the Royal Anthropological Institute). His main finding, since nicknamed "the two modes," was a change in what had previously been very tight constraints on how primate attention could be used. Once "unbundled" and "dispersed," as it were, attention was no longer just an enforcement tool—part rope and part whip—used as the principal weapon of social control. The change, when it occurred—sometime, it seems most likely, between 16 and 22 million years ago—reset the fear/explore balance in primate group relationships. Chance's terms for the two modes he had detected were "agonic" (from the Greek word for "intense combat and strife" that also gave rise to "agony"), which characterized the arrangements among the monkey species he had been observing, primarily rhesus macaques and baboons, and "hedonic" (a more familiar word; its Greek root means "pleasurable" or "sweet"), an "add-on," or additional behavior, which could be seen in all species of great apes, including orangutans, but seemed most highly developed in chimpanzees.

What are the specifics of agonic and hedonic interactions? Here's how Chance wrote about both modes toward the end of his career, in a chapter from a 1996 book, *The Archaeology of Human Ancestry*:

> In the *agonic mode,* individuals are always together in a group yet spread out ... keeping their distance from the more dominant ones to whom they are constantly attentive [glancing at them at least once every thirty seconds, Chance says in another book, and] ... ready, at an instant, to avoid punishment ... with various submissive and/or appeasing gestures. . . . [The frequent glances are accompanied by continuous] partial tension in all the limb muscles.

The *"hedonic mode"* in chimpanzees, Chance said, was characterized by "the languid, relaxed, often slow movements of these creatures except when excited in pursuit of ... hunting, throwing, climbing, etc." The mode's chief feature was flexibility:

A manifestation not only of absence of the fear of punishment in the relationship between individuals, but also of a freeing of an individual's attention from being the medium or channel of the social bond between them and the rest of society. Because it is no longer active as a bonding element, attention is freed for detailed investigations and manipulations of objects in the physical environment, thus facilitating the development and expansion of intelligence.

Putting a date on the first appearance of the hedonic mode is my own extrapolation. Baboons, unlike rhesus macaques, which date back to more than 20 million years ago, are actually a relatively "modern" species that evolved at approximately the same time as *H. erectus* (and in roughly the same kind of open African country). But baboons, like rhesus macaques, are Old World monkeys, not apes, and since apes and monkeys diverged 22 to 25 million years ago, perhaps—although this has yet to be demonstrated—any baboon behaviors, even if developed comparatively recently, are prehominoid in derivation. Whereas, since orangutans show signs of hedonic playfulness, and orangs are thought to have branched off from the other great apes something like 14 to 16 million years ago, this would open a 6- to 11-million-year-long window of opportunity for the decoupling of fear and attention and of the need to devote an inordinate amount of attention at all times to obedience and subservience. Not that species yoked to the agonic mode can't survive—after all, *H. erectus* and baboons roamed the same savannas, where baboons thrive to this day, living in groups of fifty or more (usually referred to as a "troop" or a "congress"). Nor is it to deny that modern human situations don't have painfully agonic aspects (we've all encountered them). But it is hard to imagine how the many dimensions of our larger awareness could have been activated among species where the narrow focus and many restrictions on awareness of the agonic mode, not to mention the constant muscular tension and threats of reprisal from within your own group, were all that any individual had ever known.

We know that astonishing changes in human capacities followed from becoming bipedal. As Robin Fox, a Rutgers University anthropologist, expresses it in *Conjectures and Confrontations,* a book of essays, "Concentration and persistence are there in the apes, but they had to be applied systematically and across a wide range of behaviors" for humanity to emerge. "The attention span, as we now like to call it, had to be lengthened and focused on something other than food and sex," Fox notes. To what extent was the process assisted or even accelerated by hominins' access to the "bipedal perceptual platform," the new arrangement of feelings and perceptions that standing up had made possible?

I guess I'm most inclined to think," Will Harcourt-Smith told me recently, "that the idea makes best sense if you think of this larger awareness as something that really kicked in at the time of obligate bipedalism." This, he notes,

we've roughly pegged at 2 million years ago with the coming of *Homo erectus,* or some other similar early *Homo* species, although it would be more accurate to talk about a larger span of time, somewhere between 2.5 and 1.8 million years ago. Whatever the precise date turns out to be, that was the big shift in hominin life—well, the second big shift, after the changeover about 4 million years ago from occasional to habitual bipedalism (with the appearance of *Australopithecus anamensis,* Lucy's predecessor species, sometime between 4.1 and 3.9 million years ago).

We know that obligate bipedalism coincides with the grasslands opening up, with the emergence of tools, with brain enlargement, and with having to travel farther on a daily basis for food, while avoiding different predators. So this was a really critical period. It required us—well, hominins, because up to a point these creatures were still not human—to pay attention to a wider range of stimuli just to get what was needed in terms of the search for nourishment and safety. And it was the moment when we finally had no other strategy available. It wasn't possible any longer to shinny up a tree, since our feet didn't work that way anymore. At the same time, we couldn't run like a gazelle—our new feet and legs wouldn't let us do that, either. So we had to use whatever intelligence we had. I always try to think adaptively, as you know, and think about behaviors that serve evolutionary purposes. In the circumstances we're talking about, there could be a very strong selection pressure for the ability to use this larger and more intensive awareness of our surroundings, to sustain it throughout the day, and to retain it from one generation to the next.

It could be that the first phase, the habitual bipedalism phase, set the scene for a more intense awareness of the landscape and far greater emotional involvement. And then obligate bipedalism set it in motion. It's the proportion of time you're doing anything that counts. When you're finally an obligate biped and seeing vistas to the horizon 80 to 90 percent of the day—vistas that give you an overview of the entire landscape—maybe that's when a threshold of inquisitiveness is crossed, and *curiosity* in the sense we're using it takes over. So it isn't just that vistas are known to exist that's needed—it's having them "stay there" in the present, and perhaps in memory, too, that gives a new context. Meaning that maybe continuous exposure to new conditions is the key—and at a time when, as we've said, you have to start traveling miles for tool materials as well as for food.

All of a sudden, landscape use becomes really interesting—maybe that's the point. You're moving through an environment that's changed in many respects—in its colors and smells and overall feeling—and of course you're moving through it at a different height from the ground. *And* you're taking in so much more of it, second by second. I think that most people would agree that reverie and focused attention, the forms of awareness we're most familiar with, serve evolutionary purposes. So why not say the same for the enhanced and intensified awareness that complements them? Since this was also the time when true traveling began, when hominins moved out of Africa for the first time, the implication, I'd say, is that with the advent and retention of our larger, full-landscape awareness, we gained a kind of "travel chip" in our minds that we then took with us as we spread across the globe.

Or put it another way. A new physical capacity to be more exploratory, thanks to our longer legs, overlapped with a new mental capacity to be more exploratory, the desire to range a little further that heightened excitedness and sharper perceptions bring. It's kind of scary, but it feels good. These guys were not Lewis and Clark, but travel now conferred an evolutionary advantage—and in that sense had actually become part of evolution in action. We can't say that obligate bipedalism preceded brain growth, but they do coincide. So maybe what we're really saying is that becoming bipedal helps you get smart, and I don't think many people have talked about this in that way. Your legs bring you into the savanna, but your new perceptual platform brings you into an even more expanded realm, and it's the stimulation and new information that is the precursor of smartness, the backbone of cognitive development. And the steps you start taking become the first steps on the road to intelligence—a path that a long time afterward led modern humans out of Africa, some 120 to 90 thousand years ago, and that, later still, produced the explosions of art and "symbolic behavior" that we know of in Europe 40 thousand years ago.

Harcourt-Smith, however, had a question of his own. If an expanded awareness—or a "travel chip," as he had called it—was useful enough to have been offered permanent residence in our minds something like two million years ago, why is it that people today who have inherited it often feel estranged from it, or have a hard time even acknowledging its presence, or describing it, or contacting it, or figuring out its uses? All I could tell him was that it was a question I'd frequently found myself thinking about—because it does seem so odd to be cut off from something that offers so much enjoyment and insight. So far, I said, I'd come up with several theories. Sedentism and its effects was a common theme running through these ideas.

For instance, we've said that our larger awareness is a unique amalgam of heightened feelings, characterized by a curiosity blended from vigilance and anticipation. But one of the first accomplishments of sedentism was to set up a perimeter that excludes dangerous wild animals (or at least minimizes their intrusions), thus in effect re-creating pre–obligate bipedalism conditions, except that instead of regaining a situation where treetop safety was once more available each evening, there was now a permanent zone where some parts of alertness could be relaxed—although there was still the weather and, of course, the actions of other people to contend with.

These altered circumstances, as I see it, reset the fear/opportunity balance, and so made our larger awareness less "necessary" as a constant state of mind, while offering new scope for other forms of awareness, such as focused attention and daydreaming, where any consciousness of our surroundings (not to mention the sense of time passing) virtually disappears. Although writing more specifically about brain development, John Allman, a biologist and anthropologist at the California Institute of Technology, seems to echo this understanding in a 2000 book, *Evolving Brains*. Noting that the human brain has become smaller over the past 35,000 years, Allman suggests that "the domestication of plants and animals as sources of food and clothing served as major buffers against environmental variability. Perhaps humans, through the invention of agriculture and other cultural means for reducing the hazards of existence, have domesticated themselves."

The arrival of settlements also set up the distinction we still make between "here"-ness, as we've called it, meaning places where we expect to find a relaxed state of affairs, and "there"-ness, or everywhere else. At first, even though people, once settled, didn't move around much, "here"-ness didn't occupy very much ground. Gradually, however, as humanity grew and spread, "there"-ness shrank in size, and along the way the "wildness quotient" of the remaining "theres" was repeatedly reduced, diluted, tamed. However far from a town we may be, for instance, the North America we travel through today is wildly—if that's the word—different from the presettlement world that reappeared when the glaciers receded; over a four-hundred-year period 13,000 years ago, the continent lost two-thirds of its large mammals (defined as mammals weighing one hundred pounds or more). To which we add the fact, already noted, that we've been able to turn "here"-ness into a portable commodity we can carry around with us, and that we can alter the focus of travel by imposing either a "never-left" or "still-back-here" sense, where we find ourselves preoccupied by the thoughts that had dominated our thinking before departure, or on an "already-there" quality, based on anticipating our arrival and what it is we'll be doing when we get to our destination.

Estimates of how much of the earth's land surface has been affected by human activities range from 50 to 83 percent. Since these worldwide changes—such as leveling forests to plant crops—are thought to be causing the extermination of approximately 140,000 species of plants, animals, and microbes every year, by the mid-1990s a number of ecologists had already concluded that, no matter what the actual percentage of land being diverted to human uses turns out to be, the ongoing changes to existing ecosystems have already been so extensive that we are now in the middle of a "sixth extinction event." (The "Great Dying," which proved so devastating to sessile sea animals 250 million years ago, was one of five previous mass extinctions in earth's history; the most recent one before the current "Holocene extinction" was the "end-Cretaceous event," 65 million years ago, which was most notable for killing off the dinosaurs.) Going beyond

·this, Paul R. Ehrlich, the conservation biologist, sees a further danger: "*Homo sapiens,*" he told a National Academy of Sciences colloquium in March 2000, "in addition to causing the sixth major spasm of biotic extinction, is also altering the course of evolution for millions of years in the future." Meaning, he said, that without anyone's having intended it, the wholesale modifications being made to existing landscapes are in effect "redirecting evolution" by placing unprecedented restrictions both on "the rate of evolutionary regeneration" and on "the nature of the replacements produced."

As to what we could call the "awareness implications" of all these interventions into natural processes, Ehrlich says only that "tens of thousands of future generations" of people will find themselves consigned to living out their lives among impoverished environments that no amount of travel can ever take them away from, since simplified landscapes far less diverse than the ones that still surround us will be all that the planet can sustain. But a number of America's best natural history and nature writers have addressed the subject more directly. Robert Michael Pyle, for instance, a butterfly expert whose books chronicle the changing Northwest, remembers "pottering, netting, catching, and watching" insects, crawdads, and tadpoles in the vacant back lots and leftover marshes of Aurora, Colorado, his hometown, a small town when he was growing up in the 1950s that has since become a sprawling Denver suburb. "What," he asks—in *The Thunder Tree: Lessons from an Urban Wildland*—"to a curious kid is less vacant than a vacant lot? Less wasted than waste ground?"

But then the marshes got filled, an empty lot behind the Lutheran church was paved over, and other lots became building sites. "The total immersion in nature that I found in my special spots," Pyle writes, "baptized me in a faith that never wavered, but it was a matter of happenstance too. It was the place that made me." Had it not been for the vacant lots, he says, "I'm not at all sure I would have been a biologist. I might have become a lawyer."

"How many people grow up with such windows on the world?" Pyle asks. "Fewer and fewer, I fear," he answers, concluding that "if we are to forge new links to the land, we must resist the extinction of experience." Coining an equally memorable phrase, Richard Louv, a nature writer and for many years a columnist for the *San Diego Union-Tribune,* has written in a 2005 book, *Last Child in the Woods,* that loss of casual contact with nature during childhood results in a condition he calls "nature-deficit disorder," with effects that parallel those produced by attention deficit hyperactivity disorder. On the other hand, renewed immersion in natural surroundings, he says, develops "nimbler bodies, broader minds, and sharper senses."

Similarly, David Quammen, who lives in Bozeman, Montana, and writes swashbuckling, digressive, and fact-stuffed science and travel books, in *Monster of God: The Man-Eating Predator in the Jungles of History and the Mind,* discusses another imminent "interior extinction," as we might call it, should the earth's remaining "alpha predators"—his term for the big cats and several other creatures, including some bears, sharks, snakes, and the Komodo dragon of Indonesia—disappear or survive only in zoos and aquariums. "Great and terrible flesh-eating beasts," Quammen writes (echoing Bruce Chatwin's reflections on *Dinofelis*), "have always shared the landscape with humans." But Quammen doesn't think humans have up to now had a chance to relax, even during the long years after we were no longer being tracked by *Dinofelis*. "For as long as *Homo sapiens* has been sapient," he says, "alpha predators have kept us acutely aware of our membership within the natural world," a world that included adversaries that "need to hunt and compete desperately" and at all times "must be bold, prudent, stealthy, opportunistic, and lucky." The result: "Among the earliest forms of human self-awareness was the awareness of being meat."

The loss of these creatures, Quammen thinks, wouldn't make our lives safer, because it would instead expose us to an inner danger, by removing a last bit of what we could think of as built-in, or environmental, or "situational humility." "Without them," he once told an interviewer from the *Seattle Post-Intelligencer*, "we would be freed from their reminder of our place in the natural world and the food chain. Then our level of arrogance and abuse may take off beyond what it is now, which is bad enough."

A reviewer of Quammen's book, Bill Gifford, writing in the *Washington Post*, acknowledged that even in the northeastern United States it was still possible to experience the "awareness of being meat":

> Whatever it was, it was bigger than a housecat. Beyond that, I can't be sure. It was a tawny shadow, slipping out of the woods on a summer afternoon in northern Pennsylvania. It flashed across the logging road

I'd just pedaled on my bicycle, then melted back into the trees. I knew that cougars were supposed to be extinct in the East and that the drive home would be far more dangerous, but . . . when I saw what I saw, even if it was probably just a bobcat, the woods suddenly became a very different place—watching, waiting, alive.

Extinction also affects awareness in the animals that survive it. Wolf packs, extirpated from Yellowstone National Park in the 1920s, were reintroduced to the park in 1995 and 1996. Studying the impacts of renewed wolf presence in 2004, two forestry scientists from Oregon State University retrospectively discovered that wolf removal eighty years previously had brought about what they categorized as a "trophic cascade" of ecological changes—technically, a description of a domino effect of displaced and unbalanced feeding habits, which in this case meant that without wolves, elk had lingered along streambanks, stripping them of willows, aspens, and cottonwoods and leading to a decline in beavers, songbirds, and fish, all of which require flourishing groves of these trees in order to survive. "We are just at the very infancy of understanding the importance of these apex predators sitting at the top of the food chain affecting entire ecosystems," one of the study's authors, William J. Ripple, told a reporter. Central to this new understanding is a new focus on fear as an ecosystem regulator: "When you remove the wolves," according to Robert L. Beschta, the study's other author, "the elk are able to browse unimpeded wherever they want, as long as they want. Now that the wolves are back, the ecology of fear comes into play."

If pandas have become the "face" of the Holocene extinction—representing both what might yet be lost and efforts to retrieve and safeguard the diversity of life that still abounds—the ecology of fear can claim its own emblematic species: the dodo. Found only on the island of Mauritius, east of Africa, the dodo, a kind of giant, flightless pigeon, disappeared forever less than a century after being discovered by Dutch sailors in 1602. It is already considered an international symbol twice over: of extinction and of stupidity, memorialized in the phrases "dead as a dodo" and "dumb as a dodo." But its true shortcoming was that, having never known predators, it lacked defenses. (Flightlessness emerges only in birds that live on islands without predators.) Just as dangerously, it lacked any kind of internal warning system, specifically fear. In more technical language, it had become an "ecolog-ically naive" animal, and in consequence "approached humans," as has been said, by Parrot Parrot, a Web site devoted to preventing mistreat-ment of parrots, "like a child might, open and curious."

Which means the dodo has more to teach us than we had thought, and we could start by adding a third "D" to what we say about these birds, and talk about being as "dazed," or as "damaged," or as "disabled as a dodo"—as a way of acknowledging the fate that overtakes any crea-ture victimized by having developed only a one-dimensional aware-ness, making it, though at the opposite end of the fear/explore scale from, say, *Dinofelis,* as deficient in long-term staying power as that fear-some creature eventually proved to be.

As we've already seen when talking about travel and human origins, when you open yourself up to it, there's far more "awareness data" available than appears at first. More than enough, I'd say, to suggest that an "awareness solution" can be part of a planetary approach to the biodiversity crisis. In the first place, on the local level, we need to make a distinction between the "extinction of experience," as Robert Michael Pyle refers to the lost chances of coming face to face with nature brought about by the bulldozing of nearby scraps of surviving wildlands in urban and suburban areas—the "hand-me-down habi-tats," "throwaway landscapes," and "Cinderella sites," he calls them—and any concurrent "extinction of awareness." It's clear that our wider awareness is no longer always automatically triggered by being out-doors, for the reasons we've just been discussing: loss of landscape and the "taming" of most of the landscapes that remain. But "awareness suppression" and "awareness displacement" are by no means the same thing as awareness extinction. The capacity remains intact. Shifting gears inside is now a matter that in many circumstances is up to us—we have to know it's something we can do, and then we have to do it instead of relying on unconscious prompting. But that's the only essen-tial difference.

Instead of lamenting lost landscapes, we can use our extended awareness to rebuild them, and while we're at it thread ourselves back into the picture. Because of the "diffusion factor" or "universalizing component" within deeper awareness, meaning its ability to connect us to a Larger Here and a Longer Now. Because of this, even catching sight of a single tree can remind us of what, when I was writing about New York's semiconcealed H_2O landscape, I started calling our "second address"—a surrounding "there"-ness that has been recognizable to every generation since the glaciers pulled back. It may be that this second address needs its own physical reanchoring to make it through the twenty-first century. E. O. Wilson has suggested that habitat permanence can be ensured if we declare 50 percent of the planet off-limits to further development. There are already big-picture plans under way to stabilize enormous tracts of land on all continents by rethreading them with wildlife corridors that have been interrupted in recent years by highways, buildings, and fences.

One such project, Y2Y, or Yukon to Yellowstone, a $2-million-a-year effort within what's been called the "wild heart of North America," covers a 2,300-mile-long corridor beginning just south of Yellowstone and extending to the northwest across parts of five U.S. states and four Canadian provinces and territories to the Alaska border, an area of 465,000 square miles where wolves, grizzly bears, and other Holocene megafauna, such as bighorn sheep, are still plentiful, for the most part. Its Asiatic complement is a 5,000-mile-long "genetic corridor from Bhutan to Burma" (announced in 2008 and not yet but no doubt soon to be called "B2B"), across parts of five nations—Bhutan, India, Thailand, Malaysia, and Myanmar—that will "allow tiger populations to roam as freely across landscapes as it is their nature to do."

From an awareness point of view, these and many other "countryside biogeography" or "megacorridor" or "megazoo" or "rewilding" visions, as they are variously called, could be more easily woven together by making our planetary second address feel like a seamless whole rather than a collection of parts. It's a matter of making it plain as we protect them that the regional landscapes that surround us and the continental corridors that link them are parts of the "largest here," a planetary network of densely interconnected landscapes and ocean areas.

The most promising plan I've seen for accomplishing this global vision was first put forward as a *New York Times* op-ed piece in March 2009. The authors, Scott Borgerson and Caitlyn Antrim, whose expertise is the governance of oceans, talk about turning global warming to our advantage by setting in place what they call an Arctic "great park" or "zone of peace" that could—although this language is mine, not theirs—become one half of a bipolar force field that could then connect protection work throughout the two hemispheres and act as a permanent guardian and bulwark of wildness. Here are a few excerpts from their initial proposal:

> By 2013, the entire Arctic could be devoid of ice in summer, and the region is likely to experience an influx of shipping, fishing and tourism. Russia planted its flag in the North Pole's ocean floor two years ago, and other northern nations find themselves under mounting pressure to lay claim to huge swaths of the seabed. Before the land grab goes too far, the nations most involved should turn the northernmost part of the Arctic into a great park—a marine preserve that protects the polar environment and serves as a center for peaceful, international scientific research. . . .
>
> One approach would be for the states and international organizations most involved in the Arctic to designate everything above 88 degrees latitude north—a circle with a 120-nautical-mile radius—as a marine park. This would be consistent with an idea presented in 1987 by Mikhail Gorbachev of the Soviet Union to create an Arctic "zone of peace." And it has precedent in the 1959 treaty that created an international zone for scientific research in Antarctica, and that has governed that continent so well ever since.

Although the danger is now long past, I often wonder if rooted somewhere in our sedentist heritage is a lingering shame and fear and distrust of a wider awareness because this way of focusing our attention was so much a part of the mind-set of the greatest enemy sedentist communities ever had to contend with, at least before the advent of modern warfare. For more than three thousand years, farmers and villagers endured constant surprise attacks and periodic full-scale invasions by groups, bands, and sometimes armies of nomads and wanderers, people who had remained mobile even after villages had turned into cities, and who professed an often scathing contempt for the settled life and its practices. ("Raids are our agriculture" was one of their proverbs.)

To anthropologists, these people are known as "nomadic pastoralists," since their expertise is with flocks of domesticated animals that migrate from place to place throughout the year (horses in Mongolia and Central Asia; sheep and goats or camels in southwestern Asia; cattle in East Africa; reindeer in northern Scandinavia) rather than with crops of domesticated plants, which must be cared for within the same plot, year after year. Although nineteenth-century theorists tended to dismiss pastoralists as rather primitive survivors of a "transitional" state between foraging and planting, recent anthropologists see the state as a viable alternative to the settled life—a sophisticated undertaking based on the understanding that animals can graze and move on. This makes it possible for humans to "lightly inhabit" large stretches of semiarid open country—such as the steppes of Russia and central Asia—by maintaining a shifting human presence in areas where no single piece of land gets enough rainfall to support a more permanent encampment.

The two most devastating conflicts between pastoralists and settled communities—separated by more than eight hundred years, and both still vividly remembered today—were brought about by the sudden appearance in Europe of the Huns more than sixteen hundred years ago and the rapid rise of the Mongol Empire across most of Asia and parts of eastern Europe during a seventy-year period that began in A.D. 1206. The Huns, perhaps originally a Turkic people from north of China, pushed various Germanic tribes ahead of them—Goths, Vandals, Angles, Saxons, Franks—in a series of incursions that helped destabilize the Roman Empire. (To Mediterranean historians, it has frequently been pointed out, these were "Barbarian invasions" that led to a "Dark Age"; German historians have taken a kinder view, referring to the displacements involved as the "Great Migration" and as the *Völkerwanderung*, or "wandering of the peoples.")

The cruelty of the Mongol invaders and the sound of their horses' hooves left an indelible impression on survivors, as Colonel Sir Henry Yule, a nineteenth-century Scottish Orientalist, recorded in his book *Marco Polo* (the quotation reappears in Bruce Chatwin's *Songlines*). This was the account, in Persian phrases written to echo the thud of galloping cavalrymen, set down by someone who had escaped the sack of Bokhara by Genghis Khan in 1220 (try reading the sentence out loud to yourself to hear its pounding rhythm): "*Amdand u khandand u sokhtand u kushtand u burdand u raftand*" ("They came and they sapped and they burned and they slew and they trussed up their loot and were gone"). Juvaini, a thirteenth-century Persian historian who wrote in detail about the Mongols, later said, according to Yule, that his whole book "and all the horror of those times is contained in this one line."

Perhaps it was memories of events like these that led generations of settled people to think of their nomadic pastoralist neighbors as the ultimate bogeymen, inherently dangerous to life and property and the antithesis in every way of whatever was lawful and orderly.

Disparaged for many years by sedentist scholars, the abilities of the world's remaining hunter-gatherers—people who have never adopted either planting, or pastoralism—were looked at through a new lens by anthropologists of the 1960s. Realizing that hunter-gatherers had more leisure time than modern office workers, they hailed them as the "original affluent society." Rediscovery of the virtues and accomplishments of nomadic pastoralists—who today number less than 1 percent of the world's population—has taken longer, although Eric Alden Smith, who's now a professor of anthropology at the University of Washington, has recently written feelingly about pastoralist intelligence and awareness. "A wealth of knowledge goes into pastoralist decision making," Smith says, noting that it's a product of "intensive information gathering" that keeps herds mobile in the face of often unpredictable plant growth and weather patterns. The complexity of thought involved has gone unnoticed, he thinks, because of the "ignorance of researchers who didn't understand enough . . . to ask intelligent questions."

Louis Palmer, the author of *Adventures in Afghanistan,* found himself profoundly impressed by the Kochis, or "mountaineers," the nomads of Afghanistan, horse riders and conductors of camel caravans, when in the 1980s he became one of the few Westerners to spend time with them. The Kochis led him into their country on a two-day trek north from Quetta, a mile-high city on the western edge of Pakistan:

> The scenery varied from desolate moonscapes to fertile uplands.
>
> It was almost uncanny how over a thousand people could live in that land, carrying virtually everything they needed, camping and moving on with hardly a trace of their presence, apart from the ashes of their cooking fires.
>
> I never once saw an abandoned tin can or piece of paper left behind at a Kochi camp site.
>
> These people live very close to nature but also, in some strange way,

near to what one can only call eternity. When I remarked to one Kochi how little trace there was of the caravan's passing, he immediately said that to him the caravan was like a human life. Only one breath separated it from eternity.

"The caravan is really only that breath, if you understand me," he said. In the West he would have been described as "culturally ignorant," or maybe just "illiterate." But he had the mind as well as the look of a poet: and, in addition, the practicality to be our master blacksmith. "We came and we lived, and then disappeared—we people on earth, we Kochis on the march . . ."

Another possible explanation for our estrangement from the extended awareness within us has to do with the great Galileo Galilei, the "father of modern science," who may have inadvertently solved too many problems when he investigated the properties of motion more than four hundred years ago.

It's not known whether Galileo ever, as legend has it, actually dropped objects of different weights from the top of the Leaning Tower of Pisa during the course of his motion experiments (this may have been only a gedankenexperiment), but his central insights about motion have ever since been accepted as definitive explanations of how three-dimensional bodies behave when in motion within our particular solar system.

Galileo, who, looking through a telescope he had built himself, was the first person ever to see that another planet, Jupiter, has moons of its own, is probably most famous even today for defending the idea that the earth revolves around the sun—an action for which the Roman Catholic Church eventually condemned him to life imprisonment. In the 1590s, this idea was still a hotly debated topic. Many people remained skeptical, and the central objection being raised was not theological but practical and had to do with motion.

The commonsense point of view held that if the earth was spinning on its own axis (making it seem as if the sun were streaking across the sky), then everything not attached to the earth would also be in motion. Thus "to travel to the west," as Henri Bortoft, an English physicist who writes about the philosophy of science, has pointed out, "the traveler would merely need to jump up and down, and the west would eventually arrive at his or her feet." Galileo, Bortoft notes in his book *The Wholeness of Nature*, "turned the problem the other way round," saying, in effect, that "the crucial thing is being able to move the earth without causing a thousand inconveniences" to all the things the planet supports: "Thus, indifference to motion ceases to be a 'problem' and becomes instead a *new way of seeing* motion." Indifference to the earth's motion became, for Galileo, "the fundamental postulate of a new science of motion"—which meant that "keeping up with the earth" became the essential motion of any terrestrial object. Galileo's particular breakthrough, Bortoft continues, his new, special, useful way of seeing motion, led to specific concepts and formulations that would be adopted by the science of mechanics and that continue to form the basis for thousands of kinds of practical and theoretical computations, including those made every day by transportation engineers. As Bortoft points out, if a ball could fall from the Tower of Pisa without being deflected to one side, this demonstrated that a body "can have several motions simultaneously without these getting in each other's way. They will simply add together to produce a resultant motion."

But it wasn't just that a body's motions didn't get entangled. The body itself could be "divorced," so to speak, from any and all of these motions. As Bortoft explains:

> Now in order to see that a body is indifferent to its motion, Galileo had to come to a further fundamental change in the way of seeing motion itself. He separated the motion of a body from the essential nature of the body, i.e., he saw the motion which a body had as being entirely extrinsic, instead of being intrinsic, to the body. Before Galileo, motion entailed the essence of whatever it was that was in motion. Motion itself was considered to be a special case of change, and change was considered to be whatever it is that is changing becoming more fully itself. Thus a growing plant, the education of a child, and a body falling to the ground were all instances of change in which something comes to be more fully itself. So motion (change of place) was seen as being a *necessary* feature of what it is to be the body which is in motion. For Galileo, on the other hand (and thence for modern physics), there is no such necessary connection between the kind of motion a body has and its essential nature.

Since a body's motion, in this new formulation, is no longer a logically necessary part of its very being or essential nature, it can be altogether indifferent to—or let's say completely unmoved by—its state of motion. It is still considered as something capable of change, something with the capacity of "becoming more fully itself," but moving around is no longer tied into the process. " 'Motion' is now merely a *state* in which a body finds itself," Bortoft says, whereas before Galileo, motion was seen "as the change *from* one state *to* another." This is the "key point," Bortoft emphasizes—since "if motion is only a state in which a body can be, and not part of the very nature of the body, then clearly the body itself must be *indifferent* to the state of motion which it *happens* to (not must) be in."

Although it wasn't his purpose, Galileo changed the default position of our thinking about what it is that motion makes possible; in his terms it is, by definition, an "impersonal" force, meaning one that has no appreciable effect on our personhood. Without meaning to, this approach "abolishes" the interventions that Deep Travel can bring to travel.

THE LEGACY OF AWARENESS

Transport, motorways and tramlines
Starting and then stopping
Taking off and landing
The emptiest of feelings
Disappointed people clinging on to bottles
And when it comes it's so so disappointing

Let down and hanging around
Crushed like a bug in the ground
Let down and hanging around
          —from "Let Down," by Radiohead

Dar harakat, barakat.
("In movement, there is a blessing.")
          —a saying of the Kochis, the nomads of Afghanistan

S tanding back to look across the spectrum of human awareness in all its various forms, we see one thing that stands out: the structures of awareness entrusted to us in our waking hours are a hybrid, an amalgam, an imperfect fit. These, as we can tell, are present in everyone every day: daydreaming or reverie; focused attention or pinpoint awareness; and a wider, expanded, more inclusive awareness that I've also called by several other names, such as Deep Travel and the bipedal perceptual platform. There are other forms of awareness, too, such as "flow" (also called "the zone"), the sense some athletes have of moving effortlessly in sync with what's happening and what's about to happen. But such states are more occasional visitors, and so have been omitted from this very preliminary survey.

Shifting gears between the states or lenses or tendencies that we've been tracking can be awkward, because the first two look inward and the third outward for the most part, and because a sense of time passing or slowing dramatically comes and goes when we do this. Yoking them together, or even keeping one in mind when another is present, can be even more difficult. A work in progress? That depends on what we do with our extraordinary awareness legacy from this point forward, since at the moment the fundamental question of what they're "good for" remains unresolved and still to be dealt with. Furthermore, as if that weren't enough to grapple with, there's an additional problem, this one cultural rather than biological: these days, despite daily exposure to all these awarenesses, many people have a hard time recognizing the threefold nature of the equipment they're using, since a succession of postsettlement societies, including much of what we've been brought up to revere as "classical civilization," has "settled for less," so to speak. So even now we still limp along on a foreshortened basis, and often, like a racehorse that has never galloped, confine ourselves to far less than what might be possible.

We're still getting used to the fact that when it comes to being in motion, for example, we have several ways of traveling. Like the falling objects Galileo elucidated, we can be indifferent to motion, ignore it, tune it out. We can remain "unmoved by motion." Technology makes us even better at this—iPods promote reverie; cell phones maintain narrowly focused attention. They also get us into trouble in situations when a wider awareness is something we need to stay alive, as when driving. Which is why President Obama's secretary of transportation, Ray LaHood, convened a two-day summit about "distracted driving" in Washington in September 2009, calling it a "menace to society"; a report by *Car and Driver* magazine cited at the conference had found that "texting and driving is more dangerous than drunken driving."

Or—unlike an object—we can be moved, changed, even transformed by motion. Movement can be a part of "becoming more fully ourselves."

What we need now is a "post-Galilean" approach to travel and transportation, one that makes an inviolable distinction between living cargo and inanimate objects and that recouples the art of moving people around to accommodating people in all their dimensions. Because when blinders are placed over the workings of Deep Travel by anyone—travelers themselves, the vehicles that carry them, the roads and train tracks and bridges and other rights-of-way built to support vehicles—we are starving ourselves, letting ourselves down. Soon there will be seven billion people on earth, and then eight, and after that nine or more by the middle of the century. That's an awful lot of people to cheat on a daily basis.

This is a different problem from the "traveled-through experience," the effect that travel and the structures built to support travel have either on the landscape or on formerly isolated or only lightly visited people. It also has to be distinguished from yet another problem: "travel's leave-behinds," the accumulation over time of every piece of unrecycled waste generated by any trip, many of which gather out of sight, such as the Eastern Pacific Garbage Patch between California and Hawaii that's now twice the size of Texas; 26 million tons of plastic end up in the oceans every year, and currents slowly sweep this debris into "trash vortices." Or like the "catastrophic event" five hundred miles above the planet on February 10, 2009 (the words are attributed to James Oberg, retired from NASA), when a defunct Russian military satellite and an operational U.S. commercial satellite crashed into each other at high speeds, generating "tens of thousands of pieces of space junk," according to a news report, "that could circle Earth and threaten other satellites for the next 10,000 years."

In the normal course of events, Deep Travel awareness arrives spontaneously through several channels. It can sometimes be "allowed" to return by the mind, because of a perception that there's nothing threatening nearby—a sort of "paradise effect," it might be called. Or it can be deliberately "invoked" or "summoned" because existing information reaching us through other means seems inadequate to explain the situation at hand.

But since so much of our upbringing and training steers us away from these contacts, or from noticing them when they happen, or from relishing them and seeking them out, I've thought that our best chance of rearranging the way we use our awarenesses is to start somewhere back "before the beginning," so to speak. We're in the middle of a remedial, catch-up phase, almost as if entering the twenty-first century required a quick refresher course in nineteenth- and early-twentieth-century technology, a return to a time when a car motor wouldn't start until you yourself cranked it, when a pump needed to have a little water sluiced down into it before it began working properly. Which is why there's some "pump priming" scattered throughout this book. Because the more often we evoke our wider awareness, and the easier it gets, the more eager we'll be to reclaim it. Wider awareness opens us up to the world, but first we have to open ourselves up to it, even though it's already been ours for such a long, long time.

A great deal could be written—and I think is about to be written—about the long-term health benefits of Deep Travel, once the overlap with established health data is more clearly recognized. For instance, Marian C. Diamond, a neuroanatomist at the University of California, Berkeley, who decades ago discovered that when placed in an "enriched" environment (with more to do and to explore) even aged rats grew new brain cells, has in more recent years looked at "successful aging" among people, identifying five factors she considers "essential for keeping our brains healthy and active throughout our life span," as she told the National Council on the Aging in 2001. "You are going to say there's nothing new about them," she told her audience. "Perhaps so, but we now have important scientific validation we did not always have." Two of the five factors (diet and human love) are not particularly connected to Deep Travel, but one (exercise) certainly could be, and the other two are directly relevant. Here they are with her numbering:

> Three, we must CHALLENGE the brain. It gets bored; we know that well.
> Four, we need NEWNESS, new pursuits, new ideas, new activities in our life.

Deep Travel is a bringer of novelty and the unexpected, a dissolver of boredom, even during an otherwise very routine activity, like a trip to the supermarket.

Or I could cite a 2009 experiment (first published in the *Journal of Personality and Social Psychology*) that discovered, according to a write-up in *New Scientist,* that "people who had spent time living outside their own countries" were "less fixed" in their thinking and "more able to accept and recombine novel ideas." This was evidenced by the fact that they were "more likely . . . to solve the 'Duncker candle problem': given only a box of thumbtacks and a candle and told to fix the candle to a wall, you need to divine that the tack box can be used as a shelf."

But it's not enough to present Deep Travel as something that's "good for you," because that sounds too much like medicine. The doing of it is the real reward. What's needed right away is a systematic exploration of what Deep Travel brings to exploring and, more particularly, some of the specifics about how it affects all the different ways of getting around that we know about. Let's start with canoeing. Jeff Warren happened to mention to me one day that he was heading off for northern Ontario for a couple of weeks of canoeing and was looking forward to the slowness and the quiet and the constant opening of vistas. Here's his account of that trip:

> Call it "Paddling the Stream of Consciousness." I'll even start with a famous William James quote on the subject (from his *Principles of Psychology*):
>
>> As we take, in fact, a general view of the wonderful stream of our consciousness, what strikes us first is this different pace of its parts. Like a bird's life, it seems to be made of an alternation of flights and perchings. The rhythm of language expresses this, where every thought is expressed in a sentence, and every sentence closed by a period. The resting-places are usually occupied by sensorial imaginations of some sort, whose peculiarity is that they can be held before the mind for an indefinite time, and contemplated without changing; the places of flight are filled with thoughts of relations, static or dynamic, that for the most part obtain between the matters contemplated in the periods of comparative rest.
>
> For me, the mind-while-canoeing is the essence of Jamesian flight.
> At the start of the trip the mind is filled with thoughts, with perchings—mental checklists, idle daydreams, and of course big sensory snapshots of the novel landscape. But as time goes on, something strange happens. As the movement of the paddle rises and falls, thoughts . . . soften. They become more flight-like, long transitions that glide through the mind like the canoe glides over the still water. Soon, even the flights themselves slow into longer and longer stretches of internal silence. This is more than the "zone"-like automaticity that comes with repetitive motion. There is something about being in nature

without the interfering layer of built civilization. A deeper pattern reasserts itself, subterranean, an entraining force that rises up from the earth and spreads out through the trees and water and into your body, simultaneously locking you into its powerful rhythm and also diffusing you, reducing you, absorbing you.

Being on the water exaggerates this effect. Early in the morning the mist is on the lake, and everything is quiet and still, and the wake of the canoe seems to flatten immediately so that there is no evidence at all of your passage. You feel like a ghost. Even as the mist lifts, and the sun gets higher in the sky, this feeling of insubstantiality stays, as if, so close to the water, you are really just part of the horizon, and all the real activity is happening on the shore, the forest theater, which tracks by slowly, the scale of it massive and humbling and awesome.

Jeff Warren's contribution made me wonder if perhaps it would be helpful to have some sort of chart or simple form or small, pocket-sized pad that could be carried around for making notes about the comings and goings of Deep Travel during a trip. It might look a little like a sheet of blank music paper, except that the staff or stave—the grouping of parallel horizontal lines—would be cut down to three from the normal five. To get things started, there's a blank single day form along with a blank multi-day form on the following page, which can be copied (and downloadable forms are posted at howwetravel.org). The sample form below is one I've filled in about a Deep Travel moment that has stayed with me—seeing a peregrine falcon on a fire escape in Manhattan (described back on page 10):

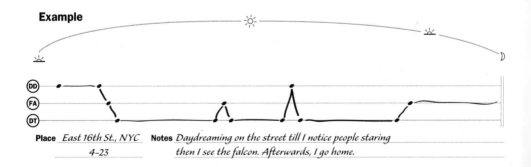

Example

Place *East 16th St., NYC*   **Notes** *Daydreaming on the street till I notice people staring*
4-23   *then I see the falcon. Afterwards, I go home.*

DD   DAYDREAM
FA   FOCUSED ATTENTION
DT   DEEP TRAVEL

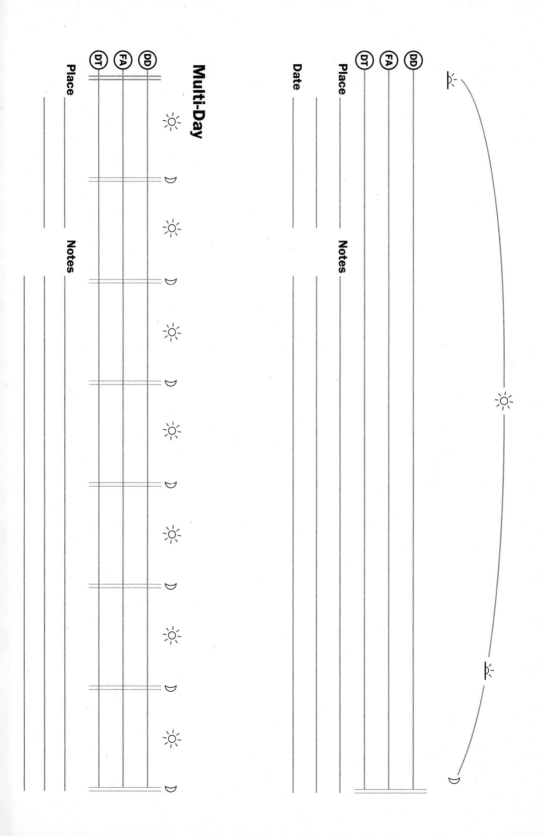

Multi-Day

DD FA DT

Place _____ Notes _____

Place _____ Date _____

DD FA DT

The printed horizontal lines on the form represent daydreaming, focused attention, and Deep Travel. You'll notice an arc over the whole stave, representing the arc of a trip. I've used musical notes connected by lines to indicate the unfolding of the scene—daydreaming until I zeroed in on the people staring upward, and then an unexpected plunge into Deep Travel, a feeling which stayed with me almost all the way home, except at street corners. (I used the whole form, though catching sight of the falcon and then walking home only took about twenty minutes.) For a longer trip, you could mark off each pause or deep breath or change of pace in a trip—its "perchings"—with a "measure line" or "barline," the vertical line perpendicular to the staff that musicians use to indicate the completion of a certain number of rhythmic beats. On the form they might indicate stopping for a meal, or changing vehicles, or waiting in an airport, or passing a notable landmark or milepost—reaching the summit of a mountain, or catching a first glimpse of the ocean, or a sudden rainstorm, or a lingering sunset when the dips in a road begin to fill with deepening pools of gloom while the hilltops still gleam brightly in the sun, or the final fall of darkness at the end of day. For a trip that lasts more than a single day, I'd suggest separating each day with a "double barline," which in musical notation means the end of a section of a piece and here would mean going to sleep and waking up again. You could fill in the sheet with any impressions that strike you—verbal notes about the music of the trip. How much of it was actually spent in Deep Travel? Did Deep Travel come by itself, or did you decide to shift over into it? Was it difficult to make the transition? Did anything happen to bump you out of it again?

The next step—trickier because it has "policy implications"—is to reexamine not just trips but the physical components of trips (vehicles, buildings, rights-of-way) with an eye toward updating them so that they can serve a post-Galilean age. They must continue to be safe and comfortable, of course, and if they're parts of working transportation systems, they must continue to offer, or aspire to offer, reliable and on-time service. But because humans are a hybrid, they have another mission as well. Each element of a trip needs to contribute to the chance that any trip at all can be an exploration of the unknown and the not-yet-known, that the time involved can be used profitably to help us become more fully ourselves.

It's not a new idea. More than twenty-two hundred years ago, the Indian emperor Ashoka, who had renounced armed conflict, "beautified" (as we would say) the roads and highways of his country. As one of his edicts records:

> Along roads I have had banyan trees planted so that they can give shade to animals and men, and I have had mango groves planted. At intervals of eight *krosas,* I have had wells dug, rest-houses built, and in various places I have had watering-places made for the use of animals and men. But these are but minor achievements. Such things to make the people happy have been done by former kings. I have done these things for this purpose, that the people might practice the *Dhamma.*

By the *Dhamma,* Ashoka meant kindness, restraint from cruelty, non-violence, tolerance. Banyan trees, close relatives of fig trees and mulberry trees, can grow one hundred feet high and spread laterally, through descending aerial roots. One famous banyan tree reportedly grew to such an enormous size that it could shelter twenty thousand people. Modern parkways, invented in the 1860s by Frederick Law Olmsted, the great landscape architect and the designer of New York's Central Park, carry forward his idea that roads, if "so planted and constructed never to be noisy," can extend outward the "tranquillity and rest to the mind" that his parks induced. A road—or any right-of-way—is a kind of "permanent caravan," if you choose to think of it that way. Like a caravan it's a guided trek, and thus in many ways a pre-shaped experience along a pathway that has been chosen in advance; only in the case of a fixed and paved highway, the caravan leaders, the highway engineers, disappeared from sight long ago and now lead you onward by bending the pavement left or right. You may think you're entirely on your own, but you're not.

In the 1880s, Olmsted and his friend H. H. Richardson, a Boston architect, launched the "Railroad Beautiful" movement, designing and landscaping thirty new commuter stations for the Boston & Albany Railroad, and setting up the B&A's "railroad gardening" program. (Olmsted had never forgotten his arrival years earlier at a little English countryside railroad station near Liverpool—a place, he wrote at the time, that was "green, gorgeous, glistening.") An article in *Railway Age* magazine in the 1920s reported that the same practice had been continued by the Lackawanna Railroad in New Jersey, creating "veritable parks" at its commuter stations that had become "the pride of every town" along the way.

Some years ago, I got the idea of "parkwaying" the existing rail lines around New York City. NatureRail, the little group I set up, has looked at several potential sites: a two-mile-long cornfield north of Baltimore next to Amtrak's Northeast Corridor line from Washington, D.C., to Boston; the small, triangular meadow next to the Spuyten Duyvil station of Metro-North Railroad's Hudson Line, for instance, in the southwest corner of the Bronx, right next to the point of land where the Hudson and Harlem rivers meet and opposite to the tall gray cliffs of the Palisades; and New Jersey Transit's new Secaucus Junction station, in the middle of the Hackensack Meadowlands, an enormous saltwater marsh with reeds seven feet high. (With only a little trail work through the cattails and phragmites just outside the Secaucus station, someone on a lunch-hour break in Manhattan could get on a train at Penn Station and be walking through the Meadowlands—which are hard to reach by car—only eight minutes later.)

Then there are the vehicles we enter—the "third skins" that we put on when we go outside, as an outer shell beyond our clothing, or "second skin." To what extent can our several awarenesses "breathe" through these skins, which are mostly made of metal, plastic, and glass? To what extent are they suffocated or simply not taken into account? "When the *California Zephyr* entered service on March 20, 1949," writes Henry Kisor, who was the book editor of the *Chicago Sun-Times* for almost thirty years, in *Zephyr: Tracking a Dream Across America,* a loving tribute to a storied passenger train, "it immediately captured the nation's imagination," even though it was ten hours slower than a second train between Chicago and Oakland, California, the *Overland Limited*:

> The difference lay not in the inherent speed of the trains, but in how they got there. The spectacular Colorado Rockies and California Sierra route was only part of the attraction. Five of the *Zephyr*'s ten sleek, silvery, air-conditioned fluted stainless steel cars featured glass-enclosed penthouses that gave the rider a fish-eye lens's 180-degree vista. The Vista-Domes, as they were called, were the brainchild of Cyrus Osborn, a General Motors executive. In 1944 Osborn was riding in the cab of a

Rio Grande locomotive (some sources say the cupola of a caboose) through the heart-stopping scenery of Glenwood Canyon in the Colorado Rockies when he had a bright idea: Suppose similar vantage points, made of glass, could be built atop passenger cars—what a view they would afford! The Vista-Domes became the *Zephyr*'s most popular feature.

Osborn's insight was based on recognizing that railroad cars assume that train travelers have eyes only in the sides of their heads—there are windows to the left and the right, but straight ahead all you can see is the door leading to the car just ahead of you. Many railroad lines were laid out with the same scenic sensibilities hikers find on long-distance mountain paths, like the Appalachian Trail. But ordinarily only train engineers get to see these sights—and nowadays the few remaining dome cars in the United States can be found only on a few short-haul tourist railroads, such as the Grand Canyon Railway and the Napa Valley Wine Train (although they still survive on transcontinental trains in Canada).

Amtrak's high-speed Acela Express trains, however, introduced in 1999, come close. Part of the Acela design team had just finished working on Spain's then-new high-speed trains, the AVE, which had been deliberately planned as an eye-catching national statement ("Spain's Concorde" was the catchphrase), a train whose unspoken message to one and all was that Spain had cast off the Franco period and was ready to join the rest of Europe as a full partner. Acela set out to speak reassuringly, if somewhat more quietly, to its own passengers—mostly East Coast businesspeople making same-day trips—through not-quite-noticed design details that indicated that almost everything a traveler might want to do had already been thought about. So, for instance, moving from car to car takes no effort, because the glass doors at either end of each car open automatically when you approach, and, as on a plane, there are laptop plugs at each seat. But, unlike a plane, the ceilings are high; there's a lot of legroom; the lights over each seat offer three settings (off, dim, and bright), not just on or off; the seats line up with the windows; and the windows are tall enough so that, although you can't look in all directions (tunnels along the Northeast Corridor are too low to permit the running of dome cars), you can look up and out and down, all at the same time.

You don't have to look if you don't want to; you can pull a curtain across the window. But if you decide to look, the effect is intense because the landscape outside is not just a distant prospect but something you've never left, since it seems to come right up to your feet and even to wrap around under the wheels. It's not a managed landscape—no NatureRail or parkwaying here. It's not even a landscape that's paying attention to you, since houses and businesses show their fronts to roads and only their backs to train lines. It's not always what you want to see, but it's what's there to be seen—every scrapyard, every weed, every abandoned tricycle in a backyard, every overgrown stream bank, invisible because there's a billboard in front of it (although you can't see what's being advertised, because the billboard's facing a highway). Every two seconds you get a new framed picture of what America looks like when no one's looking.

We know quite a bit about the physical outlines of human settlement patterns fifty years from now—in that world with more than nine billion citizens, a large majority of people will live in huge metropolitan regions where existing cities and their suburbs have grown into one another, swallowing and being swallowed simultaneously. In the United States, we can, for instance, look forward to places like "Los Diego," a blend of Los Angeles and San Diego; "Milwago Bend," a long curve of urbanized land around Lake Michigan from Milwaukee through Chicago to South Bend, Indiana; and "Baltington," a capital region that's part Baltimore and part Washington, D.C. We are assuming, probably reasonably, even though the question of how much longer oil will be available as a fuel is hotly debated, that we'll still be moving around for the most part in cars, trucks, buses, trains, and planes; the configurations of "modal share" (meaning who will be using what means of transportation), however, seem to be in flux for the first time since cars and planes became the "wave of the future" fifty or sixty years ago. We know far less, because we haven't thought about it much yet, about what experiences will be available to those billions of travelers.

We urgently need to bring more players into the design process—people who are alive to the larger possibilities of minds in motion. Years ago, for instance, the American installation artist Robert Irwin drew up detailed ideas for expanding Miami International Airport. Art critics called them his "masterpiece," but professional airport planners dismissed them as fanciful. "Art-in-Response," an essay by Arthur C.

Danto, a philosopher and art critic and admirer of Irwin's, outlines Irwin's airport thinking:

> His project assumes that the airport, the first and last part of a city a traveler experiences, should in some way emblematize the city, rather than serve some impersonal outskirt function, architecturally everywhere and nowhere. This involved him in the design of approach roads, parking, rental car return sites, and of the roads back to the metropolitan center. What is emblematic of Miami is the abundance of water. . . . The road from airport to city and back again should traverse typical Dade County waterscape, planted with palmettos and reeds. . . . Irwin designed a cool corridor through which one headed . . . and the pattern of the driver's experience was an alternation of shade and light. And he designed a marvelous "central park," filled with plant and even bird life, an amenity for spiritual restoration as needed by travelers, leave-takers, greeters. . . . In the end, the entire airport would be art . . . the users of which need hardly be mindful of the marvelous way art has been used to ease their passage. One of the goals of art in such projects is, Irwin states in a sort of flowchart, to "heighten awareness." Not to heighten awareness of art as art, but of the dimensions and features of life that art raises to the highest powers of enhancement while remaining invisible.

In a book published in 2000, *The Ice Palace That Melted Away: Restoring Civility and Other Lost Virtues to Everyday Life,* the late Bill Stumpf, a man regarded as the father of ergonomic seating—he was co-designer of the Aeron chair—proposed building a Vistadome version of a 747 passenger plane. "In spite of the million-plus air miles I've flown over the years," he wrote, "I realized I had never experienced the thrill of flying." His solution was to "relocate passengers to the edges—cargo + fuel inside," and then add on the kind of projecting Plexiglas bubbles originally created for nose, belly, and tail gunners on World War II B-17s:

> Imagine the glory of watching the sunset from the nose or leading edge of a wing. Imagine a windowed perch on top of the tail where one could view the 747's flexing wings and shimmering architecture, punching holes through the clouds, spewing vapor trails in the moonlight. . . . Imagine your own telescope scanning the stars and the moon from the clarity of the night's sky.

Early in his career, in the 1960s, Bill Stumpf, who then taught at the University of Wisconsin's Environmental Design Center, started studying how people sit. He was part of a team that included doctors who specialized in muscle development and in blood flow. "Everything," he later said, "was about freeing up the body," and about "designing away constraints." Today, as we consider how people move, the challenge is to free up the mind as well.

Because Deep Travel awareness is where we set our internal fear/explore balance, horrible events like the terrorist bombings of September 11, 2001, reach into this part of our mind as well as the rest of our being, and reset our own "ecology of fear and sadness and hurt" in ways that are not easily re-reset. It was an act designed to frighten, and it did. I remember walking around Lower Manhattan in the days after the attack—I live a couple of miles north of the World Trade Center site—realizing that the skyscrapers I'd known all my life were as temporary as tents. It wasn't a renewed awareness of the danger of "being meat." It was emptier than that, because the deaths that day when the buildings fell weren't even keeping some other creatures alive.

So Deep Travel sometimes shows you things you wish no one would ever have to see. But it's ours, and it's also a way of meeting risk bravely, which John Adams, an English geographer, defines as the constant internal weighing of needs: "The behavior of young children," he writes in *Risk,* his book on the subject, "driven by curiosity and a need for excitement, yet curbed by their sense of danger, suggests that these junior risk experts are performing a balancing act. In some cases it is a physical balancing act; learning to walk or ride a bicycle cannot be done without accident."

Sir Henry Morton Stanley advised all travelers to proceed in this uniquely human fashion. In his "Thoughts from Note-books," a chapter of his *Autobiography,* he set forth his credo: "Bidding a glad farewell to the follies and vanities of civilized cities, step out with trustful hearts ... perceiving, by many insignificant signs around, that whatever heavenly protection may be vouchsafed to us, it would soon be null and void unless we are watchful, alert, and wise."

ACKNOWLEDGMENTS

I was most fortunate to receive a series of research and publication grants at a number of critical points as I was writing this book. Profound thanks to the Rockefeller Brothers Fund, the Geraldine R. Dodge Foundation, the Surdna Foundation, and the Nathan Cummings Foundation, and to several of the past presidents and executive directors of these institutions for their generosity and support, including Colin Campbell, David Grant, Edward Skloot, and Charles Halpern; to the Furthermore program of the J. M. Kaplan Fund, and its president, Joan K. Davidson; and to the Design Arts Program of the National Endowment for the Arts.

My appreciative thanks as well go to New York University's Robert F. Wagner Graduate School of Public Service, which has welcomed me as a Visiting Scholar since 1994, giving me an intellectual home base for my work and the ongoing use of their research facilities. Particular thanks to Dean Ellen Schall and Associate Dean Rogan Kersh; to former Deans Jo Ivey Boufford and Bob Berne; and to Professor Mitchell L. Moss, who took an early interest in this book.

Thanks also to Robert E. Paaswell, former president of the City College of New York, who broadened my understanding of transportation issues by appointing me a Fellow of the CUNY Institute for Urban Systems (CIUS).

Old friends Vin Cipolla, president of the Municipal Art Society, and Robert Yaro, president of the Regional Plan Association, have also offered unstinting support and thoughtful advice. Peter C. Bosselmann, professor of urban design in architecture, city & regional planning, and landscape architecture at the University of California, Berkeley, invited me to lecture several years ago about the book as it then existed; his comments and the feedback from his colleagues and students were of immense help.

A number of good friends and knowledgeable scholars have gone out of their way to share insights and expertise and to offer comments, suggestions, and needed corrections that directly shaped and added dimension to this book. Foremost among these is William E. H. Harcourt-Smith of the American Museum of Natural History, who for several years was a wise and patient mentor, collaborator, and sounding board as I attempted to trace Deep Travel back to its hominin roots. Although many of these generous people are named in the text, here with my great gratitude is a more complete list, as their contributions appear in these pages: Hillary Brown, Martin Hanlon, Tony Frantz, Jon Natchez, Tahir Shah, Ben Hamilton-Baillie, Sheldon Bart, the late Edward S. Reed, William Mace, Christopher Meier, Chris Andrichak, Dana Raphael, the late Reginald Golledge, Jeff Warren, Ian Tattersall, Ken Mowbray, Marian C. Diamond, the late Bill Stumpf, John Adams.

Close readers of early versions of the manuscript whose comments were unfailingly helpful include Brent Oppenheimer, Anthony Perl, and Anthony C. Wood.

In addition, I've had valuable conversations and correspondence along the way with some of the best minds working in travel and transportation, in parks and open space protection, in planning and design, and in other fields. Here, in alphabetical order, is a partial listing of those to whom I am especially indebted: Gerald W. Adelmann, J. Winthrop Aldrich, Ellie Altman, Chip Angle, Carol Ash, Kent Barwick, Judith Batalion, Adrian Benepe, Scott Bernstein, R. Clifford Black, IV, Steve Blackmer, Hooper Brooks, Christopher N. Brown, Kevin Brubaker, Amanda Burden, Dan Burden, David Burwell, Peter Calthorpe, Sarah C. Campbell, Lorne Cappe, David Carol, Marisha Chamberlain, Chester Eric Chellman, Don Chen, Andy D. Clarke, Joel E. Cohen, Carter Craft, David Crombie, William J. Cronon, Grace Crunigan, Kabir Dandona, Rick Darke, Robert Davis, Wayne E. Davis, Liz Del Tufo, Hank Dittmar, Harry Dodson, JoAnn Dolan, Paul Dolan, Thomas M. Downs, Andrés Duany, Frances F. Dunwell, Joe Edmiston, T. Roberson Edwards, Christopher J. Elliman, Walter R. Ernst, Wendy Feuer, Charles A. Flink, Benjamin Forgey, Marianne Fowler, Carol Franklin, Jan Gehl, Richard Gilbert, Todd Goldman, Peter Goldmark, Roberta Gratz, Ken Greenberg, the late Rick Guttenberg, Ronald J. Hartman, Denis Hayes, Bruce Heard, J. Scott Hercik, Randy Hester, Michael Hirshfield, Jean Hocker, Mike Houck, Mark Hurley, and the late Jane Jacobs.

Also Camille Kamga, Daniel Kemmis, Roger G. Kennedy, Fred Kent, Jim Kent, Jeff Kenworthy, Roy Kienitz, Richard Killingsworth, Bill Klein, Joseph P. Kocy, Charles Komanoff, Walter Kulash, Barbara W. Lawrence, Howard A. Learner, David Lerner, Jaime Lerner, Robert Liberty, David Lillard, Amy Linden, Jeremy Liu, Gianni Longo, Marcia Lowe, Anne Lusk, Joshua Lutz, Joshua Mack, Clare Cooper Marcus, L. Richard Mariani, Barbara McCann, Jeannie R. McCloskey, Ed McMahon, Mary Means, Christopher G. Miller, Richard Moe, Darrel Morrison, Patrick F. Noonan, Michael Northrup, John G. Norquist, Doug Obletz, the late Peter Obletz, Jeff Olson, William D. O'Neill, Robert Ornstein, Lyman Orton, Enrique Peñalosa, Howard Permut, Juri Pill, Chris Pommer, Warrie Price, Richard Pyle, Jonas Rabinovitch, George Ranney, Jr., Vicky Ranney, Lisa Rapoport, Richard Register, Jack M. Reilly, James P. RePass, Michael A. Replogle, Martin E. Robins, Betsy Barlow Rogers, Will Rogers, Jonathan F. P. Rose, Brian Rosenwald, Ben Rubin, Janette Sadik-Khan, Scott Russell Sanders, Ross Sandler, Saskia Sassen, Stewart Schwartz, Lawrence A. Selzer, Ron Shiffman, Adele Simmons, Eugene Skoropowski, Richard Stangar, Peter E. Stangl, Peter Stein, Robert Sullivan, Tupper W. Thomas, Harriet Tregoning, Mary Tremaine, Ramon Trias, Roger Ulrich, Cesar Vergara, Karen Votava, A. Elizabeth Watson, Bob Weinberg, Bill Wilkinson, Steve Winkelman, and Michael Wyesession.

At Knopf an extraordinary team supplemented by remarkably talented independents and friends has surrounded me, starting with Sonny Mehta and my incomparable editor, Ann Close. Caroline Zancan and Bonnie Thompson, my copy editor, also improved the manuscript considerably; Iris Weinstein created the book's elegant design and Jeff Ferzoco (creative and technology director at Regional Plan Association) contributed the terrific Deep Travel report forms; the striking cover is the work of Jason Booher with input from Carol Devine Carson, a cover photo by Alison Gootee, and an author photo by Michael Lionstar. Thanks also to Pat Johnson, Lena Khidritskaya, Stephanie Kloss, Nicholas Latimer, Allison Myers, and Victoria Pearson at Knopf; to Charles Newman for his excellent index; and great appreciation as well to my friend Ric Pipino for his help with the cover. I have the good fortune to work with the best agent in the business, Amanda Urban, at ICM, and with her stellar colleagues Liz Farrell, Alison Schwartz, and Clay Ezell.

Robert Wilson, Allen Freeman, and Sandra Costich deftly shaped the excerpt of the book that appeared in *The American Scholar*.

Deepest thanks to my wife, Lois, and my son, Jacob, to whom this book is dedicated.

INDEX

A NOTE ABOUT THE AUTHOR

In Motion is Tony Hiss's thirteenth book and follows
H2O—Highlands to Ocean and the award-winner *The
Experience of Place*. His books have explored everything
from train travel to Hunanese cooking to the story of his
family to the future of New York City and include a
children's book about giant pandas. Hiss, who was a staff
writer at the *New Yorker* for more than thirty years, has
lectured widely around the world and is currently a
visiting scholar at New York University's Wagner School
of Public Service. He lives in New York with his wife,
the writer Lois Metzger, and their son.

A NOTE ON THE TYPE

The text of this book was set in Requiem, created in the
1990s by the Hoefler Type Foundry. It was derived from
a set of inscriptional capitals appearing in Ludovico
Vicentino degli Arrighi's 1523 writing manual, *Il Modo de
Temperare le Penne*. A master scribe, Arrighi is
remembered as an exemplar of the chancery
italic, a style revived in Requiem Italic.

COMPOSED BY
North Market Street Graphics, Lancaster, Pennsylvania

PRINTED AND BOUND BY
Berryville Graphics, Berryville, Virginia

DESIGNED BY
Iris Weinstein